REGNUM S

Three Seasons of Charismatic Leadership

A Literary-Critical and Theological Interpretation of the Narrative of Saul, David and Solomon

REGNUM STUDIES IN MISSION

A full listing of titles in this series
appear at the close of this book.

REGNUM STUDIES IN MISSION

Three Seasons of Charismatic Leadership

A Literary-Critical and Theological Interpretation of the Narrative of Saul, David and Solomon

Tamás Czövek

Foreword by Carl E. Armerding

regnum

Copyright © T. Czövek

First published 2006 by Paternoster

Paternoster is an imprint of Authentic Media
9 Holdom Avenue, Bletchley, Milton Keynes, MK1 1QR, UK
and
PO Box 1047, Waynesboro, GA 30830–2047, USA

12 11 10 09 08 07 06   7 6 5 4 3 2 1

The right of T. Czövek to be identified as the Author of this Work
has been asserted by him in accordance with the Copyright, Designs
and Patents Act 1988.

All rights reserved. No part of this publication may be reproduced, stored in a retrieval system, or transmitted, in any form or by any means, electronic, mechanical, photocopying, recording or otherwise, without the prior permission of the publisher or a license permitting restricted copying. In the UK such licenses are issued by the Copyright Licensing Agency, 90 Tottenham Court Road, London W1P 9HE.

British Library Cataloguing in Publication Data
A catalogue record for this book is available from the British Library

ISBN-10 1–870345–48–7
ISBN-13 978–1–870345–48–4

Typeset by T. Czövek
Printed and bound in Great Britain
for Paternoster
by Nottingham Alpha Graphics

REGNUM STUDIES IN MISSION

Series Preface

Regnum Studies in Mission are born from the lived experience of Christians and Christian communities in mission, especially but not solely in the fast growing churches among the poor of the world. These churches have more to tell than stories of growth. They are making significant impacts on their cultures in the cause of Christ. They are producing 'cultural products' which express the reality of Christian faith, hope and love in their societies.

Regnum Studies in Mission are the fruit often of rigorous research to the highest international standards and always of authentic Christian engagement in the transformation of people and societies. And these are for the world. The formation of Christian theology, missiology and practice in the twenty-first century will depend to a great extent on the active participation of growing churches contributing biblical and culturally appropriate expressions of Christian practice to inform World Christianity.

The Editors

Series Editors

Regnum Africa: Drs Kwame and Gillian Bediako, Akrofi Christaller Memorial Centre, PO Box 76, Akropong-Akuapem, Accra, Ghana.

Regnum East Asia: Rt Rev Dr Hwa Yung, PO Box 175, 70720, Seremban, Negeri Sembilan DK, Malaysia

Regnum South Asia: Rev C B Samuel, Post Bag No 21 Building, Vasant Kunj, New Delhi 110 057, India

Regnum UK: Canon Dr Chris Sugden, Editorial Director of Regnum Books International, PO Box 70, Oxford OX2 6HB, UK

Regnum USA: Dr Doug Petersen, Regnum USA, Vanguard University, 55 Fair Drive, Costa Mesa, CA 92626, USA.

To the community of the Oxford Centre of Mission Studies whose members, in one way or another, are all dedicated to the cause of charismatic leadership.

Contents

Foreword	xiii
Preface	xvii
Acknowledgements	xix
Abbreviations	xxi
Chapter 1 Introduction	1
Background of Study	1
Literature Survey	3
Studies on 1-2 Samuel and 1 Kings	3
"HERMENEUTIC OF SUSPICION"	3
STRUCTURALIST APPROACHES	7
A THEOLOGY-FREE LITERARY APPROACH	10
THE HISTORICO-LITERARY APPROACH	15
Studies on Charisma	20
LAYING THE FOUNDATIONS	20
CHARISMA RELATED TO OFFICE	20
CHARISMA AS A SUPERNATURAL PERSONAL TRAIT	26
MEDIATING BETWEEN THE TWO VIEWS	28
EVALUATION AND CONCLUSION	28
Methodology	31
The Biblical Text	31
The Emergence of the Synchronic Approach	32
Synchronic Approaches and Their Shortcomings	32
My Methodology	33
GENERAL OBSERVATIONS	33
SPECIFIC OBSERVATIONS	36
Style	40

Chapter 2 From Charismatic Judgeship to Limited Kingship   41
In the Shadow of the Last Judge   41
  Setting the Stage   41
    THE ARRIVAL OF THE NEW LEADER   44
    THE COMMISSIONING OF THE LEADER   49
    THE MILITARY DELIVERER   50
    THE CONFIRMATION OF THE NEW CHARISMATIC   53
    CHECKS OF POWER   54
The Fall of the Charismatic   66
  Rejected by the Prophet   66
  The Handicapped King   72
  Rejected by Yahweh   76
  The Doomed King   86
  Charisma and Character   92
  Signs and Wonders   92
  "Spring"   93
The Leadership of the Charismatic   94
  The Transition in Leadership   94
  Saul's Attempts to Resolve the Crisis   96
  To What Extent Was Saul Charismatic?   98

Chapter 3 Between Charismatic Military Leadership and Oriental Kingship   101
Attaining Power   101
  Setting the Stage   101
    IN NEED OF A NEW KING   102
    IN NEED OF A COMFORTER   103
    IN NEED OF A NEW MILITARY LEADER   105
  Who Is David?   108
    THE MILITARY DELIVERER   108
    THE STRATEGIST   109
      David's Relationships   109
      David's Actions   113
  The Confirmation of the New Charismatic   116
Maintaining Power   118
  Charisma Tested   118
    KING AT THE CROSSROADS   118
    KING IN THE PALACE   129
    CHARISMA REKINDLED   136
    POWER RE-ESTABLISHED   140
  Checks of Power   144
    IN THE SHADOW OF THE GENERAL   144
    IN THE SHADOW OF THE KING   152
    HOLY MEN   154

Contents   xi

    SUMMARY   155
   Administration   155
   A Yahwist Military King or an Oriental Despot?   156
   Charisma and Character   164
   Signs and Wonders   165
   "Summer"   167
The Leadership of the Charismatic   168
   The Transition in Leadership   168
   David's Attempts to Resolve Crises   171
   To What Extent Was David Charismatic?   173

Chapter 4 From Redefined Charisma to Royal Pretension   **175**
Attaining Power   175
   Setting the Stage   175
   The Rise of the New Leader   176
Maintaining Power   181
   Solomon's Rule   182
      PROSPECTS   182
      CHARISMA REDEFINED   183
      CHARISMA TESTED   187
      CHARISMA DEMONSTRATED   188
   Solomon's Rule Revisited   191
      SOLOMON REVISITED   191
      CHARISMA DEMONSTRATED   192
      CHARISMA RE-TESTED   196
      CHARISMA DEMONSTRATED   198
      THE KING'S WIVES   199
      THE AFTERMATH OF SOLOMON'S (MIS)USE OF CHARISMA   200
   The Axis   200
   Solomon's Rule Evaluated   205
   Charisma and Character   206
   Administration and the Checks on Solomon's Power   206
   Signs and Wonders   207
   "Autumn"   208
The Leadership of the Charismatic   209
   The Transition in Leadership   209
   Solomon's Attempts to Resolve the Crisis   210
   To What Extent Was Solomon Charismatic?   212

Chapter 5 Conclusions   **215**
And What Came Then? – "Winter"   215
Charismatic Leadership   215
Transition in Leadership   218
Signs and Wonders   220

Prospects 223
The Relevance of This Study 226

Bibliography **233**

Author Index **245**

Subject Index **248**

Scripture Index **259**

Foreword

Tamás Czövek's study of charismatic leadership in the early monarchy breaks new scholarly ground. But the breaking of new scholarly ground does not by itself justify publication in a series designed for a broad audience. What, then, might justify such inclusion, and why should the average reader be interested?

Charismatic leadership has been a feature of every age since recorded history began. The charismatic leader in earlier times was considered to be just what the name implies, one who had received a unique "gift" or "grace" (Greek: charisma), assumed to be from God or the gods. Although contemporary secular culture has debased the coinage to the point where charisma is little more than an element of personality, that has only increased the public's fascination. The present-day charismatic leader, no less than his or her counterpart in a less secular age, commands a unique authority, one that arises and operates outside humanly controlled channels of rational and legal discourse. Call it the favour of the gods, or the power of the numinous, the end result is the same. An individual who is neither elected nor appointed demonstrates, through the loyalties of followers, the phenomenon we call charismatic leadership. From military leaders like King Saul or Joan of Arc, to statesmen like Pitt or Churchill, the power to sway empires through brilliance in the field, or the power of oratory, has never been denied. To the considerable frustration of many who might feel it unfair, the charismatic's advantage over what Max Weber called "legal-rational" leadership, i.e., leadership that plays by legal and rational rules, has been demonstrated again and again.

So what is there to study, and what can be learned from this particular study? May I suggest that there is still much to be learned about how charismatic leadership works, both in its strengths and weaknesses. Whether in the secular or ecclesiastical realm, we often find ourselves or our institutions dominated by charismatic leaders, whose style can offend our rational sensitivities and whose appeal may in fact transcend, or even confound, legal structures. In other words, the topic is current.

But why go back to the early biblical monarchy to find a "trajectory", a theoretical concept which holds out promise of helping us to understand the "how" of charismatic leadership, not just in its historic particulars, but generally? The answer, of course, must lie in examining the claimed "trajectory" to see if it in fact elucidates more general principles, and whether those principles can successfully be applied beyond the specific setting of Israel's monarchy. Of course, some readers may question the entire enterprise, asking if such a study is in any sense a proper theological task, or whether the narrative itself was penned with the goal of teaching its readers something about charismatic leadership. May I suggest that these questions, though they may provoke some excellent discussion and even passable answers, are irrelevant, at least for the present context.

That there are theological lessons to be learnt from the biblical narratives, and that every narrative has some didactic function, is not to be questioned, but the present study seeks to discern from narrative experience the kind of instruction that is appropriate to the genre. That the illustrations here are drawn from an important period in redemptive biblical history, in which Yahweh is raising up leadership for his covenant people, in a narrative that contains more than its share of normative principles, is fascinating, but does not force us back to theology as a starting point. Hopefully, the present study will provide some grist for the theologian's mill, but its questions are posed, and answered, in other ways.

I must leave it to the reader to determine whether Czövek has made a convincing case, and even to say what that case may be. I will conclude this "Foreword" with a few comments on the process, and where a reading of this book may point the contemporary reader.

My own studies in charismatic leadership have focussed on the judges, so it was with great interest I learned of Tamás Czövek's desire to extend the principles of charismatic leadership into the early monarchy. That there was something to be studied was never in doubt, but that the intriguing and often contradictory evidence from the lives of Saul, David and Solomon (with Samuel as a sub-text) would yield so much fruit could not have been imagined. Whether or not we agree with each detail in the following study, we shall certainly be challenged by its careful and close reading of the text, its fine sense of having captured the essence of biblical personalities, and its ability to analyse ancient people and structures in ways germane to contemporary life. Its studies of the narrator's art are intended both to advance scholarship and stimulate the general reader, with elusive features like the ability to separate narrator and character, and thence to discern their respective viewpoints, relentlessly if sometimes controversially pursued. Never mind that along the way some favourite characters come off a bit the worse; equally sympathy may be elicited for a classically tragic figure. Traditional moral, or even theological, criteria are bypassed because it is argued that the narrative itself leads us this way. Rather than emerging as a morality play, the historical drama of Samuel-Kings is examined through the filter of charismatic leadership study and what we can learn from it.

Any of us who have worked with, or experienced, charismatic leadership in contemporary life will find areas of resonance. Max Weber tended to see the

Foreword

true charismatic leader as a creature of a bygone era prior to the rise of "legal-rational" structures, when authority was understood to come directly from the gods, or other realms of the mysterious and numinous. This of course is to ignore much of the non-western world where earlier categories continue to thrive, but it may reflect also a significant rationalising tendency in its analysis of Enlightenment culture. Certainly, with the advent of postmodernism, the older categories have not only revived but claim widespread popular allegiance. And as postmoderns would be quick to point out, the resonance today of ancient categories represents not nostalgia for a bygone age but the demonstration of the inadequacy of Enlightenment rationality.

Finally, those who look to Scripture, and supremely to Jesus Christ, for models of leadership, will naturally want to learn what can be gleaned from such a study about charismatic leaders and charismatic leadership. For, without dispute, charismatic principles of leadership dominate whole periods of Old Testament history, and in many ways reflect the only kind of leadership that can be meaningfully applied to the earthly life and work of our Lord. Whether the monarchy after Solomon, with its virtual suppression of the Spirit's overt ministry, represents a maturing or a decline may still be debated. Equally, there will always be contrasting opinions about the post-apostolic church, in which the "offices" of elder and deacon virtually displace the role of spiritual gifts in leadership. But in these days, when the official structures of both political and ecclesiastical leadership have been challenged at their very heart, it ill behooves serious students of Scripture to ignore the "trajectories" that dominate both the early monarchy and the apostolic era.

For all these reasons, and others, I would encourage a wide reading of Tamás Czövek's work. That it emerged as a doctoral thesis under my supervision, and in so doing expanded the scope of my own reflections considerably, can only be a matter for personal gratitude. It is a matter of equal satisfaction that Paternoster/Regnum has made the study available to a broader audience.

Dr Carl E. Armerding
Vancouver

Preface

Interpreting biblical texts with a particular agenda has proved a useful and rewarding undertaking. One may be referred to works such as Phyllis Trible's essays in her book, *God and the Rhetoric of Sexuality* in 1978, Robert Polzin's structuralist reading of 1-2 Samuel, *Samuel and the Deuteronomist* and *David and the Deuteronomist* (1989, 1993), or the magisterial opus by Jack Miles in 1995, *God: A Biography*, to mention but a few. The particular questions of the particular agenda enable one to see biblical passages and connections, characters and events in new light. I hope that my specific aspect of charismatic leadership will for the reader yield both new insights regarding the characters and their motives, events and interconnections of the narrative and fresh theological understandings.

For obvious reasons aspects of charismatic leadership, even though referred to differently in everyday parlance, has most of the time played a significant role in organisations like the church. When I started this research, however, my own experience in my home church was that questions regarding charismata of leaders, recognition, election and confirmation of the charismatic, transition in leadership were not faced by church members nor by leaders. Often church leaders suffer from demands they cannot meet as well as from the frustration of not being able to work on territories where they feel competent — ignorance of charisma leads to overload and frustration. Transition periods unprepared for are fraught with tension and conflict — neglect of the aspect of charismatic leadership takes its toll. In a similar vein church members, youths in particular, trying hard to make themselves useful by virtue of their God given abilities, grow irritated and discouraged of their unsuccessful attempts at getting involved in their local churches — tradition hampers attempts at inventive initiatives.

I trust that readers will not find this study as an odd one out in a series of mission studies but, in one way or another, will be able to use the insights in their various contexts. My prayer is that this study may not remain a piece of some methodological, exegetical and theological observations, however much these may be important, but lead those who endeavour to serve God in their own settings to a better understanding of the situation they find themselves in and, following this, a more competent employment of their abilities granted by the Spirit of our gracious Triune God.

Finally I wish to express my deepest gratitude towards Dr Anthony Cross who kindly assisted me through the work of typesetting of this book.

Tamás Czövek
Törökbálint
November 2005

Acknowledgements

Clearly this research has not been a one-man work, but come into existence by the support and help of people and organisations. Here I would like to acknowledge my gratitude to those most directly involved in the completion of this study.

URCO Foundation in the Netherlands financed this project in the first year as did St Andrew's Church in Oxford. This latter has also proved a place to worship the Triune God. I am greatly indebted to them. So I am to Langham Trust that has made the biggest contribution to the financial needs of the study during its more than three years. I can only hope that the investment of Langham Trust, which is committed to training leaders in the 2/3 world, will not have been fruitless.

The North Oxford Overseas Centre, with all its staff and residents, has been a wonderful place to stay. The fellowship, love and care I and my family have experienced have made us feel at home.

Of those who have helped me in the intellectual and often spiritual struggle of studying charismatic leadership I must first mention Dr Carl E. Armerding. He not only stimulated me to start this research but has been a constant source of encouragement, advice and invaluable insights. He has proved a mentor, in the best sense of the word, without whom a PhD student, unlike a charismatic leader, cannot succeed. He and his wife, Betsy, have always had the door of their home open for me. May their love and commitment to training leaders in Eastern Europe bear fruit abundantly.

Prof Robert P. Gordon has supervised me meticulously and patiently. He has drawn attention to weak points in my argument and, even though occasionally disagreeing with me, has kindly encouraged me in this research.

Marcel Măcelaru has proved a good friend whose suggestions, particularly regarding methodology and literature survey as well as editing have greatly increased the quality of this study. Dr Bernard Farr at the Oxford Centre for Mission Studies (OCMS) has read the thesis and made essential suggestions regarding literature survey, style and conclusion in particular. Suggestions by Dr Len Bartlotti at the OCMS about practice have contributed to a better understanding of leadership as well as to the final form of this thesis. My sister, Sári, and her husband, David, read the first draft. It was not only my poor English that made their job indispensable. Without their critical comments the argument could not be as coherent and compelling as I hope it is. Of course none of them is responsible for the views represented in the study.

My wife, Klári, and two daughters, Emőke and Gyöngyvér, have coped with my workload during this period. My wish and prayer are that what I have learnt may impact their lives and vision as well, so that all of us may experience signs and wonders by God's intervening Spirit.

Last but not least special thanks go to the community of OCMS. The Centre has not been a mere institute – it has been a place to experience loving support and care, a place of worship, friendship, sharing of concerns, sorrow and joy, scholarly discussion with a holistic outlook not only to missiology but theology. It has also been driven home to me that doing a research at OCMS is much like waiting for Jesus – we must be prepared at any time to give an account of what we have done. In one word, it has provided a stimulating atmosphere and vision so essential for research and life. It is one of the few institutions I have seen where not solely the brain is involved in doing theology but the whole person, indeed community. I dedicate this study to this community.

Tamás Czövek
Oxford Centre for Mission Studies

ABBREVIATIONS

ANE	Ancient Near East
AT	Author's Translation
ch.	chapter
chs.	chapters
DH	Deuteronomistic History
ET	English Translation
f	following
ff	following (plural)
FT	First Testament (a.k.a. Old Testament)
i.e.	that is
LXX	Septuagint
MT	Masoretic Text
NIV	New International Version
NRSV	New Revised Standard Version
SN	Succession Narrative
ST	Second Testament (a.k.a. New Testament)
v.	verse
vs.	versus
vv.	verses

ABBREVIATIONS OF BIBLICAL BOOKS

Gen	Genesis
Ex	Exodus
Lev	Leviticus
Num	Numbers
Dt	Deuteronomy
Josh	Joshua
Ju	Judges
1 Sam	1 Samuel
2 Sam	2 Samuel
1 Kgs	1 Kings
2 Kgs	2 Kings
Ps	Psalms
Mt	Matthew
Mk	Mark
Lk	Luke
1 Cor	1 Corinthians
Gal	Galatians
1 Thess	1 Thessalonians
Heb	Hebrews

Do not put out the Spirit's fire.

   Paul of Tarsus

Neither do men pour new wine
into old wineskins.
If they do, the skins will burst,
the wine will run out
and the wineskins will be ruined.
No, they pour new wine
into new wineskins,
and both are preserved.

   Jesus of Nazareth

CHAPTER 1

Introduction

Background of Study

My interest in charismatic leadership is related to my personal and church background as well as the situation of my church, the Reformed Church in Hungary. Between 1993 and 1996 I worked as an assistant minister in a congregation in Budapest. When, in my youth group, the question of charisma was raised, as a good Reformed I was at a loss. I had to consult a friend who was more open to the "charismatic question". I remember we were sitting on the bank of the Danube discussing the need of various charismata, "lay people" getting involved and the implications of all this for worship and service.

Later on at a youth camp in 1995, we discussed with the youth group how they could get more actively involved in the life and services of the congregation. We debated how we as individuals filled with God's Spirit and enabled by the Spirit's gifts as well as a community could contribute to the benefit of the church. Some actions followed, and it seemed that minor changes in service could be expected. However, after I had left the congregation, the views of the youths were no longer officially represented and their attempts were thwarted. (Subsequently the youth group disappeared, but nobody took any notice.)

At the weekly chapel of the colleagues in the church, we pastors took turns in leading a Bible study. When it was my turn, rather naively, I expounded Numbers 27:12-23, as this was the passage I had read that morning. Afterwards the other young assistant pastor told me how embarrassing the situation had been: an assistant pastor aged 30 preaching to two senior pastors aged 70, just before retirement, about the need of a smooth transition in leadership...

Related with the above mentioned problems is the fact that in churches where two or more pastors minister, division of duties is not based on the pastors' skills. In fact, each pastor is responsible for every duty and has to carry out every task of church life in the conventional way. In general, pastors are rarely elected because they exhibit charisma but rather because of appearance, quality of voice, marital status, etc. In short, *charisma and charismatic leadership are not in the purview*.

Another factor needs to be mentioned. In the wake of World War Two, Hungary experienced a religious renewal referred to as "The Awakening". It certainly had a strong impact on the lives of many, the Protestant churches as well as on the theological and spiritual climate of the country. This impact, however, was not long-lasting. The Communists took over and suppressed or banned anything related to religion. Fifty years on, those having been touched by the wind of The Awakening (and still alive) remember this period with nostalgia. This became evident after the political changes of 1989-90, when, with religious freedom guaranteed, people of The Awakening started to re-establish and redefine religious life in post-Communist Hungary. Although it was characterised by a rather narrow individualistic spirituality and theology, their intention was commendable — bringing about an awareness of God the Saviour. Unfortunately, the same cannot be said of method and result. Those were copies of The Awakening period. Similarly, these old warriors produced copycats, who in their turn copied their masters' method, language and approach. Leaders and followers refused to notice the milieu of a changed society, culture, language and values and canonised methods and approaches of another age. Again, *charismatic leadership was ignored.*

Also studying the book of Judges, I realised that biblical narratives do deal with charismatic leadership. I started to read studies available in Hungary by Buber, Noth, von Rad and Weisman, cultivating my interest in charismatic leadership. I also remembered that I had met a theologian in 1990 who had been studying charismatic leadership for years. So I wrote to Carl Armerding about my ideas and he encouraged me to prepare a proposal for a PhD. Subsequently he was willing to supervise my PhD research.

One word on timing. It seems that I did this study at the proper time. Fortunately my topic was neither over- nor under-researched. That is, I had essential and indispensable studies available — one of them, Jobling's 1 Samuel commentary, was published just at the right time for me — but not to the extent that nothing new could be said.

Of course, much in focus and methodology has changed since I started my research. One thing has, however, remained unaltered — this study is intrinsically related to the perceived "crisis" in Hungary and the desire for change. My background as a Hungarian Reformed is crucial and should be borne in mind when reading this study.

The Bible and experience teach that God uses leaders to deliver his people. These leaders are granted special gifts, charismata, by God's Spirit. The discussion of this study is simply structured. After the Introduction, in the second chapter I shall deal with Saul's charismatic leadership. The focus of the third will be on David and that of the fourth on Solomon. In this research I shall attend to questions such as how these charismatic leaders rise. How and to what end is charisma bestowed? How is it then used? How are the leaders designated; how do they demonstrate their charisma and leadership skills; how are they confirmed? What constitutes a charismatic leader? How is leadership transformed? How do these charismatic leaders then fall? What characterises the transition in leadership? These aspects I shall study as they are presented in the narrative. Since this is not a commentary, nor a purely descriptive study, but a study based on and influenced by my experiences and the desire for change, at the end of each chapter I shall discuss more general questions of charismatic leadership. In fact, a longer discussion will be dedicated to leadership questions in my conclusion, implying that this study is not confined to being a literary but extends to being an applied leadership study. Finally, this study is not about Saul's rejection, David's success and Solomon's wealth — it is about leadership and how charisma is used.

A word on terminology is necessary. Firstly I shall use "spirit" when referring to God's *ruach* in the FT[1], where "it" is not yet thought of as a divine person of the Trinity. I shall capitalise the word, however, when used in Christian usage or in reference to the ST.

Secondly the antonyms "static" and "dynamic" I shall use in their everyday sense in reference to charismatic leadership or characterisation. While the former is "stationary; not acting or changing; passive" (Fowler-Fowler 1990:1191), thus rather negative, the latter I take as something "energetic; active; potent" (366), so positive.

Literature Survey

In what follows I shall review the literature most useful to my own study dealing with either 1-2 Samuel and 1 Kings or charisma. I have not found studies on both. Obviously, as my work is literary-critical, I have consulted studies of the synchronic approach. Since my focus is on charismatic leadership, I cannot ignore studies on charisma.

Studies on 1-2 Samuel and 1 Kings

"HERMENEUTIC OF SUSPICION" — DAVID GUNN, LYLE ESLINGER AND PETER MISCALL

Conventional exegesis (e.g. Keil 1971; Klein 1983) has treated the narrative and its characters in a rather black-and-white manner. Some characters are regarded as positive from the beginning to the end, while others are negative. The former particularly applies to the prophet Samuel, who, after Moses, is conventionally considered the first and foremost prophet and spokesperson of Yahweh — at the expense of the baddy, Saul. With the emergence of synchronic reading, however, Saul has been given a retrial. Similarly, other characters regarded as heroes of faith, like David and Solomon, have been treated with more suspicion. I shall discuss three scholars under the heading "hermeneutic of suspicion", although this phrase is not completely accurate — thus the inverted commas.

David Gunn attempts to find an alternative method and reading, more attentive to plot and literary unity, to the conventional historical one. In his

---

[1] I prefer referring to First Testament and Second Testament to using Old and New Testaments. By so doing I follow Goldingay (see 1994:2, n. 7).

1978 volume, *The Story of King David*, he tries to break with the historical approach to the David narrative[2] by working on the assumption that it is based on oral tradition (see also his 1974 and 1974a). He criticises Rost's study (1982) and the works following it by claiming that Solomon's role in the SN is very limited, therefore any notion of political slant (*Tendenz*), whether positive or negative (see Ackerman 1990:59), necessarily lacks textual support. Too much emphasis on oral prehistory, however, resulted in an overly hypothetical framework (see 68-70; cf. Fokkelman 1981:11, n. 20). As a reaction to historical criticism and as his initial attempt at a more literary focus on the Bible, it departs from the tradition-critical approach whilst still depending upon it too much to offer a new approach.

In *The Fate of King Saul* Gunn (1980) improves on the methodology of his 1978 study in that he abandons his quest for oral tradition, which is not an invalid alternative to written tradition but, as not documented up to this date, it is very difficult to grasp. It is a very useful literary study. Taking the final form of the text for granted he does not deal with its prehistory, but instead focuses on plot development, the relationship and interaction between Samuel and Saul as well as how and why their relationship changes. Basing his arguments on the text Gunn succeeds in producing a purely literary approach. By referring to other literary examples and stressing the notion of "fate", Gunn presents the story as the tragedy of King Saul. That Gunn has made a contribution to the studies of the Saul narrative is beyond doubt. Still Exum is right in claiming (1992:18) that Gunn "unnecessarily seeks to distinguish between fate and flaw, he never treats human guilt and divine hostility as an essential combination, and in emphasizing Saul as a victim of God he sometimes loses sight of Saul as a victim of himself."

Although attempts had been made to give a subtler, less partial account of Saul's rejection (e.g. Stoebe 1973), Gunn was the first to turn the tables on Samuel. It is a pioneering attempt also because despite being not overtly applied, it is a solid study dealing with "fate", and it is not overburdened by methodological discussions and technical terms.

As early as 1985, though using a different methodology, **Lyle Eslinger** set out in the same direction as Gunn. His close reading (40) offers "a *detailed* and comprehensive descriptive reading of the narrative" (38; his emphasis). He reads 1 Samuel 1-12 as a "transition from theocracy to a theocratically subordinate monarchy", which "is a *digression* in the story of Israel's theological-political relationship with God" (50; his italics). He succeeds in presenting the various positions of the narrator and the different characters. Indeed Eslinger makes the fine and necessary distinction between different levels of "narrative ontology" and subsequently one between different voices within the narrative (1989:6-8, 81ff); and he is perhaps the scholar who insists

---

[2] By the David narrative I mean the narrative where he is the protagonist. The same applies to the Saul and Solomon narratives.

Introduction 5

most consistently on distinguishing — in his 1994 essay (see also his 1983) — the different narrative voices. He makes the essential distinction between "authorial and character rhetoric" (1994:7).

Eslinger's 1985 volume is a verse-by-verse commentary. Owing to his close attention to and focus on the verse he, similarly to Edelman and Fokkelman, is prone to ignore overarching themes, structural arrangements and developments of themes, motifs and plots — a basic difference from Gunn and Polzin. This is evident in his comment on the verb עצר in 9:17. Without discussing different possibilities he makes his choice (310) which is probably not the best.

In his 1989 study Eslinger devotes a chapter to "Biblical Narratology" (10-15), where he helpfully states his intention:

> An important aim of narratology is to describe how authors can manipulate discourse as a tool to affect the meaning of story. Narratology often devotes greater attention to the discourse that relates story because it is the only medium in narrative literature that is directly aimed at the reader. No voice within the story world of the narrative can address the reader directly without breaking the conventions that govern this literary form. (11)

Eslinger's most recent study (1994) is a rhetorical analysis of 2 Samuel 7. Following a good introduction he reveals his cards (5): "Our primary concern for the rhetoric that we find within the narrative should be the strategies and rhetorical moves by which characters seek to persuade or bend each other to their own purpose." Subsequently he deals with three basic questions (9): Why does David want to build a temple? Why does God try to stop him? How does God try to stop him? It is a most insightful rhetorical study of the literary architecture of the chapter.

If there is a hermeneutic of suspicion, Eslinger is definitely its guru. Commenting on 1 Samuel 9:15f he writes: "If Samuel proceeds to carry out Yahweh's commands it will indicate that he refused to do so previously on account of his misunderstanding Yahweh's original intention" (1985:304). This is a heavy value judgment by implication, for Samuel's previous refusal is not clearly suggested by the text. This suspicion is manifest in his interpretation of ch. 9. He resorts to gap filling in 9:22: Samuel makes the participants of the banquet guess about Saul's identity and future (313f). The text, again, is reticent about Samuel's plan, if he had one at all. On 9:23f he comments: "The conspiratorial sacrifice has transformed Saul into Samuel's compliant eater, who, for a time, swallows everything Samuel feeds him" (315). Firstly Saul was like that (see my discussion); there was no need for a transformation. Secondly it is a nice pun but the motif of eating with Samuel itself does not lead to this conclusion. And thirdly referring to a "conspiratorial sacrifice" is strong language. I shall also often use strong wording, an indispensable means in studies related to rhetorical criticism. It seems, however, that the force of his argument is not so much in his textual observations but in the language with which he communicates it.

Eslinger calls David a "murderous character instructing his son in the ways of bloodthirsty revenge and calling that wisdom" (1989:127). Once again what interests me is the language Eslinger uses. This quote, because couched in strong terms, is very persuasive, which is his aim. Provan (1995a), however, has made a good case for the relative wisdom of David's testimony. If Provan is correct, Eslinger's statement fails.

Eslinger's discussion of 1 Kings 3 is slightly biased. Right at the beginning he calls Pharaoh "the arch-villain" and "anathematic opponent Yahweh [sic]" (1989:129), which he might be in Exodus, but this view here lacks textual basis. Then Eslinger studies the rhetoric of Solomon's request from God with extreme suspicion. Whatever the king utters proves self-serving and presumptuous. Even for choosing rather "innocent" terms in which to couch his request Eslinger accuses Solomon of hubris (134f). If the king had chosen more ambitious and presumptuous language, he would obviously have been guilty. But even formulating his request prudently, as the case is, is a sign of his presumptuous attempt to hoodwink God. Solomon is caught in a "catch 22". After the demonstration of Solomon's wisdom, 1 Kings 3, Eslinger disapprovingly asks (139), "What kind of wisdom is this? Certainly events do turn out right, but is it because of Solomon or inspite [sic] of him?" The problem with this approach is that he ultimately puts the blame on God for having granted such "ineffective" wisdom.

I cannot comprehend either how one can come to a negative interpretation of 1 Kings 3:8f, as the text itself is quite unambiguous. Eslinger's hermeneutic of suspicion, always looking for hidden motives (e.g. 143), grows out of proportion. His concept is of static characters unwilling or unable to change (see 134, n. 21). The claim that Solomon first built his palace and only then the temple (141) lacks any textual evidence. One also wonders why the reselling of horses to the Hittites and Arameans (10:29) is any worse than keeping them (152).

Overstated nuances coupled with overstatements are applied by Eslinger to make his point. So, for example, there is no doubt about Solomon's guilt in ch. 11. Still to draw a chiastic congruity in v. 4 between "his [Solomon's] wives" and "his father" and then to speak of "the wicked wives of Solomon" (154f) is far-fetched. All in all, Eslinger's suspicions often result in rather twisted and tendentious explanations.

Peter Miscall's (1983, 1986) underlying agenda is to demonstrate that various, sometimes complementary, sometimes contradictory, interpretations are possible. The possibility of reading the text in different ways makes conventional interpretations relative.

He is conscious of the difficulties with the text of 1 Samuel (1986:viii) but still maintains that "text-critical study should be preceded by extended readings, wherever possible, of each version." He stresses that 1 Samuel is part of the larger unit Genesis-Kings, and is aware of the problems of focusing

Introduction 7

solely on 1 Samuel (1986:viiif).

Miscall starts by claiming that FT narratives are complex and elusive. "There is, at the same time, too little and too much of the narrative, too few and too many details, and this gives rise to the many, and frequently contradictory, interpretations of and conjectures about OT narrative" (1983:1). He can be regarded as a moderate forerunner of Eslinger's suspicious hermeneutic.

> The Lord's appearance, especially his word, may be mediated, i.e. someone claims to be reporting a speech or action of the Lord, e.g., the man of God in 1 Sam. 2:27-36, Samuel in chapter 15, David's men in 1 Sam. 24:5, and David in 1 Sam. 25:39. Inquiries of the Lord are included in this category. We have to address the issue of the reliability of the mediator when it is a person; questions of character, setting, purpose for the statement, etc., must be raised. [...] Finally, with Samuel, the question of his character and possible motives must be raised even if it means that his 'truthfulness' is impugned. (1986:xiii)

He summarises his aim well:

> I do not attempt to establish an essentialist interpretation—the true meaning, the author's intention, what it really meant, what really happened, the purpose of the text, or any of the other diverse phrases or categories employed to refer to an essential meaning. It is not my purpose to overcome ambiguity or equivocation, either by ignoring or explaining away details and repetitions or by filling in gaps and missing information. Gaps, details, repetitions, inconsistencies, and contradictions are considered to be deliberate, and their impact on the reading is assessed. (1986:xvi)

"Undecidability" is the key word of his interpretation. "It is not an attempt to argue for a 'new' interpretation of David", but rather "to demonstrate that David is both good and bad, that the text [...] supports both views at the same time" (1983:2). Miscall's attempt I think will remain a novel one for years to come.

STRUCTURALIST APPROACHES — DAVID JOBLING AND ROBERT POLZIN

David Jobling's commentary on 1 Samuel (1998) is probably the most consistent structuralist and, at the same time, eclectic (24f) approach to the narrative. It is not a commentary in the conventional sense, rather a monograph and a structuralist appropriation of themes in the book. It is understandable but unfortunate that he focuses on the first part of 1 Samuel and its particular themes and characters, hence does not deal with the book as a sequential reading.

Jobling defines his methodology as follows:

> I see the Bible performing a function close to that of myth as understood by Claude Lévi-Strauss—who, among the structuralists, has had the strongest influence on me. According to him, myth deals with a society's defining beliefs

and with fundamental contradictions in its system of belief. The work of myth is to give a sense that these contradictions have been resolved—though they are in principle beyond resolution—and thus to make existence tolerable for the society. I do not equate biblical narrative with myth, since that term is best kept for the products of societies where the sense of history is much less developed than in Israel. But when the past is viewed from a sufficient distance and for the purpose of explaining the present, as I believe is the case with the Bible, historiography functions very like myth. Lévi-Strauss insists that a society's mythic record can only be understood as a total system comprising many particular myths. In the case of the Bible the total system means the whole narrative, and eventually the whole canon. (6)

In two further respects Jobling is a structuralist in that he, firstly, insists (5; his italics) "on the *system* of meaning in the text. The text gives expression to a set of relationships of both form and meaning." Secondly, Jobling seeks

> clues to meaning primarily on a *large* textual scale. I give priority to the question of what 1 Samuel means *as a whole*. Mine is a deductive method. This puts me at odds with the prevailing trend in the narrative study of the Bible, which looks for meaning in the literary arrangement of shorter sections and build up the meaning of the whole inductively from these smaller-scale analyses. I do not regard this as simply a matter of taste. I think that my method is more appropriate to the sort of literature the Bible is. (5f; his emphasis)

The statement that his is a deductive method needs to be qualified, for he is very keen on (recurring) motifs and themes, plot and characterisation. Thus his methodology may not be very deductive. Unfortunately he fails to enter into a serious interaction with e.g. Fokkelman and enlarge upon his disagreement with the inductive method.

Jobling's deductive method is apparent, e.g., in his "deep-structural reading of Saul's rejection" (85-88). He is a true follower of Lévi-Strauss also in that he operates at and with the mythic level of "fundamental contradictions". For him Samuel is a mythic character who lives on even after his literary and actual death (86). He stresses the transitional role from judgeship to kingship of Samuel, who thus supplies "an appearance of continuity between the two systems" (69). At the same time the prophet's inconsistent and inexplicable living-on creates multiple and contradictory roles as being the last judge as well as the inaugurator of monarchy (69).

Jobling's structuralist approach, and his taking the mythic level into account, enables him to see the replacement of judgeship by kingship and their antagonism in a systematic and dynamic way. Jobling deduces his interpretation of Samuel and Saul's relationship, deeds and interactions from what they stand for. Furthermore, as a true structuralist Jobling is sensitive to contradictions — not explaining them away but trying to integrate them into his world of binary oppositions.

Introduction 9

Jobling issues a legitimate warning: 1 Samuel has always been read forwards and not backwards (33). "Backwards" aspects like the judges cycle, the competing governments of judgeship versus kingship first raised by the Gideon and Abimelech stories, and the Philistine presence and hegemony become important themes in both Judges and 1 Samuel. Subsequently he realises (32) "that the canonical books exercise a power over our reading, authorizing some ways of reading over others."[3] He then suggests new boundaries: "The Extended Book of Judges" (Ju 2:11-1 Sam 12) and "The Book of the Everlasting Covenant" (1 Sam 13-2 Sam 7). This division results in a totally new approach and novel reading.

On the other hand Jobling tends to overstate his case, particularly when narrative coherence is concerned. For example, he claims that Saul's portrayal both as a rejected king behaving treacherously and as one willing to abdicate to David cannot be sustained (92). I think this paradox often characterises, both in real life and in fiction, paranoid people such as Saul.

Jobling sometimes cannot avoid speculations for instance about "the God of the gaps" (72f). His concept of the ideal Israel (70ff) needs some clarification. His discussion of Ruth and other topics seems to be rather non-essential. His "gay reading" of the Jonathan-David relationship (161-65) is somewhat unclear about the level at which Jonathan chose David in 20:30 (161): at the historical or the textual?

Jobling's is probably the most ideological, indeed tendentious, reading of Samuel. He uses the text to make his case. This has the rather inconsistent and arbitrary result that when the narrator is in apparent opposition to his view, he takes a stand against the narrator (136).

Robert Polzin's is an ideological reading where the text is a showcase of the conflict between authoritarian dogmatism and critical traditionalism, his declared programme in his first volume (1980). The two volumes on 1-2 Samuel (1989, 1993) are a step forward from his 1980 volume towards an easier to comprehend and handle commentary. Polzin criticises textual criticism as an end in itself (1989:1f) and makes a good case for the study of the final form of the text (1989:2ff).

Working with structuralism's binary terms Polzin reveals a competence in analysis as well as in generating ideas regarding the DH (see e.g. 1 Sam 9:7-9; 1989:93-102, 124f). Another structuralist idiosyncrasy is his attention to language as the vehicle for expressing all these. For him it is a multivoiced narrative which produces interconnections at different levels. He draws parallels and contrasts, traces key words and motifs throughout the passage and the DH. The result is a coherent story.

A structuralist, Polzin is attentive to rhetorical nuances, niceties (1989:82), puns, metaphors (e.g. sight/insight of Samuel; 1989:49-54, 130, 152-55) and

---

[3] His observation might be elaborated on with Klement's study (2000) in mind, who too reads backwards.

details conventionally regarded as stemming from different sources (1989:89f). He is able to grasp the theme development and thematic correspondences in, at the beginning and at the end of the book (see 1989:216-24). He can distinguish between significant and insignificant, defining and subordinate elements in the stories and so grasp their motifs, metaphors and themes, such as the overarching theme of monarchy, political and theological developments — as reflected in the text. Overall structure and salient themes of the narrative found by identifying key terms like "pass" in 1 Samuel 14 or repentance in 1 Samuel 15 are significant for him. Therefore he sometimes ignores minor features and grammatical, structural or literary devices.

Characterisation ("character zone") is in focus throughout. Polzin stresses both implicit (see 1989:114) as well as explicit characterisation (e.g. in "Coherence and Characterization"; 1989:187-90). Even though he condemns Saul for disobedience, unlike Fokkelman, he does not fail to be consistent in the characterisation of Samuel and Saul in 1 Samuel 13-15. He is wary of anything relating to prophecy and inquiring of God, therefore his interpretations relating to this issue are prejudiced (1989:183-86). He seems to run out of steam by the end of his book of 1989; the last chapters are much shorter than the earlier ones. One would wish he had kept his stamina to the end.

Polzin's style is not as dogmatic as Fokkelman's. His readiness to leave open questions and room for different interpretations (1989:173) is less normative and more compelling. His style is amusing and playful, often employing a metaphoric-poetic language, which makes his commentary readable and enjoyable. Reading this remarkable study one wonders whether Polzin can found a school of interpretation.

A THEOLOGY-FREE LITERARY APPROACH — JAN FOKKELMAN

One of the most interesting, ambitious and complex interpretations of 1-2 Samuel is **Jan Fokkelman**'s ambitious enterprise (1981, 1986, 19990, 1993), trying to deal with the text as a literary work void of theology. It is a milestone in the literary criticism of the books of Samuel and as such merits a thorough critique. On occasions I shall compare Fokkelman's ideology-free attempt to Polzin's ideology-loaded endeavour.

Fokkelman's is both a minute and "high-flying" synchronic reading working on the assumption of the reliability and coherence of the MT (1981:7f). The textual and literary-critical discussions on the synchronic level are also excellent. To study 1-2 Samuel as a literary unit disregarding genetic questions is commendable. To subject it to detailed literary analysis is obviously rewarding. I am indebted to him for many insightful observations.

Fokkelman's presentation and methodological discussion of the structure of a literary work are helpful (1986:4-17); he regards the narrative as a network of integral components and is keen to integrate them into higher structural levels. Yet in his subsequent study the reader often cannot see the wood of the narrative, sections or book from the level he is analysing. Moreover such

Introduction

models often make the process of analysis rather mechanical and speculative.

One should expect a good commentary to help the reader understand both the details and the whole. Fokkelman excels in the first, but as for the latter the reader is left with the question, what is Samuel about? (This is a remarkable difference, again, to Polzin.) Fokkelman states his pursuit explicitly:

> The aim of the intrinsic study of literature is to understand the text from inside, guided by the obvious and quite natural question: "What do you mean? What are you saying?" This question is simultaneously the most essential question which we could ask of the text or, more generally, of any work of art or, even more generally, of any partner in conversation. (1981:1)

This "manifesto" is helpful in that it reveals Fokkelman's aim. At the same time it brings to light the intrinsic limits of it, his rather fragmentary interpretation. Since his interest lies in "what it means", he fails to appreciate and make sense of the plot, development, the whole. Again too much focus on the constituent parts (17f) makes the narrative fragmentary.

Fokkelman is very keen on analysing each part of the narrative: sections, sentences, words, suffixes. By overestimating the significance of parts he sometimes forces his structure on the narrative. I have rarely found arrangements like ABCA'C'B' (see e.g. 1993:527; 1986:55, 478, 521; see also Newing 1994:251) compelling. Rosenberg rightly observes (1986:111) that Fokkelman "seems to confuse a 'full interpretation' with belabored colon-by-colon and scene-by-scene analysis." He concludes, "It is not the totality of one's interpretation that matters, but the consequentiality." What Alter claims of Fokkelman's Genesis commentary applies also to his Samuel study (1981:16): Fokkelman "shows a certain tendency to interpretive overkill in his explications, at times discovering patterns where they may not be, and assuming with a noticeable degree of strain that form must always be significantly expressive." All in all Gunn's assertion that the more exhaustive the analysis the more speculative it becomes (1978:15) is correct. (A more structured format with more chapters, subdivisions, headings and subheadings would also have improved this vast commentary.)

Fokkelman's minute commentary is too descriptive, seldom evaluative. Unlike Polzin he is not overly concerned with the theological significance of the narrative — indeed he often betrays disdain or suspicion of theological interpretations. He rebukes Ridout (1971) for "ascribing it [2 Sam 7] an all-controlling position" and causing "the estranging impression of a theological invasion." He explains his refusal to engage in theological interpretations: "Whoever says that the decisive interpretation of the text must be theological isolates and absolutizes the religious element and is therefore only partially occupied with the text" (1981:427). Subsequently he ends up ignoring the theology, an essential element of the narrative.

Having abandoned theological concerns Fokkelman often embarks on rather flimsy psychological (and even semi-doctrinal) interpretations.[4] This is probably the unfortunate consequence of ignoring the theological intent of the text. In his very sophisticated but fragmentary literary analysis he tries to find psychological motivations instead of ones related to plot and character development.

Besides the above shortcomings what characterises Fokkelman's study is a lack of consistency. It is apparent in three areas — in method (is he working in synchronic or rather diachronic terms?); characterisation; and his view on a particular event he interprets.

Fokkelman's inconsistency in method is evident right at the beginning of his first volume. He starts his commentary with the study of the so-called SN (2 Sam 9-20 and 1 Kgs 1-2), ignoring sequentiality. This is a severe blow to literary criticism.[5] He is of the more or less dogmatic view (1981:1) that the SN is

1. "universally recognized as the pearl of biblical prose" and "the best text for exploiting the qualities and techniques of Old Testament narrative in order to develop interpretations as well as criteria";

2. "a consummate whole well-suited to synchronic reading".

I tend to be suspicious of unsubstantiated claims as #1. They need criteria in order to be regarded as valid, and scholars, including Fokkelman, have failed to provide them but have apparently taken them for granted. This is so despite his feeble attack on the supremacy of Rost's thesis (10) and the disclaimer of it (1981:12, n. 20). His inconsistency is also visible in his stance towards the SN and the complex of David's ascension to the throne (1986:3). Here he calls the SN "non-existent".[6]

As for #2 Fokkelman claims that Kings was incorrectly split from Samuel (1981:410, n. 20). What is the evidence? What about the difference in grammar, syntax and vocabulary? It is obviously a diachronic presupposition, critiqued by Gunn (1978), Keys (1996) and Stoebe (1999), and as such seems to be also in breach of his own methodology. He too acknowledges this (1990:11), but without proper justification.

Fokkelman notices the peculiarity of 2 Samuel 21-24 — its chronological ambiguity, concentric arrangement and loose connection to the preceding narrative (1990:11-13). He treats it as an appendix — a historical-critical

---

[4] See e.g. 1993:418, where he speaks of the old and new Adam in psychological terms; 1981:187: doctrinal notion of synergism; 1981:242: heaven in 2 Sam 18:9 as a place of salvation, irrelevant to the discussion.

[5] Polzin (1989:250, n. 1) claims that Fokkelman's "decision to treat the two parts of Samuel in reverse order—his vol. 1 dealing first with 2 Samuel and his vol. 2 then analyzing 1 Samuel—was, in my opinion, an unfortunate way to work through the artful construction of a text that is essentially narrative and where, therefore, sequentiality of reading is crucial to one's understanding of the story."

[6] We shall see that occasionally he is inconsistent in his view of characters and events.

Introduction

approach. In other words in his view 2 Samuel 21-24 does not organically contribute to the book, its plot and development (cf. 1990:13f). He only adds to the reader's confusion by the admission (1990:11), "By definition the function of the 'Last Words' is closure. The adjacent hymn [2 Sam 22], which also serves to round off the whole, befits a long-established king." But by including 1 Kings 1-2 in his study he has ignored the closure of Samuel, violated his methodology and nullified his own observations. Even though the thematic relation of 1 Kings 1-2 to Samuel is beyond doubt, treating it as part of Samuel rather than Kings is a weakly founded enterprise.

Fokkelman does not interact much with other interpreters. I assume this is intentional, although to do so might have been beneficial. Occasionally he engages in extra-textual or diachronic questions of what really happened, thus going beyond what the text explicitly or implicitly says (1986:592-95, 641; 1981:185, n. 34).[7] To be sure, everyone has to resort to gap filling, still it needs to be in accord with plot development, characterisation and in line with one's methodology.

As for the inconsistency in characterisation, Fokkelman pays little attention to portrayal. In the case of Saul as well as of David he fails to account for the character changes, rendering them rather static. One of the effects of his insensitivity and inconsistency in characterisation as well as of his vacuous psychologising is that one loses the sense of dealing with real-life characters, not in the sense that they were necessarily historical but that they are coherent characters in the narrative world.

As mentioned above, Fokkelman's arguments, conclusions and view are not always obvious. So, for instance, when interpreting 1 Samuel 20:35-21:1 (1986:341-51), after making the reader anticipate a solution, his preoccupation with the symbolic-literary level prevents him from explaining why, using such an elaborate system of signalling, Jonathan and David finally met at all. This reveals a basic flaw in his commentary, namely his failure to demonstrate a consistent plot, due to the disproportionate focus on literary devices.

In commenting on 1 Kings 1 Fokkelman asserts (1981:354): "We simply do not know if Nathan's words, repeated by Bathsheba, recall an actual event. Neither do we know if David, in v. 30, genuinely recalls a pronouncement once made by him or simply succumbs to the strong, suggestive pressure applied by wife and prophet." In a note he adds (n. 12): "I value this abstruseness as a literary asset and find it unnecessary to seek a 'solution'." Yet on p. 412 he recants: "[…] Nathan and Bathsheba's appeal to an oath sworn earlier by David is no concoction exposed to venomous criticism, but a true claim." And n. 1 there: "With respect to David, this means that in I Kings 1:17//24 he is not misled and, in v. 30, does not take a new, but an old oath." One has the impression Fokkelman was not quite sure what he was arguing.

---

[7] Unfortunately Polzin makes this mistake too, when commenting on 1 Sam 17:55-58 (1989:173).

Fokkelman's interpretations are frequently myopic. For instance I am not convinced that the double reference in 1 Kings 1 to Nathan's being a prophet is meant to lend "special authority to his words in David's eyes" (1981:359). It is possible but not the only option. It may just as likely be ironic — a prophet is the ringleader of the coup (cf. Walsh 1996:10).

More importantly since there are several options as to what a motif means because interpretations are often not intrinsic to the text, hence one has to resort to gap filling, it is clear that the interpretation is not merely a discovery of the text's original meaning but is determined by the interpreter's attitude and method. Thus being "open and empty" is a self-deception.

A basic characteristic of Fokkelman's project is the tendency towards literary orthodoxy. In his methodological discussion of the question, "when are we an immaculate mirror?" he asserts (1981:2) that there are "three features of the creative reader: (c) He commits himself totally; (b) his attitude is positive [Towards what? — text, narrator, author?]; and (a) he is nonetheless open and empty." Disregarding the question why he lists these in reverse order this is a positivist approach, not very different in effect from the attitude of diachronic approaches he so vehemently criticises. Fokkelman seems to be a representative of a new literary orthodoxy (see Jobling 1998:289f) — one exclusive approach is substituted by another. This impression is only reinforced by the following claim: since the narrator uses "no material other than language" the narrative's content "is ideologically neutral. It does not prejudge in respect of religion, morals or philosophy [...]" (1986:6). The implication of this statement is that any literary work is "ideologically neutral", an obvious nonsense.

Moreover,

> By committing oneself to a method beforehand the reader limits himself *eo ipso* and simultaneously furthers the reduction of his contact to cognitive aspects alone. I myself strive to derive my method from the work itself. This means that at this moment I have no worked-out system of approach but a premise which consists of certain principles, presumptions, and literary instruments; it means that my method must grow and be filled in as the work progresses. (1981:3)

This is a commendable endeavour but obviously self-deceptive, for he too, even if unconsciously, had his method beforehand, not merely "certain principles, presumptions, and literary instruments". More significantly this reinforces one's impression that Fokkelman's ultimate purpose is to determine the one true meaning of the text. His attempt to clarify what he means by correct reading also adumbrates this.

> Whoever wishes to make any assertion at all about the text can only do so after and based on the reading of the text. A sloppy or a prejudiced reading of the text gives an interpretation which is full of errors or blind spots respectively. On the other hand, the more careful the reading, the more valid the interpretation. The reader is a mirror, and his interpretation is the text's image in that mirror. From

this perspective too, the decisive importance of the reader, his qualities, and his attitude become evident. (1981:2)

I do not know how assertions like this, along with his discussion of reason (6f), were received in the early 80s. Twenty years on they sound banal (this also applies to the introduction to his 1986 volume).

My criticism above and the fact that I will frequently be referring to his observations in a positive way appreciating his elaborated analyses may seem contradictory. This is probably due to the fact that I have benefited from his observations on smaller units, whereas his analyses of larger units as well as methodological or structural observations I have often found unconvincing.

THE HISTORICO-LITERARY APPROACH OF PHILIPS LONG, DIANA EDELMAN, IAIN PROVAN AND CHRISTA SCHÄFER-LICHTENBERGER

V.P. Long's (1989) is a thorough and reliable exegetical and theological study which advocates a "synthetic exegetical approach based on a more complex theoretical model and open to fresh intuitions on both the diachronic and synchronic levels of inquiry" (18). His study of 1 Samuel 9-15 is an attempt at a synthetic approach that demonstrates the coherence of the Saul narrative.

Long correctly observes (33) that in Samuel "the favoured narrative mode is 'showing' rather than 'telling'", as, instead of straight narrative, description and comment, in FT story telling

> it is the scenic narrative mode that is nearly always preferred, with straight narrative being used primarily to introduce and close scenes and to recount action that cannot be presented scenically. Even where a biblical story contains a large amount of straight narrative, the highlights and the climax of the story are almost invariably scenic. (22)

This observation is a good starting point for a synchronic reading. On the other hand seeing the progress and profits of the synchronic approach in the last 20 years one wonders how much Long's measures up to a synchronic reading. And to be sure he is attentive to literary devices like keywords, word-play and poetry as heightened speech (25-31), repetition and analogy-contrast (34-41), but he fails to trace themes and motifs, intertextual allusions, not to mention plot and character development. By not attending to the niceties of the text in rhetorical-critical terms, Long tends to take what is said, like the rejection and condemnation of Saul, Samuel's valedictory speech and accusation at face value, without analysing — as Polzin and Eslinger do — the context and style of what the narrator says.

It also needs to be said that by not demonstrating how the passage he studies contributes to the overall theme of the book Long fails to produce an integrated reading.[8] *A Case for Literary and Theological Coherence*, the subtitle says. He does not live up to the subtitle, as demonstrated by the lack of discussion of ch. 12 and the relatively brief one of ch. 11. I also wonder whether we can have a coherent reading of Saul's rejection starting at ch. 9 so leaving out of the picture the introduction to the monarchy in ch. 8.

Since Long's focus is on Saul's rejection, he does not examine Samuel's involvement and how he manipulates Saul.[9] He simply takes Samuel's prophetic sincerity and authority at face value. Related to this is that Long does not demonstrate character development. (See e.g. comments on 14:18f where he does not consider that Saul's action and behaviour might be the consequence of previous events, 112f; and also his interpretation of ch. 15.) Thus whereas in Fokkelman's case less psychologising would have been more beneficial, in Long's more would have achieved more.

Long's word studies, more or less in the Kittel tradition, are valuable. One wishes, however, that he had carefully studied the terms in their closer as well as wider context in Samuel, in the way Polzin does. Furthermore, as a basic requirement of the diachronic approach he partly advocates, he pays attention to ANE practices like the prophetic mediation of divine will to the charismatic king. Regarding this my main criticism will be that charismatic military leadership in Israel cannot be subjected to any human authority. ANE kings might be as Long depicts them; I shall argue, however, that charismatic kings under Yahweh's guidance must necessarily be independent of any, including prophetic, control. Therefore a comparative approach cannot be applied. This is not to say that Long fails in his attempt at a synthetic approach, but rather that the diachronic approach detracts from the synchronic.[10]

Diana Edelman's (1991) is a good sequential reading of the narrative of Saul (1 Sam 8-2 Sam 1). She is concerned "with the final form of the text," thus she explores "the world-view of the last 'hand' that made adjustments to it" (13). This sums up Edelman's method with its promises and pitfalls alike. The attempt at a close reading of the final form of the text (13, 70) is commendable, but one wonders how much hers measures up to a really close reading, like e.g. Eslinger's. Firstly the portion she chose to analyse in less than 300 pages is too long. A close reading of twenty-five chapters of narrative should also make one expect a more careful character and plot development. What the reader gets

---

[8] His aim, the demonstration of the literary and theological coherence of the section, in which respect his study is excellent, apparently did not allow for this.

[9] Again this is partly understandable as it is not a synchronic approach in the strict sense. Since the publication of his study Samuel's character and manipulation have been studied.

[10] Even though I shall strictly use the synchronic I am not an advocate of a total divorce of the two approaches. I am rather claiming that had Long had the chance to consult studies by Fokkelman, Polzin or Eslinger, he would probably have come to different conclusions.

Introduction

instead is rather bits and pieces.

More importantly, one is not quite sure to what the "last hand" refers. Is it the author or the final redactor? In either case Edelman seems to be concerned with some imputed and hypothetical "world-view", the investigation of which comes dangerously close to a diachronic approach. In other words the supposed relevance of the hypothetical audience is not in accord with her declared method of close reading and literary criticism (see e.g. 73f). This suspicion is reinforced on reading her claim to approach the text as a historian trying to put herself

> in the shoes of a member of the intended ancient audience so that I can understand the author's allusions, structuring techniques, and idioms to the most detailed degree possible. My primary focus is on understanding how, when, and why the writer created this narrative about Saul, with the ultimate goal of deducing what parts might have been based on pre-existing sources and what portions are likely to have been the product of creative artistic invention and guesswork. (11)

Edelman is at odds with literary patterns such as the rise of the lowly and fall of the mighty suggested by Preston (1982). She criticises the pattern not in literary but in historical-sociological terms (34f), either because of lack of attention to the biblical text or because of inattention to the secondary literature. This is probably due to the confusion created by her double methodology. By working on two levels she cannot avoid the impression of trying to escape to the historical-sociological level when in dire straits on the literary.

Because not attentive enough to literary aspects, Edelman often produces somewhat odd interpretations. That the king was "to be the guardian of the existing revelation" (49) seems far-fetched. Similarly I cannot see any "time-frame intended" for the anointing process by either the narrator or God in 1 Samuel 9 (50). The Jonathan theme is certainly important in the narrative (35f), but not as significant as she thinks. That Jonathan "accepted *Yahweh's* decree of guilt in 14.43" (136; my italics) is very doubtful to me, as God is totally absent from the chapter. She observes that his red hair made David distinctive (116), which is not too ingenious an observation, for the narrator could have found some better characteristic of distinction for the new king of Israel. Similarly that the replacement of God's good spirit by a bad one was intended "to teach Israel the need for ongoing obedience" (117) is rather fanciful. She fails to recognise in chs. 16 and 18 the antagonism of the old and new kings, a brilliant narrative motif. Commendable is, however, that in studying chs. 16-17 Edelman's literary critic self prevails by refusing to discuss possible different traditions. That David swore an oath of loyalty on entering Saul's service (122) is at least questionable for lacking textual basis. To build an argument on this supposed motif violates every exegetical method. Similarly, after speculating when Saul learned of David's anointing (120f), Edelman simply takes Saul's knowledge thereof in 17:55-58 for granted (134). To introduce Yahweh into the paternity question of ch. 17 (134f) I think is to miss the point of the narrative and misunderstand Gooding's argument (1986:60). On ch. 18 Edelman notes: "Should David die now by his [Saul's] hand, he in turn would almost certainly be assassinated by a Davidic supporter." One wonders on what textual detail this observation (139) is based, especially when she adds, "The narrator has the audience's full attention."

Edelman assigns an overestimated and often speculative import to dress as displaying ethnic identity (236f, 267, 302). As a matter of fact she frequently falls into the trap of speculation: she connects Abishai's phrasing in 26:8 with Saul's double attempt on David's life in 18:11 and 19:10 (224f); Jabesh-Gilead's absence from the battle in ch. 31 to her "implies that they had not obeyed their monarch's summons to arms", which she takes as a loss of trust in the king (292). References such as "Wadi Suweinit" (81, 125) sound odd in a synchronic study concerned with narratology. The claim that the coronation ceremony is about "how the author envisions historical events to have unfolded" (83) is also rather arbitrary.

To study the text both as a historian and as a literary critic seems to be rather irreconcilable. This is manifest in that Edelman often operates with some reconstruction and too much gap filling. A double methodology is a slippery area, and Edelman could not keep her balance.

Edelman has shed light on various textual details and on Saul's story as a whole. Still one would expect more of a study published in 1991, and for which important studies on Samuel were available. Her study would likely have received more significant scholarly attention had she produced a more novel one.

A fine attempt to use both diachronic and synchronic methods is represented in **Iain Provan**'s studies (1995, 1995a, 1997). His is a good attempt at what Long calls a "synthetic approach" — harmonising both literary and historical approaches. His essay (1995a) brilliantly develops the argument by using both literary and historical (socio-political) insights. Though he does not mention it, his discussion of 1 Kings 1-2 (18f) implies that he operates with the assumption of a SN. 1 Kings 1-2 "is itself not so much the beginning of a story as the last chapter of a larger story" (18f). I feel uneasy with claims like this because textual criticism and the tradition of the text suggest otherwise.

Despite assuming a SN Provan urges the reader to read Kings as a coherent, continuous narrative in its final form (34-43). And that is exactly what he accomplishes in his commentary (1995), which, in a popular rather than academic form, explicates what he later outlined in his 1997 book. Provan is also interested in word-play (22f), motifs and overarching themes (27).

A word on terminology. Provan calls Kings "didactic literature" (1997:23), which phrase appears to me a little unfortunate[11] along with "historiography"

---

[11] It has been observed that biblical narrative, Genesis-Kings in particular, is not didactic but ideological (see Sternberg 1985:38).

(45ff). I would prefer the term "historiosophy" used by Israeli scholars. This term implies both purposes suggested by him, namely that the biblical book is both ideological and related to history.

The only negative observation concerns Provan's hermeneutical orientation. He frequently operates with the rather Lutheran and biased opposition of grace and law (13, 41, 92, 96), though it is not explicit in the narrative. Also he sometimes interprets Kings from the perspective of Proverbs (48, 50, 56), a popular, but questionable, approach. Are these terms those of the FT and, more particularly, Kings, or rather imported ones?

Christa Schäfer-Lichtenberger (1995) scrutinises authority and the legitimacy of successors. She criticises Rost's study (1995:232-35) and considers the Solomon narrative one unit. Thus 1:1-3:15 for her is the grounding of Solomon's authority and legitimacy (231), which assures a coherent reading. She thus reads chs. 1-2 forwards predicting changes in Solomon's character. By so doing she departs from most Solomon studies, and this is commendable, because to consider the first two chapters an introduction to 1 Kings is essential if we are to understand the Solomon narrative. In this vein she looks for signals indicating narrative and character coherence. So after God's appearance at Gibeon Solomon is changed (258-62, 282f).

Schäfer-Lichtenberger (277-323) has organised her discussion of 1 Kings 3:16-8:66 under the title "Test of the Charisma"; 9:1-9 under "Yahweh's Response"; 9:1-10:29: "Solomon's Test Period". Even though I shall differ with her when interpreting particular sections, I welcome her attempt to read the narrative in a sequential and coherent way. My only criticism is that though she uses the terms "charisma" and "charismatic", she fails to provide a definition or study the aspect more carefully (on this see below).

Obviously none of the studies discussed above are related to my topic of charismatic leadership. Indeed I have not seen a synchronic study on the charismatic leadership of Saul, David or Solomon. The studies just surveyed still relate to my study in that they, with the exception of Schäfer-Lichtenberger, approach the text synchronically, yielding valuable insights to my study as well as points of orientation to develop my methodology.

By working with the tools of the synchronic approach I assume, as scholars of this approach do, that the narrative makes sense. That is to say, I shall try to find explanations and motives in the text, whether explicit or implicit.

Similarly to Gunn, Eslinger and Miscall I shall be suspicious of conventional evaluations of events and characters, whenever they fail to provide compelling and comprehensive interpretations. Indeed, I shall be suspicious of any unsatisfactory interpretation regarding plot, character or their development. I shall follow Gunn by interpreting Saul's rejection as caused mainly by Samuel's authoritarianism. Following Eslinger I shall pay attention to whose viewpoint is reflected in a statement. I shall use Miscall's "undecidability" in my evaluation of David.

Jobling has taught me to see the Saul narrative in a structuralist framework of binary oppositions of old and new. Jobling's structuralist approach to the Samuel-Saul or judgeship-kingship transition has helped me appropriate these themes. His openness to the psychological makes the Samuel-Saul relationship more easily understood. Polzin has made me aware of the need to put 1-2 Samuel in the context of the DH. His attention to keywords, puns, motifs and themes has inspired my reading. Similarly his focus on "character zones" has resulted in a consistent characterisation, which I shall follow.

V.P. Long has demonstrated the coherence of the Saul narrative, on the presupposition of which I shall work. By his pattern of the designation, demonstration and confirmation of charisma I have found it helpful to understand the sequence of the narrative. Schäfer-Lichtenberger has demonstrated the coherence of the Solomon narrative as well as drawn attention to important aspects such as charisma and transition in leadership. Taking political and sociological motives into account can enrich our understanding of the narrative, Provan has shown.

Fokkelman's aesthetic study of sections, sentences and words has occasionally attracted me to minute analyses as well as cautioned me of the dangers of missing the whole picture by doing this. His failure in presenting a consistent characterisation and plot has made me aware of the need of both. Similarly, Edelman's proneness to speculations and failure to work consistently on the synchronic level have served as warnings to me.

Studies on Charisma

LAYING THE FOUNDATIONS — MAX WEBER

Max Weber sets out his seminal study (1968) by identifying three types of leadership, which he calls legal-rational, traditional and charismatic. He deals with the third most extensively. Because of my focus I shall not discuss the first and second categories. Nor shall I develop Weber's theory of the transformation and routinisation of charisma. I shall rather use his observations as a springboard and refer to him to support my arguments.

Weber studies charisma and charismatic leaders as a sociologist. Nevertheless, he stresses (216), "The concept of 'charisma' ('the gift of grace') is taken from the vocabulary of early Christianity." Indeed his definition of charisma as "a certain quality of an individual personality by virtue of which he is considered extraordinary and treated as endowed with supernatural, superhuman, or at least specifically exceptional powers or qualities" (241) by his followers is in line with this observation by him. Though Weber stressed the biblical origin of the concept, subsequent theological scholarship has ignored this.

CHARISMA RELATED TO OFFICE — ALBRECHT ALT, HERBERT DONNER, WALTER BEYERLIN, T.C.G. THORNTON, GÖSTA AHLSTRÖM AND RODNEY HUTTON

In two groundbreaking essays on the Judahite and Israelite monarchies (1989,

1989a) **Albrecht Alt** makes the claim that in the view of ancient Israelites the king was chosen and empowered by God. A designation by a prophet followed. Nothing played a more significant role in the formation of the Israelite kingdom than charismatic leadership (1989:188-91). The dynastic idea was not inherent to the charismatic kingship of Saul. In fact charismatic leadership and dynastic kingship were opposed to each other (204f). Israel's king,

> in the original conception, owed his authority exclusively to the fact that he was spontaneously called and endowed with charismatic powers by Yahweh (I Sam. ix. 1-10, 16). The homage of the tribes that followed the first test of his powers (I Sam. xi) signifies by contrast nothing more than a later ratification. (1989a:243)

As opposed to the judges, Saul's commission was not restricted to one single campaign, but he was to save Israel from all the enemies round about (1 Sam 10:1, LXX) (243). Alt also argues that charisma was not hereditary but only and at most for the lifetime of the one endowed. This belief was strong in the first century of the Northern Kingdom. Alt suggests that basically kingship was open to any individual whom God might choose by a prophet. In addition God may replace the king.

Alt also claims that Judah had no concept of charismatic kingship similar to the Northern kingdom's. With the king as a descendant of David, Judahite kingship embodied perpetuity through the existing royal family. It meant stability and Judah, as a dynastic monarchy, was void of charisma. Still, Alt concludes (257) that in contrast to Israel, in Judah charismatic authority is not limited "to the person and lifetime of one individual king chosen by Yahweh, but is bestowed as a permanent possession on the whole ruling house."

Alt's use of charisma illustrates the confusion of terminology in scholarship. Since charisma is considered a very volatile force, it is generally attributed to temporal and volatile leadership such as judgeship and kingship in the Northern kingdom. It is not bestowed upon persons empowered to overcome some crisis. Though I shall also claim that charisma is not static, I shall try to avoid associating it with an institution.

Herbert Donner's article (1959) is not specifically concerned with charisma, but still makes some interesting remarks. Clearly relying on Alt he states that originally dynastic bonds were alien to the Israelite monarchy. The two constitutive features of the king's designation by Yahweh and his acclamation by the people tied the monarchy rather to the charismatic leadership of the judges' era (129).

Then in a footnote, without further elaboration, he remarks that the free initiative by Yahweh to designate a charismatic can be found in the dynastic kingdom of Judah as well. The charisma of governing, however, is not limited to the person and lifetime of the king in office but concerns the dynasty; it is not an individual designated but the whole dynasty (144, n. 158). Apparently Donner abandons the concept of individual charisma. Instead he understands charisma as related to the office of kingship and ruling. This idea will prevail in biblical scholarship until the late seventies.

In an article on Saul's charisma (1961) **Walter Beyerlin** questions some of Alt's theses. In Judges he claims Yahweh's spirit empowers individuals like Othniel, Gideon or Jephthah always for single and limited actions. It is difficult to maintain that this became institutionalised and permanent in Saul's kingdom. It is even more unthinkable that the actualisation of the bestowal of God's spirit into a permanent charismatic state was accomplished through the acclamation of the people (187).

In 1 Samuel 9:1-10:16 Saul's inner transformation and Yahweh's spirit demonstrate the basic change caused by the anointing. In chs. 13-15, however, there is no sign of charismatic leadership. Saul's attempts at institutionalisation (his cousin Abner is his general, Ahijah his priest), a policy unknown in Judges, further support this view. Only ch. 11 is about a charisma and leadership typical of the judges' era, but this is not an organic part of the Saul tradition Beyerlin claims.

Saul's charisma, Beyerlin carries on, was related with a prophetic-ecstatic manifestation (10:5-16). However, the tradition did not regard Saul's charisma as prophetic in origin and character. This prophetic charisma, though a divine gift, was but ephemeral. The foremost result of this charisma was that Saul was and remained Yahweh's anointed even after David's election, making the king untouchable. His authority came from Yahweh, the anointing one, whose spirit dwelt in Saul. The acclamation of the people in 10:24 was thus the recognition of this fact: "The king lives/is filled with life!" (194f).

The difference between the major judges and Saul was that, while charisma in the case of the major judges was a talent of leadership, Saul's charisma was also linked to his personal qualities. Yahweh's life and authority had to be manifest in this way. This supports Beyerlin's claim that Saul's charisma had little in common with that of the judges, but the concept was influenced by the Canaanite environment. Beyerlin refutes Alt's claim that Saul's kingdom was not thought to be hereditary, as well as the idea that Saul had only martial tasks, while in peace he had none.

Two years after Beyerlin's essay his critique of Alt was boosted by **T.C.G. Thornton**. Thornton criticises Alt's thesis from the perspective of comparative religion by referring to the general ANE world-view, in which all kings were regarded as "charismatic" rulers and Judah was definitely no exception. Therefore he claims it is hard to maintain that in Israel there existed a special kind of charismatic kingship fundamentally different from everywhere else. Kings everywhere claimed to have divine backing, so probably also in Judah. He concludes, "There is no good evidence that prophetical designation was given greater importance in Israel than it may have been given anywhere among Israel's neighbours" (5), including Judah.

After investigating Kings he asserts that there was no significant difference between ideas of kingship in Judah and Israel. Thornton sums up his findings

Introduction

saying that the difference was not between various ideals of kingship, but in the way the people regarded their reigning dynasties.

The problem with this approach, also perceived by Thornton,[12] is that the term "charismatic" comes to refer to any ruler — hence it becomes meaningless. This does not correspond with either the biblical concept or Weber's usage.

Following Thornton, **Gösta Ahlström** studied charisma with reference to ANE ideologies (1968). He suggests that the concept of divine charisma was very common in ANE. Kingship was regarded as a divine institution both in Mesopotamia and in Israel.

Charisma is "a gift of favor", Ahlström asserts (95). A distinction should be made between human and divine charisma. As far as charismatic kingship is concerned "it is the people, or the father of the king, who choose him. This we may call the human charisma" (95). From another point of view, though, "it is the deity who chooses the king. Of course, this is accomplished through a vision, through a prophet, or through some liturgical act by which the king can be said to have received divine gifts, such as the spirit" (95). The two ideas common in ANE are not mutually exclusive but are both involved in the institution of kingship.

Ahlström criticises Alt:

> For that matter, we know that Jahweh was always more interested in order than in chaos. [...] The theory that the multiplication of dynasties in Israel was an indication of the survival of the charismatic rulership is hardly plausible. It would appear to us that the reverse would be true. Charismatic kingship willed by the deity would best be expressed in political stability. (96f)

More importantly Ahlström claims (97) that "the characteristic feature of the divine charisma should be the gift of Jahweh's spirit, *rūaḥ*, as in the case of the kings." Since not all the judges are said to have had the spirit, they lacked divine designation and charisma (97f). Saul was chosen and had God's spirit hence he was charismatic (99f). Scholars generally argue that Solomon ascended to the throne by palace intrigue and by the assistance of his father and mother. Supposedly he was not divinely chosen and had no charisma (100f). Ahlström disagrees with this view by referring to 2 Samuel 7:12ff.

> David's successor shall become the son of Jahweh, and Jahweh shall be his father. Certainly, this is charisma in the highest *potens*! The passage clearly shows the ideological (or should I say, "theological") relationship between the deity and the king. As the anointed one, Solomon is a part of this charismatic relationship. (101)

Ahlström finds in 1 Kings 1:48 "the religious motivation behind Solomon's kingship": Solomon is appointed by his father and at the same time chosen by

---

[12] Note the frequent reference to charisma in inverted commas.

God (103). That Solomon was the chosen one was recognised by Adonijah, the queen of Sheba and Solomon himself (104). Ahlström concludes

> that the ideas of divine election and "charismatic" kingship must be associated with the election and appointment of a king both in Israel and in Judah. The idea that there was a real difference between these two states relating to royal ideology is a fabrication of scholarly imagination. In both kingdoms we find the notion of divine election. In both kingdoms we find the idea of divine charisma. In both kingdoms we find the concept of divine establishment. The kingdom is always constituted by the deity, and the king is always appointed by Jahweh (Deut. 17:15). (109)

Then he adds,

> It is the individual king who is the bearer of the reality inherent within the dynasty. Thus, properly speaking, he is the one who is the divine choice and the possessor of the charismatic gifts. [...] Not only David but every king has been placed on the throne by Jahweh. Not only the king chosen at this moment but also his descendants have been selected by Jahweh to rule. (110)

Ahlström's attempt to introduce the concept of a human as well as a divine charisma is confusing and a deviation from the Weberian and biblical concepts. Moreover, Ahlström equates charisma with being elected by Yahweh hence being Yahweh's son. This makes him speak of the "charismatic relationship" between Solomon and Yahweh (101). By making divine election of dynasties and charisma synonymous, Ahlström dissolves charisma in the context of its possible scope of operation. His position "is tantamount to conceiving of charisma as embedded in an institution" (Overholt 1984:289). In other words, it is very problematic to regard being elected as equivalent to being charismatic (see my discussion on Solomon.) The aspects of endowment by the divine spirit, its purpose and, further, the way charisma is used are not addressed. By focusing on its origin and collapsing charisma into divine election Ahlström practically divides charisma from its purpose and renders it static.

Basing his arguments of Solomon's charismatic kingship on non-deuteronomistic texts, psalms in particular, and hardly referring to 1 Kings is questionable as well. Related to this is that Ahlström does not work in narratological terms, i.e. he sometimes argues out of silence and neglects evaluations implicit in the narrative.

In the most recent discussion of biblical charismatic leadership (1994) **Rodney Hutton** tries to reconcile charisma with institution. He begins by claiming that the issue of charisma is finally related to that of authority. As a good Lutheran representing "office" he downplays the tension between charisma and institution. He prefers the idea "that charisma is not a unique form of authority that stands over against other more 'regularized' forms" (5). He proposes (8): "Charisma will be understood not primarily as a personal trait exhibited by a 'charismatic' individual independent of social context but rather as an essentially social phenomenon that is a function of broader group dynamics and fixed social relationships." Thus Hutton's approach is mainly sociological, which he further clarifies in the section "Social Reconstruction and Theological Reflection" (9-16). Unfortunately Hutton fails to engage in a serious methodological discussion with synchronic approaches to the biblical text, which makes his attitude to them unclear (see e.g. 57-62). Though his analyses are often insightful, one wishes he had consulted literary critical studies by Polzin and Fokkelman, which would definitely have enriched this work. But as a matter of fact not even V.P. Long is referred to.

Hutton's sociological orientation to charisma is visible in his sympathy to Shils' theory which rejects "any notion that charisma represents an *intrusive* disordering principle that is in social tension with a 'legal/rational' or 'traditional' form of authority" (65; my italics). Indeed,

> any charisma as it manifests itself in the person of the judge is not understood to be an *intrusion* into the normal ordering principles of social leadership. The "charisma" of the judge was not exclusively located in some extraordinary *incursion* of divine power into the otherwise orderly management of "business as usual." To the extent that the judges can be spoken of as charismatic, such charisma is not associated with the divine empowerment—that is, with the momentary explosion of the "spirit of God" in the person's life. (66; my italics)

Hutton supports this view by a brief exposition of the activities of the judges (66-70). He claims that

> when we say that the judges exhibit charisma, we mean that the author portrayed them as leaders who were fundamentally "supercharged" by commitments to core values of Israelite society. Since they are also epic protagonists, they are naturally portrayed as also displaying behaviour understood to result from greed, passion, or some tragic flaw, best illustrated in the case of Samson but also seen in the cases of Gideon and Jephthah. But beyond the flaws of such normal epic characterization they are persons who represent the struggle for the establishment and preservation of Israelite national identity and the commitment to solidarity and cohesion. In spite of their forays into lamentable behaviour and near disastrous mishaps, they were received by the reader as representative of the centering of cosmos and order in the life of Israel. As soon as the note of a judge's death was announced, the next movement in the plot was once again in the direction of disorder and chaos. The attribution of charisma to the judges does not relate strictly to the note of spirit empowerment, as will be demonstrated by what follows. It is the other way around. Spirit empowerment serves as one symbol among others of confirmation of the attribution of charisma. (66)

After a brief discussion of the judges' charismatic empowerment (65-69) he dismisses the notion by claiming:

None of the judges was depicted by the Deuteronomistic historian as possessing a "charismatic empowerment" that stood over against other, more ordinary forms of legitimation. If one can legitimately speak of the judges as "charismatic," it is only in the sense that they represent the centering principles of cosmic justice and order in the mind of the author and his intended audience. (69f)

Hutton comes to the conclusion that charismatic and institutional leaderships are but two sides of the same coin.

Claims such as the one just quoted may imply that God's salvation comes about by virtue of verifiable sociological developments and without any reference to the supernatural. It does not take a Barthian to see the peril of collapsing the supernatural into the natural. This notwithstanding Hutton later claims of 10:1-13 that "the charismatic empowerment, though again temporary, is not an end in itself" (90; see also 93). One is confused as to Hutton's real view. Similarly what he means by "charismatic empowerment", a frequent term, is unclear.

Hutton's clinging to "charisma" as a merely sociological concept with little reference to God's spirit, in the DH more often intrusive than not in my view, as the origin of it results in an abandonment of the theological. Ironically the theologian Hutton ends up working as a sociologist, while the sociologist Weber was more aware of the biblical origin hence possible theological import of charisma. I shall demonstrate that it is unnecessary to restrict charisma to either an individualistic or a sociological concept. Charisma can be viewed as a personal quality dependent on the social context, i.e. emerging in crisis situations.

CHARISMA AS A SUPERNATURAL PERSONAL TRAIT — ABRAHAM MALAMAT AND ZE'EV WEISMAN

An alternative approach to office related charisma has been proposed by Israeli scholars. In an essay on "Charismatic Leadership in the Book of Judges" (1976) **Abraham Malamat** studies the topic from a theological and sociological perspective. Concerning the sociological aspect he claims that, in Weberian terms, the decline of traditional authority made the charismatic judge-deliverer emerge, nearly all of them from a socially marginal position, raised outside normal society. As for the theological factor Malamat asserts that charisma approximates to the expression "Yahweh's spirit" (157), hence it is a supernatural trait related to personality. He then lists the characteristics of charismatic judges: they emerge in emergencies; "direct contact with transcendental powers and identification with the symbols held most sacred by a people" (161) as well as public signs characterise their activity which is not necessarily linked to religious or civil centres; their authority is spontaneous as they are appointed in an *ad hoc* way; the relationship between the leader and the people is not based on coercion but on personal reverence and emotion.

Malamat's emphasis on charisma as a supernatural and personality-related trait rather than on sociological forces is a fresh impulse in the study of charismatic leadership. It is also more in accord with the accent of biblical accounts on charismatic leadership. Thus I shall follow Malamat by focusing more on the personal than the sociological.

In the following year another Israeli scholar **Ze'ev Weisman** investigated the topic (1977). In his essay Weisman raises two significant questions related to charisma. Firstly how far is it justified to identify "charismatic leadership" with a particular historical-political regime? Weisman is aware of the dilemma that

> there seems to be a paradox in the fact that attempts have been made to identify "charismatic leadership" with a particular historical-political regime. This arises from the fact that originally the term "charisma" was tied to a theocratic outlook which contradicts principally any kind of regime based on the authority and sovereignty of a human being of flesh and blood. As a theological notion it conveys the idea of God's spiritual gifts, bestowed upon people who function as His emissaries and carry out His mission upon earth. (400)

He carries on:

> Following M. Weber's definition I would suggest that there is no real justification for the application of this term to a political regime or to any consecutive historical system of leadership; it may properly be applied only to individual leaders as such. [...] There is, therefore, in the attempt to identify charisma with a certain political and historical regime a methodological deviation from M. Weber's original hypothesis, a deviation which arose from the conversion of the typological designation into a historical and political term. (401)

Secondly what was the relationship between the charismatic leaders and the historical situation of the era of the judges?

> Each of these saviours was unique, and each of them emerged in his own way to rescue his people from their enemies in the critical circumstances of the time. Whether his activity rose out of a spontaneous impulse to serve the immediate needs of his close environment, or his historical consciousness made him identify himself with the interests of his people, the charismatic saviour represented by his deeds the embryonic national leadership of the Israelite state in formation. The individual qualities which motivated these figures to rise up against oppression, coupled with the readiness of their people with the cures which the saviours could offer provide the explanation of the close relationship between the charismatic saviours and the era of the judges. Distress alone does not create charisma; charisma follows in the wake of salvation. (410f)

Similarly to Malamat, by looking for the particular rather than the general

Weisman stresses "the individual qualities".[13] He views charisma as a functional term, and I am sympathetic to it, as well as to his insistence that charisma should not be assigned to any political-historical regime but to individuals on whom God's spirit is bestowed.

MEDIATING BETWEEN THE TWO VIEWS — THOMAS OVERHOLT

Next to join the discussion was **Thomas Overholt** — a mediator between the two camps (1984). He discusses Ahlström's, Malamat's and Weisman's theses.

Ahlström, following Thornton's critique of Alt, maintains that for a "charismatic" kingship the election and appointment of monarchs in Israel and Judah were indispensable. The obvious problem with this concept is that "the term 'charisma' refers to an individual with special gifts". How is it then possible to "apply it to a king as representative of the institution of the monarchy, especially to Solomon, the archetypal bureaucrat?" (288).

On the other hand, Malamat follows Weber's categories by suggesting that authority is bestowed on the charismatic spontaneously. Charismatic leadership is therefore not dependent upon class, status, age or sex. Relationship between people and leader rests not on formal rules, administration or coercion but on emotion. Israel desired to make charismatic leadership fixed and stable, which Weber called "routinisation". Weisman followed in Malamat's footsteps by claiming that the Weberian concept of "charismatic leadership" should not be applied to a political regime or any system of leadership. The origin of the judges' charisma is their individual qualities.

Overholt tries to mediate between these views. He asserts that the judges appear to have been "charismatic leaders functioning as individuals without permanent institutional connections" (289). Overholt also argues that Weber hints at the possibility of charisma being embedded in institution, hence "a rigid distinction between individual and institutional authority" (289) is not conceivable. Overholt's conclusion is that individuals are bearers of charisma. A manifestation of charisma apart from a social context is inconceivable. Society is no passive recipient but, by recognising it, the authoriser of the charisma.

EVALUATION AND CONCLUSION

As shown above, after Weber there was a shift from focusing on the individual charismatic to the social process and environment, so that Ahlström and

---

[13] It might not be an accident that after nearly half a century reign of the sociological concept of charisma in theology it was Israeli scholars criticising it and giving a new impetus to the study of charisma. I also wonder whether their role in this may be explained by reference to Jewish theology, especially midrash, which eagerly seeks to elucidate explicit and implicit references of the text, while being unconcerned with background questions. If my hunch is right the reaction on the part of Israeli scholars to the "Lutheran excess" (see below) was something to be expected.

Thornton apply "charisma" to dynasties and virtually every ruler; simultaneously the focus has been on the *concept* of charisma with little discussion of biblical texts. Consequently studies on charisma have basically become sociological, ignoring textual and theological considerations. The consequence of this ignorance can be seen in the unfortunate tendency on the part of theologians who ignore the explicit or implicit view of the narrator. This neglect and loss of the textual-theological seems to be due to the sociological orientation, which has created a widening chasm between the Weberian and biblical charisma and the sociological one.

I disagree with scholars who seek to apply the concept to virtually any leader. The focus and basic thrust of my study are literary and theological; my methodology requires a literary-critical and theological definition of "charisma". Therefore I have sought to narrow down the application as well as the validity of "charisma".[14] I shall define "charisma" in regard to its function.

It is remarkable that almost without exception the scholars in whose view charisma and office are closely linked, whether or not they rely on the Weberian concept of office charisma, are of Lutheran background (Alt, Donner, Beyerlin, Ahlström, Hutton).[15] I wonder whether the concept of charisma being embodied in an institution or office is the predominant view of Lutherans. For them "office" is by definition decisive as regards God's activity and church life, thus linked to charisma. Similarly it would be interesting to trace the connection between prophetic designation as indispensable in the charismatic's emergence and apostolic succession and ordination.

For obvious reasons, Max Weber's work has influenced scholarship to a high degree. As a sociologist his approach and methodology were throughout sociological. Biblical scholarship has subsequently adopted his definition of "charisma" without any reflection on the question whether it is substantiated by biblical texts. Certainly there is a difference between the sociological and the theological concepts. The theological concept is that, as the term suggests and as Ahlström, despite his invalid application of it, correctly formulated, charisma derives from God's favour (cf. Malamat 1976:157). God bestows charisma on anyone he chooses (cf. 1 Cor 12:11). In this respect charisma does not apply to any influential leader as assumed when the Weberian definition as a sociological concept is accepted. Rather charisma is a biblical concept of an

---

[14] At the same time, I have tried to define "charisma" in a broader sense than Weber did, whose definition apparently does not apply to personalities unrecognised as charismatics in their lifetime, but who, like the prophet Elijah, had a great deal of impact upon later generations.

[15] I should admit that I could not check this. The fact that these German and Swedish scholars taught at universities where only Lutheran and Reformed professors are admitted makes the case quite strong though (Hutton teaches at a Lutheran seminary). Also the emphasis on *Amt* in the German Lutheran and Reformed traditions, most often referred to as evangelical, is similar in significance. Seemingly only Thornton is of a non-Lutheran background.

extraordinary quality of a leader, which, on the narrative's level, is recognised as superhuman and supernatural by the narrator and his characters. (In this way I intend to reclaim for charisma its divine origin and theological content.) The process of recognition might be called confirmation. By virtue of his/her charisma the charismatic offers a resolution to a particular crisis.[16]

Likewise I shall talk of charismatic leadership when a person, endowed with charisma and so exercising influence upon his/her followers, offers a resolution to a certain crisis situation, political, social, economic or religious. This will mean that charisma in the cases of Saul and David is closely linked to effective military leadership. This is what the crisis required. Still I do not consider the concept of military charismatic leadership absolute, but rather acknowledge the possibility and necessity of transformation of charisma once Solomon succeeded his father. I shall argue that at the beginning of his rule he was confronted with a crisis situation although one not military in nature.

It needs to be noted that "charisma" and "charismatic" are used inconsistently and rather confusingly (e.g. Noth 1984; DeVries 1985). In his insightful article Malamat speaks of "an upsurge of charismatic sensitivity among the people" in emergency situations, and refers to a sociologist's phrase of "charismatic hunger" (1976:156). Even Schäfer-Lichtenberger in her otherwise brilliant study suggests that Mettinger has noticed the significance of Solomon's charismatic endowment. And even though in his comparison of Saul's and Solomon's charisma he takes into account their changed manifestations does not consider that Saul was a charismatic whereas Solomon only a charismatically endowed king. The designation of charismatic endowment as a constant possession points to the trivialisation (*Veralltäglichung*) of the charisma. Obviously the charismatic does not dispose over the charisma. In addition there is the permanent threat for the charismatic to lose the charisma along with the recognition of followers. Wherever this happens all the charismatic's feats are forgotten. Thus in the evaluation there can only be either recognition or rejection. In this respect Saul is a classic charismatic whereas Solomon's character is much subtler. This latter, in some respect, is to be viewed as a functional charismatic. After taking the throne without charisma he is charismatically endowed in a specific way. Differentiating between the person, the position of Solomon and the charismatic fulfilment of the role is the basis for a negative evaluation of Solomon's person. Neither Solomon's specific talent nor his charismatic achievements such as administration, foreign policy or temple project call for disapproval, however (1995:280).

She is correct in pointing out the danger of "trivialising" charisma by its *Veralltäglichung*. However, the distinction between the charismatic Saul and the "only charismatically gifted" Solomon seems abstruse and speculative. To be sure in order to justify her thesis of Solomon as the negative counterpart in

---

[16] Although from a sociological perspective, Hong argues similarly (2000:63-107).

Introduction

the David-Solomon transition to charismatic Joshua in the Moses-Joshua transition Schäfer-Lichtenberger was compelled to resort to such a distinction. But her sophisticated differentiation of the concept results in a trifling one. This impression is reinforced by sentences like this (290; AT): "After Solomon's design is legitimated as one both traditional (v. 17) and charismatic (v. 18) Solomon's aspiration can publicly be pronounced (v. 19)." To me it seems that 1 Kings 5:18 (ET 5:4) is not a "charismatic legitimation", whatever that means, but merely a theological statement. More importantly I doubt whether intents can be called "charismatic". Likewise, commenting on 5:18, she talks of "the charismatic explanation (God's promise)" (290; and similarly on 5:21, 291). Such statements display the confusion in terminology.

Methodology

Apart from a couple of essays (Hutton, Schäfer-Lichtenberger) either charisma or the narrative has been the focus of biblical studies. I endeavour to study both. Furthermore the major, and almost only, concern of studies on charisma has been to establish who is charismatic. This done theologians have not been interested to pursue the investigation of charisma in biblical narratives to find out more about its nature. It also seems that so far the interest of theologians has been limited to studying the *concept* of "charisma", whilst, by not studying particular cases, persons or situations in depth textually and theologically, *charismatic leadership* has remained a neglected area of biblical research. This study attempts to address these oversights. The main scope of this research will be charismatic leadership, which aspect is crucial for an understanding of the narrative. Since I am interested in charismatic leadership, I shall study the narrative with this particular perspective in mind, which in turn will affect my methodology.

The Biblical Text

Like most literary critics I study the Hebrew text in its final form without attending to genetic or background questions. Like other literary critics I am aware of the textual difficulties of 1-2 Samuel. Also like other literary critics I shall take the synchronic route; I will not ignore them but focus on the text and only deal with them where a text-critical discussion helps my reading. I view the text as it stands now, "on its face value" (Gillingham 1998:180), with no regard to its prehistory (*Vorgeschichte*). Thus I will disregard units like David's Rise or the SN, by which I am not saying that they did not exist as independent sources or traditions.[17]

---

[17] The underlying presupposition of the viability of analysing two different literary units as a single narrative (2 Sam 9-1 Kgs 2), however, is questionable.

The Emergence of the Synchronic Approach

In the seventies and eighties literary studies were concerned with demonstrating the literary coherence and artistry of biblical narratives. This is best seen as a reaction to source oriented scholarship. From the eighties the focus has shifted to theological themes on the basis of literary coherence. Similarly literary studies at the very beginning, i.e. in the late seventies and early eighties, used to devote lengthy and sometimes acrimonious discussions to the validity of synchronic reading vs. historical criticism. The controversy about and attack on historical criticism of the 80's are now gone. Hence I will not deal with it. Nor am I dealing with diachronic questions of how and when the text came into being. I am dealing with the text as we have it now and interested in what and how the narrative says either explicitly or implicitly. Thus mine will be a strictly synchronic approach. Although not dealing with historical questions, I am not denying their relevance. The gradual decrease of Polzin's discussions (between his 1980 and 1993 volumes) of the relevance of synchronic reading and his critique of diachronic approaches may be indicative of the increasing validity of the synchronic approach in its own right.

Synchronic Approaches and Their Shortcomings

On the other hand I am not an uncritical devotee of literary criticism. My critique concerns two major and some minor aspects. Firstly I am very cautious not to idolise "my method" by making a clean sweep of any other method and so claiming exclusive rights to my reading of the Bible. (Unfortunately this has been a temptation to many.) Secondly, just like source or redaction criticism, literary criticism tends to "make do" with a purely descriptive approach. I should probably have written "tended", because it seems that this was a characteristic of earlier literary criticism (e.g. Gressmann, Caspari, Schulz, Conroy, Kenik), which was content with exploring and investigating the text solely in literary terms. In other words by refraining from drawing theological conclusions it pretended to keep away from any ideological commitment. Now the time has come to take the step towards theological evaluation and appropriation of the text by drawing upon purely literary studies.

The deficiency of literary critical studies of the mere descriptive kind is that they are satisfied with demonstrating the aesthetic values of the narrative without bothering with the question of what the aesthetics of the narrative are meant to serve: the ideological and theological content. To take this criticism a step further I have been somewhat frustrated seeing that with a few exceptions literary critics of theological training have scarcely applied what they have discovered to politics, church life and society. Are they or the publishers not interested in these issues? Or is it due to a Western framework and "descriptive theology"? Whatever the answer, I shall apply what I have found in the text.

Literary critics are susceptible to making sense of any text, even if they are contradictory (see Polzin and Fokkelman on "messenger" vs. "king" in 2 Sam

11:1; cf. Gordon 1978). For me, as for many scholars, textual and literary criticisms are not my favourite pastime but means to find answers to existential questions of life, politics and leadership.

Also by the exclusive focus on literary devices, structure and arrangement those studies often fail to see the wood for the trees, i.e. the intention(s) of the narrative. Literary criticism has fallen into the same trap as historical criticism. Given his methodology Fokkelman is particularly susceptible to this temptation, while Gunn and Polzin demonstrate a healthy balance. Preoccupation with the technicalities of structure, rhetorical motifs, chiasm and arrangement likewise render the plot, narrative and characters often incomprehensible or invisible. Neat structures and graphics can make the story, plot and most importantly the theology disappear. It seems that the more technical a commentary the less keen it is on unravelling the theological issues. They are either supposed to be "hidden" in those technical signs or denied straightaway.

My Methodology

GENERAL OBSERVATIONS

First and foremost this study is a synchronic reading and as such avoids historical questions. Since studies by e.g. Long and Eslinger have satisfactorily addressed the questions of coherence and unity, I shall not specifically deal with them. Mine is similar to Miscall's programme:

> The text, in the sense both of the individual passage or passages that I am reading and of the entire corpus [Gen-Kgs, in his case], is a material entity consisting of specific words in a particular arrangement. The readings respect the specificity and pay close attention to what exactly is said, how it is said, and also note what is not said, what the text leaves out. This respect extends to all of the details, oddities, gaps, etc., of the text. I do not remove troublesome details and statements by explaining them away in some fashion or by ignoring them; they remain even though they block a coherent and definitive interpretations. Nor do I try to fill in worrisome lacunae by bringing information from another part of the text or by conjecture; they stay empty even though they also prevent a definitive interpretation. (1983:1f)

I shall use the arsenal of literary criticism including establishing literary structures of chiasm or ring composition, finding keywords and delimiting subsections. I will read vigilantly, i.e. looking for discrepancies, unexpected turns, events, reactions, names, references, repetitions, omissions, utterances and motives in need of an explanation. I shall pay particular attention to evaluations on the part of either the narrator or characters. I shall also attend to who says what and what is explicit and implicit in what is narrated.

As much as possible, though, I shall avoid minute analyses of passages and verses, as focusing exceedingly on the particular makes one forget the overall purpose of narrative and plot, character and their developments. If I am not mistaken these features constitute what Gunn and Fewell call the "surface" of the narrative. I have found their methodological "manifesto" helpful and fitting to my method as well.

> We incline to a reading method that takes seriously the "surface" of the narrative, treating its characters (at least initially) as discrete persons and the sequential unfolding of the story as significant. We do not limit narrative meaning to the literal "surface" of the text. We are not "formalists". But we believe that interpretation becomes increasingly tenuous as it loses touch with the surface of the narrative. (1993:30)

In general my focus will not be on the informational dimension of the meaning of the text (to use Daniel and Aline Patte's terms) but I hope to get to "know something about the symbolic dimension of the meaning of this text—the system of values presupposed by the text, a part of the vision of life that the author held" (1978:4).

In more specific terms I shall read the text through glasses which bring focus on charismatic leadership to find clues as to how charismatics rise and are granted charisma. Employing the model of V.P. Long (1994), how are they designated and confirmed after demonstrating charisma? Furthermore what are the threats to charismatic leadership; how is it transformed? How does the text illuminate charismatic leadership and how does charismatic leadership illuminate the text? I assume that the text has something to say of the issue either explicitly or implicitly. I am not writing another commentary but a study with the specific focus of charismatic leadership.

I shall also try to leave room for what Miscall calls "undecidability". I consider this an opening for ambiguous evaluations (e.g. in 1 Sam 17), where I shall argue that by undecidability the narrator portrays charismatic David. It must be added that undecidability or ambiguity might be due to complexity and dynamism rather than stasis in characterisation (see Preston 1984; Perdue 1984; Bar-Efrat 1989:89-91).[18]

Occasionally my reading will come close to a symbolic interpretation resembling rabbinic midrash (see Porton 1992:820). Thus, for example, when interpreting 2 Samuel 6:6 I will initially focus on the particular (some Hebrew words), and try to make sense of their "inherent meaning", ignoring the context. Only then will I set what I have found in the context of the story.

As for psychological interpretation I have a rather ambivalent stance. On the one hand I understand Polzin's opposition to it for it has produced controversial explanations foreign to the text; on the other Auerbach has wonderfully demonstrated (1953:12f) that psychological aspects and processes of characters

---

[18] The first to draw attention to the indeterminate, the minimal externilisation, the obscure in style, plot and characterisation, "fraught with background", was Auerbach (1953:3-23); thus Miscall's "undecidability" is not totally new.

are clearly present in Hebrew storytelling. Therefore sensitivity to the psychological dimensions of plot and character definitely helps understand the narrative (cf. Gunn-Fewell 1993:47-50). Fokkelman, despite having a penchant for psychologising, does not really take psychological motives into account, i.e. has no elaborate psychological approach. In contrast, Jobling's pragmatic methodology results in a subtle commentary and enables him to reveal both underlying motifs/motives and overarching themes. One wonders whether Jobling's versatility in methodology, as opposed to the methodologically more rigid Fokkelman, is the clue to his subtle and insightful interpretation. Alter has correctly proposed (1981:17) to take psychological aspects in the David narrative into account. Since, however, in the Saul-Samuel relationship the psychological aspect is vital, I intend to apply it to the Saul narrative as well.

I shall occasionally move from a close reading to a type of structuralist interpretation, making use in particular of the binary opposition between old and new. The recognition of this opposition has been influenced by my experiences in Eastern Europe and the Reformed Church in Hungary. Were my background different, I would not have found Jobling's commentary, amongst others, as attractive as I did. On occasion I shall also move from a close reading to an imaginative interpretation, as well as use structuralism as a mode of appropriation of the biblical message. Thus my method will be eclectic, using the particular method best fitting my purpose. I see this as essential in order to understand the world of the biblical narrative and ourselves. In this respect I am much indebted to Jobling, who is probably the most eclectic of the commentators.

Is my methodology deductive or inductive? Polzin claims that "there is no such thing as a truly inductive hermeneutics" (1977:1). I think the two approaches play complementary roles in my analyses. My research question and topic definitely define my method and generate a rather deductive stance to the text — I approach the narrative with a specific mindset looking for clues to and motifs of charismatic leadership. At the same time both my synchronic method and my awareness of the dangers of tendentious readings make me cautious of an overstated deductive approach. Reading the text with specific questions in mind, looking for specific details, motifs or themes does not prevent me from taking the text seriously. On the contrary. It helps me focus on themes, details and literary devices heretofore ignored or unrecognised. How can questions related to charismatic leadership illuminate the text, narrative, plot and characters? I am convinced that what I have found is explicitly or implicitly in the text and not imposed on it by me.[19] But finally it is up to the reader to decide.

Before I turn to specific observations in which I intend to explain some of the above principles, two notes seem to be in order. Firstly often keywords are common words, such as לקח in 1 Samuel 8-9, which, however, may turn out to

---

[19] See Goldingay's helpful hermeneutical discussion, 1995:36-55.

be used to delimit passages or mark significant concepts of a section. Secondly the distinction of perfect and imperfect "tenses" in Hebrew is specious when used to argue for the narrator's temporal stand-point (Polzin, Eslinger), as the verb's temporal conjunction has been criticised by recent studies (e.g. McFall 1982; Niccacci 1990). Therefore I prefer using the terms *qatal*- and *yiqtol*-form.

SPECIFIC OBSERVATIONS

Studying Hebrew poetry as postgraduate students we were told that, in order to understand it, we should be aware that the Hebrew says everything twice. However, when it came to reading narratives, repetitions suddenly became interpolations or different sources that did not make any sense whatsoever. It is baffling that scholars, including literary critics, do not account for repetitions, i.e. they treat this literary phenomenon as if there were no real difference between the two statements. I shall attempt to demonstrate that in many cases we had better pay close attention to repetitions in order to discover clues to the plot, character portrayal and motivation. Texts such as 2 Samuel 5:10, 12 make me wonder why these two apparently very similar evaluations are necessary in the narrative (cf. Brettler 1991). It seems that the text itself leaves questions of motivation, character and development open, and we are invited to fill the gaps (cf. Gunn-Fewell 1993:50)[20]. Often gap filling is only possible by some sort of "reconstruction", psychological or otherwise.

Characters as parts of and contributors to the plot are probably the most important narrative components. It has often been observed that unlike Greek characters, the dramatis personae of the Bible are not static but dynamic, they progress and change. The significance of this observation still needs to be recognised though, because the progress and change, often subtle, are rarely considered. The change itself might be noticed without, however, giving account of how it came about. Saul's, David's and Solomon's character changes are similar in that all three presuppose some implicit factors contributing to the change. Character development with all its psychological concomitants should be considered.

It is my contention that the Saul, David and Solomon narratives can all be read as coherent stories in their own right. My aim is therefore to present a coherent and consistent narrative and development of storyline and characters. This is of course the aim of most of the interpreters, but, as I shall attempt to show, many fail. I shall also attend to what motivates characters, an important aspect of the narrative world.

Scholars of a liberal-postmodern background are critical and often suspicious of conventional assessments of characters. Thus the liberal-postmodern approach seeks to exonerate Saul while condemning David. The ironic twist is that whereas Saul's exoneration is due to the discovery of

---

[20] Unfortunately they have resorted to gap filling to the extent that it often borders on speculation. See particularly their discussion of the Abraham narrative (90-100).

neglected textual evidence, the same cannot always be said of David's condemnation, which is often a result of bias against people in power.

I am not aware of detailed discussions on the development of characters occupying large narrative space. Bar-Efrat in his excellent study offers a good but relatively brief discussion of dynamic characters depicted through indirect characterisation (1989:89-92). Though his discussion implies character change, a more explicit treatment of it could have contributed to a more powerful argument.[21] Likewise Gunn and Fewell, who discuss both characters and plot but not the combination of the two, refer to characters' "capacity to grow, to develop" (1993:75), but fail to elaborate. Apart from hints (1983:40) Berlin virtually leaves character development untreated. Characterisation is the first where the synchronic approach falls short.

When I first started my research I was convinced of Saul's sin and the correctness of his rejection. Reading the text and studies I began realising it was not a black-and-white issue nor a romantic story of "baddies" and "goodies". The presuppositions I grew uncomfortable with were:

1. Hebrew characters are basically static. This is never stated, therefore seems to be a subliminal presupposition implied in readings. As first observed by Auerbach (1953:17f) Hebrew characterisation, in contrast with that of Homer, is dynamic, i.e. FT characters are subject to outside influences and change. Even though this is widely acknowledged, the unaccountability and irrationality in the changes make them either incomprehensible (e.g. Saul's irrational change between 1 Sam 11 and 13-15; David's by 2 Sam 11; Solomon's by 1 Kgs 11) or static (Saul always had ulterior motives). My attempt will not be to exonerate Saul (this would amount to a hermeneutic of suspicion) but to make sense of the text, plot and character development. Readers are eager to learn the causes of changes in a story; a good narrator provides them explicitly or implicitly. However, most interpretations fail to give a coherent representation of plot, nor do they account for the changes of Saul, David and Solomon, even though some change is noticed or presupposed. Mine will be an attempt at a coherent reading. Popular Christian literature similarly fails when not explaining Saul's abrupt character change between 1 Samuel 11 and 13-15. Due to this failure, Sunday school teaching and the underlying Christian virtue of deference one is disposed to see Saul as the villain and do not even consider, amongst others, the possibility of Samuel's complicity in his rejection. Not accounting for change hinders dealing with real-life characters — a significant component of the story.

"Narrative criticism [...] looks for logical progressions of cause and effect"

---

[21] Bar-Efrat remarks (90), "In short stories, like most biblical narratives, there is virtually no technical possibility of gradual development. We often feel, nevertheless, that those characters who appear in many episodes change profoundly in the course of their lives." Apparently he is at odds with and hence cannot relate the two issues, i.e. the technical impossibility on the one hand and "what we often feel" on the other.

(Powell 1990:42). Powell has discussed different types of causal relationship in ST narratives more thoughtfully (40-42) and suggested three categories: possible, probable and contingent causalities. Although Powell does not apply these categories to FT narratives, character changes in general and those of Saul, David and Solomon in particular seem to belong in the second category, "in which one event makes the occurrence of another more likely" (40). I shall interpret the characters dynamically, i.e. in the light of how they relate to each other at their various appearances and how they are affected by events.

2. Sections of the narrative are inconsequential episodes with little or no bearing on preceding and following plot, development or characterisation. By not accounting for these vital aspects interpreters ignore the conventions of narrative. A case in point is McCarter who considers 1 Samuel 14 "an important anecdote about the king and the king's son" (1980:241), but fails to elaborate on its importance. Similarly McGinnis, though noticing that the chapter "contributes in important ways to the emerging portrait of Saul" (1999:257), discusses it after 1 Samuel 13 and 15. In my reading the purpose of 1 Samuel 14 is to portray a king handicapped due to the incident in ch. 13. The chapter's events and characterisation will impact the events and characterisation in ch. 15. While the surrounding chapters are "kernels"[22], ch. 14 is a "satellite" event, which should not, however, lead to it being ignored.

3. Saul's culpability. It is in most studies taken for granted, but the details of what went wrong with him have not been satisfactorily discussed. The narrative before 1 Samuel 16:14, which is the watershed between "good" and "bad" Saul, does not imply an abrupt change in his character. Is the narrative inconsistent in its portrayal of characters — when and why did Saul go wrong? Gunn and Fewell are right when remarking:

> The events of the plot are often explicitly connected by the narrator in terms of cause and effect. Where this is not done, readers tend to supply causality, or at least coherence, for themselves. In short, narrative is generally assumed by hearers and readers to interrelate distinct temporal events, involving several characters, in a coherent whole without extraneous incidents. (1993:2)

The same inconsistency can be noticed on the part of interpreters studying David. Sternberg's statement of 2 Samuel 11 (1985:529, n. 30) is representative: "Within the composition of the book, therefore, ours is a central chapter in that it pinpoints the where and why of David's change of fortune." Sternberg's inability to account for "David's change of fortune" is the more remarkable given his identification of the chapter in question as "preceded by a consistently favorable presentation of David as a God-fearing, successful, and victorious king" and "followed by a long chain of mishaps and disasters" (528,

---

[22] These "are those in which choices are made that determine the subsequent development of the narrative." "Satellite events do not involve choices but simply describe the working-out of those choices made at the kernels" (Powell 1990:36).

n. 30). The popular and otherwise correct view of David's turn of fortune is succinctly rendered also by Polzin: "There are not many places in the Bible where a character's reputation is so *suddenly* and effectively demolished as in 2 Samuel 11" (1993:117; my emphasis). Of course characters and their reputation can be demolished in an instant. Not being prepared for it, however, readers, expecting coherence in plot and characterisation, will be confused. Thus what I question is not the change in David's character and fortune. I question the suddenness or, more precisely, unexpectedness of change which thus renders plot and character incomprehensible.

I have similar difficulties with studies of the Solomon narrative. My first problem is that, following Rost's thesis, 1 Kings 1-2 is generally read backwards and not forwards, these chapters are considered a part of another narrative. Nor is Solomon's change by ch. 11 accounted for by scholars — they do not explain at which point of the narrative and, more importantly, why he changed for the worse.[23] Again it is correctly noticed but as far as coherence of plot and characterisation are concerned left unexplained. Dividing Solomon's (or David's; Carlson 1964) rule into two clearly distinguishable parts creates a neat and schematic arrangement (see Porten 1967:121 in particular), which, however, results in a tendentious interpretation subjecting the various parts to the underlying ideology. Regarding 1 Kings 3:7-12 the focus of Solomon's wisdom is rarely taken into account by interpreters.

4. Prophet Samuel's unquestionable character. Samuel is viewed in a rather positive light, even though his manipulations have clearly been exposed by interpreters. This is manifest even among perceptive scholars such as McGinnis (1999:250-52) and Bar-Efrat. The latter, by an appeal to authority, claims:

> Amongst the judgments of actions pronounced by the characters, a special place should be allotted to those made by a prophet. Because of his special standing as God's emissary, whatever a prophet says carries particular weight, and it can be assumed that the author identifies fully with the prophet. There are abundant examples of this, such as Samuel's condemnation of Saul's actions, Nathan's of David's, Elijah's of Ahab's. (1989:84)

This attitude is frequently at work either subliminally or consciously. Therefore it is refreshing to read Amit's observation just before her discussion of Samuel's role in 1 Samuel 15 (2000:53): "The prophet of the Lord who speaks or acts against God's will, and not in accordance with the narrator's stances, is made to be seen as unreliable, and his words as unrepresentative of the stance in which the author is interested."

5. Charismatic leadership in Israel compared to kings in ANE who were often subject to prophets in warfare. As I shall hopefully demonstrate this is hardly applicable to charismatic leaders in the FT.

---

[23] Even Parker leaves the change unaccounted for as he does not discuss chs. 6-8 at length.

6. The narrator's view is not always separated from that of characters, whether God's, Samuel's or a messenger's is concerned. This is so to a certain degree in 1 Samuel 13 and certainly in ch. 15 as I shall show. Eslinger's warning (1983) has not been heeded.

The above observations have led me to study and evaluate carefully
- the narrative, its development, portrayal and ideology;
- the characters' motives;
- other, sometimes contradictory accounts (e.g. 1 Sam 14:47ff vs. ch. 15);
- in general the narrator's view on events, characters and explanations. What I am primarily interested in is the *narrator's view* on what and how he narrates.

This study will also attempt to demonstrate the critical attitude of the biblical narrator to those in power, whether Samuel or Saul, David or Solomon.

Style

Though mine is not a rhetorical study as far as method is concerned, I shall often resort to persuasive wording as employed in rhetorical criticism. Literary critics in general are more rhetorical in both wording and titles. So shall I be. If the reader finds my style provocative — that is how rhetoric works.[24] Therefore I have attempted to phrase my headings and arguments in a rhetorical rather than descriptive form.

I shall follow the narrative as much as possible. This explains both the similarities and the differences of the structures of the chapters. The discussion of Saul is disproportionately long in comparison with those of David and Solomon. There are a couple of reasons for this. Both the personality and the narrative of Saul are extremely complex, that make a more elaborate discussion necessary. Secondly my discussion of Saul will prepare the typology of charismatic leadership. All biblical quotations are from the NIV unless otherwise noted.

"One could engage in endless debate on theoretical questions in literary criticism, but ultimately one must expose oneself to the risk of actually dealing at length with a concrete text", Conroy once remarked (1978:7). So I shall now turn to the text of Samuel and Kings and offer an attempt at a coherent reading of the narrative — from the perspective of charismatic leadership.

---

[24] Here I refer to James Barr's criticism of Brueggemann's rhetoric (1999:544-47). Barr is definitely correct in his observation — except that he does not understand the function of rhetoric.

CHAPTER 2

From Charismatic Judgeship to Limited Kingship

A crucial moment in the life of God's people — Israel chooses to replace charismatic judgeship, sanctioned by Yahweh, with kingship. It is Samuel the prophet and judge who is commissioned to usher Israel into this new season and implement the change of government. The last and greatest charismatic judge, opposed to the constitutional change, willy-nilly sets out to anoint a king, the new charismatic leader.

According to Max Weber, charismatic authority rests "on devotion to the exceptional sanctity, heroism or exemplary character of an individual person, and of the normative patterns or order revealed or ordained by him" (1968:226). So far Samuel has been in charge of setting the norm and revealing the God-given order for Israel. However, this must change. Samuel should yield his authority to the king's. Will he? And will the king be able to acquire the same charismatic authority?

It is spring, the season of a new beginning.

In the Shadow of the Last Judge — The Rise of the New Charismatic Leader

Setting the Stage — The Crisis of Leadership, 1 Samuel 8

For long years Samuel has led Israel. He has been an exemplary judge and delivered Israel from the Philistines. But Samuel is growing older. His attempt to establish hereditary judgeship casts the first shadow on his integrity. Ironically, by making his corrupt sons judges, Samuel unwittingly hastens the emergence of monarchy, a nightmare to the prophet (cf. Jobling 1986:51, 54, 63; 1998:63f).[1] When it becomes clear to the elders of the tribes that the matter of leadership has not been settled in a favourable way, they turn to Samuel (ch.

---

[1] Corruption is a triggering factor in the emergence of the new order. Preston has observed a pattern of (worthless and hence) rejected sons in 1 Samuel (1982:29). "Sons in disagreement with their father" is, however, more inclusive applying also to Jonathan. Thus in 1 Samuel the fall of the houses — Eli's, Samuel's, Saul's — was partly caused by the second generation's corruption or disagreement with their father. Even David's sons were corrupt but his house was spared because of God's everlasting covenant (2 Sam 7). McCarter has rightly observed (1980:160) that "succession is shown to be undesirable because of the character of the sons."

8)[2], voice their concerns and demand "continuous, uninterrupted leadership" (Edelman 1991:37).

After stating the problem, which is one of leadership crisis, the elders express their demand: "... now appoint a king to lead us, such as all the other nations have" (v. 5). Although the last part of the elders' petition is often considered the underlying reason for his embarrassment, Samuel does not mention it to Yahweh. This suggests that the main cause of his annoyance was the people's displeasure with his administration and judge-leadership and a demand for their different sort of leadership by a king. This seems to be underlined in 12:12 where the prophet recalls the people's demand — but only the part offensive to him. In 8:7 Yahweh makes clear that the elders were not discontent with a particular judge, Samuel, but with judgeship as form of state. Something in Samuel's perception went wrong, therefore God needs to remind him that "it is not you they have rejected". On the other hand it is understandable why Samuel, who has made every effort to maintain a functioning theocratic judgeship, becomes angry when seeing his dream disappearing.

As far as Yahweh is concerned, "straight through to the end of II Kings, the Lord God is never referred to as a king." Neighbouring nations had kings "but all were defeated by kingless Israel and its unroyal God" (Miles 1995:168). Therefore Israel's demand implies "a lack of respect for God's sovereignty and of trust in God's ability to save his people out of the hands of their enemies" (Thornton 1967:421).[3] Still, in contrast to his prophet, God is rather calm. Despite Yahweh's disapproval of the people's motivation for demanding a king he does accede to their demand by commanding Samuel three times (8:7, 9, 22) to appoint a king. Thus, as Ackerman neatly puts it, "Hannah's *sha'ul*" (see 1:20) is "forced by the deity to anoint Israel's *sha'ul*, and we are left wondering which of these, if either, is God's *sha'ul*" (1991:9).

Conventional interpretation regards Samuel's speech as focusing on the dreadful consequences of the people's choice, and, by doing so, faithfully representing Yahweh's view. A close reading of the text, however, will challenge this interpretation. On reading מִשְׁפַּט הַמֶּלֶךְ (8:9) stipulations and limitations of the power of privileged Israelite groups (such as the priests, 2:13;[4] kings, Dt 17:14-20) should come to mind (Ackerman 1991:10). God is

---

[2] Unattributed Bible references in chapter 2 are to 1 Samuel.
[3] Yahweh's rule was manifest in crisis related judgeship. Israel's existence was "unstable", for their national existence and freedom always depended on Yahweh's intervention and grant of charisma as well as on a reliance on this on their part. Yahweh's charisma was granted when needed. Once the crisis was resolved the charisma was not needed and was thus "suspended". Concerning this Buber is correct in claiming that the shift from theocracy to monarchy was a "removal of the direct primitive theocracy by the indirect one" (1964:759; AT; cf. Klaus 1999:79-83).
[4] And Dt 18:3.

referring "to the curbs on kingship given through Moses in Deut. 17:14-20; and the stipulations are duly transmitted to the people in verse 10" (Ackerman 1991:11). Although God was uneasy about the request of a king, he was willing to grant it. But being cautious of the potential of the change, he is keen to stipulate the king's rule.

Vv. 11-18, however, indicate that Samuel's perspective is rather different from God's. The speech is not introduced by "thus says Yahweh" (cf. 10:18) but by "and he said", which would not have been necessary if his reported speech were a continuation of v. 10 (Ackerman 1991:11). Indeed commenting on the change from וְהִגַּדְתָּ and הָעֵד תָּעִיד (vv. 9f) to וַיֹּאמֶר Eslinger claims that instead of prescribing Samuel describes "the manner of the king" (1985:270f; cf. Edelman 1991:40f; Steussy 1999:36; Uffenheimer 1999:277f). Moreover v. 19 emphasises that it is his voice and not Yahweh's the people refuse to heed, which suggests that they know that kingship with stipulations is permitted (Ackerman 1991:10). By his rhetoric Samuel intends to cause the people to change their mind. They get the point but refuse to reconsider (v. 19). Samuel stresses a kingdom's drawbacks by painting a negative picture and ignoring positive aspects such as external-internal security or administration of justice (Garsiel 1985:65; see also Polzin 1989:87).

The main subject of Samuel's speech is the future king. Verbs emphasise the king's superiority to the people and how he will exploit or abuse them. He "will take", a keyword in the speech (also noticed by Fokkelman 1993:348; cf. Garsiel 1985:68), the people's sons, daughters, best fields and gardens, menservants, maidservants, best lads[5] and asses (vv. 11, 13f, 16). He "will make" the free sons of the free people his attendants (v. 11). He "will take a tenth" of the people's grain and flocks (vv. 15, 17) which practice, bearing in mind the religious significance of tithing, could be considered "an encroachment upon Yahweh's prerogative" (Gordon 1986:111). He "will give" his servants and eunuchs what he has taken from the people (vv. 14f). He "will take" the people's belongings "for his own use" (v. 16). The effect of all this will be obvious to all: "You will be his slaves" (v. 17), which Fokkelman calls "the ironic reversal" (1993:349). "The election of a king will return Israel to the slave status from which Yahweh originally freed them" (Eslinger 1985:276). The king will be invested with power and authority by the people to do all these — against the people.

Here Samuel draws attention to the lapse from the democratic theocracy represented and led by him to the exploitative monarchy chosen by the people. For the prophet this lapse is all the harder to stomach because the constitutional theocracy provided equality. What Samuel stresses is that whereas in the theocracy Israel has held on to communal values and interests, in the impending monarchy individual values and interests will replace them — those of

---

[5] Retaining בַּחוּרִים over against the LXX is of significance as will be demonstrated below.

centralised royal power.

The speech creates a distance between people and king. Not only are the verbs carefully chosen and applied but also the nouns and suffixes. Everything will appear as "his" personal property and private matter. Even wars will be "his" (v. 12) and not those of the nation. The democratic-charismatic institution of blowing the trumpet will be replaced by the power politics of the king.

Samuel's objection to monarchy seems to be justified if the excesses and abuse of power in ANE are taken into account. His anger is understandable, since as "regards society power would be permanently institutionalized and invested in a man who ruled by the grace of the people" (Tsevat 1980:91). In other words the king would be elevated nearly to a position so far only occupied by Israel's Sovereign.

The abusive and oppressive nature of monarchy is emphasised by the choice of the verb זעק which in related passages (9:16; 12:9f) as well as in other parts of the FT (e.g. Ex 2:23; 3:7, 9), occurs in contexts of socio-political oppression. Ironically, whereas in 1 Samuel 9:16 and 12:9f Israel cries out because of the oppression caused by not having a leader, the implication here is the very opposite: they will cry out because of the oppression by the leader they chose. And while previously they experienced Yahweh's merciful intervention, now they are assured of receiving no deliverance by Yahweh in due time.

The problem with Samuel's rhetoric and presentation, however, is that he has not been ordered to tell the people of their wickedness and the evil consequences of demanding a king (Polzin 1989:85). He even intimidates the people by warning them of future refusal if they cry out to God (v. 18). God's prophet seems to act on his own — not for the last time.

The people refuse to listen to Samuel (v. 19), "stress the positive functions of monarchy which are ignored by Samuel" (Garsiel 1985:68) and insist on becoming like all other nations (v. 20). They speak of "our" case and wars in contrast with Samuel's use of personal suffixes in v. 12. Did they not grasp the prophet's warning, or did they refuse to accept its relevance to them?

In 1 Samuel 8 God's people arrive at a crossroads. Israel's elders are not content with the nation's prospects. So far judgeship brought insecurity and instability with its non-hereditary leadership. They want kingship, a more predictable and stable government. Samuel's view is that judgeship allows for Yahweh's initiative: Israel's God comes to his people's help by raising charismatic deliverers endowed by his spirit. Will the new system change this or will Yahweh be able to maintain his role as the only source of help?

THE ARRIVAL OF THE NEW LEADER, 1 SAMUEL 9:1-10:8

In ch. 9 a new scene is introduced with the same opening words as the book and its first scene in 1:1. A new story begins, another story concerning the rise of the low (see Preston 1982:31; Martin 1984). Since the beginning of a story sets the scene and reveals much about characters and plot, I shall study carefully how Saul's story begins.

From Charismatic Judgeship to Limited Kingship 45

The man introduced here (vv. 1-4) is from Benjamin, the least significant and powerful tribe in Israel after its near extinction. We may recall their involvement in Israel's civil war (Ju 20-21) and what preceded it (Ju 19).[6] Benjamin is a suspicious tribe. Yet we know that in the past this very tribe was able to "produce" deliverers such as Ehud (Ju 3)[7]. Remembering what we read in ch. 8 the unlikely question arises: Will this tribe be the one to provide a candidate for kingship?

The answer seems to be yes; in v. 2 we learn his name, Saul, "The One Asked For". Is he the one in whose person the petition of Samuel's mother is going to be fulfilled (see Ackerman 1991:2-4, 9; Fokkelman 1993:346f)? Saul is an "impressive young man", one בָּחוּר וָטוֹב[8]. Steussy even suggests that both occurrences of טוֹב in v. 2 may refer to Saul's spiritual quality: he was "a good man" and there was none in Israel "better than he." Consequently the last part of v. 2, "He stood head and shoulders over the entire people", may also be taken in a spiritual sense (1999:51). Learning of the new hero's excellence the reader is full of expectation: Is Saul the one to be elected king? He seems to be an appropriate candidate. Recalling the phrase's occurrence in 8:16, however, where it was applied to young men taken by the king "for his own use", the budding hope for a deliverer is overshadowed. Now what will this young man be, a deliverer or an oppressor? A military king or an oriental despot? With this question a challenge to the possible king as well as one of the main themes of 1-2 Samuel has been announced.

Saul and his servant set out to find the lost donkeys. We read of their itinerary in detail (v. 4). The mention of the hill country of Ephraim is a reminder of the ignoble events in Judges 17-19. Shalisha is probably related to the numerals "three" (9:20; 3:8; see also the three signs in ch. 10) and "thirty" (9:22). Shaalim is reminiscent of שְׁאָלִים in 8:10, which contains the name of our main character. We have already come across the tribe name Benjamin in v. 1. Finally Zuph (v. 5) recalls the very beginning of the book and Samuel's story (1:1). These names heighten the expectation of a new beginning as well as prepare the reader for subsequent events.

9:5-10:8 is composed of five scenes. Each scene is introduced by the personal pronoun "they" followed by a movement-related verb, the exception

---

[6] I assume that the author was familiar with the Pentateuch, Joshua and Judges.

[7] Ehud's physical characteristic (he was "left-handed", Ju 3:15) is just as emphatic as Saul's appearance here.

[8] The juxtaposition of the two phrases derived from the verbs בחר and שאל is too extraordinary to be taken casually (Buber 1956:123), and will resound in 12:13 on Samuel's lips: "Now here is the king you have chosen, the one you asked for". Being aware of his attitude to kingship and the new king, it sounds like a complaint, as if the prophet were cross in recognising the loss of his leadership role (that it was not he who will fulfil his parents' petition), his fall as well as the rise of a בָּחוּר whose name, irritatingly, is *Saul*.

being scene four which is introduced by וַיִּקַּח (v. 22).[9] This exception is of high interpretive significance as will be demonstrated and gives a clue to the chapter's perspective on the relationship between the future king and his mentor, Samuel. Moreover what we learn at the outset of Saul's story will have important bearing on the prophet-king relationship.

The first scene (vv. 5-10) focuses on the main characters of ch. 9 and their relationship. Firstly Saul is presented as one dependent on his father (v. 5). His father in turn is portrayed as protective of his grown-up son.[10]

Saul's dependence is further elaborated on. It is his servant who takes the initiative and makes the most important decisions (vv. 6, 8) about their destiny of which they are as yet not aware. The servant appears "indispensable" (Fokkelman 1993:379, n. 27). He even proposes: "I will give[11] God's man the silver I have" (v. 8; see Deist 1993:13). Saul, the master, only reacts to the servant's initiatives. Even though he is supposed to be in charge, he only agrees to the servant's suggestions. He is passive while the servant is the active character (also noticed by V.P. Long, 1989:202f; and Deist, 1993:13). Thus Polzin (1989:103) rightly claims that Saul's "character zone is filled with doubt and uncertainty", which is manifest right at his first appearance. He raises questions throughout (vv. 7, 18, 21 twice). "Saul, therefore, is a seeker of answers as well as asses, a traveling question mark" (Polzin 1989:103). In the light of ensuing events, even his very first statement, which is not a question (v. 5), is notably insecure.

The servant suggests to visit God's man who "is highly respected, and everything he says comes true" (v. 6). What will he say that will come true? "Perhaps he will tell us which way to take", he adds. And indeed the prophet will (fore)tell Saul's way, who expects guidance for his immediate problem, "while the narrator hints at a somewhat different significance for the path that the two characters have taken" (Eslinger 1985:293). In fact the prophet will tell the king at decisive moments which way to take.

---

[9] Fokkelman (1993:356) has also observed the essential role of "they" and the pivotal placing of וַיִּקַּח in 9:22 (360). His interpretation of the movements and the whole scene differs very much from mine, however. See 356-435.

[10] I think one does not have to resort to source criticism to explain the alleged discrepancy between a youthful Saul in chs. 9-11 and a grown-up Saul of chs. 13ff. In my view Saul is deliberately portrayed as dependent at his appearance. Similarly to Kish, Jesse is somewhat "protective" of his presumably grown-up sons in chs. 16-17 (see especially 17:17f), which makes David's autonomy the more remarkable. In this way the narrator points out the difference of Saul's and David's personalities at their appearances as well as the difference of their destinies affected by the different appearances.

[11] The MT is to be preferred here over against other manuscripts reading either second singular or first plural in an attempt to put Saul in charge.

From Charismatic Judgeship to Limited Kingship

The second scene (vv. 11-14a[12]) reaffirms our first impression of Saul as one greatly dependent upon others' initiative and decision-making. He is mentioned along with his servant ("they") again. And it is "they"[13] who ask the girls "they" meet (v. 11).

By now the reader has been prepared for the encounter between Saul and Samuel, scene three (vv. 14b-21). Ironically, despite the girls' clear instructions, Saul is unable to identify the seer. Concerning this V.P. Long (1989:204) states that "the reader has an uneasy sense of a certain incomprehension and ineptitude in Saul's actions."[14] This is the first instance Saul takes the initiative. He puts a question to the stranger who will turn out to be the seer (v. 18). This first initiative is answered in a startling but characteristic way.[15] The stranger's answer is short: "I am the seer." And not bothering to ask why Saul is looking for him he immediately takes control of the situation and the lad by briefing Saul in what to do (v. 19). The seer does not listen to Saul's question — a peculiar demeanour impacting and overshadowing their relationship from the beginning to the end and eventually causing Saul to fail.

After introducing himself Samuel promises to tell Saul "all that is in your heart" (v. 19). What exactly is in Saul's heart waiting to be disclosed by the prophet? Is it the whereabouts of the lost donkeys, about which Saul is concerned? Samuel immediately reveals their whereabouts. His announcement of the finding of the donkeys is a prophetic declaration. It is not quite clear why he announced it in such a solemn way. Why did he not just state the recovery of the donkeys? Did he want to impress Saul?

Saul's modest answer to Samuel (v. 21) pictures him as a reluctant candidate to the throne (Fokkelman 1993:404). By his self-portrayal a major theme is introduced, elaborated on in the subsequent narrative: Saul, the "worthy refuser" (Jobling 1986:84, 87).

Scene four (vv. 22-26) summarises in a nutshell the prophet's suppressive attitude towards Saul and sets the scene for what is yet to come. Instead of "they", הֵמָּה, the scene begins with Samuel "taking" Saul and his servant (v. 22). One of the key words in Samuel's speech in ch. 8 was the phrase וַיִּקַּח

---

[12] In referring to verses I follow Muilenburg's (1956) way of dividing verses into subverses by considering each clause an independent unit. 9:14, for instance, consists of four clauses.

[13] Again the MT is to be preferred to other manuscripts reading third person singular.

[14] Then he adds "that 'not listening' is one of Saul's major failings in ch. 15." I would concur with his portrayal except that, since I interpret ch. 15 quite differently, it is to be viewed not as much as a "major failing" of Saul but rather as a preparation for future misunderstandings of what Samuel looks like and what he wants from Saul (see esp. chs. 13 and 15), which is so characteristic of our narrative.

[15] Notice that the prophet's last words to Saul (28:16-19) will be similarly overwhelmingly authoritative. Commenting on ch. 28, Beuken (1978:5) states that Samuel "refuses a consultation as pointless."

warning of the abusive actions of the future king. Here it is Samuel who takes possession of Saul and the servant. As a consequence "they" referring to Saul and his servant is never again applied. The "idyllic" journey is over, *their* relationship is destroyed by Samuel's appearance. He takes the בָּחוּר just as the king will take the בַּחוּרִים (see 8:16) "for his own use"[16]. He also takes the servant but only to replace him and to lay claim to the office of the king's mentor.[17] From now on he will act as the king's mentor making suggestions and decisions. Thus the servant is not only used to provide Saul as well as the reader with information (so Eslinger 1985:291), but to prepare the change of cast.

Scene five is the climax of the story, reporting on an essential recasting. It is introduced by "they" again, conspicuously referring to Saul and Samuel, as underlined by the narrator in v. 26, and not the servant who is sent away by Samuel never to reappear[18]. His being sent away symbolises Samuel's success in eliminating him and taking his place. These are the main motifs of the chapter. "All in all Saul appears to be exactly the kind of man whom Samuel would have every hope of molding into a compliant king who would least limit the prophetic and judicial powers Samuel has been accustomed to exercise in the past and now sees threatened" (Polzin 1989:104).

A recasting has taken place due to the events in scene four. The altered "they" (Saul and Samuel) is the effect of וַיִּקַּח in 9:22. Up to scene four, it had been the servant taking the initiative for his master. From now on it will be the prophet. From now on their lives will run together; their fates can no longer be

---

[16] This picture of Samuel as an abusive leader is reinforced by the occurrence of the noun טַבָּח, cook (v. 23). In 8:13 the king was said to take "your daughters to be [...] cooks" (feminine). What is the purpose of the banquet? Samuel's intention is not quite clear here either. Eslinger (1985:313) observes, "Samuel continues to honour him [Saul] in a way that is mysterious to the characters but transparent to the reader." Eslinger even refers to a "theocratic conspiracy" (313); that the meal was used by Samuel "especially to convince Saul of his destiny" and as such it was a "psychological manipulation" (314). In addition to the motif of the suppressive mentor we shall deal below with another proposed by V.P. Long (1989). One may argue that 9:22 can be interpreted in Long's terms, i.e. the prophet takes Saul as his protégé. Even so Samuel's leadership will turn into authoritarian and manipulative mentoring.

[17] I might have overstated the significance of וַיִּקַּח. What caught my eye in v. 22, however, was the departure from the established structure as well as the new cast of roles. In addition 22b, וַיְבִיאֵם לִשְׁכָּתָה, is the more natural rendering of what 22a has already stated. Therefore 22a seems rather redundant. See also Linafelt's article (1992) on לקח as a verb implying power.

[18] Disregarding 10:14 (on this see Fokkelman 1993:433) where the servant is mentioned. The uncle addresses Saul as well as his lad as if assuming the "old configuration" of Saul's being subordinate to the lad. He is obviously mistaken — the lad is silenced by his master. Fokkelman has also noticed the servant's elimination although he draws out different emphases and comes to a different conclusion (1993:408).

separated. Only when dead will the prophet cease to mentor him but even then he will haunt the king (ch. 28).

The recasting is reiterated by the application of וַיִּקַּח in 10:1. Here again it is Samuel *taking* "a flask of oil", and so the initiative, to anoint Saul. The prophet acts (emphasised by three verbs in 10:1) and speaks (highlighted by his long commission speech), prophesies and commands. As the new "they" is the effect of וַיִּקַּח in 9:22, so is the וַיִּקַּח in 10:1 the effect of the altered subject of 9:27.

In order to become the future king's mentor Samuel turns Saul's life upside down. Saul left his home to find his father's asses and returns home as Israel's anointed king. He set out on a family business and finds himself entangled in a national one. The simple farmer is appointed a national leader in a matter of hours. Obviously, however, this has not changed his character; he is portrayed in chs. 9-10 as irresolute, one in need of another's advice and leadership — an inauspicious start. After his anointing he is still an undetermined peasant under the protective wings of his father (cf. 10:2). Will he change? Will he measure up to the task he has been assigned to?

The aspect of character — taking initiative, being in control, self-confidence — is linked to the success of a charismatic leader. If handled in a way as to support the charismatic in his/her endeavour, she/he will succeed. If not, failure is inevitable. The narrative deals with this question, so shall I.

THE COMMISSIONING OF THE LEADER

Whether the crisis of government is resolved depends on the charismatic leader's qualities. What was needed in the context of 1 Samuel 8? Just before Samuel's encounter with the future king Yahweh specifies what he expects of and entrusts to Israel's future leader. He is to deliver Israel from the Philistines (9:16).[19] The need and meaning of delivering Israel is obvious. Israel has long lost its national independence and is being suppressed by other people, therefore a charismatic military leader is in demand. Eslinger noticed (1985:306) that in 9:16 Yahweh quotes his own words from Exodus 3:7-9 concerning Israel's deliverance from Egypt, which indicates that God views the present situation as reminiscent of that preceding the exodus. Saul is to be the new Moses, the new charismatic leader delivering Israel — this time from the Philistines.

V.P. Long has studied the narrative from the aspect of prophetic mediation. Saul's commissioning is mediated through a prophet, unlike previous charismatic leaders (Moses, Gideon) who were appointed by Yahweh without human assistance (1989:60f). The prophetic mediation becomes "particularly evident in three areas: in the divine election of kings, in their rejection when this became necessary, and in the conduct of war" (61f). Long finds support in R. Bach's study which contends that the early monarchy experienced a division

---

[19] Saul is also commissioned to "restrain", עצר, Israel. The verb never recurs and is somewhat obscure. But see Rudman 2000:523.

of function of charismatic leaders whereby the king became the executor of the military function while the prophet mediated the divine initiative and will (1962:111f).[20] Prophets were involved not only in pre-battle rites but their function "often extended beyond the ritual aspect to the advisory and supervisory" (V.P. Long 1989:63).

In 10:5-8 the prophet,

> as co-inheritor of the charismatic tradition and as mediator of Saul's call, commissions Saul to challenge Philistine domination by an initial act of defiance, assuring him of divine assistance in the accomplishment of this feat. As we have argued, not only the Philistine focus of Saul's commission, but also the reference to the Philistine governor at the site of the third and final sign confirming Saul's appointment, strongly suggest that Saul's first action should be against the said governor [10:5]. The effect of such an action would, of course, be mainly provocative, flinging down the gauntlet to the Philistines and placing the Israelites in a state of revolt. The major conflict would remain to be fought. And since it must not commence independently of Yahweh's spokesman, Saul is commanded in 10:8 to follow-up his first action by repairing to Gilgal to await the arrival of Samuel, who will come not only to consecrate the battle but also to *instruct* the new appointee as to what he should do. (64; italics his)

Thus Samuel commissions Saul with both a military action and obedience in the form of submission to the prophet, which will be manifested in Saul's waiting for him at Gilgal. In 15:1 Samuel reaffirms his mediatorial role in the king's election (135). Both 10:8 and 15:1 precede and stipulate a task of Saul, the former the insurgency against the Philistines, the latter the war against Amalek.

The division of power established by Samuel is decisive in both the narrative and Samuel's mind, leading to conflicts between king and prophet (chs. 13, 15). I shall argue that the twofold commission, even though obvious in itself but uttered in an obscure way and accompanied by ambiguous signs, confused Saul.

THE MILITARY DELIVERER

Saul's next problem was that Israel had no army, no military leader and no arms. He had not had any training to take on the oppressors' superior military equipment and trained troops. How will the country boy live up to the enormous expectation, how will he face the challenge?[21] Will he prove himself a new Moses? Will he liberate Israel?

---

[20] See also Abramski 1984-85 and Culpepper 1987. We shall see that this hardly holds true for David.

[21] Saul's commission is similar to that of Gideon who also without any military experience was raised to a leadership position. Garsiel (1985:78-82) has drawn an analogy with Gideon in addition to one with Moses.

The future king will deliver Israel; this is the primary role God assigns to him (9:16). Hence the king as military deliverer is a major theme in the narrative. Strangely enough the theme does not explicitly recur until the end of ch. 10 (v. 27), not even in the commissioning of Saul. The passage on Saul's election ends with the question: "How can this fellow save us, יֹשִׁעֵנוּ?" Even if it is "troublemakers" giving voice to their scepticism in this cynical way, we should not miss the narrator's point. With this rhetorical question he reintroduces the significant theme of delivering Israel, and by doing so establishes a literary link to Judges. In the book of Judges ישׁע and its derivatives function as keywords. 1 Samuel 11, as will soon be demonstrated, is about deliverance by a charismatic judge-like hero. Will Saul be able to deliver Israel? And if so, how? How can a peasant rescue Israel from the hands of its powerful enemies? The question has been raised and ch. 11 will provide the answer.

First we read of the siege of a town in Gilead by the Ammonites. It appears to be a local crisis affecting the population of the town only.[22] Jabesh Gilead is beyond the Jordan, far away from the lives of Hebrews living on the West bank of the river. Israel's fragmented tribal federation has made the town an easy prey to Ammon. Jabesh's inhabitants desperately hope someone will deliver them. In v. 3 the people of the besieged town pick up the word and theme of deliverance, "If there is no מוֹשִׁיעַ you can do whatever you want to."[23] Nahash is so self-confident that he accepts the proposal and sits back. In its desperation the town turns to the newly elected king for relief. Will he be willing and able to help besieged Jabesh? And if so will the help arrive in time? The recurrence of מוֹשִׁיעַ in 3d reinforces the rhetorical question raised in 10:27: Will a deliverer be raised and against all odds save Jabesh?[24] Bearing in mind the events of tribal jealousy and civil war narrated in Judges an affirmative answer seems as distant as Jabesh Gilead from Gibeah.

On learning Jabesh Gilead's plight the people "all wept aloud" (v. 4). This remark calls to mind Judges 2:4,[25] where after a messenger's rebuke Israel wept. Whereas there it was stated that Yahweh was not willing to save them, the reader is pondering about Yahweh's willingness here.

In v. 5 Saul appears as an ordinary man. V.P. Long (1989:231f) views Saul's farming activity as a further sign of his reluctance to assume his office after his election. He concludes "that, due to Saul's inaction since his appointment to

---

[22] See Fokkelman's convincing argument (1993:438, 459-61) for retaining the MT. But even if the text is corrupt (so Cross 1983) this emphasis in the narrative is obvious.
[23] Sawyer (1965:478) has correctly stated that a מוֹשִׁיעַ is needed "in a situation of injustice, and in particular unjust oppression of the chosen people".
[24] See also the correspondence of יצא in 11:3 and 10 and the implications noted by Fokkelman (1993:456f).
[25] In this regard the way 1 Sam 10:18f reminds us of Ju 2:1-6 and 6:8-10 may be considered a preparation for ch. 11.

'save Israel', the situation has not yet much improved" (232). To be sure throughout the narrative he is reluctant to assume kingship and take up his mandate to deliver Israel (see Good 1965:56-80). As I have argued this is normal to a degree — before the turning point in 11:6.

On hearing Jabesh's distress, God's spirit comes upon him in power (v. 6) — the same phrase employed in 10:10 — and he becomes a charismatic leader who can perform extraordinary acts. Notice that in Judges 14:6, 19; 15:14 (cf. Ju 3:10; 6:34; 11:29) this term is used in a dynamic sense describing the work of God's liberating spirit; Yahweh's spirit qualifies Saul for the tremendous challenge of delivering Israel. Therefore unlike the people he does not weep — weeping is a sign of impotent despair; but rather gets very angry — a sign of power and competence; the more so if we remember that his anger comes from God. Saul "is angered by the situation because he has just been given the means to surmount it" (Eslinger 1985:366). The shy farmer is all of a sudden transformed into a different person. His fierce anger signals his endowment by God's spirit, which in turn is the *conditio sine qua non* of a charismatic leader and deliverer.

Saul's resolute action is an essential aspect of charismatic leadership. Hesitant Saul of chs. 9-10 is transformed into a leader taking determined and independent action. I shall show how abandoning his resoluteness will cause the end of his charisma and his fall.

Cutting the yoke of oxen in pieces intimates "what is going to happen if the paralysis isn't shaken off and brotherhood takes no tangible form. Saul wants to make the loose tribes into a unit; the people have to rally behind their leader without any divisions. A torn body is no longer a body. Does Israel realize that?" (Linden 2000:99).

Saul summons the whole nation to rescue Jabesh (v. 7): "This is what will be done to the oxen of anyone who does not follow Saul and Samuel." His call to follow him and the prophet proves his leadership skills as well as his awareness of what is at stake: the nation needs to be united under political (Saul) and religious (Samuel) authorities. He acts charismatically, i.e. independently.[26] The local crisis of a remote Gileadite town becomes a national crisis through Saul's perception and summons. Fokkelman (1993:467) rightly asserts that "the narrator highlights him as a hero, as the true leader and inspirer of the nation." After Saul's summons all Israel is united as one man (v. 7) — the very opposite to the attitude of the judges' era. Jabesh Gilead once again becomes a case uniting all Israel (cf. Ju 21). "The fear of the Lord sweeps away fear of the enemy and gives the people complete confidence in the campaign's meaningfulness, and that it will be crowned with success" (Fokkelman

---

[26] Even if Eslinger's (1985:366) suggestion that Saul now "is reminded of Samuel's instruction to do what comes to hand" is accepted Samuel presumably was not present in Gibeah thus Saul did not consult with him. Note also that Saul gives the order to follow him first and only then the prophet.

1993:470). Will the curse of Jabesh (Ju 21) and the fate of Israel as a nation (Ju 21:25) be reversed? The signs are auspicious.

In v. 9 Saul promises deliverance and reassures the inhabitants of Jabesh. Hope replaces doubt and despair. Israel mounts a surprise attack on the oppressors (cf. Ju 3:15-30; 4:17-22; 7:19-23; Ackerman 1991:13). The judges' success frequently required quick action often accompanied with deception or ruse (see Ehud and Gideon), so Saul in ch. 11 steps into the judges' footsteps. By the end of the day Saul has established himself as a charismatic deliverer, a מוֹשִׁיעַ. In a matter of hours the country boy we met in ch. 9 has been transformed into Israel's leader capable of the extraordinary task of uniting Israel's tribes and bringing deliverance — by God's spirit. 11:1-11 depicts Saul "as someone who, like the judges of old, leads Israel to victory under God's inspiration" (Polzin 1989:113).

A domestic crisis almost spoils the joy of deliverance; but something remarkable happens: even though the people address the prophet in v. 12, it is Saul who responds to them (v. 13; MT). In this way he manifests autonomy and wisdom. Thanks to his intervention amnesty is declared and bloodshed avoided. Saul appeals to God's deliverance to explain the pardon. He thus restates Samuel's, albeit differently meant, claim in 10:19: Yes, it was Yahweh who delivered us today. For the people it is obvious — through the charismatic leader Yahweh raised. In the Ammonite crisis Saul demonstrates his skills to deliver Israel. Will he be able to deliver them from the Philistines as well?[27]

Saul is transformed in this chapter from a commoner into a military deliverer, evident from the demonstration of his leadership skills. He reveals these by performing what was needed and what his countrymen could not do. In averting both outside and domestic crises he exhibits autonomy. All these are essential for a charismatic leader such as Israel needed at the time and was given in the person of Saul. Thus it is only from a diachronic viewpoint that Beyerlin can consider Saul's charismatic judge-like bravery irrelevant to the nature of his kingship (1961:189). From a synchronic point of view it is indispensable and essential, not merely in ch. 11 but throughout the entire plot. As Weber observed: "Kingship originates in charismatic heroism" (1968:1141).

THE CONFIRMATION OF THE NEW CHARISMATIC

In his study on the Israelite kingdom Soggin observes that the basis of the monarchy was the charismatic principle, i.e. only a person elected and bestowed with specific skills by Yahweh could be made king (1959:403). As is apparent from his comment the early kingdom in Israel was laid on a charismatic foundation. It might be appropriate to refer now to my definition of charisma, which is an extraordinary quality of a leader, that is recognised, on the narrative's level, by the narrator and his characters. Now I shall investigate

---

[27] In anticipation of the answer I notice that the term מוֹשִׁיעַ is never again used of Saul after 11:3.

how Saul's charisma was recognised and confirmed.

When Saul is chosen he is hiding. V.P. Long considers this a negative sign of timidity and reluctance (1989:217f), which he traces throughout the narrative. I think his reluctance is negative only so far as it is a character defect. Regarding the enormous challenge of kingship the simple farmer faces it is quite understandable. His reluctance will change after 11:6 — as much and for as long as Samuel allows it.

The narrator concludes ch. 10 with an unexpected remark. After electing their first king, the people including Saul are sent home by Samuel "each to his own town" (10:25f). It is the rejected old prophet who is still in charge, not the king (Gordon 1986:120). Saul is portrayed here as one of the people, not as a king in ANE terms.

The charisma God himself mentions (9:16) and then grants Saul (ch. 11) is that of military leadership. Saul had to be transformed from a farmer into a skilled general and military strategist — a מוֹשִׁיעַ. This is what both the crisis required and the elders had demanded. In ch. 10 Samuel designates Saul (V.P. Long 1994; see also Edelman 1991). At the decisive hour and in contrast with the people crying in their despair, Yahweh's spirit comes mightily upon him and transforms him in a matter of seconds. Saul demonstrates his leadership skill by becoming angry and delivering Israel from Ammon through his charismatic exploit (11:1-11). The reluctant farmer has been transformed into a capable military leader by Yahweh's spirit. The people recognise and confirm his judge-like charisma of a מוֹשִׁיעַ after the victory (11:12) and at the assembly at Gilgal by renewing the kingship (11:14f).

CHECKS OF POWER[28] — THE CASE AGAINST THE PROPHET

In the early chapters of 1 Samuel, Samuel is depicted as a humble lad serving God under the guidance of Eli in a very sinister situation. The prophet presented from ch. 8 onwards is quite different.[29] The once young charismatic leader, who was first a vehicle of God's judgment on Eli's house (ch. 3; 4:1ff)[30] then led God's people in the battle against the Philistine oppressors (ch. 7), has grown old. At his emergence Samuel was deferential — now in leadership position, he is authoritarian and clinging to power. With the years passing by his experience of leading Israel, the crisis of leadership and a rival's appearance

---

[28] Polzin (1989:89) has also noticed Samuel's function as the "institutional and personal check" of the king.

[29] In terms of Samuel's change Jobling (1986:85) remarks that Gideon attained the high point of his judgeship in Ju 8:23, when he utters his anti-monarchical confession and just before acting as a bad king. Similarly Samuel reached the zenith in 1 Sam 7, immediately before precipitating kingship.

[30] In my view 4:1 is the introduction to the following rather than a summary of the preceding so forming a preface to God's judgment on Eli's house announced in ch. 3 and executed in ch. 4. Understood in this way Samuel unconsciously prepared the fall and extermination of Eli's house.

on the scene seem to have affected his character and the way he leads Israel.

In order to understand the narrative, its development and portrayal of characters, it is imperative to deal with Samuel before we turn to Saul's rejection in chs. 13-15. A reassessment of Samuel's personality has gained ground in the wake of studies by Gunn (1980), Polzin (1989) and Ackerman (1991), to mention but a few. Now I shall analyse Samuel's leadership status and his motivation, because these two are pertinent to the theme of Saul's charismatic leadership.

There are obvious expectations on the prophet's part as well as hidden motives. Clearly, Saul had not only a military task but also to obey Samuel (10:5-8; V.P. Long 1989:63f). What concerns me is Samuel's expectation of Saul to obey him. To the prophet the election of Saul announces a new form of government, in which the king, Yahweh's military leader, is supposed to obey the prophet, Yahweh's religious representative. In this power structure the prophet is superior to the king, which Saul must acknowledge by carrying out the commission in the way Samuel dictates it.

The elders' request to Samuel (8:5) "however sinful seems not entirely impractical" (Polzin 1989:83). But Samuel is worried about his own power and influence rather than those of the potential king or Yahweh. Polzin has also noticed the startling and effective way the narrator reports Samuel's speeches to Yahweh and to the people. The story

> is constructed in such a way as to keep the reader in the dark—or at least suspicious—about whether the directly quoted words of God in verses 7-9 and the directly reported words of Samuel in verses 11-18 are supposed to represent *all* that God and Samuel said on these occasions. (82; his italics)

Polzin goes so far as to question Samuel's motivation. He claims the problem with the speech is that it warns the people only of the restricted nature of their future life under the king's rule. It is hardly conceivable that Yahweh, instead of reminding them that for him founding a monarchy was tantamount to idolatry, instructed Samuel to warn the people. Thus the speech is an attempt on Samuel's part to delay or even to subvert Yahweh's decision (85f).

If Polzin is right then from now on the reader needs to be on her/his guard regarding any action and speech Samuel performs and delivers. The suspicion is reinforced on reading the conclusion of the chapter, where he repeats the people's words to Yahweh (v. 21) "as if this superfluous act of telling God what he obviously already knows might, as a last resort, give God an opportunity to change *his* mind about allowing the monarchy" (Polzin 1989:84; italics his). Samuel, "the imperceptive lad of chapter 3 now appears a stubborn, self-interested judge, who for his own reasons is slow to do the LORD's will" (83). Not only his words characterise him negatively but also his refusal "to report back to the people that Yahweh has granted their request. Instead, he sends everybody home (8:22)" (Deist 1993:9).

If this assessment of Samuel's character is correct then one may assume that the elders' demand (8:5) was probably triggered by a basic character flaw of the prophet. In an evident contrast to his early ministry (1 Sam 2-7) he became authoritarian in his leadership style and in executing justice. "Samuel grew old" (8:1) amounts to his having become different, i.e. incompetent in leadership (see also Fokkelman 1993:326-29).

In ch. 9 the narrator depicted the changed relationships. The prophet took the lad's place, hence the initiative and control over Saul's life. V.P. Long, in favour of the prophet, suggests (1989:60-65) that Samuel wanted to establish prophetic control over the king. I have viewed it negatively. Miscall distinguishes between "the authoritative and stern prophet" and "the authoritarian, harsh, and bitter leader" (1986:72f). Which aspect was predominant in their relationship and in Samuel's attitude and how much the prophet was aware thereof are difficult problems. As the narrative unfolds the question is whether the Samuel of ch. 8 remains the same or changes in ch. 10.

The prophet introduces the anointing[31] of Saul with the words (9:27), "Stay here a moment, and I will tell you the word of God." In 10:1 he adds: "The LORD anoints you prince over his people Israel..." (NEB). Fokkelman observed that the structure of the two verses

> raises a subversive question: is perhaps (the uttering of) the anointing, i.e. the one line giving the verb *mšḥ* to the Lord, already the full content of God's word? The consequence of this equation, which is suggested by the chiastic connection and the closed nature of the figure, is in that case that the entire mass of 10:2-8 is primarily Samuel's view and is not an oracle in the strict sense. This does not alter the fact that in vv.2-6 Samuel has a surplus of divine knowledge at his disposal. (1993:416)

If that is the !case then we are witnessing the very moment when Samuel's "prophetic overkill", to use Polzin's phrase (1989:105), of Saul began — not in announcing the signs but announcing the action the king is assigned by Yahweh to perform.

After anointing Saul in 10:1 Samuel reassures him by predicting three events about to happen to the newly anointed leader. At the emergence of Israel's first charismatic leader in Exodus 4:1-9 there were signs marking Moses' commissioning too. But whereas his three signs were meant to convince his compatriots, "Saul's signs are for his own encouragement" (Gordon 1986:117).[32] The reader wonders why these signs are important to the king-elect. In view of Saul's character and position as Israel's new leader some instructions on what to do, avoid or strive for would surely have been more

---

[31] Edelman (1991:51) observes that Samuel used a "bottle" to anoint Saul while in other cases (16:13; 2 Kgs 9:1-3) a "horn", a symbol of royal strength and power, is mentioned. Was this intentional?

[32] In contrast to Gordon I regard this as negative.

helpful. But nothing in Samuel's briefing, apart from the highly ambiguous references in vv. 7f, points in that direction.

The signs are arranged in a definite order from the vague to the more tangible, at least in form. They contain more and more details, adding more and more importance to the particular sign with increasing tension. The first sign comprises only one verse (v. 2), the second two (vv. 3-4) and the third three (vv. 5-7; whether or not vv. 7-8 belong to the sign, it is the most extensive). In similar fashion the first encounter will be with two men, the second with three and the third with a "band of prophets" (AT).

The first sign relates to the family business Saul was sent on by his father. Here there is no mention of God (cf. vv. 3 and 5). The family matter is underlined by the place of the announced encounter with the two men — it will happen "near Rachel's tomb", "on the border of Benjamin", which must have reminded Saul of Rachel's death when giving birth to Benjamin, the father of the tribe (Gen 35:16ff) as well as of the fact that the sign will happen in Benjaminite territory. As if the prophet said to Saul, "Your tribe will acknowledge you" (Buber 1964:766-68).

All the information Saul learns from the two men is already known to him. In 9:20 he was told by Samuel not to be concerned about the asses which had been found. Saul himself had expressed his concern about his father's worry about himself in 9:5. What is the point of the message? The only new information in 10:2 is that of Kish's worrying question: "What shall I do about my son?" which can be rendered, "What shall I do/prepare to/for my son?" The reader is left contemplating this.

In the second sign, in its first half in particular, there are abundant religious overtones. The three men Saul is to meet, as contrasted with the two of the first sign, will be involved in some religious business, probably a pilgrimage to the sanctuary "founded" by the father of the nation (Gen 28:11ff). Being greeted by them means national recognition for the anointed leader. The reader is given a response to Kish's question — in a vague form for now.

If there was no religious characteristic in the first sign, and only a few in the second, religious features abound in the third. As a climax to Samuel's prophecy and the signs reassuring Saul of his election Saul will encounter a band of prophets "coming down from the high place". That the encounter is about feast and joy will be obvious. Saul will join them in prophesying after he has been empowered by Yahweh's spirit. Joining the prophetic band will certainly show Saul "how impressive a prophet's powers can be" (Polzin 1989:105).

By mentioning Yahweh's spirit coming down on the newly anointed leader of Israel, however, a confusing element has been introduced into the third sign. What Samuel meant by the "change into a different person" (10:6) is unclear. What the narrator meant, however, is increasingly obvious — a dupe at the prophet's disposal, created with God's assistance, as 10:9 suggests. Saul is no longer "the son of Kish and in his father's service; from now on he will be the son of Samuel" (Linden 2000:95). This is also what Jobling (1998:117) proposes by referring to the substitute father motif, picked up in 10:11f.

The content of the sign has been religious so far, the phrase צלח רוּחַ יהוה עַל, however, occurs in the previous "volume" of the DH in the Samson narrative in reference to Samson's enabling by Yahweh's spirit for military exploits (Ju 14:6, 19; 15:14; cf. the similar terminology of Judges on emerging charismatic military leaders in Ju 3:10; 6:34; 11:29).[33] Saul must be perplexed. Will it be a sign related to a religious experience or to a military commissioning? If Saul "is not to carry out such a function, why did Samuel guide the prospective *king* toward receiving the *prophetic* spirit in the context of his call (10:5-7)? Samuel is responsible for mixing the charismatic roles of the prophet and the military leader, not Saul" (Ackerman 1991:15; his emphasis). The ambiguity of the description referring to either a religious experience or a military exploit is the more apparent when noticing Samuel's mention of the Philistine garrison/governor at Gibeah coupled with God's (or "the deity's") presence promised. Because of its vagueness the commission in 10:7 amounts to the command: "If you listen to me you will do whatever you would like to."[34] That the command "must have had a slightly confusing or misleading effect on Saul" (Fokkelman 1993:423) is thus an understatement.

Whatever Samuel's instruction in v. 7 was meant to refer to the answer to Kish's question in v. 2 is given, and the answer is just as confusing as the reference to the third sign, which precedes it. After the first sign the reader was left pondering the answer to the question, "What shall I do/prepare to/for my son?" So far the second and third signs have pointed to a (religious) feast, which led one to expect that the signs would eventually be related to some sort of religious experience, thus the response should be, "Prepare a sacrificial feast for him in the company of the family!"

The confusion increases on learning the instructions in v. 8 about a sacrifice — but unrelated to a family feast. In addition the same phrase is applied in v. 7 (עשׂה לְ) as in v. 2 ("What shall I do...?"). If the connection is intended, then the answer to the question in v. 2 is implied in v. 7, "Do nothing, Saul is in

---

[33] If the comparison between Saul and Samson is intended, also suggested by the same terminology, one question still remains: Why is Saul compared to Samson and not to another judge? The question is even more burning with Polzin's observation in mind, that 1 Sam 11 displays several aspects reminiscent of Judges (1989:108ff). The expectation for a deliverer is voiced in the naming and its aetiology of Samuel (Ackerman 1991:19; see also Polzin 1989:24-26), which was not fulfilled, but foreshadowed the appearance and activity of Saul, who, similarly to Samson, was supposed to deliver Israel from the Philistines. This motif might be a good starting point to answer this question. My answer for now is that here the Nazirites Samson and Samuel are compared as well as Saul who is about to replace Samuel. Also Saul resembles Samson in that he too died a heroic death by suicide. For more on the two stories see Brooks 1996 and Exum 1992:18-44.

[34] Even if it refers back to v. 5, as V.P. Long (1994:278f) claims, it is very vague.

charge of the events." And in fact this is the obvious content of Samuel's instruction here: "Once these signs are fulfilled, do whatever your hand finds to do, for God is with you." Regarding the confusion the prophet has caused

> Samuel's series of signs to Saul in verses 1-8 amounts to something like prophetic overkill. [...] Samuel exhibits his prophetic clairvoyance like a strong man publicly flexing his muscles in an excessive or unseemly fashion. [...] So this prophetic show must be for Saul's benefit. (Polzin 1989:105)

Furthermore the signs are "examples of how Saul's divinely guided career will proceed. In all three examples, Saul is a passive respondent to the circumstances into which he is led" (Eslinger 1985:324), which is quite startling regarding his newly obtained leadership status. Thus it is not far-fetched to conclude: "Personal control appears to be what Samuel is after; Saul as both king and prophet offers a double warrant for royal dependence on Samuel, who himself leads the prophets" (Polzin 1989:106; cf. Weisman 1981:230f). Even at their last encounter Saul will reveal his dependence (cf. Craig 1994) by conjuring him up and asking what he is supposed to do (28:15).

The reference in 10:5 to the Philistine garrison/commander at Gibeah, where Saul is going to prophesy, moreover, strongly suggests that the anticipated military feat is to take place just after the prophesying. Strangely Saul's military commission is linked to a prophetic manifestation so that both Saul and we "who have already noted Samuel's generalized declaration to Saul about his specific responsibilities as 'king-elect' in 10.1 will tend to wonder if Saul will indeed be able to decipher and carry out Samuel's vague and cryptic command" (Edelman 1991:54). I shall soon demonstrate that Saul will not.

Regarding Samuel's two commands (10:7f), V.P. Long (1989:59-66) has claimed that bearing the division of royal and prophetic powers in mind they are not contradictory but rather express the twofold commission of the king. More recently literary critics have substantiated the signs' confusing effect on the two offices. Ackerman has blamed Samuel "for mixing the charismatic roles of the prophet and the military leader" (1991:15). So in 10:5-8 Samuel encourages Saul's prophetic independence, while at the same time commanding "strict royal dependence upon prophetic direction. In other words Samuel is shown placing Saul in a double bind" (Polzin 1989:107). Thus Samuel's command in 10:7 is in profound tension with that in 10:8. "Verse 7 does no more than state what it is to be a king, but anyone to whom the words of v. 8 can be addressed is no king at all. Verse 7 is a tautology, v. 8 a contradiction" (Jobling 1998:85).

At the assembly at Mizpah Samuel continues with his manipulations (10:18f). On previous occasions in Israel's history God often referred to his saving act to highlight the unfaithfulness of the chosen people. Of them Judges 2:1-3; 6:8-10 and 10:11-14 correspond most with 1 Samuel 10:18f as they are very similar in content and structure. Also their "chronological" proximity within the DH makes the comparison feasible.

The condemnations in Judges compare well with those in 1 Samuel in another respect too. Judges 2:1-3 reports the first instance of Israel's infidelity in the book. They fail to drive the Canaanites out, thus Yahweh's punishment will be to keep them so that "they will be thorns in your sides and their gods will be a snare to you" (Ju 2:3); and exactly that happens. By ch. 6 Israel grows desperate and cries out to Yahweh who angrily reminds them of what he has done for them (vv. 8f), states their covenant relationship and Israel's disobedience (v. 10). God's judgment abruptly ends with "But you have not listened to me", the effect of which is: "If you do not care nor do I." The angel's arrival in the very next sentence to appoint Gideon to deliver Israel, however, disproves this. When the situation further deteriorates in ch. 10, God's response to Israel's repentance is terse and harsh (vv. 13f): "But you have forsaken me and served other gods, so I will no longer save you. Go and cry out to the gods you have chosen. Let them save you when you are in trouble!" Yahweh's unwillingness is only changed by the appearance of Jephthah. This sequence is a decrescendo of Yahweh's commitment to his people and the severity of punishment proportional to Israel's sin. The punishment of Judges 2:1-3 is a test (cf. Ju 2:22) and Yahweh is still personally involved. After the condemnation in ch. 6, however, Yahweh withdraws. Though his withdrawal is only ostensible, his refusal to help is real in ch. 10.

If there is a decrescendo in the Judges passages, there is a crescendo in Samuel's three speeches of his commitment to Israel and its king. He ends his first speech with a warning of sombre prospect (8:18): "When that day comes, you will cry out for relief from the king you have chosen, and the LORD will not answer you in that day." 10:18f anticipates a harsh denunciation. Instead a summons to the tribes to present themselves follows. As I shall try to show, Samuel's speech is an attempt to retain his leadership status; therefore, after reproaching the people of having "done all this evil" (v. 20), he admonishes them of obedience to Yahweh (vv. 20f). The prophet even assures them of God's commitment to them (v. 22) and volunteers to pray for and teach Israel (v. 23). Apparently God's relationship to his people, impaired by the request for a king, has been restored. The events of chs. 13-14, however, shed doubt on Samuel's volunteering; Israel's first king is abandoned at his first fault, and when he enquires of God, he encounters only silence — the day has come when Yahweh does not answer.

The three speeches in Judges are introduced by a reminder of how Yahweh brought Israel out of Egypt followed by a stipulation and/or condemnation. The subject of the speeches is consistently God. In Samuel's speech, however, the introduction of God is succeeded by the prophet's denunciation, the tone of which is utterly accusatory (cf. Fokkelman 1993:439). In addition, all the three condemnations in Judges follow detailed accounts of Israel's covenant disobedience. The request of a king offended God (1 Sam 8:8), who nonetheless granted it. Israel's option for monarchy is not depicted as grave a sin as those in the Judges sections. Therefore the style and tone of 10:18f are disproportionately severe. The reader has the impression that in this way Samuel vents his anger on the people, just as he did after they had requested a king (ch. 8) and will in his farewell speech (ch. 12). All three speeches by Samuel are marked by a reproachful tone.

Savran (1988:73; his emphasis) has also noticed that Samuel's speech (10:17-19)

> is structured along the lines of the prophetic oracle of judgment: call to attention (17), messenger formula (18a), recitation of YHWH's saving acts (18b), and the accusation (19a) [...]. Absent, strikingly, is the judgment that generally follows such accusation both in prophetic speech and in narrative quoted direct speech situations. Thus, in the redacted version of 10:17-27, the story of the choosing of Saul occurs precisely at the formal point where we expect judgment to be pronounced. The implication is clear: Despite Samuel's overt praise of Saul in 10:24, kingship *itself* is to be Israel's punishment.

Then Samuel summons the tribes for the lot. When Saul is chosen king[35] Samuel recommends Saul's stature.

> The crowd has already been manipulated so much through the steps which have just been made in Mizpah, and through it are so sure of God's conducting the meeting that, without a moment's hesitation, they observe the large frame of Saul to be the proof of his destiny. (Fokkelman 1993:448)

What Samuel wanted to achieve he now has. At the request of the elders he appointed a leader over Israel, a king in total dependence upon him and in the grip of his control.

After Saul demonstrated his charisma and his competence for leadership by defeating the Ammonites the people want to confirm him (see V.P. Long 1994) in his office. Polzin has shown that the features of 11:1-11, reminiscent of Judges, direct the reader to expect a judge-like leader to be confirmed by the people — not as a king but as a judge. But Samuel, who holds on to power by manipulating the people (11:14), intervenes and Saul's kingship is renewed (1989:114-17). Indeed Polzin claims that it was Samuel's design to resurrect (119) the kingship. The irony is that the very day Yahweh rescued Israel in the fashion of the judges the people prompted by Samuel renew the kingship instead of abandoning it (11:13f).

At that point Samuel delivers his speech of farewell (ch. 12). It is "a daunting monologue" (Fokkelman 1993:483) which could also be entitled "The Rhetoric and Manipulation of an Indignant Prophet". Samuel's posture is self-defensive as he manipulates the people (Polzin 1989:118f); his protestations of

---

[35] Conspicuously in 10:17-27 there is no explicit mention of "making Saul king". Did Samuel deliberately avoid this as Ackerman suggests (1991:12)?

innocence (vv. 3, 5) are irrelevant to the section's emphasis (118). Samuel, by virtue of his rhetoric in 12:6-17, implicitly blames the people (120f).

The speech is divided into four sections each introduced by גַּם־עַתָּה/וְעַתָּה (12:2, 7, 13, 16).[36] The outgoing leader "has been walking before you" (AT) just as the king is now (v. 2). The point of this remark is that Samuel certainly did not harm anyone in Israel confirmed also by the people (v. 4). However, by having warned the people in ch. 8 of the king's transgressions he implicitly challenges Saul not to make the mistakes of a king — an impossible expectation to meet.

Dragga (1987) has observed that Samuel's speech is not simply retrospective but rather designed to place the newly chosen king in the shadow of the judges. By doing so the prophet destines Saul to inevitable failure. "There is likely to be little room for error in Saul's conduct as king, and if fault is to be found in him it is likely to concern 'disobedience'" (Gunn 1981:93). "The implication seems to be that unlike him the coming king will indeed do all these misdeeds—as he prophesied in 8:11-18" (Ackerman 1991:14). Acknowledging the prophet's innocence the people are trapped in the implication that nothing was wrong in Samuel's leadership of theocratic mediation in the pre-monarchic period (Eslinger 1985:388).

It is not obvious why Samuel mentions his sons. Are they, as Eslinger (1985:386) suggests, juxtaposed to the king with the particle הִנֵּה and in association with the people to make them joint heirs, along with the king, to the prophet's heritage? Or is it his last desperate attempt to establish a dynasty? And if so is he appealing to the hard core of the right wing intent on retaining judgeship and theocracy and opposing monarchy? If so, he is dividing the people.

In the second section of his speech (vv. 7-12) Samuel recounts Israel's history. The point of the section is that Yahweh managed to ensure Israel's security through judges (v. 11). Why did they then ask for a king? The indicting tone of Samuel is all too obvious. Here Samuel's main concern is formal vindication for Yahweh as it was for himself in the previous section and not a fair review of faults (Eslinger 1985:394). When recounting the story of the exodus he stresses the mediators' agency and excludes Yahweh. By doing so he draws attention to his own agency and criticises his replacement by a king

---

[36] On the use of the interjection see Brongers 1965. The sections are: vv. 2-5, 7-12, 13-15, 16-17 with vv. 1 and 6 preceding the particular section to be juxtaposed by what follows. The sections make up an ABA'B' pattern by being introduced with וְעַתָּה הִנֵּה הַמֶּלֶךְ (vv. 2, 13) and גַּם־וְעַתָּה הִתְיַצְּבוּ (vv. 7, 16). As Eslinger (1985:393f) pointed out vv. 2-5 are on Samuel's conduct while vv. 7-12 on Yahweh's conduct. To this I add that vv. 13-15 deal with the people's, including the king's, conduct with vv. 16-18 being the climax of the chapter (highlighted by the emphatic גַּם) where the prophet arrives at the point and effect he has aimed at in his manipulative speech — through Yahweh's assistance he reclaims and re-establishes his power and control over the people.

(Eslinger 1985:395f).

The third section forms the climax of Samuel's self-defence and indictment. As Israel chose (אֲשֶׁר בְּחַרְתֶּם) foreign gods in Judges 10:14, so they chose (אֲשֶׁר בְּחַרְתֶּם) a king, Samuel condemns them, ignoring the failure of his sons (Savran 1988:55). "Now here is the king you have chosen, the one you asked for..." (v. 13). Again the tone is accusatory. The accusation is followed by stipulations set by God's prophet. The people are warned not to rebel against "Yahweh's mouth" (vv. 14f; MT). By now the audience has been convinced that rebelling against Samuel, Yahweh's mouthpiece, amounts to rebelling against Yahweh.

The fourth section is introduced by the emphatic גַּם־עַתָּה. The people have been convinced of their sin in demanding a king and when upon Samuel's call God sends thunder and rain they stand "in awe of the LORD and of Samuel" (v. 18), to which end the whole show was staged (Eslinger 1985:484, n. 20). Another purpose of the demonstration "is to prove the strength of Samuel's ties with Yahweh and their agreement concerning the monarchy" (411; cf. Steussy 1999:38). Samuel wants deference demonstrated in loyalty — not towards the king but towards him the spokesman of Yahweh. And this is what he now receives along with a manipulated and forced repentance (see also Polzin 1989:121f). "On account of his intimacy with this powerful God and their shared antipathy towards the request for a king, Samuel is a man to be feared by the people alongside God" (Eslinger 1985:413). In contrast to 7:8 ("our God") in 12:19 the people ask Samuel to intervene on their behalf with "your God" (415) — they are intimidated and alienated from Yahweh.[37]

On the people's request (v. 19) Samuel promises to pray for them. Indeed by his promise to mediate between God and the people he re-establishes his leading position and influence (vv. 20-25). "Threatened with retirement, Samuel has emerged from the crisis with a public vindication of his integrity (v. 4) as well as the public recognition of his indispensability as mediator" (Eslinger 1985:422). Concerning his speeches in chs. 11-12, in

> both cases, a desire for personal power at the expense of communal welfare seems to underlie his actions and self-justifications. Samuel diverted the people away from repentance in chapter 11; he now diverts their attention away from his central failures by speciously concentrating on areas of responsibility unrelated to his actual failures of leadership. (Polzin 1989:119)

Whereas Samuel did his best in ch. 8 to dissuade the people from choosing a king, in chs. 11-12 he prevents them from returning to the more direct form of Yahweh's leadership — and he succeeds. Thus from ch. 8 on Samuel has been more concerned with his own power, influence and control over the people than

---

[37] "Your God" (sing.) throughout the narrative seems to be a sign of being intimidated (see 15:15, 21, 30; cf. Fokkelman 1993:526).

with God's. However, the newly elected king is an impediment in his attempt to establish control. Therefore the prophet will do his best in chs. 13 and 15 to assert his authority.

Another emphatic aspect in the section that I have already touched upon is the relationship between the prophet and the people, and Yahweh and the people. The narrator, by a careful choice of related phrases and demonstrating the effect of Samuel's speech, gives different accents to different effects of these relationships. After the military victory, in 11:12, 14, it is "the people" with whom Samuel interacts: a people led by and dependent upon their prophet-leader. Samuel's proposal draws the people's attention to his prophetic leadership.

As a result of Samuel's intervention "all the people" go to Gilgal (11:15). Arriving at Gilgal and holding "a great celebration" they are referred to as "all the Israelites". The phrase will recur in the next verse,[38] when Samuel addresses "all Israel" in his farewell speech. Here we encounter Israel as God's people celebrating their long awaited unity.[39] Only one, the prophet, does not join the celebrating masses.[40] And when delivering his address "nowhere does the tone of his speech in 12:1-25 reveal joy. On the contrary, the prophet is still as sour as in ch.8 [...]. Samuel is not even mentioned as a subject/participant of the crucial kingmaking in 15b [ch. 11]. No, the prophet is sure not to take part in the celebration…" (Fokkelman 1993:485). The effect of the address in this context is, therefore, "Do not be happy. You are a wicked people." This is the tenor of 12:9-25. The prophet spoils the joyful celebration of Israel, Yahweh's

---

[38] The slight difference is that in 11:15 it is כָּל־אַנְשֵׁי יִשְׂרָאֵל whereas in 12:1 כָּל־יִשְׂרָאֵל.

[39] The phrase, which is most emphatic in 11:15 and 12:1, is stressed in ch. 11. Nahash's intention is to "bring disgrace on all Israel" (11:2). The "assumption" on the basis of which he launches his attack on Jabesh Gilead is that Israel is disunited and weak. This is the literary reason, I suggest, for the terms in v. 3. Israel's national identity is underlined by the phrase "(throughout) Israel" (11:3, 7). We are reminded that the unity of Israel, which is essential to its national identity (see Ju 20-21), is at stake here. Nahash's "assumption" and assault, however, backfire. By the end of the chapter "all Israel" is united (v. 15) and the Ammonites are utterly defeated. Israel stands the trial and demonstrates unity. For the second time in their narrated history, after Ju 20-21, they stand up for the common good and interest of the nation and demonstrate a sense of belonging together, being one nation under Yahweh's guidance. They have become Yahweh's people by interpreting a local crisis as a national one. And while the *casus belli* in Ju 20:3 was נְבָלָה, "awful thing", here it is חֶרְפָּה, "disgrace" (1 Sam 11:2). What the two have in common is their attack on the nation's identity as well as the effect: they cause outrage and war, and as a result Israel is united. The clear difference between the two narratives is that whereas Ju 20-21 concludes with the ambiguous sentence, "In those days Israel had no king; everyone did as he saw fit", here we have Israel with its king elected. In this respect 1 Sam 11 may be considered the reversal of Ju 20-21 even if Polzin (1989:115), otherwise correctly, regards it as ambiguous.

[40] The MT of 11:15 is to be retained.

reunited covenant people.

In 12:6 the emphasis again is on "the people". Having been reminded of their wickedness by their leader "all the people stood in awe of the LORD and Samuel" (12:18). Forced by the prophet "all the people" are willing to repent and ask for Samuel's intercession on their behalf (12:19). "The people" (12:20) are still under Samuel's manipulative leadership. Immediately after frightening the people Samuel assures them, "Do not be afraid", but by adding, "You have done all this evil...", he makes the people even more frightened and dependent upon himself. He concludes his speech by referring to the duty of his leadership status which he will voluntarily and conscientiously carry out (12:20-25). By the end of his "farewell speech", Samuel has re-established his leadership. "The scene thus ends with Samuel totally in control" (Gunn 1980:65). "The question remains as to whether he himself is pleased with the fact that the freshly inaugurated king turns out to be an excellent 'judge' (in the specific sense of charismatic deliverer)" (Fokkelman 1993:534). This question will be answered in ch. 13.

Samuel's motivation has frequently been jealousy or resentment. Therefore the reader's suspicion is on high alert as he/she is presented with the prophet manipulating either the people or Saul.[41] Has Samuel acted like this because he has become used to power and is therefore intent on keeping it? In other words is his manipulating "merely" the habit of an inveterate leader or is there some other motive for his manipulation and claim to leadership?

I have referred to studies by R. Bach (1962) and V.P. Long (1989) who claim that in the early monarchy a division between the functions of charismatic leaders was established. The king was endowed with military function, while the prophet mediated the divine will. Thus Samuel's dominance over his protégé was justified. I have asserted, however, that for a charismatic leader such as Saul it was essential to retain independence. The prophet, by his high-handedness as well as demand of obedience, and a wait which will prove fatally illogical, pushed the king into the abyss of hesitation and ritual strictness. Dependence on Samuel irreversibly damaged the charismatic's character and prepared his doom. Samuel "could not prevent kingship but he has achieved the next best thing—a king he can control, a king who is less than a king. Samuel has won his battle with Saul, so he wants to keep Saul as a figurehead who conforms to his (i.e., judgeship's) idea of what a national leader should be" (Jobling 1998:87).[42]

---

[41] Whereas Jobling (1998:60) sees Samuel showing "a real enthusiasm" for Saul in 9:22-24; 10:7 and 11:14, in my interpretation even these sections portray him as harbouring selfish or manipulative intents.

[42] All the judges were successful with no mentor on their sides, with Barak being the exception who proves the rule. It is ironic that Samuel achieved what he did not intend — to make Saul, often considered the last judge, an anti-judge by subjecting the king to his prophetic control.

The prophet obstructed Saul's leadership in many ways. In the shadow of the greatest judge the first king was doomed to failure. Conspicuously Saul's other commission to restrain Israel is not referred to after 9:17, nor does the verb עצר, with the possible exception of 2 Kings 17:4, recur in the DH in reference to kingdom. This might be explained by Samuel's effort to restrain the king, so that Saul was unable to fulfil his commission of restraining Israel. The one who was supposed to restrain God's people was the one restrained by the mediator of the divine commission. Samuel made great efforts to protect his authority and subject the king to his prophetic control. Seen from this perspective Samuel was more than a check of power — he was its obstacle.

Apparently Samuel could not cope with the changed system. For him the only *modus vivendi* was theocratic judgeship. His old skin could not bear new wine. He was intent on establishing prophetic control by any means, but this was not merely occasioned by jealousy and rivalry — his ultimate aim must have been to retain theocratic judgeship. Samuel's multifaceted motivation affects the question of Saul's rejection, to which I now turn.

The Fall of the Charismatic

Rejected by the Prophet, 1 Samuel 13

To correctly evaluate this chapter, often considered Saul's first sin and subsequent first rejection by God, it is important to bear in mind how Saul's charismatic authorisation has been presented so far as well as related aspects of leadership such as charisma and success. I shall also relate this chapter's events to those preceding it in ch. 10.

Samuel's farewell speech in ch. 12 marks the end of the judges' era. In the same vein 13:1 inaugurates the beginning of a new era — that of Israelite monarchy (cf! Noth 1991:5, 23). Saul's reign is introduced with the regnal formula, standard in Kings, which commentators tend to either ignore (e.g. Brueggemann 1990) or discuss in isolation from the context (e.g. McCarter 1980:222f). I shall try to make sense of the verse in its wider context.

Obviously the MT does not make sense whatsoever; it must be corrupt. Saul could not possibly be just one year old when becoming king, and did not reign for two years only. This absurdity, however, is so blatant that one is forced to wonder whether this statement might be intentional, with some non-literal intent[43]. I have suggested that Saul emerged as a dependent person. In the shadow of Samuel, who kept him under his prophetic control, the king could not gain autonomy, so essential for a charismatic leader. I shall soon demonstrate that in chs. 13-15 Saul will not be able to win independence of his mentor. The king started his reign as a one year old completely dependent upon others, and did not reach maturity — Saul remained a child till his death. His

---

[43] For metaphoric interpretations of the verse see Sternberg 1985:14; V.P. Long 1989:74f.

short reign implies that it must have been unsuccessful, as in two years one cannot accomplish much, particularly if an infant. 13:1 thus serves as a summary of Saul's kingship. Indeed 15:35, "Samuel mourned for him", announces the end of Saul's rule, even though he will *de facto* rule Israel apparently for many years. By the end of his two blundering campaigns King Saul is considered dead.

At the outset of his military campaign against the Philistines Saul is able to mobilise Israel (13:2-4). As will be shown his following will scatter when their leader is compelled to wait (13:6-8). Along with his following, his charisma and charismatic leadership will also fade away.

When commissioning Saul, Samuel vaguely hints at the Philistine governor (10:5). In 10:7, "do whatever your hand finds to do, for God is with you", the prophet seems to refer to the Philistine menace which Saul was to take on as well as the governor to be assassinated, and these are what he apparently did in ch. 13. Thus 10:7 can be regarded as a command to a provocation with 13:3 being its realisation, while 10:8 is the command to convocation, which is fulfilled in 13:7b-15b (V.P. Long 1989:55).[44] Even if the Ammonite crisis prevented Saul from waging war on the Philistines, 13:2 suggests that he soon started his military campaign,[45] even though not in the manner Samuel expected him to. At the beginning he is determined "to act charismatically and surprisingly" (Fokkelman 1986:27). Once he had military support he declares war by having Jonathan kill the Philistine governor at Gebah (13:3; Fokkelman 1986:18). Obviously, "the intent of Jonathan's action is to precipitate an Israelite insurrection by provoking the Philistines" (V.P. Long 1989:79). To gain the support he needs Saul mobilises Israel by having the trumpet blown (v. 3). This act makes Saul appear like a charismatic judge.[46] The armies on both sides take positions (13:4f). Although "Saul apparently anticipated some sort of military activity, an all-out military engagement was not immediately in view" (V.P. Long 1989:82); it seems he was counting on Samuel's quick arrival.

Until now events have been developing rapidly. With Saul waiting in Gilgal (13:7), however, events slow down and get out of his control. The aspect of waiting/delaying and all the corollaries are emphatic in the story. Due to the delay lasting as long as seven days the people with Saul suffer a dramatic and "complete process of disintegration" (Fokkelman 1986:34). Those summoned

---

[44] On why Saul did not act immediately when the signs in ch. 10 were fulfilled, V.P. Long (1989:209) mentions "reluctance or incomprehension, or a combination of the two" as the possible reasons. By attributing his reluctance partly to Samuel's failure to clearly clarify his commission I view Saul in a more positive light. See also Edelman 1991:54f.

[45] Saul's commission, charisma and the crisis did not allow for a large time interval between the events of chs. 8-12 and the declaration of war on the Philistines.

[46] One wonders whether implied in the mobilisation was to let Samuel know the war has been started and so to make him come to Gilgal, where the king subsequently moved to (13:4e), to approve of the battle as well as to instruct the king (cf. 10:5-8).

to Saul in 13:4 were probably enthusiastic at first, then are pictured in a critical situation (13:6), then "quaking with fear" (13:7) and, unsurprisingly, eventually scattering (13:8) due to Samuel's delay as stated by both the narrator (13:8) and Saul (13:11). Thus the situation has become worse. Saul has to abandon his position at Bethel and Michmas and withdraw to Beth Aven, then Gilgal (Fokkelman 1986:31). Despite the Israelite disarray and the superior Philistine military, however, Saul "is evidently full of heart and has confidence in his own might" (Fokkelman 1986:28). He is obediently waiting for Samuel as instructed in 10:8 in order to consult him, even if it defies military strategy and common sense. "Just as in cap.11, he is the only one to remain calm and is not diminished by the pressure of the military situation" (Fokkelman 1986:36). In retrospect he portrays the situation and his response to it using the verb אפק (13:12). V.P. Long paraphrases it (1989:89; italics his): "'Though the situation was falling apart around me, I *restrained myself* (i.e. *pulled myself together when the temptation was to flee*) and offered the burnt offering.'" Interpreting the verb in this way Saul is not admitting to a bad conscience as often understood but rather claiming "to have acted in a self-controlled and even heroic manner" (89f). This is supported by the narrator's remark that Saul approached the prophet to be blessed (v. 10).

Better late than never and with "no room to manoeuvre" (Fokkelman 1986:36) pious Saul takes the initiative and prepares for the delayed action by offering the sacrifice (13:9). At that very moment the prophet suddenly arrives. Unsuspecting Saul goes out "to greet him" (v. 10). "Saul's action appears to be properly and guilelessly deferential. Samuel's answer to Saul, by contrast, is harsh, unresponsive, and accusatory: 'What have you done?' (v. 11)" (Brueggemann 1990:99). Whatever Saul's response might be, the prophet announces the judgment (vv. 13f). A look at a previous judgment on a previous house may aid our understanding of Samuel's denunciation.

Not long before another prophet appeared and declared Yahweh's verdict on Eli's house (2:27-36). Similar to the anonymous prophet, in 13:13f Samuel denounces Saul's transgression; then speaks of Yahweh's repentance of his plan about Saul's house, which Yahweh would have established forever; and a new, reliable appointee. Different, however, is the manner in which the verdicts are announced. Whereas the judgment on Eli's house bears the full authority of Yahweh (introduced by כֹּה אָמַר יְהוָה; the whole verdict in first person singular by Yahweh; the judgment twice supported by the authoritative נְאֻם־יְהוָה in 2:30), in whose name Samuel is speaking is doubtful; his denunciation lacks authority. Like Saul the reader is not certain to which command of Yahweh Samuel refers that Saul is said to not have kept, therefore in what his foolishness consisted.[47] Whether the judgment originates from Yahweh or

---

[47] Notice that even Samuel's condemnation in 13:13f is very vague as to what Saul's foolishness and his breaking of Yahweh's command consisted of (cf. Mauchline 1971:113). Samuel just touches on the king's sin (the case) and then rushes on to the

merely the prophet is ambiguous.

Apparently Samuel is keen to denounce the king and prevent him from both apologising and proceeding, i.e. from taking any action on his own. Samuel does not investigate or pay attention to Saul's defence and his circumstances but rather arrives with a prepared script of accusation — in spite of his own commitment declared in 12:23 (Ackerman 1991:15). The question is, what exactly was Saul's sin in Samuel's eyes? Why did he become so angry and condemn the king without proper investigation?

Popović blames Saul for breaking a cultic-ritual command (1993). Focusing on Saul and so ignoring his mentor's fault is missing the narrative's point. Saul's innocence and veracity are carefully established (Polzin 1989:129; see also Fokkelman 1986:38). My contention is that Saul, by taking action on his own, unintentionally issued a challenge to the authority structure established by Samuel. Saul did not prove to be subservient. That the king may become independent of the prophet by establishing a second centre of power not under his control posed a real threat to Samuel.[48] "The commandment that seems to have been broken is, 'Thou shalt not violate Samuel's authority'" (Brueggemann 1990:100). Indeed Robinson (1986:42) sees a back-reference in 13:10 to 9:13, where "Samuel attaches great importance to other people's waiting for his arrival at sacrifices". This reference might be hinted at by the note in 13:10 that "Saul went out to be blessed" (AT).

Saul's sin in Samuel's eyes was lack of deference: he did not wait long enough. Saul "acts as a king acts, but his doing so brings Samuel back quick [...] to tell Saul that he has committed the ultimate sin, the sin that means divine rejection. [...] What he feels guilty of is not a cultic blunder, but *acting at all in the absence of Samuel*" because "his real obligation is simply *to do nothing without Samuel*" (Jobling 1998:86; his italics).

Samuel finds Saul guilty of "foolishness, נִסְכָּלְתָּ" (v. 13), which verb usually denotes misperception of reality (Stoebe 1973:252f; see von Rad 1962:265). V.P. Long is accidentally correct in claiming (1989:90) that the reality Saul misperceived was that of "the subordinate nature of his own kingship"; he did not conform to reality — as perceived by the prophet. That is the reason for Samuel's harsh and relentless condemnation: he wants to subdue the king again, to make him aware of the obligatory reality of being under the prophet's

---

denouncement (the verdict) totally ignoring the king's defence (vv. 11f). By doing so, however, he pushes the king into strict religiosity as will be shown below, which the accusatory tone of Samuel's question, "What have you done?" (13:11; cf. 14:43; Gen 3:13; Jo 7:19) only aids. Of course this "is not an open question but a rhetorical one, spoken in a reproachful tone" (Fokkelman 1986:37).

[48] See Ackerman's (1991:15f) similar explanation. Fokkelman (1986:44) also claims "that Saul's decision to make offerings himself really was the last straw to the prophet", and the clash was therefore a "contest of competence". However, he overestimates the significance of Saul's "disobedience".

authority. This the prophet achieves by calling Saul "stupid" (so Goldingay 2000:96f).

Thus the real reason is to be found in Samuel's rather than Saul's attitude. Having seen how vague his instruction was in the decisive moment (10:5, 7f) as well as regarding his delay one is compelled to conclude that all this was *intentional*. That is to say Samuel was intent on holding the king under his prophetic control — by vague "prophetic" formulations, delay and prophetic denouncement. At the slightest sign of independence the prophet is keen to crush autonomy.

David Gunn (1980:39f) has asserted that even if the instruction in 10:8 was ambiguous and therefore in Saul's understanding no sin was committed, in Samuel's view the "immediate cause appears to be Saul's breaking" it. What is relevant to the discussion here is that 10:8 was *ambiguous*. And although Gunn does not mention the possibility my conviction is that it was intentionally ambiguous. Why did Samuel not anoint Saul amongst the guests of the sacrificial feast but rather in privacy the next morning? Did he want no witness to the ambiguous commissioning? Furthermore why did he require Saul to wait seven days and not, say, one or two only?[49] Such a request is irrational. Did he intend to obstruct Saul's military campaign? I cannot see any other reason for the prophet's command or for his delay, which therefore must also have been *intentional* (see also Polzin 1989:252, n. 12). In other words the prophet uttered an ambiguous instruction (10:8) with different possible interpretations, of which he was aware. Then he intentionally delayed for the period Saul had to be waiting, i.e. not acting, and just when the deadline was expiring he, being aware of the odds Saul and his troops were facing, appeared on the spot expecting to catch Saul at some action he could be condemned for (see Preston 1982:34; Amit 2000:176).[50] Seen this way it is almost immaterial when exactly, i.e. before or after the deadline, the prophet arrived at the scene (see Gunn 1980:39f). What matters is that considering the odds he arrived too late. "One suspects that Samuel has set up Saul for this 'failure'" (Alter 1999:73). "Teachers set their pupils difficult and even unfair tests just to see what they will do. It is in this vein that Samuel arranges to be a bit late" (Jobling 1998:120). The prophet's instruction was unfair and inappropriate in that it was impossible to obey.

---

[49] 10:8 is best understood as referring to Saul's waiting for Samuel when already in Gilgal, and not the time to elapse between 10:8 and 13:7.

[50] V.P. Long, in his otherwise excellent study (1989), fails to explain why Samuel delayed which in my view is significant in understanding the passage and requires an explanation anyway. A division of labour between king and prophet might have been "fundamental" (see 60-62) but not at the expense of other factors. It seems to me that in Saul's case rather the opposite of Long's claim is true: that fundamental division claimed constantly by Samuel led to Saul's rejection. Furthermore by failing to differentiate between Samuel's view and Yahweh's, to which the narrator in the chapter never refers, Long equates Samuel's with Yahweh's judgment.

One more aspect of the problem needs to be mentioned, which in my view is most significant in understanding Samuel's motive and action — that of charismatic leadership. As I have shown Saul emerged as a charismatic military leader. As such he was to act resolutely and without delay, especially in the emergency situations of the Philistine crisis. What paralyses his military campaign is the greatest peril of any military action — delay. On the basis of 10:7, which is an apt summary of his charismatic commission, the king might have felt entitled to launch an attack on the enemy but was compelled to delay his offensive — for seven days! — because his mentor said so in the next sentence. No wonder that he had to withdraw and on the seventh day, to avoid total military annihilation, consider taking military action in the prophet's absence. It may appear that what Saul did was exactly what Samuel was counting on.

It is a consensus among scholars that the prophet did not read studies on charismatic leadership. Being a charismatic leader himself, however, he was certainly aware of the "rule of the game", i.e. how a charismatic leader succeeds or fails: *Charisma and a charismatic only prevail if not hindered in or prevented from immediate and urgent action.* In Weber's words (1968:242): "If proof and success elude the leader for long, if he appears deserted by his god or his magical or heroic powers, above all, if his leadership fails to benefit his followers, it is likely that his charismatic authority will disappear." After the victory in ch. 11 and the successful assassination of the Philistine governor marking the start of the uprising, 1 Samuel 13:5-15 is the best case of elusive success, God apparently deserting (13:13f) and followers not benefiting from, the charismatic leader — Saul is hindered as מוֹשִׁיעַ and his charismatic authority shaken.[51]

Saul's delay and unsuccessful military campaign were the result of a weakened charisma destined to be extinguished. I have claimed that the secret of Saul's success in ch. 11 was resolute and independent action. To the extent he was successful there he fails here. The reason for his failure has become clear. He failed because at Samuel's behest he compromised his charismatic leadership by suppressing determination and independence. My suggestion therefore is that the prophet's intention with his ambiguous instruction (10:8) and deliberate delay was to make the king fail and ruin his career by killing his charisma. Samuel intended to rob the "rival" king of military success, hence political power and authority.[52] He knowingly caused Saul's alleged rejection

---

[51] Note that in ch. 15 he will be announced to have been rejected by God. In ch. 19 he will be ridiculed by his mentor again. By then he is no longer considered charismatic by the narrator.

[52] In ch. 11 he miscalculated by not foreseeing the Ammonite crisis where Saul — consciously or not, in accord with the prophet's instruction in 10:7 — did not hesitate but took immediate action. By so doing he proved a charismatic deliverer and was subsequently confirmed by the nation as such. Since the crisis's location was given, i.e.

by God by driving him into an attitude of living up to the prophet's standards and concept of true religion. It need be underlined, therefore, that in ch. 13 Saul was rejected only by the prophet and not by Yahweh. The king sinned only in the prophet's perception but not in Yahweh's (so also Good 1965:67; Jobling 1998:86). Note that Yahweh neither acts nor speaks in the chapter (observed also by Fokkelman; 1986:93), and the reader is left wondering about Yahweh's view. The narrator utters no single word of condemnation of Saul either.[53]

The chapter concludes with a description of the state of affairs in Israel (13:17-22). Thus the tenor of ch. 13 is Saul's rejection by the prophet (vv. 8-16) framed by the deterioration of Israel's position (vv. 2-7), and the Philistines' superiority (vv. 17-22).

> We wonder what is worse for Saul: his men's lack of arms, the superior force of the enemy, or the demoralization which makes great holes in his ranks. The composition, however, shows what is even more serious: the conflict which stands at the centre, the undermining of Saul's position by the prophet. (Fokkelman 1986:46)

The Handicapped King, 1 Samuel 14

In the previous paragraph I suggested that in ch. 13 Saul was rejected by Samuel. To understand the development and sequence of the narrative I shall first deal with Saul's perception. How did he experience the rejection announced by his mentor? What did he attribute his rejection to? And what resulted from his perception of being rejected?

Since ch. 14 is the direct continuation of the story it can best be understood against the backdrop of the antecedents. In contrast to ch. 13 the prophet is absent and does not act or speak. Still his ghost hovers over the king, to whom his presence is tangible. The king cannot get rid of his mentor's heavy spirit. His actions are determined by what he thinks Samuel, and by implication his god, expects him to do. The chapter must be interpreted in these terms, i.e. as

---

beyond the decision of the king or the prophet, Saul could not go to Gilgal to wait, hence could not be prevented by the prophet from taking immediate action. In 11:15 Samuel reveals his disappointment about the king's success that spoiled his anticipation. One also wonders whether his suggestion to go to Gilgal (11:14) was not a cover-up of this miscalculation by a back-reference to 10:8.

[53] Unfortunately David Gunn (1980:40) in his seminal study fails to recognise this and subsequently thinks that Samuel's condemnation equals that of Yahweh. Similarly Fokkelman despite his valuable observations dares not draw the right conclusion but rather claims that to conclude "that Samuel contrived the leaden words of 13:13sq. form too great an involvement and that he is the only one responsible for them would be going too far" (1986:93). I believe my "radical" interpretation is in good accord with the text.

an episode between two rejections and portraying a handicapped king.

As observed above Samuel did not go into details concerning Saul's sin. He pronounced the rejection without investigating or indicating what the king's sin consisted of. As already seen and as will be shown, in several instances (10:5, 7f; 12:2f; ch. 15) he avoids clarification in cases when this would be indispensable, and makes ambiguous statements. Regarding 13:13f it

> is important to note that the judgement also is ambiguous: at the least it means that Saul will not establish a dynasty; at the most it could be taken to mean that his kingship will come to an immediate end — for a successor is already chosen. Thus Saul acts henceforth knowing that unless he can manage to defy this destiny, he has himself no certain future as a king, while Jonathan his son has no future at all. (Gunn 1980:67)

I have also claimed that ambiguity was a weapon in Samuel's armoury of manipulation to which he often resorted. Saul's final rejection in ch. 15 too will partly be caused by a "misunderstanding" between Saul and Samuel. What might have contributed to Saul's reluctance to act was his waiting (13:10-15) for the prophet's instruction promised in 10:8, but finally not disclosed. The prophet left the king (13:15) without instruction for further action. This apparently paralyses Saul to such a degree that he becomes passive while his son takes the initiative throughout the chapter.

Ch. 14 begins[54] with Jonathan's surprise attack which causes turmoil and disarray amongst the Philistines and eventually their utter defeat by Israel. That the section still does not end in triumph but nearly in tragedy is due to the king's strict religiosity[55] forced upon him by his mentor's vague hence effective denouncement — effective because it caused Saul's further hesitation, insecurity and strict ritual legalism. In Saul's perception Samuel denounced him because of some sort of cultic failure. Though the prophet's denouncement is obscure its effect is clear: Saul becomes overcautious in cultic matters (cf. Gunn 1980:38; Robinson 1986:43). Being frightened and intimidated he dare not take any action on his own — he hesitates so showing his old, non-charismatic self. Though this is not stated in the narrative it is obvious from how Saul subsequently acts. Whenever he is supposed to make a quick decision it is preceded by some kind of cultic performance meant to assure Yahweh's presence and good will[56] and helping him in his pursuit defy his "destiny".

---

[54] Actually it begins with a long list of geographical and military data as well as Ahijah's genealogy. As for this latter Fokkelman (1986:48f) has demonstrated its inauspicious purpose.

[55] Saul was probably prone to this attitude as suggested in 13:9, 12, which in turn might have been caused by Samuel's manipulative speech in ch. 12. Any commentator portraying him in rather negative terms, however, has to explain the alleged sudden change in his personality.

[56] Also noticed by Polzin (1989:135), although with different implications.

Thus the prophet's denunciation opened to Saul a window on the terrible possibility of God's turning his back on him (Fokkelman 1986:39). The prospect of Yahweh's abandonment keeps the king under the prophet's terror. In the following chapter Saul is mesmerised by his mentor; in ch. 14 we are witnesses to "Saul's extended decline" (Fokkelman 1986:33) announced in ch. 13.

Seeing the tumult on the Philistines' side Saul orders Ahijah to perform some cultic act, probably to obtain Yahweh's assistance or an oracle (Fokkelman 1986:58), but he suddenly changes his mind (14:18f). Here he falls short of the charismatic Saul of ch. 11, who needed no oracle to act with determination. He does not exploit the splendid possibilities of the situation but hesitates (Fokkelman 1986:59). This is the first consequence of his rejection (Edelman 1991:86; Fokkelman 1986:59). Then, to secure victory, he binds himself and his troops under an oath (v. 24). By doing so "Saul creates a handicap" (Fokkelman 1986:62) and makes his own troops fatigued and so unable to carry on the pursuit. Saul is increasingly obsessed "with ritualistic insurance against possible defeat" (Polzin 1989:135). He seems to be preoccupied with ritual and cultic flawlessness rather than military success. This is hinted at already in the introduction of the chapter where Jonathan is accompanied by his נֹשֵׂא כֵלָיו (v. 1), while Saul by Ahijah the נֹשֵׂא אֵפוֹד (v. 3).[57] The "same Saul who was initially too preoccupied with the military aspects (in 13:8sqq.) now pays too little attention to them and a deficit of religiousness has now become a surplus" (Fokkelman 1986:64).

In vv. 33f he is concerned about his men committing cultic sin. Thus he changes the slaughtering into a ritual. He apparently wants to make a good impression on Yahweh, and to demonstrate his zeal he builds an altar (Fokkelman 1986:68). Here he functions as a priest mediating between God and the people.

At sunset Saul must make a decision whether or not to go on with the enemy's pursuit.

> The man who would not allow the people to eat during the day now allows them no rest during the night: v.36. Since he himself has made the day unproductive by an obstructive taboo, the job is still unfinished and Saul intends to continue the pursuit during the hours of nightfall — are not those hours themselves unproductive? The man who found ritual perfection more important than the military requirements of the situation now cannot get enough of the battle. How hopelessly Saul has lost his balance! (Fokkelman 1986:70)

---

[57] These two phrases function as epithets in portrayals. Jonathan's feat is introduced by the young man's epithet as Saul's failure through that of the priest. Of course each epithet discloses something beyond it — the person's character and main concern respectively, in this way depicting Jonathan as a competent warrior and his father a cultic "fanatic" preoccupied with rituals. Since Jonathan is not my focus I shall not deal with aspects related to his person and actions.

Prompted by the priest he inquires of God again (vv. 36f) — unsuccessfully this time. Lawton (1993:40) remarks that being prompted by the priest renders Saul's piety doubtful. I differ from him by seeing here a stage in the development of Saul's character. I see the transition from charismatic-determined Saul to his legalistic-hesitant alter ego. Gunn (1980:68) claims that God seems to have thrown the oath back in Saul's face. This is true not only of the oath but the whole enterprise: the severe pursuit of the enemy, the initial success, piety — all prove hindrances to Saul; he himself impedes victory. "Saul in fact becomes increasingly the great obstacle to the gaining of the victory, through his delaying (14:17-19) and sabotaging (14:24sqq.) interventions — an *opponent* in actual fact!" (Fokkelman 1986:77; his italics).

Being intent on figuring out the cause of God's silence, a dreadful experience to him,[58] he solemnly vows to find the sinner (vv. 38f, 41). He demonstrates great determination to fulfil his vow by not sparing his son (v. 44).

> At this point the narrator presents us with another great irony, for Saul behaves now towards Jonathan, his own son, in just the same unbending way as Samuel had earlier behaved towards him, Saul, in the matter of his "breaking" Samuel's instruction to wait for him at Gilgal. No allowance is made for the circumstances of Jonathan's sin. (Gunn 1980:69)

Does Saul wittingly or unwittingly identify with his mentor? Is he under his influence? Or is he reacting to Samuel's insult in this way? Is he frightened by the prospect of rejection (see Linden 2000:103)? All these motives, as well as the fateful pursuit of the enemy, point in one direction: regarding ritual Saul is overcautious. In chs. 9-11 Saul was an average Israelite, he did not betray any sign of cultic fanaticism. Even in the hour of a crisis (ch. 11) he was merely concerned with and focused on the military aspect of the emergency. There is no mention of any cultic activity whatsoever. After ch. 12 a different Saul acts. In ch. 13 due to Samuel's instructions (10:8) he is merely concerned; in ch. 14 due to his rejection by the prophet he becomes overcautious regarding ritual.[59] This attitude will also characterise him in ch. 15. The problem on the day of the battle seems to be Saul's piety: religion has become his highest priority, not the battle (Fokkelman 1986:69). No wonder that Saul is consistent in making wrong decisions. The king, having been

> robbed of his security by Samuel, is now hypersensitive to anything that he can interpret as insubordination, and that he really does feel his subordinate's absence

---

[58] Do we witness in 14:37 the first instance of God's disapproval of Saul as a charismatic leader? Is it the first instance of Saul going mad and having persecution complex, later in the narrative (16:14 onwards) reinforced by God's bad spirit?

[59] Two back-references (28:3; 2 Sam 21:1f) about his policies also suggest that Saul's activity as a king was interestingly hallmarked by strict religious policies.

as a loss of prestige and an attack on his authority. Spasmodically, after losing his credibility in Samuel's eyes, he wants to enjoy total authority over all the others; a compensation which is to cancel out the disturbance of his internal equilibrium. Saul is now on edge. (Fokkelman 1986:59)

Sam Dragga (1987) demonstrated how Samuel in his farewell speech (ch. 12) set an impossibly high standard for the king and destined him to fail. Saul followed in the footprints of the judges in ch. 11; endowed by God's spirit he acted on his own and delivered Israel. In the next chapter, however, Samuel stood him in the shadow of the judges.

What the prophet "envisioned" in ch. 12 was manufactured in ch. 13 and actually happened in ch. 14: Saul did not live up to the standard of the judges. As Fokkelman (1986:33) puts it "the very first clash between them [Samuel and Saul] at once forms the point of reversal of the king's fate, so that from being chosen he becomes rejected." "Rebuked by Yahweh, forsaken by Samuel, at odds with Jonathan, Saul ultimately finds himself completely isolated, alienated by his obduracy even from his own troops" (V.P. Long 1989:129).

Still Saul is portrayed rather sympathetically. The king "in this story is not so much wicked as foolish and frustrated. His intentions are good, indeed thoroughly pious, but he pursues them in self-defeating ways, and events thwart them" (Jobling 1976:368).[60] Saul's

> show of force was religious fanaticism and betrays inner weakness. Its revelation (and, first and foremost, its cause) through the confrontation with Samuel throws him completely off balance. Just as everyone's organism reacts to shocks and changes by seeking a new homeostasis, so Saul must now try to find a new balance. (Fokkelman 1986:77)

As the narrative continues into ch. 15 we shall see whether Saul finds his balance.

Rejected by Yahweh, 1 Samuel 15

I have shown how Saul's charisma was killed by the shrewd manipulations of his mentor and how an intimidated and ritualistic Saul emerged with his charisma bound to be extinguished. Even though Saul was innocent in his actions, and despite the prophet's condemnation, an "aura of doubt and suspicion" (Polzin 1989:130) already surrounded him in ch. 13 that only increased in ch. 14. In ch. 15 the king is tested again, and readers are left to

---

[60] Even later in the narrative it is not always evident what force controls him. Does his paranoia cause him to execute the priests in ch. 22 or is it his foolishness so depriving himself of the ephod (cf. Weiss 1965:187f)? Or is paranoia accompanied by foolishness? Is Saul destined to failure to be cursed so that even after his death his house cannot escape his fate of being a pious blunderer (see 2 Sam 21)?

wonder whether their doubt is unfounded.

Ch. 15 is arranged in an ambiguous way. The chapter is a very intricate network of reported events and assessment, and though I do not believe there is an explanation resolving all the difficulties, the crux of interpretation is to see the difference between direct and implied judgment. The chapter is made up of two parts, vv. 1-12 and 13-35. In the first Saul is presented and "narrated", while in the second he is presenting and narrating his case. The narrator portrays Saul negatively in the first part, whereas the second part, on the basis of *audiatur et altera pars*, presents the king's quite different version. Since the devil is in the details I shall pay due attention to them in order to grasp the narrator's intention and view. By making sense of the details in a consistent and comprehensive way I hope to offer an alternative interpretation to the conventional one which sees Saul in a negative light. Since it is more consistent with the narrative's development and portrayal, I shall argue that the charges against Saul can be dropped.

Obviously there are two options for the interpreter. The first is to take Saul's condemnation at face value and thus ignore coherent characterisation and story line. Alternatively one demonstrates coherence and tries to interpret ch. 15 in the light of the preceding portrayal and story line. An imperative for interpreters is to demonstrate the narrative's consistency and coherence, including that of characterisation. Unlike most interpreters I shall take the latter route.

The chapter has no introduction specifying time and space, which suggests that it is linked to the antecedents (Fokkelman 1986:86). The governing theme is marked by an inclusio. In v. 1 Samuel reminds the king that it was he who made Saul king. The chapter concludes with the note on Samuel's mourning because of Yahweh's repentance of having made Saul king (v. 35). Thus the chapter is about Saul's election to be king, and Yahweh's repentance and undoing of it (so also Fokkelman 1986:91f).

In 15:1-3 Samuel commissions the king to eradicate Amalek. What catches the eye is the prophet's long introduction (v. 1) to the commission proper (vv. 2f). Why is he referring to his mission of anointing Saul (10:1ff)? The quintessence of Samuel's claim and attitude towards Saul seems to be this: "Yahweh has sent me, i.e. I am in charge of telling you Yahweh's word and mediating Yahweh's message to you — you must obey (15:1d). Though you are Israel's king, I am the kingmaker, hence superior to you." Given the clash between the prophet and the king in ch. 13, Samuel probably regards the king as one ignoring Yahweh's commands, i.e. the prophet's authority, and refusing to obey. Understood in this way Samuel may also attempt to re-establish his authority, which he thinks is vanishing.

15:2f refer back to Dt 25:17-19 which, however, qualifies *when* the action against Amalek is due: "When the LORD your God gives you rest from all the enemies around you" (25:19). Why Saul is to eradicate Amalek before fulfilling his commission of delivering Israel from the Philistines is perplexing (contra

V.P. Long 1989:137).

The verb וַיְשַׁמַּע, *piel*, in reference to summoning in v. 4, is rare and strange (see V.P. Long 1989:138, n. 25). Reading without punctuation (as was read by the first readers), however, it is identical to the *qal* stem meaning "listen" which recurs in v. 24. Is the first doubt cast upon Saul here by hinting at his alleged collusion with the people?

The narrative appeals to the reader's suspicion aroused in the antecedents. A shadow is cast on Saul's action when he magnanimously — a sign of religious devotion? — offers the Kenites exemption from the *herem* (v. 6). By speaking in sovereign terms and thus making himself God's equal Saul's generosity is rather negative (Fokkelman 1986:91).

Two observations regarding Fokkelman's interpretation are necessary. Firstly I share his evaluation of the Kenite incident as being damaging to Saul. Secondly my interpretation slightly differs from his in that I believe fully in Saul's benevolent intention and do not see any "high-handedness" (1986:91) in his action. This is an important point because, as I shall argue, the king is portrayed in this first section as one performing well-intended but dubious actions, which, lacking qualification, characterise him as in opposition to God.

The reader's distrust is alerted in v. 7 where we learn of Saul's utter defeat of Amalek "to the east of Egypt". The exodus from Egypt was referred to by God in v. 2 and taken up by Saul in v. 6. The geographical location and the extent of Saul's victory seem to hint at the possibility that the king reversed the exodus and returned to Egypt (cf. Dt 28:68). The king is more and more implicated in his "wrongdoings".

Accumulating the charges vv. 8f unambiguously state that Saul, in an obvious breach of Yahweh's command, spared Agag and the best of the livestock. What was Saul's plan with the captured king and the best of the livestock? Did he intend to keep them as a trophy and as booty? Since the narrator does not present motives, one is compelled to conclude that the king failed to execute God's command. By "one is compelled to conclude" I mean that this is the force of the narrative as it impinges upon the reader. Thus Fokkelman's conclusion (1986:90) that Saul is pictured here in opposition to God is only correct if seen from the angle of how the narrative functions. The narrator does not view Saul in opposition to God, but this is the narrative's effect upon the reader by being "not empathetic enough with Saul" (Brueggemann 1985:45).[61] This strategy is meant to raise suspicion. In line with the interpretation so far Samuel's anger in 15:11 might be understood as one against Saul triggered by his disobedience to God. I am not claiming that this is Samuel's real motive but this is what the reader is led to believe (cf. Fokkelman 1986:93f). The climax is reached in God's normative utterance over Saul (v.

---

[61] This result, albeit with the opposite effect, is similar to that of *The Godfather*, where the portrayal of the head of the Corleone clan forces the viewer to sympathise with the vicious Mafioso.

11). Yahweh has rejected the king, and by now one is convinced that he deserved it. But did he?

I believe a negative view of Saul is due to the strategy of "intended ambiguity" in the narrative. That Saul's explanation and attitude throughout the chapter can be interpreted to be the very opposite of what I have been suggesting (see e.g. Fokkelman 1986:95ff) is due to a literary technique by the narrator to make the impression that Saul is the culprit. The narrator avoids clear depiction and evaluation of the events[62] and characters in order to make the reader identify with Yahweh's judgment.[63] V. 12 merely concludes the section. Seeing him erect a monument the reader views Saul negatively (Ackerman 1991:18) — obviously he erected a war memorial of his glorious victory.

The distrust of the reader towards Saul is reinforced when learning of his journey to Gilgal. What is he up to there? Is he preparing for a new consecration of his kingship (see 11:14f) to re-establish his rule over against the prophet? Since Saul has become the culprit this is one possibility coming to mind. Whatever the king does he is guilty by suspicion.

Since "evaluation" of Saul's motives is withheld until v. 15, the reader's suspicion about his guilt is reinforced (see Savran 1988:71). Because of the narrator's failure to provide information about Saul's motives, the king has lost any chance of acquittal. The effect of this composition, overlooked by commentators, is not only that the reader is forced to see Saul negatively but more importantly that she/he unconsciously takes Yahweh's point of view in condemning the king.[64] By v. 11 the reader has identified with Yahweh's viewpoint and judgment, which are not, however, those of the narrator.[65] I shall

---

[62] Jeremias (1975:31) has also observed that Saul's fault is not discussed *in concreto* but in general if at all, although he offers a different explanation. Berges (1989:183) takes God's unqualified judgment at face value by considering it a sign of Saul's "basic attitude" manifest in his breach of the ban, so revealing the interpreter's prejudice.

[63] Sternberg (1985:484) has noticed a "series of repetitions" in the chapter functioning "as a battering ram against Saul and, indirectly, the possibly doubtful reader", though he draws a different conclusion.

[64] Clearly this is the effect of 15:1-12, manifest in popular, as well as commentators', perception. People with whom I have discussed Saul's rejection on the "popular level" strongly disapproved of Saul without, however, giving proper justification. On the historical and semi-theological causes of the "popular perception" see Gunn 1980:23-31. As an epitome for the second V.P. Long claims (1989:145) that "to insist on Saul's integrity at this point is to deny that of the narrator, for the narrator's description in v. 9 makes a clear distinction between 'all that was good (כל הטוב)' and everything that was 'despised and worthless'." Here one sees the result of taking Saul's wrongdoing, dishonesty and rejection as well as their declaration first by Yahweh, then by the prophet at face value.

[65] If so this is a remarkable case of disagreement between the narrator and Yahweh. Sternberg erroneously equates the narrator's view with God's who "speak here with one

elaborate on this point later.

Actually the previous report on booty (14:32) may be interpreted as foreshadowing the events in ch. 15 (see V.P. Long 1989:121). To understand Saul's possible intention with the sparing of Agag, however, a similar account in Joshua comes to our help. In 8:2 God's instruction to Joshua reads: "You shall do to Ai and its king as you did to Jericho and its king, except that you may carry off their plunder and livestock for yourselves." Since Joshua 6 reports on Jericho's total destruction the command must mean: No prisoners of war! 8:29, however, implies that the execution of the *herem* was open to Joshua's interpretation. It is very likely that by sparing Agag Saul imitated Joshua, as the phrase in 1 Samuel 15:8, חַפֹּשׂ חַי, borrowed from Joshua 8:23 indicates.[66] V. 32 (MT) also implies that Agag did not expect "anything but evil in Saul's hand" (Nielsen 1997:128).

This interpretation may help understand Saul's intention of building the monument. We should not miss that "in his own honour" is not the narrator's report — he keeps quiet — but the messenger's impression. On the narrative's level again this report functions to confirm the reader's suspicion. Nevertheless the text may be read in a quite different way. Foresti (1984:56) has drawn attention to Moses' building an altar after the defeat of Amalek (Ex 17:15f) with the explanation כִּי־יָד עַל־כֵּס יָהּ. Whatever the phrase means, Saul's intention by building a יָד, in an attempt to meet the "expectations" of the prophet and his god, associates him with Moses. Like Moses Saul did his best to express his gratitude for the victory. In this interpretation both the erection of the monument and Agag's sparing portray the king as a pious Israelite who "read the Bible on a regular basis" to find patterns to follow.

And now the story from a different perspective — from Saul's. Section two starts with the prophet's arrival at Gilgal. The king gives him due respect when greeting him (v. 13): "The LORD bless you! I have carried out the LORD's instructions." His claim is the very opposite to Yahweh's, though both characters use the word הֵקִים. This is a "radical conflict of perspectives" (V.P. Long 1989:144). The doubt of the reader is aroused — after all Saul cannot be right. Bearing in mind the strained relationship between prophet and king, however, the *captatio benevolentiae* of an intimidated Saul eagerly waiting for Samuel's approval of his "performance" can be heard.[67] Instead he receives

---

voice" (1985:502). On this and the notion of "omniscient narrator" see Gunn's (1987 and 1990) and Jobling's (1998:141f, 289-96) criticism.

[66] On "back-references" to the Pentateuch in the DH see Alter 1992:107-30.

[67] While I have throughout tried to portray Saul as well as Samuel consistently, Fokkelman (see especially 1986:95ff) is apparently unable to avoid inconsistency in portraying Saul negatively and Samuel positively in ch. 15 in contrast to ch. 13. For this I see no reason but that mentioned above, the "deceiving" force of the story. Any interpretation of the narrative should take account of questions pertaining to narrative coherence, logical story line, consistency in attitude towards Saul and the monarchy, clear rationale of Saul's rejection, compatibility of Saul's failure as depicted in ch. 15

disapproval in a humiliating accusation (v. 14). As on previous occasions, the prophet, without paying attention, condemns Saul (cf. 13:14f), throwing cold water on the expectant king (contra V.P. Long 1989:144f). Again the prophet has an explanation ready so he does not need to listen. He repeats his mistake of 13:11-15.

We must not fail like Samuel but carefully listen to Saul's defence. Startlingly Saul gives a different and plausible explanation from Yahweh's (v. 11), and we learn why he has come to Gilgal. V. 15 seems to suggest that sparing the livestock and bringing it to Gilgal was the troops' idea, as assumed in v. 13 and confirmed in vv. 20, 24. As to Agag, we are not explicitly told what Saul's intention with him was, except that in v. 20 Saul mentions his capture and removal to Gilgal as, at least in his understanding, in accord with Yahweh's order. "Why waste the animals when the best of them could be offered to YHWH? Why not make an example of Agag to show what YHWH does to his enemies?" (Jobling 1998:83). Samuel learns of Agag only through Saul's voluntary and unsuspecting information (Hertzberg 1964:127). In addition the fact that we do not know Saul's intention may be the narrator's literary technique. That is to say we do not learn what Saul intended with Agag because Samuel failed to ask him. Likewise the reason why we do not know why Saul built the memorial (v. 12) is that the prophet did not ask. In both cases we only have inklings based on the references to Joshua 8 and Exodus 17.

Saul did not get a fair trial. The evidence against the king was the result of the prophet's failure to investigate the case; his procedure cannot be justified by claiming that he "already knows the truth" (so Sternberg 1985:505). According to the king it was the people who have spared the livestock in order to sacrifice them to Yahweh at Gilgal (v. 15). Saul's claim is questionable. The unequivocalness of v. 9 points to Saul's responsibility (Alter 1992:150), which he denies here. Thus the king is lying. Maybe. But is this a "desperate movement of a guilty liar" as Alter claims (150f), or rather a last-ditch attempt to save face and avoid the prophet's condemnation? Saul's psychological disposition, his relation with Samuel as well as the events so far make the latter option highly conceivable. In agreement with Gunn (1980:49), therefore, I see no other convincing explanation than what Saul is claiming. What other reason can we find for him to go up from the Negeb (or Carmel) to Gilgal (some 50 miles!)? In fact Saul may be trying to correct his "sin" at Gilgal in ch. 13. Seen in this way his claim is

---

with the depiction in preceding chapters and consistent portrayal of characters (see V.P. Long 1989:135). Long has succeeded in portraying Saul in a consistently negative light, even in ch. 11. I think many details and the narrative as a whole contradict this negative depiction. The decisive change in Saul's character is clearly marked in 16:14 where his negative portrayal starts. In this way the narrator associates Saul with the major judges (cf. von Rad 1962:329).

a remarkable and dramatic shift in Saul's favour. The king replies, apparently without embarrassment [sic], by volunteering the information that the noise issues from the best of the Amalekite livestock which has been brought here — to sacrifice to Yahweh. Now we have a completely different view of what is going on: to be sure, Saul and the people had not "devoted to destruction" the best of the livestock on the spot, at the scene of battle (or wherever), but that was because they had decided it would be more appropriate to "devote" it to Yahweh at his own sanctuary. Seen in this light, of course, the sparing of the best of the spoil makes excellent sense, for how could they bring what was despised and worthless back to Gilgal to sacrifice formally to their God? (47; Gunn's emphasis)[68]

Gunn quotes the LXX (50) to back up his interpretation. As to Fokkelman's (1986:95) psychologising interpretation, I am unable to see the evidence apart from a negative attitude to Saul. Thus it is rather he than the "omniscient narrator" who "immediately sees through the façade" and "'sees into the heart'" (1986:95) — again of himself and not Saul. I think his negative stance is the basis for his interpretation (see 95ff). Ignoring Saul's defence is a common failure of interpreters, causing them to see it as hypocritical, which in turn unavoidably forces them to view him negatively throughout the chapter.

I have tried to present Saul's motive for going up to Gilgal positively. Since Samuel's condemnation in 13:13f was provoked by the king's independent action (not waiting for the prophet) here Saul appears to right his sin. Once again he has come to Gilgal to offer sacrifices but this time under the prophet's guidance, whom he awaits patiently.[69]

The issue between Samuel and Saul on the matter of the spoil and Agag seems to be similar: a matter of interpretation (Gunn 1980:51). It is a power struggle in which the king is not allowed to interpret the command (Miscall 1986:98-114). Being cautious as he has ever been since the fiasco in ch. 13, Saul tries to verify himself by over-performance. The prophet, however, is not impressed at all. He is not listening: "Stop!". God's mouthpiece does not listen but — what else is to be expected from an orthodox prophet — rather tells Yahweh's message.[70] "I shall not listen to your excuse but you listen to what Yahweh is telling you."[71] "Samuel asks Saul to explain his disobedience to the

---

[68] His voluntary information in v. 15 using the two key verbs חמל and חרם refers back to v. 3 and verifies his integrity.

[69] Also suggested by Edelman (1991:105). Her subsequent interpretation seems to be inconsistent in terms of characterisation and rationale.

[70] Edelman (1991:106), commenting on the contrast of vv. 17-19 to v. 11, raises the question "whether Samuel's comments in v. 17 are his own elaboration and interpretation of Yahweh's message or part of an additional, unreported message that accompanied the quoted statement."

[71] Does this arrogant attitude reveal something about the prophet's leadership style? If so were the elders (ch. 8) discontented with Samuel's leadership? Note also that in 16:4 the elders are frightened when he visits the little town. Indeed Gunn (1981:111) claims that

divine command, but the king's fate has already been decided in v. 11" (Savran 1988:71). Samuel emphasises the theological aspect — at the expense of the matter of fact. And — what else is to be expected? — Saul submissively complies (v. 16): "Tell me."

Samuel keeps stressing that Saul was disobedient and refers to his humility. The Hebrew of 15:17 can be understood as pertaining to the past, especially 9:21 and 10:22, meaning that although Saul was shy and humble when made king he has become arrogant and insubordinate (NIV). Alternatively it may refer to the present condemning the king of his allegedly subservient attitude to the people in that he complied with them by pouncing on the plunder and thus disobeying God's command: "Though you are little in your own eyes, are you not the head of the tribes of Israel?" (15:17; NRSV). Instead of being directed and controlled he should have led and restrained the people. Indeed Seebass (1980:123) identifies Saul's sin in that it consisted of the refusal of his royal duty as well as that of Yahweh's order to be the head of Israel's tribes (v. 17). In either case in Samuel's view the king obviously failed. Moreover Saul is charged with disobedience to Yahweh's word for taking the booty (v. 19). Now I shall examine whether he really failed.

I have claimed that Saul has been meticulous in maintaining his integrity and subordinate status to the prophet. He has not become recalcitrant. On the contrary. He was forced into a servile position before the prophet; what handicapped him was his dependence upon Samuel.

Saul politely and humbly tries to present his case again (vv. 20f). He insists he did obey and reiterates what he has already said, for Samuel might not have got the point. The way he responds refutes the prophet's charge of arrogance (if the NIV's rendering is followed). Because of Samuel's superiority and attitude, Saul's fear of disapproval, which he eventually receives, is tangible. But the prophet is relentless. Again he moves from the matter-of-fact level to that of universal truth (vv. 22f).[72] The prophet's attitude prevents him from thoroughly investigating Saul's case.

Saul has been left no alternative but admitting his "sin"; he realises that he will lose the argument. He confesses (v. 24) — this is what the prophet wants to hear (contra Frisch 1996). Although with a different evaluation of Saul, Polzin asserts that the king "is doubly repentant: of his sin and of his attempt to conceal that sin from Samuel" (1989:143). The king humbly begs the prophet's mercy, intervention and mediation before Yahweh (v. 25). Samuel, however, is

---

Samuel is considered "a dangerous man (16:4), for in him one comes perilously close to God himself."

[72] V.P. Long (1989:167) claims that "Saul's 'not listening' is presented as the moral equivalent of rebellion, which in turn is likened to divination and idolatry", hence "Saul's specific misdeed in ch. 15 is but a symptom of a more deep-seated ill." With this conclusion, however, he falls short of his second goal of presenting a coherent story-line (165f) not so much of ch. 15 but of the whole narrative in its portrayal of Saul.

determined about God's rejection (v. 26). It is final and irreversible, highlighted by the verb מאס (see Fokkelman 1993:337).

Samuel wants to leave but Saul in his despair tears his robe.[73] The robe is "*the* characteristic of Samuel's eminence. Saul reaches out to what he sadly lacks: unswerving faith, power, authority" (Fokkelman 1986:105; italics his)[74] — because he had been robbed of them and not in arrogance. At the same time Saul's grasping the robe is a symbol of perseverance to be pardoned. His tearing of the prophet's robe (v. 27) grants Samuel opportunity to declare how the kingdom has been torn from the king (v. 28), a judgment "as ambiguous as the first rejection uttered at Gilgal" (Gunn 1981:99), and more importantly to declare the truth about Yahweh's inability to repent (v. 29)[75].

In v. 30 Saul admits his "sin" again and asks the prophet to return with him to worship Yahweh. The king is still intent on reversing Yahweh's decree. Despite the declared divine decision he wants to worship God. So far v. 30 corresponds with v. 25. There is, however, a new element providing fuel for commentators not in favour of Saul. The king wants to be honoured before the elders and Israel. Is this a sign of hypocrisy? Does Saul intend to have his authority upheld before those present? If we have a negative view of the king, like Fokkelman (1986:108) and V.P. Long (1989:164; 1993), this seems to be inevitable. But having recognised the prophet's attitude towards him why would Saul call for Samuel's honouring him in a situation clearly worsening for him? After the tearing of the prophet's robe and the harsh announcement of final rejection it is rather peculiar. From this perspective his plea would rather fit in v. 25. Samuel should have been outraged on hearing his "impudent" call. But nothing of this kind follows.

Seeking a more positive representation, however, his desperate request might be interpreted differently. Samuel has exploited every opportunity to subdue the king (see 9:22; 10:6; 12:2f). Subdued and mastered by the prophet Saul's appeal is a desperate attempt to reclaim his position. At last he tries to re-establish himself as a king respected by his people. But his bid for forgiveness remains unanswered. V.P. Long's claim (1989:164) that Saul's

---

[73] On grasping the hem as being a sign of submission see Brauner 1974 and its detailed discussion by V.P. Long (1989:157-63) as well as G.R. Stone 1995.

[74] While Saul's deed in Fokkelman's view I think is negative, I see in it the king's desperate appeal to the prophet not to abandon him – another sign of his dependence on Samuel. Since it was the prophet who made the king dependent (to lack "unswerving faith, power, authority"), the scene is ambiguous and Saul in my view portrayed rather positively.

[75] Fretheim (1985:597f) claims that 15:29 "almost certainly has reference to David" which I am unable to see. In line with my portrayal of Samuel I rather view it as a universal statement of the orthodox prophet — in Fretheim's words (597) "a general reference regarding divine repentance" — with little bearing on the particular situation. "There is no doubt that in this story the stance of the prophet, that is inconsistent with that of the narrator or with God, is unreliable" (Amit 2000:53f).

hypocrisy is manifest in the lack of asking for forgiveness is unsatisfactory as v. 30 amounts to what Long misses. That he did not repeatedly ask for forgiveness should not be a puzzle: he had been refused, indeed silenced. The proposed worship before Yahweh (v. 30) should also be understood properly. Without forgiveness a ritually preoccupied Israelite as Saul apparently was would not have dared worship Yahweh.

Moreover why does the king insist on worshipping Yahweh (vv. 25, 30)? It seems to be vital to him. In 13:12 he is shown as one concerned about Yahweh's favour, without which he dare not start the battle. I have shown that since 13:13f, the first rejection, he has become overcautious in cultic matters. The effect of Samuel's declaration of Yahweh's rejection there was the fear of God's turning away from him (Fokkelman 1986:39), which he experienced subsequently, in ch. 14. With impending judgment in sight Saul wants to prevent rejection (15:25), and when it is announced (v. 26) his last desperate hope is to reverse it by obtaining forgiveness. Samuel's willingness to worship Yahweh with him would be a sign of that forgiveness and of rejection reversed. The prophet returns (contra Alter 1999:93 who ignores a ב in v. 11) — with no confirmation of forgiveness. With the king the reader is left wondering whether Saul's petition for forgiveness has been granted. Finally the prophet departs from the king (v. 34) without assurance in regard to Yahweh's declaration: has Saul been pardoned? Has Yahweh repented? Since the prophet leaves the king for good (v. 35), Saul receives no answer to his tormenting question. The king is abandoned both by the prophet and his god.

Before leaving, however, the prophet executes Agag (v. 33). Whereas in v. 17 Samuel reproached Saul for not asserting himself as king, now he, by correcting Saul's failure to execute Agag, humiliates him for having attempted to act as a king. No doubt by so doing Samuel publicly reprimands the king. Thus "whenever Saul gets a bit bigger in his own eyes he is rebuked, and he is not able to do anything about it" (Jobling 1998:87).

Fokkelman (1986:110) contrasts v. 33 with another event "before the LORD in Gilgal", 11:15, and notes the apparent dissimilarity. The phrase designating the commencement of the Israelite monarchy after Saul's charismatic deliverance here refers to the rejection and commencing demise of the first king and perhaps his final deprivation of charisma. This is reinforced by the note of Samuel's mourning (v. 35).

> Mourning usually *follows* death, but here it precedes it! From the combined use of words such as *mōt* and *hit'abbel*, and particularly from the meaning of the latter, we realize that Saul as king is already dead; no stronger expression of the termination of his monarchy can be imagined. (Fokkelman 1986:110; his italics)

The commencement of Saul's monarchy was announced in 13:1 and here its death sentence — even if its dying will take a long time. Saul's brief charismatic leadership has come to an end.

The Doomed King — An Assessment

Here Saul's sin and rejection as well as repentance will be assessed as major themes in the narrative. An evaluation of the main characters (God, Samuel, Saul) will also be necessary. Finally I shall attend to the question of how these different aspects relate to Saul's charismatic leadership.

First I shall review Saul's sin and rejection from the perspective of charismatic leadership. When Samuel commissions Saul (10:5, 7) he vaguely hints at a military task. Saul, however, for reasons mentioned above, fails to immediately execute the task. After the fulfilment of the signs he returns home as if nothing had happened. His inauguration as king (10:17-27) does not change this (11:5). In fact he only begins his mission in ch. 13, probably after several days or weeks have elapsed, which points to Saul's reluctance and failure (V.P. Long 1989:231f). Regarding this I have claimed that the prophet's ambiguous signs and instructions made failure inevitable.

Ch. 14 depicts Saul as one increasingly concerned with ritual at the expense of military efficiency. The prospective victorious champion becomes a bungler. In ch. 15 he fails to execute Agag for reasons we are not told. Likewise we do not know why he "set up a monument in his own honour" (15:12) — a remark by the messenger virtually contradicting Saul's portrayal and open to interpretations. What is clear is that due to Samuel's rejection — ostensibly related to Saul's cultic activity in ch. 14 — the king became meticulous in cultic matters, making him ineffective. In ch. 15 Yahweh's command mediated through Samuel is unambiguous and indisputable — just as Saul's subsequent sin and rejection are problematic as recognised by most commentators. The problem is caused by the narrator's failure to clearly define Saul's sin. In addition to what has been said so far 14:48 further complicates the picture by referring to Saul's action in the next chapter in rather positive terms. Is this the narrator's real view of the Amalekite campaign? If so is it the narrator's intention to pay tribute to his tragic hero?

I have also suggested that religious caution led to Saul's "sin", hence rejection by God. He intended to offer sacrifices in Gilgal, apparently to appease the prophet and God, whereas Samuel demanded a *herem* on the spot. Likewise it is probable that he intended to build a memorial to Yahweh as well as to execute Agag in a way similar to that of Ai's king. Meticulous religiosity would be quite negative in other instances. Saul, however, receives our sympathy (see Powell 1990:57; Amit 2000:173-75). The reason for this is that he was transformed into a religious bungler and made to blunder. He ostensibly failed to obey God and demonstrate deference to the prophet. But most importantly, due to the delay Samuel imposed upon him, he failed to carry out his commission of delivering Israel from the Philistines (chs. 13-14). He could only partially fulfil his mandate. Curiously the rejection is not really related to this failure. No matter if deserved or not, his punishment appears to be out of proportion (Gunn 1980:44). Saul seems to have not committed any particular sin, but he made the mistake of asserting himself vis-à-vis the prophet by encroaching upon Samuel's territory of interpretation. "This time his fault is to *interpret* the law of the 'ban,' the obligation totally to exterminate conquered peoples (e.g. Deut. 7:2), instead of just obeying it" (Jobling 1998:86; his italics).

Still Saul cannot be exonerated of the charge of being directed or controlled by the people rather than he himself directing and controlling them, a weakness Saul admits himself (15:24). In this respect Samuel is correct in blaming the king for being little in his own eyes despite his being "the head of the tribes of Israel" (15:17; NRSV). This reveals a basic flaw in Saul's character. He was easily influenced and was not determined in decision making and leading the people. "But whereas Saul is guilty, he is not really evil" (Exum and Whedbee 1985:34). Reluctance characterises him throughout the narrative (contra McGinnis 1999:255-57), and this is a fundamental fault in a person in a leadership position (see Goldingay 2000:97, 101f). If a leader is not resolute and firm but rather prone to be easily influenced, he/she is likely to fail. Again this begs the question whether Saul was a good choice.

The question of repentance is of no less significance. I deliberately avoid saying "Saul's repentance" for in addition to that the narrative stresses another repentance — Yahweh's. Polzin has noticed that the "clearest penitent in the chapter is, of course, Saul himself" (1989:142). After failing twice to convince the prophet of his guiltlessness (vv. 15 and 20f) Saul admits his sin (v. 24), a sign of submission. This is what the prophet really wants. That Saul's intention to restore his relationship with the prophet and Yahweh is genuine is indicated in 15:25: he begs the prophet's pardon as the precondition of worshipping Yahweh. But, with a universal declaration of God's immutability (v. 29), Samuel refuses.[76]

Saul's effort does not obtain the pardon from Yahweh that he so much hoped for. A "repentant Saul at odds with an unmerciful God" is presented here (Polzin 1989:141). He may repent yet cannot remain Israel's king because Yahweh has repented and does not repent (Polzin 1989:147). "The scene, like that in chapter 13, discloses to the reader that Saul when 'tested' is bound to fail. That is his fate" (Gunn 1980:71). And that fate is a tragic one (see Humphreys 1980 and 1982). With his repentance rejected, Saul's simultaneous attempt to save his status as a charismatic king of Israel is also crushed.

The term "before the LORD in Gilgal" "is like a refrain in this story, for before Yahweh in Gilgal take place the key events in these first formative episodes. The phrase thus speaks of Saul as well as of Yahweh and his prophet" (Gunn 1980:72). I shall now evaluate these characters, their involvement in the

---

[76] Saul's assumed sin could have made God, with some self-justification, argue: "Now you have seen yourselves that I was right in objecting monarchy. This is what you asked for." That he does not say so may point to Saul's innocence and compunction and a sense of justice of Yahweh.

story and their relation to each other.

As regards the king the "sense that Saul is acting in 'good faith' is more pronounced in the earlier section [chs. 13-14] though in the latter parts of ch. 14 a darker side of Saul begins to show itself" (V.P. Long 1989:168). I have also stated that Saul is no doubt pictured here (esp. 15:13, 16, 20f, 24) as intimidated by, hence under the control of, Samuel. In line with his portrayal in chs. 9 and 13 he is dependent on the prophet, he keeps trying to measure up to Samuel's standard and, unsurprisingly, fails. Subsequently he "loses hope, not faith" (van Praag 1986:424). Indeed his failure was that in the shadow of the prophet he was not able to establish himself as an independent charismatic leader. His doom and the death of his charisma in turn were caused by Samuel's expectation of total dependence.

Throughout the narrative Samuel's motivation and attitude towards the king have been all but admirable. In ch. 9 he established his prophetic control over Saul and then kept exercising it. His overwhelming authority is voiced in the tautological order of 15:1: "Listen now to the voice of Yahweh's words!" (AT), with key words of the chapter (שָׁמַע, קוֹל, דָּבָר) applied. These words recur at essential points in the conflict between prophet and king.[77] What is most significant is 15:24 where Saul admits his sin in a startling way. He confesses to have violated Yahweh's command and the prophet's words, דְּבָרֶיךָ. So far דָּבָר has been used only in reference to God's word. By referring to the command as Samuel's rather than Yahweh's, Saul unwittingly betrays his uneasy dependence on his mentor. Like latter-day interpreters, the king equates the prophet's words with Yahweh's. In a similar way he speaks of "your God" (vv. 15, 21, 30), pointing to his dependence on the prophet's religious authority (cf. 12:19).

As in ch. 13, the prophet interprets Saul's different view and execution of his will as a lack of deference. Samuel does not want to hear Saul's defence. He communicates God's words but does not listen to those of a human. He demands absolute obedience to what he communicates but is unable to hear what others communicate to him. Samuel is a born-to-be-tough man (Goldingay 2000:7-24).[78] Just as Saul is deferent and submissive to Samuel, so Samuel is authoritarian. He "is a strict instructor, not patient with failure but deeply attached to his pupil" (Jobling 1998:120). He is "the author's spokesperson for the errors of authoritarian dogmatism" (Polzin 1989:146). His intervention on Saul's behalf (15:11) reveals his attitude. The prophet "prefers the royal devil he knows to the one he does not know" (252, n. 13). If understood in this way he intervenes on behalf of himself. His intervention is the more ambiguous if his perception of the rejection is considered. Just as he

---

[77] On שמע see vv. 4, 19, 20, 22, 24; on דבר/קול see vv. 16, 19, 23, 24, 26.

[78] See also Simon's article on ch. 28 (1988), who argues, albeit not consistently throughout, that the self-righteousness of the "stern prophet" is counterbalanced by the witch's kindness.

felt offended when the people demanded a king (ch. 8) he feels wounded by Yahweh's repentance and rejection of Saul (15:11). God's regret, "that I have made Saul king", in Samuel's perception might well be referring to a mistake made by him in anointing Saul, hence an implicit condemnation of his prophetic activity (so also Miscall 1986:103). Even if one is not that negative towards the prophet, a "profound ambivalence toward Saul, whose downfall he works to bring about in 1 Samuel 13-15, but whom he mourns deeply in 15:35, 16:1" (Savran 1988:74f) should be recognised in him.

Samuel has proven to be the main culprit. Still, Yahweh avenges himself on innocent Saul. Are Samuel and Yahweh accomplices? Up to 13:14 only the prophet was definitely against the king. In ch. 15, however, he is accompanied by Yahweh. Having such antagonists Saul has no chance. What can we say about God's motives? Instead of being presented with compelling evidence we are left guessing. "Can we say that God had committed an error in choosing Saul and now [in ch. 15] repented of it, i.e. was sorry for it?" (Mauchline 1971:123). Or did he get angry and envious about the request of the people for a king other than he? Did Yahweh intend to teach Israel a lesson of the cost of such a request (see Polzin 1989:87)? Indeed Cohen (1994) suggests that by giving them a bungling king God punished Israel.[79] That is what Hosea 13:11 implies (Gordon 1984:58; V.P. Long 1989:240).[80] Was Yahweh negligent or indignant towards Saul because of the monarchy — a new centre of Israel's power (cf. Exum 1992:38f)?[81] Was he therefore intent on rejecting Israel's first king regardless of the consequences? Was he inexorable to the extent of not being able to repent and change his mind in regard to Saul (ch. 15)? These all imply that Saul, even though making mistakes, should be considered a victim — a tragic victim of an authoritative and resentful prophet and his jealous god (cf. Fokkelman 1986:690f). In fact Nielsen considers Saul the scapegoat of the monarchy (1997:135).[82] The king "is Yahweh and Samuel's dupe; the success of their operation depends on their total control of him. As soon as Saul shows signs of going his own way (ch. 15) he is rejected as unfit for office..." (Eslinger 1985:312). Eslinger's statement is reverberated in Fokkelman's

---

[79] Despite his correct claim that Saul's tragedy is first and foremost not individual but one representing that of his people, who deny Yahweh in their demand for an earthly king, Cohen unnecessarily contrasts the "tragic hero" view with that of the "divine dupe". In my opinion they are two sides of the same coin.

[80] This verse, if a reference to Saul, suggests that by the 8th century, roughly 300 years after Saul's kingship, Israel had not yet come to terms with this painful memory. Apparently it took Israel a long time to recover from this trauma.

[81] Miscall (1993) argues that the different appearances of Moses and the major characters in 1 Samuel respectively foreshadow the ominousness of monarchy.

[82] Jobling (1998:60) notices that "by the end of ch. 12 it is a kingship nobody wants— Samuel, YHWH, and the people of Israel all agree that the demand for a king was bad. (Saul's opinion is not asked.)" On Saul as victim, indeed scapegoat and sacrifice for kingship, from the perspective of ritual, see Williams 1994 and Hawk 1996.

conclusion, "Saul is the victim of a God whose rationality is beyond our ken and, secondarily, whose possible reasons are kept concealed by the narrator" (1986:691). This conclusion is logical, despite Jobling's observation that by ch. 15, when Yahweh takes the stage, the issues at stake in the mythic battle between old and new orders are too difficult and contradictory, hence he gets embroiled in a disturbing theological contradiction over whether he is able to change his mind (1998:88).

Some illumination may come from another direction. Miles notices that it is in 2 Samuel 7:14 that Yahweh speaks of himself as a father for the first time in the FT. "Fatherhood is an absolute, not a conditional, state. The father of a son cannot, in the nature of things, cease to be such" (1995:170). The tragedy of Saul lies in the fact that he did not have Yahweh as his father.

Now who is the victim and who the villain? Samuel's motives are quite clear. He sees his authority and influence threatened from the very moment Israel turns to him demanding a king. His jealousy of the king is only fuelled at seeing Saul's charismatic success against Ammon. He sees a new charismatic leader emerging in the fashion of the judges. From his point of view their relationship is a power struggle and the rival must be subdued and eliminated. Throughout chs. 13-15, Saul's benevolence is consistently thwarted and condemned by Samuel's malevolence. The prophet is the very opposite of old and indifferent Eli (see 3:18) — he just cannot tolerate different views and forms of government to those conceived in his theocratic world. In addition, just as the young Samuel was unconsciously a vehicle of God's rejection of Eli's house in ch. 4 (see esp. 4:1), so is the old Samuel consciously the vehicle of God's rejection of King Saul. Returning to where he started his ministry the prophet has come full circle.

There is a remarkable twist in the relation between Saul's failure and rejection. "Rather than his failure (some sin or other) being the cause of his rejection, his rejection—his not being allowed to be a real king—is the cause of his failure" (Jobling 1998:85). Now it "is difficult to avoid seeing the LORD as the one who ultimately sets up Saul for proximate rejection" (Polzin 1989:125). Yahweh and Samuel alike are parts of the problem. And the problem from Saul's angle is not merely that he failed to carry out Samuel and Yahweh's orders, but rather that he failed to assure himself of God's good will. Obviously without this a charismatic is bound to fail.

Soggin (1967:57) claims that the author is not concerned about the disproportion between sin and judgment. In my reading Saul's rejection seems to have been a puzzle for the narrator to the same extent that it is for us. He was confronted with the same questions we are, hence we can only guess the motive for Saul's rejection by evaluating his account and portrayal. Did the narrator not know the real cause of Saul's rejection? Did he therefore resort to a reconstruction of his own with no firm evidence against Saul? Did he portray Saul's case and Yahweh's specious rejection in this ambiguous way because he did not clearly see, or more horrendously, did not agree with Yahweh's view?

And did he contradict it by arranging the material in this subtle way to express his embarrassment and uneasiness about Saul's rejection? If so the narrator did not exclusively lay the blame at Samuel's or Saul's but to a significant extent at heaven's door.[83]

"Saul, a warrior and man of action, of dominating will, asserting his royal position and chafing at his subordinate rank in relation to Samuel", Robertson claims (1944:31). In the light of what has been established, this observation, accurately reflecting the stance of earlier scholarship and popular view, is disproved point by point. I have suggested that Saul's failure consisted not in cultic blunder, self-aggrandisement, arrogance or lack of submissiveness towards Samuel, as commentators are keen to demonstrate, but rather the very opposite. Despite being a charismatic leader as he was he fell short of establishing himself as such, did not demonstrate independence from his mentor but rather subordination as a submissive apprentice to his mentor. Saul did not appropriate his calling and commissioning, he was "unable to assert himself as king" (Jobling 1998:85).

Saul might have made mistakes (reluctance, inaction), but Yahweh's punishment nevertheless was disproportionate. Dependency on Samuel, as foreshadowed in 9:22, was one of the most significant factors determining Saul's fate (cf. Marguerat and Bourquin 1999:64f). Samuel did not let Saul go. He pushed the king into the abyss of "inescapable stress" (van Praag 1986:428)[84]. Saul became a victim of Samuel's "personal resentment" (424) and, regarding the psychological process, "a victim of losing hope, of despair" (425). Regarding my definition of charisma with God on his side and prompted by God's spirit Saul performed unexpected actions in 11:6 (and 10:7). Subsequently, however, he was consistently obstructed by Samuel which in turn resulted in the death of charismatic Saul. In this light we should not

---

[83] Protesting at God's unfair actions is not rare in biblical literature. One may argue that it is unusual for the narrator to disagree with or protest against God's decision in narratives. This is a correct objection but there are narratives of a similar mould. In my view the fall-story (on this see Barr 1992:8-14) is a kind of countertestimony (see Brueggemann 1997 as a framework to my argument here; see also Linafelt 1992) protesting against God's incomprehensible treatment of mankind in a daring way, thus setting the scene for human history and God's ambiguous relationship with mankind (cf. Levenson 1994; Miles 1995). Though interpreting the story quite differently and rather in historical-critical terms Seebass (1980:123; AT) has also observed its closeness to Gen 2-3, "in that both describe the total loss of confidence through offending a privilege without, however, talking about a deed directly reprehensible."

[84] The psychological aspects of Saul's motives and experiences need further investigation. A good case has been made by the psychiatrist van Praag who deals with Saul's feelings generated by his rejection insightfully. Whereas the king was unlikely to feel anger towards God or the prophet he was possibly angry towards innocent others and himself. Suspicion was likely to develop. And after his world became insecure and threatening, feelings of despondency were inescapable (419f).

wonder why he failed but rather why he did not go mad prior to 16:14.

Charisma and Character — The Deuteronomistic Criterion

The Deuteronomist appraises kings according to a socio-politico-ethical standard. I shall measure the three kings of my study by this standard. The list in Deuteronomy 17:15-17 states that the king should
- be chosen by God and should not be a foreigner;
- not rely on military power (implied is dependence upon Yahweh's intervention);
- not have an oriental harem;
- not accumulate wealth.

In other words the king should not be an oriental despot. Saul was chosen by God. I have argued that he was a military king until the end of his life. Even after his rejection he tried hard to appease God and demonstrate his dependence upon him. Also the narrative witnesses to a rather puritan king, who apparently, apart from Rizpah, did not have concubines. Neither did he accumulate wealth. He is presented as a king who lived up to the Deuteronomistic standard.

Signs and Wonders

Jobling (1998:257) perceptively observes that in 1-2 Samuel God's interventions gradually decrease. I shall develop Jobling's observation by slightly modifying it: charismatic movements/leaders are in need of and approved by God's interventions. These abound at the beginning of their activity but then decrease. The more they experience the stronger their claim and authority are. And vice versa: if God's interventions decrease the movement or leader is doomed to failure.

Here manifestations of God's intervention through Saul's charismatic leadership should be discussed briefly, which may contribute to a better understanding of charismatic leaders and movements in general. The timing and incidents leading to Saul's encounter with Samuel already anticipate that something extraordinary is beginning. This is confirmed by the signs after Saul's anointing, culminating in his prophesying. The events reach their climax when, with Yahweh's spirit transforming him into a charismatic leader, Saul takes the initiative and miraculously delivers Jabesh. Signs and wonders accompany charismatic Saul's emergence.

After the climax, however, the signs cease altogether. Indeed Craig claims (1994) that Saul's reign is bracketed by God's twofold silence. The first military campaign of the confirmed king (ch. 14) becomes the action of an intimidated bungler unable to make God respond. His last and fateful military campaign is preceded by a similarly unsuccessful attempt to contact God (ch. 28). As Saul the judge-like deliverer has Yahweh on his side (ch. 11), so is Saul the king deprived of God's presence, word and intervening assistance. After ch.

13 signs of God's change of heart multiply, and Saul is finally rejected in ch. 15.

At the new beginning, in direct continuation with the judges' era, extraordinary phenomena confirm that God's spirit had raised a charismatic. I shall elaborate on this later. Whether God's interventions as a basic characteristic of charismatic leadership should be replaced by institutions to uphold continuity, stability and God's presence remains to be seen.

"Spring" — The Israelite Monarchy in Blossom

Parallels and comparisons between literature and the arts have previously been proposed (see e.g. Berlin 1983:13ff; Petersen 1986). Now in a kind of intertextual reading I shall take the step of relating the movements of Vivaldi's *Four Seasons* to the movements and developments of the characters and plot I have dealt with, because I have found remarkable analogies. In concluding my discussions of the three major characters I shall view the three seasons of Israelite monarchy, each season embodied by the respective king and his rule, from the point of view of how my characters relate to each other, how the climate of the season changes and how the particular season is depicted.[85] Not being a musician myself I shall rely on Paul Everett's recent monograph (1996).[86]

"The cycle's brightest, most optimistic music is heard first, as befits the season" Everett observes (80).[87] In the first movement spring is announced with all its splendour — pleasures of country life are vividly depicted. Similarly in the narrative Israel looks forward to a new season of its life. The monarchy is announced and the first king appointed. Saul proves himself by his military prowess over the Ammonites. The events up to 1 Samuel 11 constitute a proper beginning of the new venture.

The mood of the second movement, however, is different: instead of the happiness of E major it shifts into C sharp minor. To be sure pleasant flowers, the rustle of fronds and trees still abound — it is springtime. Nonetheless in the background the *ostinato* of the viola stirs an uneasy feeling: the barking dog may represent Samuel vigilantly supervising the sheep and the "dormant" shepherd, King Saul.[88] As the dog's barking stifles the shepherd's slumber so does Samuel's personality that of Saul.

---

[85] It is tempting to refer to Oswald Spengler's monumental work *The Decline of the West* (1926-28), except that it is too conservative in its values and outlook.

[86] My referring to Everett's study only when it supports my interpretation may appear arbitrary. As opposed to him I shall interpret *Spring* and *Winter* rather pessimistically.

[87] Page references in these sections are to Everett's study.

[88] There have been performances in which the role of the shepherd dog is underlined by a loud and almost unpleasant rendering of its barking in accord with Vivaldi's caption for the viola: *"sempre molto forte"*, i.e. very loud throughout.

In an exuberantly festive dance the third movement resumes Spring's celebration, as Everett gives the telling title to his discussion, "Spring's raptures" (80). Indeed the year, as well as the monarchy, starts in rapture. In the midst of this gladness, however, the discordant voice of the stern prophet, who even though retired keeps guard over monarch and monarchy, could be noticed. This anticipates the fate of the first king and the rather gloomy atmosphere of *Summer* alike.

The Leadership of the Charismatic

The Transition in Leadership

As Max Weber first realised the transition in any leadership is of enormous significance. An ideal transition can be imagined as well as a real transition observed (Armerding, oral communication). In an ideal case the transition takes place in the form of a smooth process: the charismatic leader recognises 1. that his/her time is over; 2. the appearance of another charismatic leader; and 3. the need for change in leadership. 4. Finally the old charismatic leader gives way to the new by preparing her/him for leadership and relinquishing power in due time. The real transition, however, generally is a different story. As witnessed in the text Samuel could not cope with retirement, nor was he willing to abdicate at the emergence of the new charismatic leader but rather held on to his leadership position. The Samuel-Saul mentorship[89] was unsuccessful because of the jealousy and dominance of the prophet. The prophet, the emblem of the previous "awakening", has become the main obstruction to the emerging one.

In Jobling's view Saul's failure was that he did not accept his kingly commission — he kept acting as a judge (1998:66f, 85f). Indeed Jobling claims that Saul became king only after his rejection (89). 16:2 seems to support this: Saul is finally ready to get rid of the representative of the old order (see also 19:4 and the implications of 22:18f). In fact 7:15 may be understood literally, i.e. Samuel kept acting as a judge after Saul's anointing. My reading of the narrative has confirmed this. The real transition progressed through conflicts and eventually tragedy.

Concerning the old and the new orders Jobling in his structuralist interpretation has claimed that "in the presence of Samuel, central symbol of the old order, Saul can never assert himself" (1998:87); this was the king's major failure. Jobling continues:

> What this means is that kingship has not begun at all, nor judgeship ended. This is the meaning not only of Saul's failure but of Samuel's living on. While he lives,

---

[89] I have found "mentorship", even though a non-word, the most appropriate in reference to Samuel's mentoring with its allusions.

> the transition does not really happen. Saul cannot make it happen. He is willing to submit to the laws of the old order, and so he does not bring in a new one. (87)

In this regard the statement in 15:35, "Samuel did not see Saul again until the day of his death" (NRSV; cf. 19:24), takes on an interesting import. The phrase applied here is equivalent to that in Exodus 10:29 (cf. Ex 12:31ff). I suggest that this expression means that from that time on Samuel representing the old order is not at the king's disposal any longer as his "adviser" (cf. Exum and Whedbee 1985:37, n. 9). The new order is left alone, no assistance by the old is available (see Samuel's unwillingness to be consulted in ch. 28). Since the prophet declines to relinquish power, this comes about by the king's rejection (cf. Exum 1992:161, n. 41).

As for the prophet, his fault is to live on even though the narrative's rule would require him to die after 1 Samuel 7 or 12 (Jobling 1998:69, 77). Thus "while he lives he must also continue to represent and struggle for the old order that is passing, trying to maintain that order even if it means resisting YHWH's will" (69). The prophet makes every effort to uphold the old and constrict the emerging new. He does it by all the means at his disposal, one of which is the delay in ch. 13. Samuel

> is late because he is dead. He has become, as we say, "the late Samuel." He has completed his life as a judge (ch. 7). He has lived on to make a king, and he has made a king. He has delivered his valedictory. Now it is time for the king to be a king, to "do whatever he sees fit, since God is with him" (10:7). This is what Saul does in 13:8-12. He judges the situation and takes action. He acts as a king acts, but his doing so brings Samuel back quick (as opposed to dead) to tell Saul that he has committed the ultimate sin, the sin that means divine rejection. (86)

In the overshadowing presence of the old, the new order is unable to take root. "Sidelined" by the prophet (68) Saul does not measure up to becoming a king — a dependent chief never measures up to charismatic leadership.

Contrasting Saul's reign with David's from the perspective of organising state government may also highlight Saul's inability to become king. Grottanelli has observed that, by having a quite wide range of officers such as Abiathar the priest, Nathan the prophet, Joab the commander-in-chief, David allows for "diversification of specialized functions" in his government. "In contrast to David, Saul is never presented as an organizer (but rather, as unruly and 'disorganized')" (1999:100). In other words Saul, a transition figure, cannot contribute much to the formation of the monarchy. The corruption of 13:1 also suggests that Israel's first king was an enigmatic monarch. We do not know how old he was when he became king and for how long he ruled — the tradition fails the first king. Unlike David he was doomed to failure as well as to "being forgotten" in Israel's memory.[90]

Saul's Attempts to Resolve the Crisis

I started this chapter by depicting the crisis of leadership under Samuel. By drawing the contours of an emerging charismatic leader I suggested that in the person of Saul a response to the crisis was given. How did Saul face the crisis? Did he take proper steps to resolve it?

Most references to Saul in the narrative mention his military activity and depict him as a military king. I have discussed his leadership as a מוֹשִׁיעַ. In addition I ought to deal with his military achievements within the summary of his rule (14:47-52) for some insight into his accomplishments.

Saul's military achievements (14:47f, 52) form an inclusio bracketing the list of his family members (14:49-51). The structure itself emphasises the portrayal of a military king. From a text-critical perspective 1 Samuel 14:47cd is questionable. The MT's יַרְשִׁיעַ portrays Saul in a negative light, whereas the effect of the LXX's reading (ἐσῴζετο) is, at first glance, quite the opposite. The attempt at a reconstruction of the Hebrew on the basis of the LXX results in a slightly different rendering from that of the MT: יִוָּשַׁע, a *niphal* stem of the verb ישׁע, meaning something like the NIV footnote translation: "he was victorious".

The need for textual emendation is supported by another account, that of David's military feats within the summary of his rule (2 Sam 8). V. 6, repeated verbatim in v. 14, states: "The LORD gave David victory, וַיֹּשַׁע, wherever he went." In this way the comparison between the military achievements of the first king and his successor becomes obvious. Both kings were victorious; the basic difference between the sentences is the subject. This is not to be overlooked. Meir Weiss has suggested that not mentioning the name of God may be a literary technique used to imply the absence or even the non-existence of God in the character's thinking (1963:474f).[91] Thus a passive verb can occasionally have heavy theological implications to indicate the absence of Yahweh hence becoming a *passivum divinum*.[92] Moreover most of the time in the FT the appraisal of persons and deeds is not obtained by a simple negative or positive statement but rather by artful hints and implications.

---

[90] This seems to be the fate of transition figures. Despite their unquestionable contribution to the political changes in Eastern Europe, Michail Gorbachev and Lech Walesa did not even get 1% in recent elections. And who remembers Károly Grósz (I am not even sure about the spelling), the Hungarian premier in 1987-88, or Lothar de Mazière (I had to ask my German friends for his name) of East Germany in 1990?

[91] Though he did not elaborate on it Weiss first suggested this in his article on Ps 46 in a reference to Ps 12 (1961:291f).

[92] I refer here to a seminar led by Weiss in Budapest in 1991. He claimed that the passive of Ps 1:6, תֹּאבֵד, reflected the mindset of the wicked.

Bearing these two aspects in mind a peculiar portrayal of Saul in 14:47 is offered. The peculiarity lies in the application of יֹשִׁיעַ.[93] I have claimed that Saul is consistently pictured as a pious Israelite; throughout his life he tries hard to appease God.[94] Is then 14:47 positive or negative towards Saul? It belongs to the narrator's equivocal presentation claiming that Saul was victorious, but by concealing the possible source of such victories (Yahweh; cf. 2 Sam 8) it sheds doubt on them. "First, a summary here and not at the end of his reign hints that his reign is already over. Second, there is no mention of the Lord or of God in 1 Sam. 14:47-52; Saul is on his own" (Miscall 1986:98). In a striking contrast to David, Saul was victorious without having God on his side and was conscious of it as seen in his activity from ch. 16 onwards.[95] Yahweh's absence from someone's life is a judgment in itself. Just as 2 Samuel 8:6 and 14 have proven to be the antidote to 1 Samuel 14:47 so the grammatical difference has turned out to bear on theological import. My reconstruction of 14:47 has given to Saul's portrayal a specious import while the next verse, the other side of the coin, is clearly positive (another antidote?) and boldly contrasts the effect of the next chapter. Jobling also claims that

> this passage shows an unexpected resilience in Saul. He is doing quite well for a rejected king. 1 Samuel 14:47-52 demonstrates Saul's ability, after all, to grasp kingship—at least in the absence of Samuel. These verses counteract the expectation that the rejection accounts create, that Saul's reign is virtually over, and prepare us for the long reign he has still ahead of him. (1998:88; cf. Abramski 1984-85:9f)

The second part of the inclusio, 14:52, suggests that Saul's army consisted of skilled warriors rather than conscripts. This is probably characteristic of emerging states, which, however, does not alter the image of Saul as a charismatic warrior. This image is supported by the narrative of the king's last hours. Though in terror (28:5), he does not flee from the battlefield (cf. 17:11) but chooses to die there (ch. 31). Saul "displays heroic greatness in his refusal to acquiesce in the fate prophesied by Samuel, taking extraordinary steps to hold on to his kingdom" (Exum 1992:41; cf. Simon 1988). In 2 Samuel 1 David commemorates him as a warrior king (cf. Preston 1982:37). That Saul was probably more successful than usually assumed can be deduced from the fact that after his death no-one wanted to abolish the monarchy (Cannon 1932:334).

His military leadership was probably the most significant facet of Saul's

---

[93] For Weiss's thesis I think this would be an exception confirming the rule.

[94] A qualification is necessary here. Saul is consistently portrayed as a pious Israelite as well as a paranoid (see e.g. 1 Sam 22). In the course of the narrative he is increasingly overpowered by his madness at the expense of his piety.

[95] In 17:11 and 33 Saul is dismayed and terrified, the very opposite to his charismatic self of 11:6; 13:8,12. Moreover Saul's answer in 17:37 may imply, "...as Yahweh is not with me."

activity. Keeping the Philistines, Israel's strongest enemies, at bay was Saul's most important achievement. As 14:47 and 52 state, during his lifetime the Philistines could not subdue Israel. Saul's rule secured Israel's independence to some extent, and as will be shown David was able to defeat the Philistines and establish a strong monarchy only because of his predecessor's military achievements. Indeed Hauer (1969) argues that Saul's success as a military king was facilitated by his strategy. He first secured Central Israel, then the South, but his attempt to conquer the North failed. Still, in the long run his strategy proved beneficial for the monarchy.

On the other hand by failing to establish institutions Saul apparently falls short of the expectations of a monarch. Like the judges before him, Saul did not ensure continuity and stability of government. This certainly contributed to the civil war-like situation and the superiority the Philistines regained after the king's death (2 Sam 2-5). Exum (1992:36) may be correct when claiming that "instead of resolving the crisis he exacerbates it."

To What Extent Was Saul Charismatic?

I have called Saul the reluctant king. His reluctance is alluded to right at the beginning of his story. Though he is described as a giant (9:2), he displays insecurity and a lack of leadership capacity from the very beginning. In 10:23 the giant reluctant to accept his commission is hailed with ovation. Only by Yahweh's spirit coming upon him is Saul transformed into a resolute and effective military leader (ch. 11).

Ch. 11 highlights how charismatic Saul was. I have claimed that here Saul emerges as a charismatic leader by taking decisive and independent action. In fact it is Saul who declares clemency to his opponents — a royal act of a king. At this point Samuel takes the initiative — he sidelines the king and makes a powerful comeback. Then the prophet reclaims his vanishing authority. Therefore Saul's charismatic leadership is limited to ch. 11. At the end of ch. 11 the king's authority starts dwindling and the prophet's is becoming stronger so that by the start of the military operation in ch. 13 the king dare not take action independently from the prophet. This configuration of royal vs. prophetic authority foreshadows the fate of Saul's charismatic leadership.

Due to Samuel's repressive manipulation Saul was reluctant to act as a charismatic leader leading and delivering Israel in ch. 13. He failed to capitalise on his commission. His major mistake was his dependence on Samuel the prophet. With and due to his first rejection Saul ceased acting resolutely and independently. In fact by acting as if haunted by the prophet and as a blunderer in ch. 14 he surrendered to his mentor's leadership which a charismatic should never do. Ch. 15 is only the last stage in this development. Saul wanted to prove himself by over-performance and inadvertently challenged Samuel's authority. When questioned by the prophet the king kept acknowledging and endorsing the status quo, i.e. the prophet's unquestionable authority. By doing so he sealed his own fate as Israel's king and as a charismatic leader.

Last but not least Saul was able throughout his life to mobilise the army. Whether this is a sign of being charismatic or rather some sort of routine is hard to decide. Keeping in line with my definition of charisma as a divine gift Saul (cf. Malamat 1976:157), in spite of his brave military leadership, should not be deemed charismatic after 16:14. Yet he must have appropriated the basics of effective military leadership. Thus after Yahweh's spirit had departed from him he remained able to lead Israel's army.

Everything considered an emerging charismatic leader such as Saul cannot prevail in the shadow of a mentor and outgoing charismatic like Samuel — particularly if the mentor is determined to thwart the actions of his protégé. The charismatic leader of the new order fails if he acts in submission to the leader of the old. Unlike a PhD student a charismatic leader cannot afford to have a mentor and be guided by someone else, therefore a submissive and sidelined leader, a charismatic under the guidance of someone else by definition is not charismatic. For that reason the mere notion of mentorship in this respect is a contradiction in terms as a charismatic is not subject to anyone's control.

I have claimed that Samuel contributed a great deal to the death of the king's charisma. Therefore it is telling that in ch. 31, deprived of Samuel's "assistance" (v. 4), Saul re-establishes his autonomy, takes the initiative and braces himself to face his fate.

Saul's failure generated a new crisis of leadership evident in chs. 16-17. In the next part of this study I shall turn to the new charismatic leader emerging in this crisis.

Chapter 3

Between Charismatic Military Leadership and Oriental Kingship

> It is the fate of charisma to recede before the powers of tradition or of rational association after it has entered the permanent structures of social action. This waning of charisma generally indicates the diminishing importance of individual action. (Weber 1968:1148f)

Spring has given way to summer. The transition from judgeship to kingship is irreversible, and as such needs be achieved more decisively and effectively than attempted by Saul. There is no way back; kingship must firmly be established. I shall show that this takes a charismatic, a resolute and autonomous leader. Saul failed to acquire charismatic authority. Will his successor succeed? Or will David's charisma too recede and wane?

Attaining Power — The Rise of the New Charismatic Leader

Setting the Stage — The Crisis of the Old and the Rise of the New

In the previous chapter I discussed Saul's charismatic leadership. I have also touched upon the issue of how his rejection affected the king in chs. 14-15[1]. The effects, however, are most obvious in chs. 16-17 and onwards. Ch. 16 presents Saul "endowed" by God's bad spirit (see Goldingay 2000:119). Subsequently ch. 17 portrays a situation where Saul is unable to face the Philistine menace. Thus Saul's rejection made him unable to carry out his mandate in 9:16. From ch. 16 Saul acts in reaction to his emerging rival, which also indicates that Saul is not a charismatic anymore as charismatics by definition do not react but act.

David Gooding (1986:64f) has observed an underlying pattern in the emergence of David. After Saul's rejection Israel needs a king, so Samuel anoints David (16:1-13). Secondly, the king needs musical relief and David is introduced into Saul's court (16:14-23). Thirdly, when Israel faces Goliath's challenge David establishes himself as a new charismatic champion (ch. 17)[2].

---

[1] Unattributed Bible references are to 1 Samuel.
[2] For reasons of convenience I apply Gooding's observation to the entire chapter, although he speaks only of 17:1-11.

Since these aspects with their implications play an essential role in David's emergence I shall follow Gooding's scheme.

IN NEED OF A NEW KING, 1 SAMUEL 16:1-13

Saul's rejection has created a bizarre situation. Israel has a king — without Yahweh's approval. God's people need a new king. Thus Samuel sets out to Bethlehem to secretly anoint the new king. The prophet musters Jesse's seven sons but none is chosen by Yahweh. Eventually David is fetched and anointed. Alter (1999:95) claims that, in contrast to Saul's election, the "present episode unfolds systematically through repeated dialogue between God and Samuel, and so God's judgments are rendered with perfect, authoritative transparency." It may follow that God was intent on keeping David independent from the prophet. Later on, when elected by all the tribes of Israel in 2 Samuel 5, David is anointed by the elders, with no prophet involved, but still "before the LORD" (2 Sam 5:3), which I take for a good sign of autonomy (*pace* Goldingay 2000:203).

In 16:12 his good looks are described with three terms, all related to visual perception. The second phrase contains "eyes" and the third is related to the verb "see". The first phrase, "ruddy", even though somewhat obscure, fits this list well. I take it as a reference to his beardless face, hence to his youth. In 17:42ff this appearance of David proves deceptive disguising a shrewd tactician.[3] In this light 16:7 might well be God's caution that David's appearance cloaks his strategic cunning, a prerequisite of a charismatic leader as I shall argue. Eslinger (1988) contends that God chooses David in spite of his own statement in 16:7. Eslinger expects the narrator to make clear the reference point of 16:7 straight away. The narrator does so, in my view, only in v. 18, a qualification of v. 7 as to what might be in David's heart. In other words, Eslinger correctly points out the "need" of the change of Saul's heart, but fails to realise, or draws inaccurate conclusions, why there was no need to transform David.

If my interpretation is correct, the obscure reference in 16:7 sheds light on what a charismatic leader should look like, or rather what his/her physical appearance will not reveal. Physical appearance is deceptive because it does not disclose whether the person is up to the leadership task. By considering

---

[3] McCarter has observed that Saul's tall stature is deceptive (1980:185f) — just like David's. The difference not to be missed is that Saul's impressive appearance did not lead to success; indeed it occasioned failure. As opposed to him David's ruddiness "with a fine appearance and handsome features" (16:12) will bring about victory and deliverance. Another interesting contrast between Saul and David is worth observing. Although the narrative is rather reticent, the reader has the impression that Saul was the only child of his parents; in spite of his stature he is shy and irresolute. David is the smallest of eight sons — still no inferiority complex can be seen in his actions and speeches; indeed his very first words and deed divulge his destiny (cf. particularly 1 Sam 9:1ff and 17:12ff).

appearances Samuel exposes a rather general human attitude of orienting oneself according to the visible. What one needs to become an effective charismatic leader is, however, inner qualities, invisible to the eyes. That is what God looks for in the heart, what tall Saul lacked and David had.

After the prophet has carried out his task he departs for his home town (16:13). That Samuel did not remain with David may stress that the prophet did not mentor the newly anointed king — in contrast to Samuel's relationship with his former protégé. This might already be alluded to in the anointing. Whereas at Saul's anointing Samuel used a flask here he has a horn, which connotes power and authority (Edelman 1991:51).[4] Thus David was anointed with power and to independence, which were totally absent in Saul's anointing and early rule. "When YHWH's Spirit came upon David, his anointer left since he was no longer needed" (Howard 1989:476). Moreover "Samuel never speaks to David" (Miscall 1986:128), which I take as a narrative device pointing to a different prophet-anointed relationship (cf. how much Samuel instructed Saul). That David retained autonomy is suggested throughout the narrative. He is independent even when in the service of Achish (Miscall 1986:164-67). Now Israel has an acting as well as a prospective king.

IN NEED OF A COMFORTER, 1 SAMUEL 16:14-23

Saul's rejection becomes manifest in Yahweh's spirit departing from him and a bad spirit tormenting him (16:14). This develops into an acute depression needing remedy. At the same time David is permanently endowed by Yahweh's spirit (v. 13). Howard (1989:481) has noticed the chiasm in vv. 13f:

A. Yahweh's spirit comes upon David;
   B. Samuel leaves David;
      B' Yahweh's spirit leaves Saul;
A' A bad spirit comes upon Saul.[5]

There is another inclusio in vv. 13f — Yahweh's good spirit comes upon David; Yahweh's good spirit leaves Saul; Yahweh's bad spirit comes upon Saul. Howard sees here a motif of the transfer of (spiritual-political) power from Saul to David. "It can fairly be said that the three movements were part of one larger event and that the coming and going of these spirits are symbolic of the larger issue of the transfer of the kingship" (480f).

At the king's request for a comforter David is introduced into the royal

---

[4] "Samuel took, לקח, the horn of oil and anointed him" (16:13). Bearing in mind the negative connotations of לקח the reader is alerted. It is all the more conspicuous that the follow-up is very different from the Samuel-Saul relationship.

[5] I disagree with Howard in my estimate of Samuel and his influence. In my view David's loss of Samuel is definitely positive.

court. One of Saul's servants portrays David (v. 18) as
- יֹדֵעַ נַגֵּן: a musician;
- גִּבּוֹר חַיִל וְאִישׁ מִלְחָמָה: a man of war — David's epithet;
- נְבוֹן דָּבָר: an effective speaker (Rose 1974:63-65). This is a most significant characteristic of David, who "knows well the public and political impact of speech and therefore chooses his words carefully, wisely, for maximum public and political benefit. His speeches are wise, accurate, and beneficial, but for himself and not necessarily for others or for the nation" (Miscall 1983:68). Dietrich (1996:175) remarks that in the discussions with Eliab, Saul and Goliath David moves to a new, higher level by referring to Yahweh and so proves to be the winner.[6] Because this trait of David is exhibited positively in ch. 17 and in the following narrative, it can be considered a virtue (see Wenham 2000:89). Indeed the effective use of speech is essential for the success of a strategist as David was;
- אִישׁ תֹּאַר: smart and good looking;
- יְהוָה עִמּוֹ: the hallmark of a charismatic military leader in the DH.

A few more features in ch. 16 are worth mentioning. First the use of שׁלח. Samuel sends for David (vv. 11f) to anoint him — and to take possession of him (לקח, v. 11) as he did to Saul in 9:22. Notice that between these two references Yahweh's spirit is bestowed on David. In line with my interpretation above it implies that David is endowed with independence. This is so even if 18:2 claims that Saul took him, וַיִּקָּחֵהוּ, and would not allow him to go back to his father's house, as if to keep an eye on him. Saul is now in the shoes of Samuel, intent on taking, guiding and mentoring the young charismatic. His efforts, however, will be unsuccessful.

In 16:19 Saul sends for him. At both "interviews" David is portrayed as passive, the one sent for. In the subsequent narrative, however, David will turn out to be very active, taking his destiny into his hands and resisting attempts at controlling or dispatching him. The verb שׁלח introduces David's transfer from his father's house to the royal court. With the verb's recurrence in v. 22 the transfer is drawing to its conclusion and by 18:2 is completed.

This motif is reinforced and further developed by the verb בוא. In v. 12 David is said to have been brought, וַיְבִיאֵהוּ, before Samuel. Similarly Saul wants a musician to be brought to him (v. 17). Interestingly enough, however, David enters, וַיָּבֹא, Saul's court (v. 21). Put it differently whereas David is made to come on the first occasion, he "refuses" to do so on the second. He

---

[6] Concerning speech as a powerful means of influence I wonder whether being an effective speaker is not a *conditio sine qua non* of charismatic leadership (see Moses' excuse and Yahweh's response in Ex 4:10-16).

"voluntarily" enters the king's service.[7] As ch. 9 set the stage for Saul and the prophet-king relationship so does ch. 16 for David and his relationship with the prophet and the king. From the very beginning David cannot be restrained — a basic characteristic of a charismatic.[8]

The unsuspecting king mentions him as he was first introduced to the prophet, אֲשֶׁר בַּצֹּאן, v. 19, ironically unaware of David's previous anointing. When the prospective king arrives at the court he honours the acting king with presents — similar to the presents Saul received just after his anointing (10:4).

The irony of David's introduction into the royal court is obvious. The king, unaware of God's behind-the-scenes operation, prepares his own demise by taking his successor to himself, a motif richly exploited in the story.

IN NEED OF A NEW MILITARY LEADER, 1 SAMUEL 17

After ch. 14 we do not read of a Philistine defeat by Saul. In ch. 14 the deliverer was Jonathan, the victory, however, was hampered by the handicapped king.[9] Due to Saul's failure to deliver the nation from the Philistines Israel finds itself in a predicament in ch. 17. The Philistine army attacks them and Saul cannot control the situation (see George 1999:399-401). Goliath's appearance and challenge only increases Israel's trouble. In his powerless fear Saul is a shadow of his former self (ch. 11). Israel's impotence is best captured in v. 11: "Saul and all the Israelites were dismayed and terrified."

The next scene shifts the spotlight back to Bethlehem. Between chs. 16 and 17 David probably divided his time between the king and his father (17:15). The following events will put an end to his dividedness for good. David is reintroduced as "the son of the Ephrathite named Jesse" (v. 12). Nowhere else is he referred to like this. This reference, however, recalls the emergence of the first charismatic leader in the book, Samuel, whose father was referred to in this way (1:1). By comparing David's to Samuel's and not to Saul's emergence (cf. 9:1f) the question is raised: What will this new leader be like? Will he be as Samuel was?

David is "the little one" (17:14, AT; 16:11; cf. 9:21 and 15:17 on Saul), the first characteristic of David (Fokkelman 1986:131), entrusted with some minor

---

[7] Only to be freed from serving the king, at least according to the king's pledge in 17:25. Even if the pledge was not kept, due to his persecution David (and his family, cf. 22:3f) obtained some independence. It is also noteworthy that on entering the king's service David presents bread (16:20), while by taking bread from Nob (21:3-6; ET 21:2-5) "David considers his employment terminated" (Fokkelman 1986:356).

[8] One of the implications of David's characteristics may be that Yahweh's choice of a charismatic leader is not haphazard but rather reasonable. Cf. Gideon's implicit portrayal in Ju 6:11-24.

[9] Just as he will nearly hamper David's defeat of Goliath by giving him his armour, vv. 38f (cf. Fokkelman 1986:167). That the Philistine defeat in ch. 17 is not ascribed to Saul is a clear sign that he is not a charismatic leader any more.

family business (16:11; 17:15, 17f; cf. Dietrich 1996:174) as opposed to Eliab, "his big brother" (17:28, AT), in the nation's service on the battlefield (17:19). David, however, will not let himself be mastered by his big brother and diverted from his goal (v. 35). He is determined to retain his independence even at the cost of a confrontation with Eliab (see Rosenberg 1986:178). Moreover, his lack of modesty, indeed his exhibition of resolution and courage before the people, the king and the enemy (17:26, 32-37, 45-47) makes him appear as one with high ambition. To be sure he could achieve nothing without ambitious resolution. Behold, a new charismatic leader is emerging! By these motifs a new story about the rise of the lowly and the fall of the mighty[10] has formally been announced.

Having been "commissioned" by his father (vv. 17f) David leaves, נטשׁ, "the flock with a shepherd" (v. 20) and sets out to the Israelite camp. He arrives just as the army is taking battle positions (vv. 20f). Again he leaves, נטשׁ, his things with a keeper and runs "to the battle lines" (v. 22). נטשׁ can emphasise David's concern for property but the verb can also mean "abandon" (Miscall 1983:59). What is his motive to leave/abandon his things? The second phrase, וַיָּרָץ הַמַּעֲרָכָה, is ambiguous as well. It recurs at a decisive point of the story with David in action, 17:48. What makes him run to the battle lines? Altruistic patriotism, courage and religious zeal, or mere curiosity on the first occasion and fear on the second (cf. Miscall 1983:70)? I shall come back to this soon. What suffices for now is that by abandoning his family business David abandons his previous life for a military career. "In a broader sense, of course, it is the whole structure of primogeniture and patriarchal obligation that David sheds" (Rosenberg 1986:177)[11]. From now on his charismatic career will be characterised by military bravery.

Another of his basic attributes is revealed in the duel with Goliath. In 17:43 Goliath curses David by his gods because he apparently sees only the stick in David's hand but not the sling (see Gooding 1986:68). In his response David picks up the themes of weapon and god[12] (v. 45). He claims that it is not arms that ensure victory but Yahweh. At first glance this seems to be a pious theological statement which as such will prove correct. His rhetoric may be a stratagem, however. By focusing on "sword and spear and javelin" (v. 45) as well as Yahweh's power to save (v. 47) David might aim to conceal his weapon, the sling, that will before long prove a fatal one. The question of which view is valid is irrelevant. David succeeded through his shrewd ruse *and* because he trusted in Yahweh.

Miscall has introduced an alternative interpretation to the general view that Goliath was a frightening and invincible warrior: a "sitting duck" (1983:61).

---

[10] The latter had begun with Saul's rejection.
[11] "… as well as obsolete and inefficient weaponry", Rosenberg concludes (177). However, I cannot see why he extends the relevance of נטשׁ to 17:38f.
[12] Or "God" if referring to Yahweh.

Dietrich (1996:185) even considers him a symbol for being over-armed. This aspect is highlighted by Goliath's and David's respective movements. Whereas Goliath is said to move "closer to attack him" (see also v. 41), David runs "quickly towards the battle line to meet him" (v. 48; cf. Fokkelman 1986:185). The Hebrew emphasises the contrast between the two characters by having Goliath move sluggishly while David moves with agility. Thus David's putting off Saul's heavy armour and option for his shepherd kit might be a deliberate tactic. He realises that in his agility he can outflank the Philistine who, though heavily armoured, is vulnerable from a long distance. David abandons conventional warfare and embarks upon an operation of deception. I shall show that deception will characterise his career contributing a great deal to his charismatic achievements.

That opaqueness, along with deception, belongs to David's "character zone" is suggested at several points. I shall pick only two. Firstly when Goliath "saw that he was only a boy, ruddy and handsome, [...] he despised him" (17:42). But David's boyish appearance, a back-reference to 16:12, conceals a master of deception and strategy, Goliath's hasty perception will prove fatal. Secondly the enigmatic inquiry of David's identity in 17:55-58 dramatically underlines David's elusive character. Even after David has for some time been in Saul's service, the king and his most senior officer divulge their ignorance about David. They are at a loss for not having the information needed, hence are to rely on the young lad's self-identification.[13] David declares independence and freedom both from the king's and his father's houses (Rosenberg 1986:179-81). The uncertainty about David's motives will continue to disturb the reader until the end of the narrative.

Edelman proposes (1991:124f) that ch. 17 functions as a demonstration scene, in which David is tested to prove his suitability for the throne. The similarity in purpose to ch. 11 is unmistakable. In ch. 11 hearing the news of Jabesh Gilead all Israel cries in despair. As opposed to them, Saul empowered by God's spirit gets angry and acts, thus resolving the crisis and establishing himself as a charismatic military deliverer. In ch. 17 Israel faces a new crisis. Again Israel's despair and impotence are described in vivid terms. When hearing the Philistine's challenge, David, who was given Yahweh's spirit at his anointing (16:13), gets angry as 17:26 implies, which makes him act in contrast to his terrified and paralysed countrymen.

In this respect the study by Auld-Ho (1992) merits our attention. They compare eleven correspondences between Saul's and David's emergences. Although their main interest lies in genetic questions of the MT and LXX texts, which is not my focus, their observations bear on my topic. Even though they do not draw the conclusion, their study elucidates that from the very beginning Saul is doomed to failure while David's success is anticipated. This becomes increasingly obvious as the narrative progresses and David's emergence can be

---

[13] Though dealing with Abner, Exum (1992:98f) has inspired my interpretation.

compared to Saul's.

I conclude that just as chs. 9-10 were essential to Saul's portrayal and emergence so are chs. 16-17 to David's (see also Rudman 2000). By 18:5-7 and 13-16 David is clearly established as the new charismatic military leader replacing Saul. David's competence along with Saul's incompetence is confirmed by Israel's elders in 2 Samuel 5:2 (Campbell 1986:38).

Who Is David?[14]

Commenting on 17:26 Berges (1989:234; AT) makes an observation which has by now achieved general recognition: "As soon as with his first words David offers a realisation of his character. On the one hand he forces his career towards every risk; on the other hand he is consciously dedicated to Yahweh's cause." Many scholars have shown this discrepancy in David's character. Who is David: a careerist or a pious Yahwist? I shall argue that the question cannot be answered with certainty and this is a characteristic of a charismatic leader.

THE MILITARY DELIVERER

David's characterisation is introduced in a similar way to that of Saul (see my remarks on 9:1f). He is described as a גִּבּוֹר חַיִל[15] (16:18) which, again, recalls 14:52 and reintroduces the question: Will this young lad be taken, this time, by the king? And indeed we learn that the king takes him to himself (18:2), not for good though. That is to say that while Samuel took and manipulated his protégé, Saul will not be able to do so because David will declare his independence by leaving the royal court.[16]

As observed above, in ch. 17 David emerged similarly to Saul in ch. 11. Both chapters describe national crises as well as the people's impotence and utter despair. Both characters respond to the crisis in an unexpected way. Hearing of Jabesh Gilead's plight Saul bravely summons and unites all Israel and takes Ammon by surprise, thus averting the crisis. Similarly David confidently faces the giant's challenge and defeats him by a ruse.

Rosenberg (1986:179-81) has noticed that in addition to defeating Goliath David establishes himself as a free man. David's speech in 17:45-47

---

[14] I am hinting at headings in Borgman's essay (1980), which alludes to Nabal's question in 1 Sam 25:10.

[15] My supervisor Carl Armerding drew my attention to the fact that the term, whether denoting physical strength or material wealth or both, is often used in reference to military deliverers like Gideon (Ju 6:12), Jephthah (Ju 11:1), Saul's father (1 Sam 9:1) and Jeroboam (1 Kgs 11:28).

[16] Noteworthy is Polzin's comment on 20:29ff (1989:189) that Saul's anger is kindled by the alleged violation of his "prohibition of David to return to his father's house (18:2)."

depicts wholly the Israel that Israel would like itself to be, and it takes Israel out of the domain of ineffectual politics and imperfect self-defense into the transcendent realm of Exodus typology and the freedom of slaves redeemed, a freedom they apparently taste sufficiently to rally courageously in battle and pursuit against the Philistines after David's miraculous strike… (180)

By killing Goliath and so paving the way for Israel's defeat of the Philistines, David has established himself as a charismatic champion. This anticipates his military career. His military leadership is increasingly acknowledged by Jonathan, the nation, and Saul's officers (see Gooding 1986:71f; Brueggemann 1993:232). Even Saul's jealousy indirectly confirms David's military prowess, so that Alter (1999:119) rightly notes, on 19:10, that הכה and נס "are the very two verbs used in verse 8 to report David's military triumph over the Philistines: as David battles Israel's enemies, the distraught king battles David." Furthermore יצא in 18:13 and 16 implies that David does what Israel expects its king to do (see 8:20) and what Saul has failed to (Berges 1989:247). They "had wanted a king with military capacity (1 Sam 8:20). Their man is surely David!" (Brueggemann 1993:240). Indeed for the better part of his life David is a military deliverer and a strategist of first rank. For this reason he is several times referred to as one fighting the battles of Yahweh (17:45; 18:17; 25:28; 30:26). By wanting to have David killed on the battlefield Saul only achieves two things: he, the military king, is absent from the battlefield and at the same time "promotes" charismatic David and makes him successful. With Yahweh on his side David is portrayed as *the* military deliverer.

Fokkelman (1989:32) has noticed that the arrangement of the last four chapters in 1 Samuel (28-31) makes Saul's death and David's victory adjacent, by having Saul's defeat and David's triumph over the Amalekites in a desperate situation happen on the same day. This arrangement explicitly contrasts Saul's military incompetence and its disastrous consequence with David's prowess. This is not the only occasion when this is the case. Saul is unable to deliver his people, whereas David is portrayed as one fulfilling this expectation. Thus he leads the nation in its wars and delivers, ישע (23:2, 5; cf. Hertzberg 1964:190), Israel from oppressors and plunderers (17:50f; 18:30; 23:1-5; 27:8f; 30:17-20). In a word, David is doing what the king is supposed to but fails to accomplish. One wonders whether the Philistines' words in 21:12 (ET 21:11), "Isn't this David, the king of the land?", are to be understood as the narrator's view.

THE STRATEGIST

David's Relationships

I have argued that David's transfer from Jesse's to Saul's house is a metaphor of shifting commitment and loyalty. Interpreters (Jobling 1986a, 1998:303; Rosenberg 1997:130f; Lawton 1993:41) have noticed this. Saul becomes

David's surrogate father at the expense of Jesse who is eliminated[17] from the story. As mentioned above 17:26 is the narrator's first statement about the "inconsistency" intrinsic to David. I shall nonetheless draw attention to another, previous motif.

Thompson has contended (1974) that the verb אהב in 1 Samuel implies political loyalty, so that "we may suspect that already in 1 Samuel xvi 21 the narrator is preparing us for the later political use of the term" (335). Although the general opinion is that the subject of the verb in 16:21 is Saul, this is highly questionable. The three other verbs have David as their subject, and Wong (1997) has convincingly argued that אהב is no exception. Thompson's and Wong's arguments, pertaining to the same verse, have implications that no-one seems to have recognised so far. I suggest that since אהב is to be understood in its political rather than emotional sense and most probably the subject is David, this is the first instance in David's portrayal of his commitment to Saul's house as opposed to his father's. No wonder then that the very next sentence informs us about Saul's response to David's loyalty. The king merely concludes the movement by transferring David to his house.[18]

Although I have used different terminology it is nonetheless true that Saul was also transferred from his father's house to Samuel who became his surrogate father.[19] Is there any difference between Saul's relationship with his surrogate father and David's to his? David's relationships with other characters of the narrative are of paramount importance. In order to understand David's motivation I shall first analyse his relationships.

I have shown that Saul's relationship with Samuel amounted to subordination. This is what the prophet required and what the king did. In this respect David was different. As I suggested above he established his independence from Samuel, who anointed him early on, and maintained this independence consistently. David's relationship with the king is more complex. It is true that Saul takes David to himself but no attempt to take hold of him succeeds. Even though David is his subordinate he cannot be controlled or manipulated. In fact, as I shall demonstrate, Saul's attempts often backfire in that David takes advantage of the situations (cf. Brueggemann 1993:236). "Saul's every effort against David yields a consequence he does not intend, anticipate, or desire. Throughout the narrative, David is the one for whom 'all

---

[17] This is a returning motif in the narrative. Saul inquires about David's father in 17:55-58 (see Gooding 1986:60). In 22:3f David ensures his parents' safety, or, alternatively, gets rid of them to strive for his own objectives without their interference.

[18] Notice that in addition to the verb אהב the other phrases of v. 21 also connote political loyalty. As my supervisor Carl Armerding has noticed, throughout the Bible the verb operates on several levels of meaning (religious, political, social).

[19] Gooding (1986:63) has noticed the transfer motif in the cases of Samuel and David. It is not quite clear whether the reason that he did not apply it to Saul was that he was not dealing with him or that he saw it as inappropriate.

things work together for good.' For Saul, conversely, nothing works 'for good'" (Brueggemann 1993:231; see also Weisman 1998:50-54). The king, becoming envious of his young rival, attempts to eliminate him — to no avail. David's promotion and success are — apart from God's assistance — to a great extent due to Saul's envy and obstructions. David's career depends on Saul and the king's attitude to his rival, just as the king's decline is partly caused by David's success.

With their relationship deteriorating, however, David becomes increasingly detached from the king so that he is finally forced to flee. This is a basic difference from the Samuel-Saul relationship which was characterised by increasing dependence and attachment on Saul's part in direct proportion to his deteriorating relationship with his mentor. In contrast to Saul, David "knows how to veil his motives and intentions" (Alter 1999:115) — a characteristic helping him reach his ends. Interestingly David's flight does not put an end to his career as a charismatic leader. Even on the run he remains one and is recognised as a leader by people (cf. 25:28-30; 2 Sam 5:2). Indeed his fugitive status is a major factor enhancing his charisma.

Prouser (1996) has studied the function of clothes in the narrative. Regarding David's cutting off the corner of Saul's robe in 24:5 (ET 24:4) she observes:

> Although David claims that this act is a sign that he has no designs to kill Saul and is thus being pursued for naught, the symbolic meaning of cutting the hem of a cloak is unmistakable. Even Saul took this as a sign from God that his kingdom was being given over to David. (29)

As opposed to previous instances here

> David is not simply the recipient of clothing, but he actively takes it himself. In addition, Saul is not even aware of the fact that the hem of his garment has been ripped. Thus, David is successful at taking by stealth. When he makes the deed public, he does so to his own benefit. (33)

Prouser's observations are invaluable, except that she too suspects self-interest in David's declaration. David's act is not necessarily selfish. It can be considered a deliberate but ethically correct step of making public both his innocence and his claim for the throne (see Gordon 1980:54-57). And who would blame him for hoping to benefit from his declaration by making Saul stop pursuing him? 1 Samuel 24-26 emphasises that David did not intend to eliminate Saul and his house (Edenburg 1998:78-80; Borgman 1980).

That David did not plot to kill Saul when he could is also suggested by Marcus (1986:168f, n. 14). He claims that David, addressing Achish as "my lord the king", so far used by David only when addressing Saul, in 1 Samuel 29:8, actually has Saul in mind. "Thus it is reasonable to assume that David, if permitted to join the battle, would have fought against the Philistines, 'the enemies of my lord the king,' i.e. the enemies of Saul, and not with them, against Saul" (169, n. 14). This is supported by the fact that instead of Israelite villages he raided non-Israelite settlements, whether for ethical or political reasons, or perhaps both.

On the other hand David is not dependent on Saul. David often deceives the king, the weak tricks the powerful (see Hagan 1979:324f; Marcus 1986:164). Even when on the run David controls the situation. Even though David can be blamed for the tragedy at Nob (chs. 21-22; see Roberts 1999), he exits the crisis with Goliath's sword, food and Yahweh's guidance slyly secured. The king is never able to catch David who is portrayed positively, as the narrative is rather sympathetic to the weak and critical of the powerful.

It has been observed (Jobling 1986a:12; Brueggemann 1993:233) that Jonathan gave David legitimacy by offering him his royal garment and armour (18:4). This was a symbolic renunciation of the throne. It has also been noticed that in ch. 20 "David comes to Jonathan with no specific plans in mind, but to see how he might 'use' Jonathan and his friendship and covenant with him to further his own designs on the kingship. […] David senses that Jonathan can be an effective, although unwitting, spy for him" (Miscall 1983:113; cf. Kapelrud 1955:200).[20]

Moreover the narrative states that while Jonathan (18:1; 20:17)[21] and Michal (18:20) loved David, it is never stated that David loved them in return. Indeed David used both of them to escape death (chs. 19-20). Was his relationship with them motivated by friendship and love or political expediency? Or both? It is difficult to find an unequivocal answer, as the narrative is reticent. Still to claim that David is portrayed as a cunning and calculating man, using his personal relationships for his own benefit to achieve his political objective, is probably not an overstatement (cf. Miscall 1983:83). For the success of charismatics love demonstrated towards them is more essential than love demonstrated by them (cf. Weber 1968:242).[22] Later in 2 Samuel 3:13f David remarries Michal — again, as in the first instance, for political expediency (see Bowman 1991:103-6; Clines 1991).

Obviously David was very resourceful. In order to get his way he resorted to all possible means like symbolic acts, ambiguous rhetoric, using friends for his own ends and deception of allies and sovereigns. In all this David demonstrated that he was a shrewd tactician and strategist.

---

[20] Jonathan was most probably aware of his friend's opportunism and recognised his "unspecific plans", since in 20:14-17, 23, 42 Jonathan repeatedly wants David's loyalty to himself and his house confirmed (cf. Saul's similar utterance in 24:21; ET 24:20).
[21] Again the political aspect of Jonathan's love should be recognised.
[22] If that is true it is striking, maybe for that very reason, that Jesus' love in the ST is frequently and emphatically underlined.

David's Actions

Evaluating David's prowess in ch. 17 Keil (1971:183) claims, "Whilst Goliath boasted of his strength, David founded his own assurance of victory upon the Almighty God of Israel, whom the Philistine had defied." Similarly Klein considers the story "a classic example of what can be accomplished through the person of faith." He quotes Sirach 47:4f to drive home that "repeatedly in vv 37-47 David made clear that Yahweh alone was the real source of victory" (1983:182f). These scholars aptly represent the conventional, sometimes idealising, approach to David. On various occasions the narrator does portray him in a favourable light. This, however, is not the only possible way of viewing David.

Scholars of a liberal/postmodern background and conviction on the other hand are naturally suspicious of him as one in power. The more power and success one has, the more suspect he is. This stance may help one discover motives but it often results in tendentious rewriting of biblical narratives and a prejudice depriving one of critical and balanced evaluation. This suspicion and subsequent bias can be sensed in the studies by Lemche (1978), VanderKam (1980), Cryer (1985), Cargill (1986), Ishida (1993) and Malul (1996).

To clearly ascertain David's motives has been a major endeavour of scholars. Since some view David as the pious and Yahwist king *par excellence* while others deem him a "tough practitioner of *Realpolitik*" (Lemche 1978:18) this attempt has had a divisive effect. Because my purpose is to establish what the text says about David and his motives I shall be attentive to the narrative's portrayal as well as sensitive when reading studies on it. I shall try to show how David's motives, hence actions, at his emergence can be seen differently from conventionally understood, without falling into the trap of making him the scapegoat for each mishap.

Commenting on David's qualities Miscall (1983:54-57) considers 16:18 an ambiguous portrayal foreshadowing David's troubles. In his view נְבוֹן דָּבָר can

> be taken in an ironic sense, i.e., David knows well the public and political impact of speech and therefore chooses his words carefully, wisely, for maximum public benefit. His speeches are wise, accurate, and beneficial, but for himself and not necessarily for others or for the nation. (68)

In this fashion Fokkelman claims that 17:25-40 is the realisation of David being a man of נְבוֹן דָּבָר (1986:166), which point has nicely been accentuated by Ceresko's rhetorical analysis of David's boast in 17:34-37 (1985), showing the ambitious youth to be a commanding orator whose skill with words is "essential to a successful leader" (69).

Similarly, commenting on the contradiction of 17:50 and 51, Miscall (1983:78) wonders whether David's use of the sword is "just the first sign that David is a man of violence, a man of the sword. Or is it a test and mark of something else?" Certainly the subsequent narrative depicts David as a "man of the sword". Miscall even speaks of David as a man between חֶסֶד and חֶרֶב (1986:121). Here caution is recommended, however, as without the sword, even if he occasionally misused it, he could have achieved nothing. In general terms the "sword" as a metaphor of radical and successful action accompanies all charismatics of the David kind. Flanagan has grasped the clue to the charismatic's success (1983a:38): "Personal charm, agility with the sword, a keen sense of timing, patience in defeat, and magnanimity in victory were among the talents the successful tribal leader had to have in order to win and hold the coalitions that would assure his survival."

Miscall has also noticed that 1 Kings 2:9, David's last reported words, portray him as a man of blood (1983:91). Thus David's career runs between the implications of his first and last self-portrayal: between sincerity, innocence and ambition on the one hand and vengeance and murder on the other (see Gunn 1975). Furthermore 17:30 pictures David showing Eliab his back and focusing on his own interest (Fokkelman 1986:165).

Now are David's motives altruistic and pious or is he an opportunist? How is he to be viewed? Since both views of David are present in the narrative it is curious that the narrator does not take sides. "The text does not resolve the problem" (Miscall 1983:84), it is throughout "ambiguous and equivocal" (85). This ambiguity is achieved by frequent direct speech on David's part, instead of reported speech, which leads the reader "to ponder the different possible connections between his spoken words and his actual feelings or intentions" (Alter 1981:67). The ambiguity of motives is fundamental to David's character, and the narrator consciously applied and consistently exploited this. My reading, with Miscall's, remains undecided. I

> will not resolve it by convicting David of sin, of cunning, and effective scheming to attain the throne. This goes beyond the specific evidence that the text provides for the characterization of David. The narrative raises the questions of David's motivations and intentions, both immediate and future, but leaves them indeterminate. David is a cunning and unscrupulous schemer, and he is also an innocent "man of destiny" for whom all goes right. The text supports a spectrum of portrayals of David and thereby does not support any one definitive or probable portrayal.[23] (Miscall 1983:83)

This is not to say that David is so elusive that any attempt at drawing a moral from the narrative is futile, as Payne (1984:62) (mis)interpreting Miscall concludes. The "moral" of the narrative is that a charismatic leader as David was has an ambiguous character with obscure motives. David is an ambitious hero assisted by God — but assisted only so far as he remains within the covenant boundary. Unpredictability and opaque motives contributed to

---

[23] In a general observation Sternberg mentions "the characteristic mixture of David's motives" (1985:343). Cf. Polzin's extensive discussion of David's complex character (1989:266-68, n. 3) and Fokkelman's justification of David's morality (1986:568f).

David's independence and success. Unpredictability and unclear motives up to the point of causing misunderstanding and confusion occasionally characterise an emerging charismatic leader.[24] I wonder whether we would have the David story had he disclosed his motives and objectives right at the beginning.

Moreover is it necessary or possible in a charismatic's case to distinguish sharply between public and private benefits? Charismatic leaders think of themselves as forerunners of an emerging new order. As such they require total commitment, while at the same time subordinating themselves to their ideal of the new order which they firmly and persistently pursue (cf. Weber 1968:1112f). Their action is both for personal and public benefit, which are therefore hardly distinguishable. Determined charismatic leaders are, wittingly or unwittingly, intent on establishing themselves by every possible means. They recognise no constraint.[25]

Stating this I have touched on the core issue. In addition to talking of ambiguous motives it has become fashionable to speak of David as an opportunist. The word "opportunist" has negative overtones and has been used in a rather derogatory way in relation to David who was not particular about means to grasp power.[26] Because of the negative implications I shall avoid the word "opportunist" and propose "strategist" as a more neutral term, depicting people who, wittingly or unwittingly, seize the opportunity to prove and establish themselves as charismatic leaders — without necessarily resorting to

---

[24] Fokkelman's comment on 17:56 is insightful. He claims that the rare word עֶלֶם is cognate to the verb of the same radicals, "to conceal", and concludes that "the identity of the boy *conceals ('lm)* his destiny" (1986:192, n. 75). There is an interesting parallel to this in the Saul story. In the enigmatic scene about Saul's uncle (10:16) Saul conceals his anointing before his דּוֹד, or, punctuated differently, דָּוִד. Similarly David does not tell Saul of his anointing; Saul can only guess it which makes him even more frustrated and angry (Samuel also conceals David's kingship from Saul). Note that both "concealments" take place just after the designation and before the confirmation of the protagonist. Concealment is the very attitude characterising the relationship between Saul and charismatic David, the declining old and the emerging new.

[25] I am referring to Miscall's observation (1986:132). Commenting on David's taking the sacred bread and Goliath's sword from behind the ephod in ch. 21, he ponders whether this is a hint at David's recognising "neither secular nor sacred constraints". Cf. Jesus' similar actions in Mt 17:24-27; Mk 2:23-28; 3:1-6.

[26] There have been speculations about his involvement in Saul's (Malul 1996), Abner's (Cryer 1985) and Ish-Bosheth's (VanderKam 1980) deaths. These studies about David's possible motivation and means are not conclusive, as narrative evidence is admittedly scarce. In short, in these presentations David is suspect whatever he says or does. Unfortunately scholars fail to differentiate between narrator and characters, and pretend to know the events better than the narrator. Wesselius (1990) does not doubt David's innocence but contends that the specific stress is "a device to draw our attention to the political aspects of these crimes and the advantage gained from them by David" (340). For a sophisticated literary approach to David's responsibility for Saul's death and its implications see Polzin 1989:221-23.

illicit means. David Gunn (1975) has brilliantly elaborated on these two aspects by studying the theme of giving and grasping. Though using different terminology, he has observed that David, like Joab and Abner, is involved in power politics.

> Nevertheless, it remains the case that his restraint in the matter of gaining the kingdom is remarkable. It is something which cannot easily be assimilated to a doctrine of political expediency. *David is prepared to risk allowing the kingdom to be the gift of others.* It is this that singles him out qualitatively from the others. (18; my italics)

Having said this I am not claiming that David never used illicit means, but rather that charismatic leaders are marked by consistent strategies. Charismatic deliverers, if they are to prevail, are to be strategists — taking advantage of every opportunity.[27]

Closely related to this aspect is another, that of determination. Josipovici examines a number of passages in 1 Samuel where David acts resolutely while previously charismatic Saul does not, and sums up his observations: "All we can say is that David is good at taking decisions — and will go on being good at it to the end of his life[28] — while Saul is not" (1988:201). Determination is definitely a non-negotiable characteristic of charismatic leaders without which they never succeed.[29]

This also explains partly why Jonathan, who was introduced as a potential charismatic leader in chs. 13-14, was not after all the man after Yahweh's heart (cf. 13:14). In the subsequent narrative Jonathan is consistently portrayed as naive, admiring emerging and successful David (see Polzin 1989:187-90). His naivety makes him the very opposite of David. Instead of seeing a rival in him, Jonathan assists David in his pursuit to the throne. Jonathan does not act as strategists do, taking advantage of every opportunity. He remains David's foil, on whom David can rely.

David did not hesitate to use every possible means to attain his political objectives. By saying this I am claiming that this characteristic is not optional but a hallmark of a charismatic, as David was.

The Confirmation of the New Charismatic

Ch. 18 reports that due to his military exploits David enjoyed increasing

---

[27] Charismatic judges like Ehud, Gideon and Samson are depicted as leaders who take advantage of the enemy's weakness. By delivering Jabesh Gilead in the way he did Saul also proved to be a strategist, who took the opportunity to establish himself. His failure was, however, that he could not and did not assert himself in the face of Samuel.

[28] We shall see that this parenthesis does not hold for David in most of 2 Samuel.

[29] Ch. 27 portrays a strategist David who, with his eyes on the throne, deceives his current master.

popularity, first with Jonathan (vv. 1-4), then the military including officers (v. 5), Saul's attendants (v. 22), the women (vv. 6f) including Michal (v. 20) and "all Israel and Judah" (v. 16) so that by 18:30 David's "name became well known" (see Gooding 1986:70f). The unfolding narrative presupposes David's popularity with the people leading eventually to his election. The textual evidence shows David's popularity as well as an increasing awareness and support of David as a charismatic leader. In what way did different people recognise David's charisma? And what was the significance of their recognition?

As David's close friend, Jonathan was the first to recognise David's charisma (see 20:14-17; cf. 18:3f). The Philistines, being the unwilling objects of David's emergence and success, must have realised David's charisma of a military deliverer early on as well (see 21:11; ET 21:10). Distressed people perceived that they could count on David and took refuge with him (22:2). Even Saul at one point expressed his conviction (and fear) that David would succeed him (24:20; ET 24:19). This view seems to have been common amongst the people, asserted by Abigail (25:28, 30f).[30] After Saul's death Judah just took the proper step by anointing David over themselves (2 Sam 2:4). Judah elected David because he was from their tribe, which David exploited by his generous and politically motivated presents from his raids (30:26).

David had been preparing to assume power in Judah for some time (see 25:7f; 30:26; 2 Sam 2:1f). Of course he had designs on the throne, as implied in the text (30:26-31; 2 Sam 2:7; 3:13), but according to the narrator, he did not resort to any illegitimate action or means to achieve it. This in turn means that a charismatic leader and good politician, as David was, is resolute in his plans and does not subject himself to unpredictable events but rather controls them. Finally, after no rival was left, all Israel unanimously voted for David (2 Sam 5:1-5), so designating him as the deliverer and "commander of the twelve tribes" (Cross 1973:230)[31]. David's charismatic exploits and political manoeuvres paid off. Again these two seem to be inseparable. David's success was predicated on both, whereas Saul's failure was that he did not take into consideration political aspects.

To apply V.P. Long's model (1994) David was first designated for the throne by Samuel and bestowed with Yahweh's spirit as a token. Subsequently he demonstrated his charisma by military bravery both as Saul's general and on the run. The nation's confirmation followed in due time.

---

[30] It is also probable that David required increasing recognition of his anointed status in the area where he operated (cf. Weber 1968:242). Nabal's failure to do so explains David's harsh intention towards him in ch. 25. Seen in this way it was not necessarily Nabal's refusal of protection money that he reacted to as Gunn suggests (1980:98).

[31] This is how Cross interprets 2 Sam 5:2 where נָגִיד is used for David in this way. If he is correct, my thesis that David struggled throughout his life between the concepts of military leadership and oriental kingship gains a new perspective.

Maintaining Power — King David

The major theme I shall investigate here is that of David the king. How does he see himself in this position? How does the narrator see him? In 1 Samuel he regarded himself and was depicted as a military deliverer. Will he change after his election? The motif of military king versus oriental monarch was scrutinised by Preston (1982; see also McCarter 1983). I shall develop the motif.

Charisma Tested

My primary question here concerns character portrayal and development, similarly to my investigation of the tension between the Saul in 1 Samuel 11 and that in 13-15. It is a commonplace that biblical characters, in contrast to their Greek counterparts, are dynamic. It is this dynamic characterisation of which David is an excellent example. Something must have gone awry by 2 Samuel 11 with David, the archetype of charismatic deliverers. What and where? Is the remark of 2 Samuel 11:1, "But David remained in Jerusalem" — generally considered ominous — accidental, i.e. lacking any narrative interconnection, or is it a stage in the portrayal of David developed by the narrator previously? What made David stay in Jerusalem? I shall set out to study narrated events prior to ch. 11 in order to understand interconnections and demonstrate overarching motifs in the narrative.

I shall also study the "house" motif, clearly a governing one. In line with my focus on charismatic leadership I shall concentrate on David in different phases of his reign: between his election and the crisis of his rule (antecedents); the crisis itself, which did not start with Absalom's uprising, although culminating then, but with David's incompetence as king and father; David's re-emergence from the revolt; and finally how he is re-established. All these stages are in one way or another associated with his palace.

KING AT THE CROSSROADS — ANTECEDENTS, 2 SAMUEL 5-10

With David's election as king by all Israel (5:1-5)[32] the question is raised: What will he do in his capacity as Israel's new king? The following narrative sees David waver between the images of military and oriental king. The basic difference between the two is that while a charismatic military king considers deliverance his call and relies on Yahweh's intervention, an oriental (absolutist) king is keen on controlling everything by centralising power. To this end reliance on material wealth and military power is inevitable. Last but not least the royal image must be nurtured. These two concepts will keep challenging David.

First we read of the capture of Jerusalem (5:6-8) and the defeats of the Philistines (5:17-25). David seems to have carried on with his duties as a military leader. The record of military victories, however, is interrupted by a

---

[32] Unattributed Bible references in the remaining of the chapter are to 2 Samuel.

paragraph on David's palace and family (vv. 9-16),[33] making the structure of the chapter somewhat curious. In addition there are two references to Yahweh's support (vv. 10 and 12). What is their function?

After Jerusalem's capture, to which I shall return in a minute, David starts a fortification project. At this time he stays in the fortress (v. 9) — the proper dwelling of a military king. Then the narrator claims that David's increasing success came from Yahweh (v. 10). This is a powerful statement, and may be rendered as "David successfully went on and Yahweh the God Almighty along with him."

This is, however, only the beginning, and the next account of the court will present a different portrait. Namely by juxtaposing military victories with the royal court the reader gets the impression of two different lives — the life of the military king is contrasted with that of an ensconced monarch "settled in his palace" (7:1). Indeed בַּיִת functions as a place of settledness, as I shall argue.[34] Just after his election David is portrayed as standing at a crossroads, with one signpost pointing towards being a dynamic-charismatic military king delivering Israel, the other towards becoming a static-oriental king confined to his palace, the epitome of royal privileges. Until his death this dilemma will accompany the king, who will never be able to resolve it sufficiently.

At this crossroads Hiram, an ally to David, comes to his help. As the text stands it suggests that sending all the building material was Hiram's initiative, without a previous agreement with the Israelite king. Considering that it was he who later supplied Solomon with timber for the palace and the temple (1 Kgs 5:1-10), he impersonates a tutor of young kings, encouraging his protégé at the start of his career: "Now you have become one of us — join the peers!" Indeed David acquires royal decorum by building a palace (cf. Rosenberg 1986:197).[35] At this juncture Yahweh's support is mentioned for the second time. Whereas, however, in v. 10 it was the narrator's clear voice, the assertion in v. 12 is qualified by "David knew". Now by what does David know that Yahweh established him? And whose people is he concerned with — David's or

---

[33] Although we learn of David's family during their residence at Hebron (2:2), no palace is mentioned there. Whether or not he was living in one, it was not typical as opposed to the Jerusalem years when "palace" is referred to several times (see 5:11; 7:1; 11:2, 9; 12:20; 13:7; 20:3). In this regard the note on David's tent in 1 Sam 17:54 is noteworthy. Goliath's head is brought to Jerusalem, his armour to David's tent, metonyms for David's military leadership and its challenge, just as his royal projects will be linked with the palace.

[34] The house motif has been recognised and analysed at length by a number of scholars, e.g. Rosenberg 1986:113-23; Murray 1998. Polzin treats chs. 5-7 under the telling title "Houses" (1993:54-87), and his evaluation of the DH's view on "houses" (54-66 in particular) is fascinating. His criticism of David's projects is rather general and implicit, purporting to the DH, while mine is intended to be more particular and explicit.

[35] Hiram's tutorial role is corroborated by a minor observation. Whereas in v. 9 it was David who built the fortress, בָּנָה in v. 11 seems to have Hiram's men as its subject.

Yahweh's (Goldingay 2000:209)? The placing of the statement suggests that his perception was based on the building of the royal palace — not on his military achievements, so much commended by the narrator (5:10; 8:6, 14). Thus while the narrator's assessment regards David's military triumphs (5:10), David's perception seems to be based on the palace project and perceived as a token of success and God's blessing (5:12; similarly Steussy 1999:58). He thinks he knows but his perception will prove self-deceptive.[36]

By David's self-deception a major change in his value system has been put in motion. Instead of focusing on his royal duty he becomes preoccupied with establishing a royal image. This is underlined by the next note: "David took, לקח,[37] more concubines and wives" (v. 13), probably of Jebusite origin. The narrator makes clear that this demonstration of royal power by a harem happened after "he left Hebron" — the residence of a moderate tribal chief (cf. Flanagan 1981). In contrast Jerusalem is the residence of presumed royal privileges. More importantly by the juxtaposition of vv. 10 and 12 the major theme of 2 Samuel has been introduced: Will David remain a charismatic military king or become an oriental monarch?

David's first narrated military operation as Israel's king is now to be viewed in the light of what David intended and did to the capital. As the account is

---

[36] Weiss (1963:461f; his italics; AT) discusses this literary device at length, which he calls "interior monologue":
"It is one way of reporting someone's speech or thoughts in a narrative. In interior monologue the narrator or a character describes what someone said or thought, but uses neither the form of *direct* speech (A says: 'I cannot do this') nor of *indirect* speech (A says he cannot do this), but writes from the perspective of that particular person, as if it was an objective description in the third person (A cannot do this). We read it as if it was a fact, while the narrator does not actually want it perceived as such. As said earlier he wants to mirror the (mostly unuttered) words or thoughts of a character in the story. In the form of the statement itself there is no indication at all that it is a reported speech or thought. To summarise internal monologue (i.m.) looks like a description of a fact, while in reality it is a sometimes empathising, other times ironic reflection of a person's words or thoughts.
Interior monologue derives its effect from three things:
First it makes it possible to represent unspoken thoughts and emotions in a pointed way. Using it objective circumstances can be drawn into the character's experience and portrayed subjectively. Alternatively things happening in the character's mind can be reported as if they were facts.
Second there is the dubious ambiguity of the narrator presenting something as fact while he does not consider it fact at all. It looks as if he was just echoing the character's words or thoughts, but in reality he is making fun of it.
Third it is extremely lifelike, directly evoking sympathy and a vicarious experience. It gives flexibility by changing perspectives — from the narrator's perspective we switch unobserved to the particular character's perspective without an introductory 'he said' or 'he thought'."

[37] See my comment on the verb in 1 Sam 8-9 and 16.

structured, Jerusalem's siege is rendered insignificant (Fokkelman 1990:157f). "The king and his men marched to Jerusalem" and "David captured the fortress of Zion" (5:6f) are all that we learn of the siege (Fokkelman 1990:157). 5:7b only foreshadows the subsequent narrative, when Jerusalem becomes the residence of an oriental monarch — a place of royal misconduct.[38]

David's wavering is further shown in 5:17 where, by moving again into the fortress mentioned in v. 9, he faces the Philistine onslaught. He resumes the military king's duty.[39] As a sign of reliance on Yahweh's intervention David twice enquires of him (vv. 19, 23). This appears to have been a routine of the military leader (see 1 Sam 23:9-12; 30:8); so the section makes clear that David counts on Yahweh's help in military operations. Victory is granted through reliance on Yahweh's initiative, and the scope of the victory, by the use of כנע, alludes "to the greatest triumph in the period of the Judges" (Carlson 1964:57; see Ju 3:30; 4:23; 8:28; 11:33). As opposed to this there is not one case of David's seeking God in matters related to centralisation or his oriental king image. No doubt there was no need; the king was quite determined to reach his ends — even without Yahweh. Ch. 5 portrayed David as standing at a crossroads of military and oriental kingships.

In keeping with what has been said so far as well as the general view, I consider chs. 6-7 David's attempt at centralisation by trying to establish a religious centre under royal control and with Yahweh's blessing secured. Of course centralisation is not all negative. As an attempt to unify the loose tribal federation it was certainly well intended. Still the final outcome under Solomon, I shall argue in part three, will not be entirely beneficial for Israel's tribal system and religion.

Ch. 6 sets out with a strange back-reference, וַיֹּסֶף עוֹד דָּוִד. What did David carry on with the 30,000 troops? The question is even more pressing as after the first failed Philistine attack their second attempt is introduced with וַיֹּסְפוּ עוֹד פְּלִשְׁתִּים (5:22).[40] Israel's arch-enemy carries on its military operation; David is forced to react and triumphs. In ch. 6 "the reader may naturally be led to expect that David will mount a more sustained campaign against the Philistines"

---

[38] 5:7b is not an explanation of the name of the City of David (in 2 Samuel only in 5:7, 9; 6:10, 12, 16), but a reference to the centralisation motif (see McCarter 1983). As is generally recognised, the choosing of the capital on neutral territory affirms David's political insight. This is definitely true historically, hence the more curious that, apart from the centralisation project, it is not emphasised in 2 Samuel. Is the narrative's silence about the city's national significance a sign of David's political incompetence to exploit Jerusalem's strategic location? Indeed I shall argue that when regaining control after Absalom's coup David ignores the mounting tension between Israel and Judah.

[39] Chronologically the events most probably preceded vv. 11-15. By this arrangement the narrator seems to indirectly criticise David for the palace project which he started before fending off the Philistine threat.

[40] For more thematic and phrasal correspondences between 5:17ff and ch. 6 see Murray 1998.

(Murray 1998:116). In addition to ritually repossessing former Philistine territory (119f), to the reader's disappointment David resumes his "oriental king project" begun in 5:11, and not that which would have been obvious after the Philistine defeat — military kingship. He will only resume the Philistine campaign in ch. 8. In this way the text has introduced subtle hints at David's looming oriental kingship, which will, explicitly or implicitly, be elaborated on in what follows.

The attempt to subject Israelite religion by bringing the ark into the capital to the king is as ironic as it is disastrous (see Zakovitch 1999:18-21; Linden 2000:157f). After his first attempt is foiled by Yahweh's wrath, David recognises the terrifying responsibility of housing the ark and abandons his centralisation project (6:9f). 6:7 reinforces the irony by reapplying the verb נכה from 5:20, where David is said to have struck the Philistines. Here it is Yahweh striking his own people — for the ill-conceived centralisation? Obviously for the king the incident was a public relations disaster.

When the ark takes residence in the house of Obed-Edom, probably a Philistine whose name makes him even "less entitled" to God's blessing, Yahweh blesses the countryside household. This is the only case of God's blessing a house in the entire DH (Polzin 1993:65). David, of course, is not to be left out of Yahweh's blessing (cf. McCarter 1983:276). He changes his mind — economic-political expediency disperses David's fear that only lasted "that day", as succinctly expressed by the time adjunct in 6:9. The king takes security measures (vv. 13f; see Fokkelman 1990:194f) and pursues his project — this time successfully. The first references to the destination of the ark in 6:9 ("to me") and 10 ("to him" and to "the City of David") reveal David's self-interest in the project (Murray 1998:235). Vv. 13, 17-19 make clear that the master of ceremonies was David, which reveals his, and foreshadows his successor's, ambitions (1 Kgs 8) — a king controlling not only politics and society, but also religion (cf. Eslinger 1994:14-19).[41] This is a serious deviation from the idea of

---

[41] Campbell has noticed the thematic development in 1 Sam 4-6 and 2 Sam 6 (1979:41, n. 30): "The narrative of the defeats (chap. 4) raises the question of who is responsible, Dagon or Yahweh. The answer to this (chap. 5), showing Yahweh—who has departed—exercising power in a foreign land, raises the question whether he will return to Israel. The answer to this (chap. 6) raises the question whether he will bestow favor on Israel as of old. The answer to this (2 Sam 6) is affirmative, and brings the narrative to rest." Although the narrative does not give an explicit statement of Yahweh's view, it seems to implicitly condemn David's project. Thus the "affirmative answer" proposed by Campbell is illusory. Campbell may unintentionally be right in his claim though, that in 2 Sam 6 God bestows "favor on Israel as of old." It is God's favour as of old — unexpected and unpredictable (1 Sam 11; 2 Sam 17:14), capricious and inconsistent (1 Sam 13-15; 2 Sam 21, 24). I am sympathetic to Polzin's interpretation of 6:16-23 (1993:66-70). After establishing links between 6:16, 20, 22 and 1 Sam 2:27, 30 he states (69f): "In the royal story of 2 Samuel 6, it is David, Israel's idolatrous replacement for God, who reveals himself, is honored, appears lightly esteemed, and is despised." It is

devolving power in early Israel (cf. Rosenberg 1986:207). Samuel's worst dreams (1 Sam 8:6) are taking shape.

The ironic and condemning implication of David's centralisation project may be hinted at by a back-reference to a similar episode in Judges. After having delivered Israel from the Midianites, also in an attempt to unify Israel's fragile and malfunctioning tribal federation, "Gideon made [...] an ephod, which he placed, יצג, in Ophrah, his town" (Ju 8:27). This third occurrence of the key-verb יצג, without the reference to deliverance, ישע, as on the previous occasions (6:37; 7:5), marks Gideon's, and with his Israel's, turning fortune (see Czövek 1997:14-20). The disastrous outcome of Gideon's attempt to unify all the tribes of Israel is manifested in the idolatry of all Israel (8:27). What is noticeable is the employment of יצג, a rare verb occurring only 6 times in the DH out of 16 FT occurrences, in 2 Samuel 6:17, as well as the almost identical syntax of the verses. Judges 8:27ab: predicate, object, subject, adverb, predicate (יצג), object (אותו), two place adjuncts. 2 Samuel 6:17ab: predicate, object, predicate (יצג), object (אתו), two place adjuncts. Judges 8:27cd, 30f describe the disastrous outcome of Gideon's project in vivid terms. Is then what follows 2 Samuel 6:17 to be regarded similarly?

Ironic implications have become the imprint of David's project marking the ambiguity inherent in such imperial undertakings. This will be apparent in ch. 7. What makes David come up with the idea of a temple is similar to the motivation of the palace project in ch. 5 in that both have to do with perception — the leitmotif in both sections.[42] In David's perception the royal palace and the harem were manifestations of Yahweh's help and blessing — kingdom established (5:11f). I have shown how he fell victim to his misperception.

The king is "settled in his palace" (7:1), where he "can properly exercise his mind on rehousing the ark, because he is not engaged with the paramount kingly activity of fighting wars. He may thus turn his attention to another fitting preoccupation for a *melek*, the appropriate housing of the tutelary deity" (Murray 1998:164). David perceives a tent as a primitive dwelling place, inappropriate for God (7:2),[43] as the fortress was for himself, and "wants the housing of the ark, that is, of the ark's god, to emulate the status of his own splendid palace" (Murray 1998:212). Therefore he makes, what at first glance appears, the benevolent proposal to build a house for Yahweh. "But Uzzah's

---

also noteworthy that after ch. 6 references to the ark decrease with its importance diminishing, while the house gains significance at the same time (Flanagan 1988:230-32). See also Rosenberg's discussion of the house motif (1986:113-23) as well as Clements 1965:55-60.

[42] It seems unnecessary to note that in Hebrew one word serves for "palace" and "temple".

[43] On the allusion to Dt 12:10f in 7:1-3 Sternberg notes (1985:539, n. 4): "Far from needing a reminder to build a temple 'when the Lord had given him rest from all his enemies round about,' David takes the initiative at the earliest possible moment." On the ironic implications of 2 Sam 11:11 in relation to 7:2 see his n. 16 on p. 527.

death has taught him caution: this time, David consults a prophet before launching into his project" (Steussy 1999:61), and he meets Nathan's approval, "the Lord is with you" (7:3). A closer reading, however, exposes the irony. The phrase, used for military usage in the DH, is redesigned to support royal claims.[44] The prophet has become a royal official in His Majesty's service. Without prophetic autonomy, he is "on the king's payroll" as "a full-time state employee" (Goldingay 2000:220). Now it is Yahweh's turn to take the initiative (see Murray 1998: *passim*) and reveal the king's misperception (vv. 6f).[45] God does not approve of the concept of the temple,[46] but taking the initiative voluntarily promises the king a dynasty (Murray 1998:279). David gets the point and, in the very tent he intended to replace (201), royal "pretension submits without reserve to divine prerogative" (211).[47] The ironic conflict between David's royal pretension and Yahweh's concept of kingship is visible when,

---

[44] Out of twenty-six occurrences in the DH (Josh 1:5, 9, 17; 3:7; 7:12; Ju 1:22; 2:18; 6:12f, 16; 1 Sam 3:19; 10:7; 16:18; 17:37; 18:12, 14, 28; 20:13; 2 Sam 5:10; 7:3, 9; 14:17; 1 Kgs 1:37; 8:57; 11:38; 2 Kgs 18:7), with the possible exceptions of 1 Sam 3:19 and 1 Kgs 8:57, this is the only one not purporting to military activity. (Nathan's usage is very much like that of the Chronicles.) It is telling that after 2 Sam 5:10 the narrative never refers to Yahweh supporting David.

[45] See how Yahweh refers to himself in 7:6: "I have not dwelt in a house from the day I brought the Israelites up out of Egypt to this day." Yahweh claims that he will not stay in the capital, where David wants him to. Contrast the application of העלה, the verb used in reference to Yahweh's saving act from Egypt, with that in 6:2 about David's abortive attempt. Characteristically Yahweh adds in 7:6: "I have been moving from place to place with a tent as my dwelling," i.e. he has not needed a permanent and fixed dwelling. In 6:2 and 1 Sam 4:4 Yahweh "is enthroned between the cherubim." These references to Yahweh's elusive presence amongst his people constitute the basis of his uniqueness. On this see the discussion of Solomon's temple in part 3. For a similar reading of the chapter see Polzin 1993:71-75, Eslinger 1994 and Murray 1998:160-230.

[46] Note that the DH never claims the temple was built at God's behest. Conspicuously no reference can be found to Yahweh's blessing of the project.

[47] Murray later adds (229) that "Yahweh also cedes ground from the position set out in 5b-11a. He embraces dynasty as a means to secure the future welfare of his people, and, by implicature from his exposition of the promise of dynasty (12, 14-16), he concedes royal status." Schwartz (1991:43) comments on 7:4-10: "In this passage, God clearly suggests that the idea of a house, of permanence, of stability, is abhorrent, and yet he offers David a house as though it were desirable indeed; as the passage reads, the promise of a House is far from an unequivocally welcome one." Is this because a permanent house would impede charismatic activity? If so, scholars, e.g. Alt, happens to be almost correct in their claim that Judah was not charismatic, whereas the northern kingdom was. Later Schwartz (44; her italics) observes on 11:14-27: "It seems that a House is a bad idea after all. Conflicts like these are frequent because this text is not simply about the people, the nation, or its king *amassing* power, but because instead these narratives express ambivalence about power."

far from having Yahweh visit him in his splendid new cedar palace to bestow his blessing upon it, David fails dramatically to vouchsafe the blessing of Yahweh of Hosts to his household (6.20). It is only when he forsakes this grand symbol of his royal pretension so as to defer fully before Yahweh that he gains the assurance of that blessing as freely bestowed by Yahweh of Hosts (7.29). (Murray 1998:280)

I hope to have cogently argued that one of the themes linking chs. 5 and 7 is that of perception, more precisely misperception. In 5:12 David thinks he knows the cause of Yahweh's blessing, but the narrator claims the king is wrong. In ch. 7 David's misperception about an appropriate house for Yahweh is exposed. Unless one makes sense of it ch. 6 is quite redundant in this arrangement. To start with I take 6:6 as a parable of David's failed attempt at centralisation, the topic of the chapter. As such it is a succinct rendering of the theme of the surrounding narrative. 6:6 refers to a heretofore unknown man named נָכוֹן, a derivative of the verb "establish". כון is used at different junctions to refer to the monarchy's durability, and 5:12 and 7:12f are particularly important in this respect.[48]

The symbolic interpretation is supported, at a closer reading, by the victim's name, Uzzah, meaning "strength", a feminine noun, quite strange of a man. But abstract feminine nouns in Hebrew often have symbolic meanings (e.g. "Qohelet"). Since "strength" may allude to "kingdom", another feminine noun, by taking hold of the ark Uzzah, whose innocence in handling the ark is undeniable (Murray 1998:125f), acts as a royal agent (Polzin 1993:64). Taken into account the semantic range of אחז, "seize, take possession of", the monarchy's infeasible action becomes evident.[49] The kingdom laid claim to religion, intending to take possession of Yahweh's abode, which provoked Yahweh's anger, to which David also reacts with rage. This is revealing. "David, far from being plunged into mourning over the striking down of Uzzah, or being concerned at its cause, is instead mightily peeved at the baulking of his project!" (Murray 1998:126, n. 49).[50]

With 5:12 denoting a false perception of the kingdom's establishment, and the conditional statement of Yahweh's commitment to it in 7:12ff, 6:6 serves as a subversive parable on the kingdom between these two assertions. The disaster strikes when "they came to the threshing floor of Nacon", or alternatively, "when they (Israel) came to be established" through centralising religion. When they thought they had arrived (i.e. were established), the kingdom came to

---

[48] Notice the similarities between 5:12 and 7:13 achieved by the repetition of words "establish", "kingdom" and the similarly sounding נִשָּׂא and כִּסֵּא.

[49] Notice the similarly sounding nouns עֻזָּה and אֲחֻזָּה, "possession", which is not in the text but might be hinted at (cf. Polzin 1993:64).

[50] The wording of 6:8, וַיִּחַר לְדָוִד, is reminiscent of 1 Sam 15:11, וַיִּחַר לִשְׁמוּאֵל. The comparison is the more apparent, as both cases report a leader's frustration after his failed project — here David's oriental kingship is thwarted, there Samuel's first choice of a submissive king.

nothing — an anticipation of what will happen to the monarchy. At the precise moment that David thinks he has brought Yahweh under control, the deity wreaks havoc (Goldingay 2000:214).

Something else may buttress this interpretation. Semantically 5:10 is a dynamic formulation of Yahweh's support. It consists of the *verbum finitum* הלך supported by two infinitives. All three verbs express movement or change of state. Given its connotations of "stability" and "immovability", however, כון denotes something rather static in 5:12 and 7:12f (and 6:6). By choice of words and artful formulation the narrator draws attention to a significant aspect of the political establishment.

This is further supported by the underlying theological theme. In ch. 7 David thinks that the tabernacle is not good enough for Yahweh. What is needed, in his perception, is a proper shrine. The irony lies in the fact that a temple is by definition static, its building immovable. By contrast the tent represented a dynamic religion, an institution on the move, pointing to the elusive One who cannot be domiciled and controlled.[51] With the temple, religion becomes an institution of control — an infringement upon Yahweh's sovereignty, which is tied to his non-locatable, dynamic character. The temple project is linked to kingship, hence it is as ambiguous as the monarchy and calls for Yahweh's displeasure. "Thus what Yahweh rejects here is בית *tout court*, house = temple in its entirety, because בית is through and through characterized by ישב, and ישב is an infringement of his sovereign freedom of movement among his people (התהלך)" (Murray 1998:214).

David's perception of success is contrasted with the narrator's. Where is Yahweh's help to be experienced? In military exploits or in imperial building projects?[52] David thinks he has to be successful for the sake of the royal image; the narrator claims success must be for Israel's sake.[53]

Ch. 8 sets out by claiming continuity with the foregoing narrative (see Conroy 1978:41f).[54] 8:1-14 directs the spotlight back on to David, the military king. Vv. 1-6 list the countries David defeated and end with a statement of Yahweh's support. Vv. 7-12 deal with the booty. Regarding its fate vv. 7-10

---

[51] See Polzin's observation (1993:77f) on movement related words describing the tent's mobility as well as those on the future temple's stability.

[52] Polzin (1993:86) contrasts David's misperception of God's blessing of his house in 7:29 with the narrator's perception of divine blessing.

[53] This juxtaposition of perceptions will recur at the end of the book. My analysis of chs. 5-7, by throwing light on the underlying theme of centralisation in chs. 6-7, partly answers the question of why ch. 7 is placed here and not after ch. 8.

[54] Ch. 8 might be interpreted as "God, seeing how David's idle hands have made room for mischief, puts him back to work" (Eslinger 1994:17, n. 2). Yahweh's prohibition that David is not to build the temple has an interesting implication. Yahweh wants David to remain a charismatic deliverer, to which the temple, or any "house", is an impediment. That Yahweh did not succeed in making David continue with his charismatic assignment is a separate issue.

keep the reader in suspense, with only v. 11 mentioning that "King David dedicated these articles to the LORD, as he had done with the silver and gold from all the nations he had subdued". David here does not accumulate wealth but appropriately expresses his gratitude towards God, who has granted him success. So Fokkelman correctly deems the middle section the focus of the chapter (1990:255). The theme of military exploits is recapitulated in vv. 13f and concluded by the verbatim repetition of 6cd. It is important that in this structure the assertion of God's help comes after the military victories and not after the report on the ransacked goods. Thus similarly to ch. 5, Yahweh's help is linked with military success and not material wealth. Since ch. 8 is a summary of David's military exploits during his reign, his success cannot be viewed as a major motif in 2 Samuel. Hence I take it as the narrator's "yearning" for David the military king: If only the king had continued! By commenting on David's victories the author has begun to examine how David established himself, a theme further elaborated in chs. 9-10.

David's victories are interrupted by the list of David's officials (8:15-18).[55] This hints at some attempts at institutionalisation on David's part. As opposed to the judges' era and Saul's reign, David has made a significant step towards an organised and centralised court at the heart of the monarchy.

Ch. 9 at first glance interrupts the theme of military king versus oriental monarch, but actually does not deviate from the main thread but rather explains how David establishes himself. Ackroyd correctly observed the relevance of 1 Samuel 20:15f to the removal of David's enemies in 2 Samuel 8, so that David is now obliged to protect Jonathan's family (1981:390). By what means does he achieve this?

The covenant between David and the house of Saul is an underlying theme in 1-2 Samuel (Armerding, oral communication). Saul first offers his older daughter Merab, but then reneges. He does the same with Michal (1 Sam 18:19; 25:44), in spite of David's every effort to obtain her. Later on, Jonathan makes a formal covenant with David with regard to his offspring (1 Sam 20:14-17). David shows his loyalty to Saul and his house on a number of occasions (1 Sam 24; 26; 2 Sam 1; 4:9-12). While David remains loyal, Saul keeps breaking the covenant with David. As observed one can never be sure about David's motivation, still the fact stands that David is intent on keeping his part of the covenant. This aspect should be remembered when reading about David's dealing with Mephibosheth. David's covenant loyalty to Saul's house, however, is on a collision course with his oriental kingship.

The story begins by quoting David who intends to "show kindness for Jonathan's sake". The "threefold repetition, coupled with an increasing intensification of the claim of truthfulness, immediately attracts attention" (Perdue 1984:75), as the narrator could have presented the sincerity of David's intention by gradually applying the loyalty motif, which he does not. Is his

---

[55] More on the section see under "Administration".

intention genuine or a ruse? Ziba is introduced as "a servant of Saul's household" (9:2). He, however, identifies himself as David's servant (v. 2). This would merely be a court etiquette if "servants" did not dominate the chapter (see Polzin 1993:88-108). Now in whose service is he? Is he reliable? In v. 11 he twice assures David about his servant status. When Mephibosheth meets the king, David first makes sure his identity. Using the term "your servant" twice (vv. 6, 8) Mephibosheth humbly points out that he is a subject of the king (cf. Polzin 1993:96). David graciously promises to restore him his family estate. Why then does the king want him to eat at his table when he is catered for from his land (v. 10)? Previously Mephibosheth was referred to as one crippled who need not be a concern for the king (v. 3). Does David still perceive him as a threat to his rule?[56]

It is likely that the king acts from both proper and expedient motives, as Sternberg (1985:255) suggests. Still, the negative side of David's opaqueness is further amplified in vv. 9f, which stress Ziba's dependent status on his new master — a reversal of Ziba's fortune. This will obviously create tension between warden and master, the more so as there is a prospect of inheritance, hinted at by the notes on sons (vv. 10, 12). More importantly this seems to be a matter of prestige. The former landowner, who had twenty workers (v. 10), now himself becomes a subject of the new owner. V. 12 aptly summarises the change of fortune. Ziba's grudge and his uneasy relationship to his master will be revealed in 16:1-4 and 19:24-30 (ET 19:23-29; see Fokkelman 1980:30-39) as well as the king's intention.[57] There the narrator makes clear Mephibosheth's innocence. Yet David does not bother to investigate. His order in 19:29 (ET 19:28) reinvigorates the tension by playing master and caretaker off against each other.

The opening of ch. 10 is reminiscent of that of ch. 8, linking the two chapters and anticipating war (cf. Polzin 1993:107). Ch. 10 further elaborates upon David's increasing power and establishing himself as an internationally recognised king. After the death of the neighbouring monarch David intends to "show kindness" (10:2), which in turn is an almost verbatim repetition of the phrase in 9:1 (see Ackerman 1990:44). Again the question arises: is David's intention genuine or is it merely a pretext, as the Ammonite nobles suspect (v. 3)?[58] The narrative does not explicitly answer this question, but the

---

[56] Note that neither the narrator nor Ziba has named Mephibosheth, still the king calls him by name when they first meet (v. 6). This confirms our suspicion. Did the king know about his existence and only wanted to "kidnap" him? This possibility may gain weight considering Mephibosheth's whereabouts in Gilead (9:4), perhaps out of the king's reach.

[57] By dividing the land between the two David not only reneges on what he said to Mephibosheth and Ziba (9:7, 9), but also incites them against each other.

[58] It may be argued that the nobles are presented as aware of the "narratological link" between 9:1 and 10:2, i.e. of the cynical nature of David's kindness.

correspondence of 10:2 with 9:1 and David's handling of the Mephibosheth case sheds doubt on the king. Even if the king's intention is genuine, seeing the result it becomes a ruse, as the Syrians are brought to their knees and the Ammonites into David's empire (Perdue 1984:76).

Despite his portrayal in ch. 8, David, for the first time, opts for the palace. Instead of being at the front line he oversees the Ammonite war from Jerusalem and sends Joab with the army against Ammon (10:7). The change in his leadership style will have a fundamental impact upon the subsequent flow of events.

On ch. 10 Polzin (1993:108) remarks that what "follows in the chapter happens by halves", although he does not know why. I suggest that the "narrative purpose for all these halvings" (108) is Israel's dividedness between military and royal governments due to David's half-heartedness, i.e. his wavering between the battlefield and the royal palace. In 10:17 David briefly resumes military leadership and leads his troops to victory, only to abandon them in 11:1.

The theme linking chs. 9 and 10 is David's equivocal kindness, first to Jonathan's son, then to the Ammonite king's. Chs. 8-10 addressed the question of how David established himself in his foreign (military victories, ch. 8; sometimes with dubious intentions, ch. 10) and domestic affairs (ambiguous orders, ch. 9). Since his election in ch. 5 David has undergone a fundamental change in his personality and leadership style. From the end of ch. 6 he has gradually been confined to his Jerusalem palace, which has become a place of power politics and machination. David is becoming an oriental monarch. This is most apparent in ch. 11, where the shift from the covert to the overt and the culmination of the king's character development will be visible. I now turn to the Bathsheba incident and its aftermath.

KING IN THE PALACE — THE CRISIS, 2 SAMUEL 11:1-15:12

The Absalom revolt is the narratological aftermath of David's sin with Bathsheba (see 12:11; 16:10f). Therefore I shall investigate what went wrong in the royal palace that Absalom's conspiracy gained so much support (15:1-12) without coming to David's attention. How was it all possible? What did David do that he should not have? And what did he fail to do? Moreover how did David overcome the crisis? What can one learn of charismatics and charisma?

Since David was elected king things have changed. He has subdued the neighbouring nations (ch. 8), accumulated some wealth (8:7f) and moved from the "stronghold" to a palace (7:1). The turmoil of the early years is gone, everything appears, for better or for worse, to be predictable. This is the dream of every ruler. No unexpected change means stability. On the other hand David has only occasionally had great military deeds to his credit in 2 Samuel. The initial crisis triggering his emergence has been overcome. There is now no need of charismatic proficiency. I have also claimed that "palace" is a metonym for

David's perception of royal duty as well as settledness. [59] This misperception will inevitably lead to adultery and murder in ch. 11.

Ch. 11 is the *visible* turning point in David's character and fortunes. When reading 11:1a, "In the spring, at the time when kings go off to war...", the reader is forced to ponder the question: "That is what kings customarily do. But what about David? Will he follow suit?" Our naivety is immediately exposed: "David sent Joab out with the king's men and the whole Israelite army", and he "remained in Jerusalem" (11:1be). Fokkelman (1981:58f) draws attention to the use of the latter phrase in 9:13 (Mephibosheth), 10:14 (Joab), 11:12 (Uriah; plus 10:5 of the envoys in Jericho). "What has gone wrong with David in the meantime that he has so hopelessly lost his worthiness?", Fokkelman asks and blames the cruelty of war (59). This sounds rather fanciful to me, for David, as I have shown, has become inclined to be absent from war. My suggestion instead is that the pattern, if there is one, serves to highlight the startling difference of conduct of the king ("staying in Jerusalem") and that of other characters. This is the more remarkable as this is "the first place in the Bible that a leader of Israel stays off the battlefield in time of war" (Rosenberg 1986:126).

The textual problem of v. 1 is well-known. MT reads "agents", "messengers", which most of the interpreters amend to "kings", a reading based on, amongst others, the LXX. Rosenberg takes a mediating position by commenting:

> Since a king, as defined in I Sam. 8, is *himself* an agent of the people, and his exit to battle a constitutive moment of his authority, we find ourselves with an oddly convoluted inversion of kingly function in the king's preference of agents to represent him. In this transition to a sedentary monarchy, the agent within the king and the king within the agent seem at war with each other... (1986:126; emphasis his)

By 11:1, keeping away from wars has become the king's habit. As opposed to his former charismatic self, who led "the troops in their campaigns" (1 Sam 18:13, recalled in 2 Sam 5:2; see Sternberg 1985:194), David, by gradually abandoning the military king ideal, has become a titular military king sending his general for himself (contra Garsiel 1993:249f).[60] Here David is "inactive, no

---

[59] Conspicuously the events in chs. 11-12 do not change this. Between 10:17 and 15:16 only in 12:29-31 does David leave Jerusalem — "under duress". He does not go to Hebron to celebrate with his son (15:9), nor when Absalom specifically asks him to go with him (13:25). David's preferences are hinted at in 15:16 when he leaves ten concubines behind to take care of the *palace* (cf. 20:3).

[60] In 12:27f Joab aptly reminds the king of his duty, just as David's capture of the Ammonite king's crown, עֲטָרָה, 12:30, affirms his oriental king image. As opposed to this crown, about 34 kilograms, Saul had only a נֵזֶר, 1:10, which was obviously not designed for royal ceremonies, and, being a derivative of "dedicate", probably highlights

longer a fighter or outlaw" (A. Bach 1990:35). The lifestyle that such a disposition results in is visible in 11:2 (cf. Fokkelman 1981:51), which in turn shows the conduct of an oriental despot, denoted by the keyword שלח. In ch. 11 the verb occurs twelve times (Simon 1967:209). By having the king seven times and Joab four times as its subject and powerless Uriah and Bathsheba as its most frequent objects, the verb is applied in reference to power, notably royal power. The king is an oriental monarch dealing with his subjects, women and troops as he likes (cf. K. Stone 1996:93-106).[61] Samuel's nightmare (1 Sam 8:17) has been fulfilled.

This, however, is not the end of the story. As predicted by Nathan (12:10-12), the king's transgression will bring revenge on the royal house; calamity is yet to come. A powerful but discredited charismatic leader often causes the emergence of another. That is what David is about to invoke.

Ch. 13 gives some clue to what was going on in the royal palace. The heir apparent falls in love with his half-sister Tamar, who happens to be Absalom's sister. His lust drives him almost mad, only rape relieves it. Then, adding insult to injury, he expels her. Relationships are strange in the royal court,[62] and Tamar's rape is not the only strange thing in David's family.

I have claimed that the king frequently resorted to ruse. Deception has become the main factor determining relationships and fates in chs. 11-17. While, however, it was the king who deceived Uriah in ch. 11 and will deceive his enemies in 15:13-17:29, during the crisis (13:1-15:12) he is on the receiving end (cf. Marcus 1986:164). Following the advice of David's nephew, Amnon first deceives the king (13:6f), then Tamar, who becomes the first victim in the series of deception. The second casualty is Amnon himself, who is deceived and murdered by Absalom, his brother. Sexual offence followed by murder (see Bar-Efrat 1980:169) has become the scourge of the palace. The primary victim of deception, however, is David himself. On hearing of Tamar's rape King David "was furious" (v. 21). Two years later Absalom succeeds in deceiving and persuading his apparently prudent father to send the heir apparent for himself (vv. 26f; see Fokkelman 1981:115f). When learning of Amnon's murder David "and all his servants wept very bitterly" (v. 36). Ironically it is

---

Saul's commitment to military leadership — he died on the battlefield. My analysis has also shown the intrinsic irony of 12:28 and 11:1, which was "open to doubt" for Simon (1967:209).

[61] The oriental king aspect is reinforced by Nathan's condemnation for transgressing the limits of Yahwist kingship. Conspicuously, however, the prophet does not mention adultery. David gets the point and confesses his sin "against Yahweh" (12:13), again, not against Bathsheba or Uriah.

[62] The peculiar state of the palace is supported by the discrepancy between Tamar's desperate plea, "Don't rape me! Such a thing is not done in Israel" (v. 12; AT), and his father's action in ch. 11.

Jonadab who "responds" (ענה, v. 32)[63] correctly to the news (see Fokkelman 1981:118).

In ch. 14 the king is deceived by the "wise" woman from Tekoa acting on Joab's instruction. Since father and son are reunited in 14:33 the king appears to benefit from this. Appearances, however, prove deceptive, as Absalom has one more trick up his sleeves. After having shrewdly prepared the coup he once again leaves Jerusalem with the excuse of a religious obligation (15:7f).

It appears incredible that these deceptions went unnoticed by David, himself a shrewd strategist (cf. Pyper 1993). Be that as it may, the motif is foreshadowed in Nathan's encounter with the king after his double crime. Suspecting nothing, David fell victim to Nathan's ruse (12:1-6).[64]

8:15 claimed that David administered justice "for all his people." He might have done so as a king, but certainly failed as a father (see Gunn 1975:21; Petersen 1986:137f).[65] After the rape the reader wonders what will be done to the victim. How will David and Absalom react? Apart from getting furious David deals with neither sinner nor sin. Consequently Tamar has to live all her life in Absalom's house , "a desolate woman" (13:20; cf. 13: 13; Ex 22:16; see Anderson 1989:175), i.e. abandoned by her father and protected by her brother (contra Smith 1990:40).[66] While the king did not show care, as if Tamar had not

---

[63] As there are two ענה stems, Jonadab's "answer" in v. 32 is the repercussion of Amnon's "rape" (v. 14), which in turn was his suggestion.

[64] David as powerful but deceived is suggested by Sternberg's reading of ch. 11 (1985:193-222).

[65] Absalom must have harboured some grudge against his father because of this failure. Still Absalom's rapidly growing support suggests that his claim in 15:3 was well-founded. The people must have been discontent with the administration of justice (see Ishida 1982:182f; McCarter 1984:359), otherwise Absalom's attempt would easily have been exposed and frustrated. On this Gressman observes that the people's desertion to Absalom might have reminded David of the discontented people seeking refuge with him in 1 Sam 22:2 (1991:30f). One can argue that this view of David is not compatible with 8:15. My response is that the verse is true — *in its context*. That is to say the statement of David's righteous rule is linked to David's military achievements and early rule, and, startlingly, is not repeated in 20:23-26. Since David's administration of justice is dubious, the claim of 8:15 in my opinion is limited to the period of David's being a "predominantly" military king. Rosenberg (1986:160-63) argues that whereas David, by rising above the aspect of blood feud, was able to deal with Joab's murder of Abner as an offense against crown and state, in his later reign, in the Ziba-Mephibosheth and Absalom-Amnon conflicts, he abandons this principle, which "is a tangible attack on the system of justice that the crown represents" (162). Thus David's failure in Tamar's rape reveals his characteristic attitude (183). Whedbee (1988:160) rightly observes that the Absalom coup breaks "the covenantal bond of king and people, which was to issue in a reign of justice and righteousness (cf. 2 Sam. 8:15)". These considerations contribute to a subtler portrayal of David, possibly as double-sided as Saul's.

[66] This aspect is aptly rendered by two literary means. First v. 20 is about Absalom's caring response to his sister's assault by taking her to himself. V. 21 in turn informs us

been his daughter, Absalom did his best for his sister. "How appropriate that the story never refers to David and Tamar as father and daughter!" (Trible 1984:53). Amnon's murder was ironic in that he executed justice when David failed to.

The blame for these aberrations should be laid at the king's door, who apparently did not care about palace morals and justice, or about his children. They seem to have lacked nothing,[67] except their father's attention. Deceitful and abnormal family relationships, lack of self-restraint and bad temper seem to have been accepted court etiquette, so much so that Rosenberg (1986:141) rightly speaks of "the sinister aura about the court", in which a "uniquely textured hybrid society seems purposefully chosen as a means of epitomizing a moment of crisis in Israel's institutional history."[68] The king did not do anything about this crisis. The incest proved — as Absalom's actions will later — that the מִשְׁפַּט הַמְּלֻכָה had changed since first declared by Samuel (1 Sam 10:25). The royal family's "law" resumes the code of the judges' era, "Do as you see fit". It was exactly of these excesses of kingship that Samuel warned in 1 Samuel 8.

The sequence of tragedies is marked by a recurring term. וְלֹא אבה + לְ infinitive occurs in 13:14, 16, 25 and 14:29, quite remarkable for a rare phrase to be used so often so close together. Its message is no less remarkable.[69] The

---

about David's "indifferent anger" — a paradoxical response, to say the least. Thus at the end of v. 20 Tamar is embraced by her brother's attention and her father's inattention. This interpretation also explains the seemingly awkward placing of v. 21. The second means is the employment of זעק (13:19), often used in association with social oppression and injustice. Notice that David and his servants weep with their clothes torn (13:31, 36), as Tamar did in v. 19. However, for the king's weeping בכה is employed. Tamar's (out)cry belatedly causes David's wailing, so the chapter portrays a cause-and-effect relationship, predicted by Nathan. In addition Hushai's distress in 15:32, similar to Tamar's, pursues the theme by connecting the grief of the two, so relating the plight of David and his loyal men to Tamar's distress.

[67] This is seen in the wealth and lifestyle of the king's children (see 13:23; 15:1). Tamar was wearing a "richly ornamented robe", a "symbol of her royal worth" (Fokkelman 1981:110) along with the king's daughters (13:18). In Gen 37:3, 23, 32 Joseph is said to wear a similar robe, a sign of paternal favouritism. Tamar received a sign of "royal worth" but no paternal attention.

[68] See also his discussion on "good and evil" as a motif connoting the failure of royal administration (182-88).

[69] The verb אבה, with the exception of Job 39:9, occurs exclusively in negations in the FT (52 times). In the DH the phrase in *qatal* form occurs 27 times. As for the outcome Dt 25:7; 1 Sam 31:4 and 2 Sam 12:17 are more or less neutral. Ju 11:17 and 1 Sam 15:9 are foreboding for the parties involved. In 1 Kgs 22:50 (ET 22:49), after a failed attempt, Jehoshaphat seems to have learnt the lesson of accumulating wealth. Only Dt 23:6 (ET 23:5) and Josh 24:10 are unambiguously hopeful for Israel, although both are set in contexts of stern stipulations and a recollection respectively. 2 Kgs 8:19 and 24:4, when read in tandem, are inauspicious, pointing to the final destruction of Davidic

first two occurrences portray a lust-driven Amnon refusing twice to listen, לִשְׁמֹעַ, to Tamar's desperate pleas. The first precedes the rape, the second Amnon's ensuing wrongdoing by her expulsion. Amnon "was stronger", חָזַק, so "he raped her" (13:14). Then he orders his servant to "send, שׁלח, this" away (13:17). The object of Amnon's lust has become the object of his hatred, just as Bathsheba and Uriah became the object of Amnon's father's despotic arbitrariness. However, Amnon's fate is foreshadowed in this report. In the preparation of Amnon's murder the two verbs recur. Thus David "sends" Amnon with Absalom (v. 27). Amnon is then overpowered, חָזַק, by Absalom's men (v. 28).[70] The villain, having become the object of Absalom's hatred (see Fokkelman 1981:114), becomes the victim.

In 13:25 it is David who refuses to go with Absalom.[71] Amnon's death is, however, not merely his own tragedy. It forebodes both Absalom's and David's tragedy. Absalom will suffer a violent death, similar to his brother's. In 13:28 Absalom orders, צוה, his servants, נְעָרִים, to be vigilant, ראה, and kill, הִכָּה, Amnon once his "heart, לֵב, is merry" (NRSV). These terms are re-employed in connection with Absalom's murder (18:10-15). David's tragedy is that of the father deprived of two of his sons, both heirs apparent.

Joab's refusal to comply with Absalom's request (14:29) fits well in this sequence. What catches the eye is the use of two verbs, שׁלח and בוא. They are employed five and six times respectively in *qal* in 14:29-33 in reference to the

---

kingship. These four verses have only Yahweh as their subject. Thus the DH is bracketed by these verses on Yahweh's will towards Israel. (See also Dt 10:10 and 2 Kgs 13:23, which, by using שׁחת, also contribute to the auspicious-inauspicious opposition at the beginning and end of the DH.) Dt 1:26 is an explicit rebuke, 2:30 an implicit warning. The fatal consequence of the Levite's unwillingness to stay another night in Ju 19:10 is made tangible by the application of the phrase in 19:25 and 20:13. 1 Sam 26:23, David's refusal to lay hand on Yahweh's anointed, is the positive counterpart to 22:17, the guards' refusal to lay hand on Yahweh's priests, slaughtered in the next verse by Doeg. 2 Sam 2:21 I shall discuss later. 23:16f are ambiguous. First they show David's genuine remorse after recognising his despotic disposition. In the next chapter, however, he will reveal a similar despotic attitude towards his people and then repent. In the broader context of 2 Samuel this is reminiscent of 6:10 (note the same term) where he first abandons his centralisation project only to renege in 6:12. Moreover 6:10 is set in the context of a doomed endeavour, hence its effect is similar to that of 14:29 (see my comments on both passages above). The motif thus also serves to reveal David's dilemma about kingship. Asking the what-if question may strengthen the negative perspective of the verse, for seeing later developments and the end of Israelite monarchy in Kings one wonders: Could it have been avoided if David had given a different start to the monarchy from that in 2 Sam 5-7?

[70] חזק marks the violent fates of David's children. See also Absalom's death, introduced with the verb in 18:9. Joab's end, through the use of חזק (see 1 Kgs 2:28, which conspicuously mentions Absalom), also recalls his vicious means, although the key verb marking his violent death (1 Kgs 2:34) is פגע.

[71] This I take as a narrative device of David's unwillingness to leave the royal palace.

Absalom-Joab-David triangle. In 14:29ae Absalom sends for Joab, mentioned by himself in v. 32b. He wants to send Joab to the king (vv. 29, 32e). The subject of the verb בוא changes. First it is Joab refusing (vv. 29dg, 32), but eventually willing (v. 31), to go to Absalom. Following his visit to Absalom he goes to the king (v. 33a), through whose mediation Absalom finally gains entrance (v. 33d). The verbs highlight the pericope's focus on the relationship between the three characters. The irony lies in the fact that, by sticking to his plan and using rather violent means to reach his objective, Absalom prepared his own death through Joab's hands, whose mediation he had used to be rehabilitated. Joab is as much involved in Absalom's rehabilitation as he will be in his murder. The question the narrative raises by this arrangement relates to fate again. Since Absalom's rehabilitation paves the way for his conspiracy, then through civil war to his death and finally to David's mourning for his dead son, one wonders whether the rehabilitation and the reunion of father and son are good or bad, unnecessary or inevitable. And whose fate is foreshadowed here, Absalom's or his father's? Or possibly both? As Nathan foretold, misfortune has caught up with the royal house. However, the worst is yet to come.[72]

In ch. 15 a new "charismatic"[73] emerges. Absalom's appearance, with David

---

[72] The "worse-is-yet-to-come" motif is achieved very artistically, by almost cinematic means and effect, at important junctures. The placing of 13:22 after v. 21, and not v. 20 where it would fit better, gives an ominous ending to the story and an inkling of what will follow. It suggests that "it is Absalom who has the last word" (Fokkelman 1981:113). Stressing Absalom's hatred towards Amnon in v. 22 (see the fourfold reference to Amnon's hatred towards Tamar in v. 15) forebodes the showdown. That Absalom is not yet out of the picture after the murder is hinted at by repeated references to his flight. Thus in 13:34, again not the most appropriate placement, only his escape, nothing else is mentioned. In v. 37 we learn where he fled. The very next verse states the duration of his exile in Geshur, three years. The effect of this accumulating disclosure is: "I will be back!" Note also that the object of David's mourning in v. 37 is ambiguous, just as v. 39 (see different translations), which in turn prepares Absalom's rehabilitation by the king.

[73] In 14:25f Absalom is introduced as a potential charismatic leader (cf. 1 Sam 9:2 on Saul and 16:12 on David). But being a troublemaker without any moral scruples he ends up as a usurper, an unworthy leader. Absalom is not considered charismatic in the narrative as he is not raised by God's spirit. Thus the inverted commas. Strikingly Absalom meets his end "hanging between heaven and earth" (18:9; NRSV) — a metaphor of his failure, as opposed to his father, of not being in touch with either reality and abandoned by both. Furthermore "this emblematizes his fate. The judgment that falls on him and his brothers derives ultimately from both heaven and earth" (Ackerman 1990:51). Also he is not said to have been caught by his hair but by his head (2 Sam 18:9; see Conroy 1978:44, n. 4). Obviously that was the organ causing the trouble by treacherous and deceptive talk. The enigmatic reference to Goliath's head taken by David to Jerusalem might be understood as the utter humiliation and defeat of the very organ that was engaged in defying Yahweh (1 Sam 17:10), which eventually ends up in

still in power, makes the crisis evident. Having said that, I am claiming that the crisis did not start with Absalom's emergence but, as I have argued, with David's gradual inclination towards oriental kingship. Now David must reassert himself as a charismatic leader if he is to survive, over against the emerging Absalom. David becomes aware of the crisis quite late (15:14) — a sign of being out of touch with political and social reality. The king has lived in seclusion from the lives of ordinary Israelites (see 15:3f). This appears to be the only explanation for how Absalom's conspiracy gained so much support unnoticed by the king (cf. Cohen 1971; Crüsemann 1978:94-104). At the same time the revolt will serve as a shake-up. With Absalom's emergence the question is raised: How will David face the challenge? Will he regain control of the situation and overcome the crisis? Will he be swept aside or rather re-emerge with renewed strength?

CHARISMA REKINDLED — THE RE-EMERGENCE OF THE CHARISMATIC, 2 SAMUEL 15:13-19:1

I have claimed that David did not notice Absalom's machinations, his deceptive talk and acts. His son's revolt appears out of the blue and takes the king by surprise. Despite being caught unawares he acts promptly and properly on hearing the bad news (15:14). David decides to abandon the city of royal indulgence (contra Goldingay 2000:288); the emergency prompts the king to action.

The king's predicament is captured in 15:16f by the application of יָצָא, which makes the scene ironic and auspicious at the same time. The "static" king, who has become an oriental despot, is forced to "go out", to flee with his loyal men. On the other hand the potential of David's re-emergence, leading his people in war, is envisioned by the military connotation of the verb.[74] He has not "gone out" since 1 Samuel 19:8. Now he has been given the opportunity to re-establish himself as a charismatic and regain the dynamic quality of leading Israel.

David was not willing to leave Jerusalem at Absalom's urging in 13:25, nor in 15:9 — now seeing Absalom's advance he is forced to go. David is on the run again, as he was in 1 Samuel. King Saul pursued him then; now it is a self-styled king. He refused to grasp power by illicit means then, nor will he now. He is well aware that now he can only be given the kingdom (see Gunn 1975). He subjects himself to God's mercy (15:25f).

That David does not face Absalom's onslaught in Jerusalem has perplexed commentators. I interpret it in line with my argument so far. From the end of ch. 6 he retired to his Jerusalem palace and only moved to the battlefield "under

---

his (Yahweh's?) tent. Seen from this perspective Absalom's end is reminiscent of the Philistine's.

[74] The effect of the introduction to Shimei's cursing in 16:7, יֹצֵא יֹצֵא, is similarly equivocal, because of the lack of reference as to where from. Shimei may well be the narrator's mouthpiece.

duress". I have argued that in this way the narrative portrays David as an oriental king. In ch. 15 he flees, as in the early years, to succeed on the front once again. He cannot overcome the crisis in the Jerusalem palace, the place of indulgence and static, centralised kingship. That Jerusalem has become a royal resort is suggested by David's reference to it as "the city" (Bar-Efrat 1989:40f), which may also explain the king's unwillingness to expose it to a siege and possible destruction. In order to succeed David has to leave the palace.[75]

Despite his unawareness of Absalom's machinations David does not hesitate, but immediately decides to flee (15:14). He does so by giving orders, which he has probably not done for a long time, having been absent from military operations (see also 18:1f). It is he who is in charge at last and not one of his officers (see 10:10f). He realises the danger and prepares to face it. The king is assured of his officials' loyalty (15:15) — without their support he can achieve nothing.

Right at the beginning of the revolt David proves to be an eloquent rhetorician (cf. 1 Sam 16:18). He "persuades" Ittai to serve him while checking his commitment at the same time (15:19-22). Ittai is tested and David is reassured, so the Gittites can march on. Then he sends the ark back to Jerusalem. I have shown David's attempts to centralise and control Israel's religion by bringing the ark to the central shrine as well as planning to build a temple (chs. 6-7). I have claimed that these were the policies of an oriental monarch. Here David is aware that he cannot force Yahweh, the Sovereign of Israel, to accompany and help him (15:25f). His sending back the ark is the very opposite of Israel's superstitious arrogance in 1 Samuel 4:3f, and demonstrates the king's humble reliance on God. David has also re-emerged as a theologian, as he had not been involved in any unequivocal theological statement or action since chs. 7-8.

David acts, however, not only on theological grounds but for political expediency as well. His theological recognition of God's power does not prevent him from taking measures to block his fall (see Brueggemann 1974). He employs the priests[76] as secret agents (vv. 27f) and Hushai to thwart Ahithophel's advice (vv. 32-36). By doing so he acts as a strategist once again, which is a characteristic of a successful charismatic.[77] The effect of David's measures is that by the time Absalom enters the capital David has in a matter of hours cleverly established his reserve there. This stratagem will cause

---

[75] This may symbolically be hinted at by the phrase בֵּית הַמֶּרְחָק, "the distant house", v. 17.

[76] Similarly to the situation here, Abiathar first appeared and helped David when on the run (1 Sam 22:20ff).

[77] Notice the two different readings of 15:31a. The MT reads וְדָוִד הִגִּיד, which may point to David's "prophetic capacity". The alternative reading, ולדוד הוגד, testifies the reliability of David's intelligence. David's wish in 31e comes true by Hushai's appearance in the next verse.

Absalom's conspiracy to collapse and help David back to power. Marcus (1986:164) has observed that in the narrative powerless David often deceives: "In some respects this is only to be expected. If deception is a weapon of the weak against the strong, then David out of office and power will have greater need to dissemble and deceive than he will when he is in power and can more easily get his way." The conspiracy might have taken David by surprise but it also awakened his dozing charismatic spirit. This will prove fatal to Absalom. The fleeing king is setting the stage for his comeback by preparing for the role of military deliverer and by re-assuming his charismatic attributes, introduced at his first appearance.[78] Will he resume acting as a charismatic?

The way in which David regains control of the crisis is also made apparent through narrative devices. On his departure from Jerusalem David meets his loyal people. The encounters divide 15:18-37 into three sections. These are vv. 18-22 (Ittai), 23-29 (the priests) and 30-37 (Hushai), each beginning with a participial-nominal clause. The crisis gradually overpowers the people and they become desperate, as clearly stated at the beginning of sections two and three. In v. 23 it is the "whole countryside" that weeps aloud. Their despair infects David and the fleeing troops, so that in v. 30 they proceed weeping, with heads covered.

Conspicuously the beginning of the next section (16:1) breaks this pattern. 16:1 is different from another viewpoint too. Although it uses עבר, a keyword of the previous sections (see 15:18, 22f), the clause is not nominal but verbal. While nominal clauses are designed to express states, verbal clauses indicate action (see Waltke-O'Connor 1990:#37.6). In other words 15:18, 23 (and 30) hint at some sort of standstill (no movement) due to despair, while 16:1 implies that it has been overcome by showing David in action.[79] Apparently, by organising his reserve with resort to his old deceitful means, David has composed himself and regained hope. As a favourite strategy of his fugitive years he once again manoeuvres in a calculating way. This in turn redraws the map of military possibility. With a "last minute recovery so characteristic of him" (Savran on 1 Kgs 1; 1997:155), shrewd David has regained control — he is back on the stage with charisma rekindled.

In 16:1-14 David encounters two men, both linked to his predecessor. By providing for the king and his men Ziba's intention appears benevolent, but in fact it is selfish as 19:25 (ET 19:24) makes clear. Though Ziba's contention about Mephibosheth is not credible, David betrays no sign of doubt, but makes a rather rash decision. Is the king still suspicious of Mephibosheth or just does not want to waste time arguing? David's motif might be doubtful the result is clear. David earns Ziba's full support, as his privilege depends on David's kingship. David has reinforced his reserve.

As opposed to Ziba, Shimei's intention, words and action are malignant,

---

[78] Hushai's portrayal of David (17:8; cf. 1 Sam 16:18) is fitting.
[79] Cf. the movement-related verbs, each in verbal clauses, in 16:5, 14.

because, as I have claimed, David is not to blame for the fall of Saul's house. From the narrator's point of view, however, they are correct. First Shimei's cursing is introduced by the messenger formula, כה־אמר, 16:7. The cursing thus commends itself in an authoritative way; it accurately fits the state of affairs — of David's house. While being innocent of the fall of his predecessor's house, David is well aware of, and perceives Shimei's accusation as referring to, the failures and sins in his own backyard. This is why he prevents Abishai from killing Shimei (v. 10).

After learning how God, with David's back-up team operating in Jerusalem, is frustrating Absalom's plans, David and his troops arrive at Mahanaim (17:24). "Mahanaim" was introduced in reference to Ish-Bosheth's rival kingship at the beginning of the book (2:8, 12, 29). Fokkelman observes that "Two-camps" is an allusion to the division of Judah and Israel (1990:39; cf. Ackerman 1990:47f). By David's election as king over all Israel the split was healed. With another civil war, however, the wound has been re-opened, and this imagery is reinforced by the association of "Mahanaim". It also serves to make clear that the tables have been turned. The once-aspirant David now runs for his life and sets up his headquarters in the town where his rival used to reside. The new aspirant Absalom begins his conspiracy in Hebron, which a long time ago was David's capital (Polzin 1993:183).

Even in Gilead David has his back-up team, apparently consisting of influential men, Shobi an Ammonite, and two other people, probably Israelites (17:27-29). Did David secure his powerbase through privileges or are these people really loyal to him? Whether they volunteer or are compelled to help him, the king can count on help in adversity.

Preparing for the battle, the king musters his troops and announces (18:2): "I myself will surely march out, יצא, with you." But his men easily persuade him not to (18:3f). He has not been out on a military operation since 10:17. Hence his volunteering, however emphatic, is unconvincing and waiting to be refused. Thus the army marches out, יצא, as usual without their king (18:6), to defeat Israel. Absalom's defeat has been anticipated by the means of David's re-emergence as a charismatic leader: effective rhetoric, strategic planning and deceit. Absalom is no match for his father (Sternberg 1985:360).

Emergency situations such as the Absalom rebellion are opportunities when charismatics can prove themselves. In the crisis David re-emerged as a cunning strategist, organising his reserve and deceiving his powerful enemy. I have claimed that these are signs of charisma rekindled. In one regard, however, David falls short. As opposed to Saul, by not going out to battle he does not resume his status as military king. He re-establishes himself as a charismatic strategist but, by not taking the opportunity presented by the situation, fails to do so as a military king. As I shall argue this will lead to the resumption of his image as an oriental monarch.

POWER RE-ESTABLISHED — "DO I NOT KNOW THAT TODAY I AM KING OVER ISRAEL?" 2 SAMUEL 19:2-20:26

Following his victory David realises that defeated Israel is still alienated, in need of a leader (19:9; ET 19:8). Will they be reconciled to Judah and the king? Will Judah and Israel be reunited? Will the monarchy be restored? To overcome the differences and rivalry the king needs diplomatic skill and sensitivity. It is he who is to take the initiative, which he does in 19:12f (ET 19:11f).

Verbs drive home David's restoration to kingship. שוב (both in *hiphil* and *qal*) stresses the restoration aspect. First it is the northern tribes realising their failure in "bringing the king back" (v. 11; ET 10). Then the king encourages his tribe, Judah, "to bring the king back" (vv. 12f; ET 11f). Finally Judah is won over and asks the king to "return" (v. 15; ET 14), which he does (v. 16; ET 15).

When both parties reach the Jordan, a diplomatic act bordering on ritual takes place. To this end עבר (in *hiphil* and *qal* again) is employed. The men of Judah come to "meet the king and bring him across the Jordan" (v. 15; ET 14). Their eagerness is highlighted by a *figura etymologica*: וְעָבְרָה הָעֲבָרָה לַעֲבִיר (v. 19; ET 18). Just after that, before the king "crossed" the river, Shimei arrives and falls prostate before him (v. 19; ET 18), paying David obeisance.

As mentioned above the narrator gives a ritual flavour to the crossing. The verb עבר is charged with the implications of Israel's first crossing in Joshua 3-4. The crossing "carries with it heavy ritualistic and ideological baggage relating to God's gift of the land to Israel" (Polzin 1989:127; cf. 1980:91-101; 137). Like Israel then, David now arrives home. As Israel received the land, he receives kingship as God's gift. He "refuses to grasp violently what is not yet (or any longer) his, he is prepared to let the initiative pass beyond his control" (Gunn 1975:26f). As Israel's journey ended at the Jordan, so does the king's flight. And as Israel arrived back home after centuries, so does David after weeks on the run. His exile has come to an end.[80]

The ritual effect is enhanced by a reference to Gilgal (2 Sam 19:16; ET 19:15), where centuries ago Israel was circumcised (Josh 5:3ff). After the circumcision Yahweh declared (Josh 5:9; my emphasis), "*Today* I have rolled away the reproach of Egypt from you." The day of his re-installation appears to David to be of special significance. He mentions it three times in v. 23 (ET 22; my emphasis), summing up its relevance in the rhetorical question, "Do I not know that *today* I am king over Israel?" With all the troubles of his rule behind him, at this juncture one ponders what he means by this question. How will he

---

[80] It is worthwhile to refer to Flanagan's conclusion of his analysis of the "representational model", highlighting the negative side of David's re-establishment. David's return to Jerusalem makes the cycle from Moses to David complete. "The days of wilderness and wandering are ended. David is now the symbol of Yahweh's presence in Jerusalem. He is the new Moses, the new Joshua, and the new ark, the permanent representative of Yahweh among the people" (1988:231).

resume reigning? Has his attitude to kingship changed or will he continue to rule as an oriental monarch? Will he take pains to unite the nation? The following narrative will answer these questions.

The first signs are auspicious. As recognised by many commentators (e.g. Conroy 1978:89), David's encounters on the homeward journey (19:17-41; ET 19:16-40) form the counterpart of those on the outward journey (15:19-16:13). When he left Jerusalem Ittai, the priests, Hushai and even doubtful Ziba pledged loyalty to the king, while Shimei revealed his hostility. On the way back David's rule is reaffirmed by Shimei, doubtful Ziba and Mephibosheth and finally by his friend Barzillai. People both loyal and previously hostile to the king unanimously welcome him back. However, there is "an undercurrent of deterioration" of enthusiasm in welcoming the king back, which makes David's re-establishment far from triumphal (Gunn 1980a:113), and suggests beforehand the impending troubles. I shall soon demonstrate how David actively discouraged Israel's enthusiasm.

David rejects Abishai's suggestion and pardons the Benjaminite Shimei (19:23f; ET 19:22f). Even if only by recognising that because of the thousand Benjaminites "it is not an auspicious time for dispatching his rival" (Perdue 1984:78), the king passes the first test, "thus healing for the moment the threatened bond between the two rival houses" (Whedbee 1988:161; cf. Mettinger 1976:118f). When Mephibosheth meets him (19:25-31; ET 19:24-30), however, David resorts to his old scheme of *divide et impera*, so anticipating the measures he is going to take in terms of the rivalry between Israel and Judah. He settles the argument (that he had caused), by reminding "Mephibosheth who now has the real power in Israel" (Perdue 1984:78). His decision is beneficial only to Ziba, while Mephibosheth is deprived. In spite of his humiliation Mephibosheth behaves in a much more dignified way than the king himself (Fokkelman 1981:39). Again David is portrayed with ambiguous intentions, not refraining from malevolence. By failing the second test David is on the way towards being an oriental despot (see Ackerman 1990:51f).

The biggest challenge for him, however, is the controversy between Judah and Israel. The conflict is far from over, the tribes are still on the brink of civil war. The narrator pictures the quarrel (19:42-44; ET 19:41-43), which threatens to become uncontrolled. Nothing indicates that the king reacts by doing or saying anything. David is unconcerned with the tension.[81] The only measure he takes for reunification is Amasa's appointment as general over the army (19:14; ET 19:13). Fokkelman even argues that the king ignorantly stimulates the rivalry by favouring Judah and neglecting Israel (1981:292). David's indifference and insensibility will backfire before long when Sheba incites Israel to secession (20:1). His action and Israel's mutiny are a response to David's inaction. The change of fortunes is aptly summarised: וַיַּעַל כָּל־אִישׁ

---

[81] I do not see why David should in this situation resort to *divide et impera*, as Crüsemann suggests (1978:101), as he, to be sure, occasionally does.

יִשְׂרָאֵל מֵאַחֲרֵי דָוִד אַחֲרֵי שָׁבַע (20:2). The situation is critical with the re-ignition of war looming on the horizon. Why does David not take action? Is he not interested in winning back Israel?

The reason for David's inaction will be transparent once we see what his aspiration in the process of restoration is. This is hinted at by the בַּיִת motif again. 20:3 reads, "When David returned to his palace in Jerusalem, he took the ten concubines..."[82] In 15:16 the king abandoned the palace and his harem, metonyms, I claimed, of oriental kingship and royal image, to face the crisis. With the rebellion overcome he returns to his pre-war disposition, signalled by the same phrases. Thus the revolt is bracketed by the points of departure and arrival.[83] Unfortunately they coincide. In the royal palace David finds his old self, the oriental king. I have shown that this did not happen all of a sudden but rather gradually.

Fokkelman has analysed the narrative also from a psychological point of view. He has noticed that the confrontation with Joab, who drove him out of the safety of the "house" in 19:6 (ET 19:5) after the death of Absalom, makes David desperate to return "home" (19:12; ET 19:11), which is meant "above all personally, on the level of the psyche. [...] The dimension of being a public figure is now too much for him" (1981:296). David not only returned to his pre-war seclusion but withdrew to a fortified privacy. Although his throne is at stake, by 19:44 (ET 19:43) David entirely disappears from the scene, so abandoning the disputing parties "to a polarization process" thus the "schism between Israel and Judah is [...] the direct and expected result of the schismatic David" (Fokkelman 1981:316), i.e. the schism of being father and king (281).[84]

When David realises the threat posed by Sheba, he sends his general, this time Amasa, to fix the problem (20:4). Business resumes as before: David in his palace, Joab running the kingdom and dispatching his rivals. The subsequent narrative (chs. 21-24) will see the king wavering between sceptre and sword again, as in the early days (chs. 5-10). He will occasionally leave the palace for the battlefield (21:15-17) or to build an altar (24:18ff), but primarily will be confined to the palace.

The explicit rationale for this is given in David's last military account (21:15-22), reporting on four battles against the archenemy, the Philistines. When saving their king's life, who, as a sign of not being fit to fight, became

---

[82] Fokkelman nicely observes (1981:321): "Just as the women were unable to safeguard David's house, David has proved unable to preserve the house of Israel." For other devices contrasting the departing and returning David see 321-23, the essence of which might be summed up (322): "David the refugee is composed, strong and adequate versus David the conqueror who is broken, not composed, and inadaqate."

[83] That David will return from where he fled is on occasions indicated, again, by the "house" motif and wordplay. So 19:19 and 42 (ET 19:18, 41) imply that the king's "household" belongs in the "palace".

[84] David's indifference here may contribute to our understanding of the causes of his son's coup.

exhausted, his men appeal to him not to "go out with us to battle" again (v. 17). He complies. The effect is that though v. 22 partly assigns the exploits to David, we know that he has not been in battles for who knows how long (since 10:17; 18:3; 21:17?). What Israel demanded in 1 Samuel 8:6, "a king to lead us", has been abandoned in two generations. But all this is "justified".[85]

David's rule made charisma static. Absalom's revolt, making the crisis evident, made David's charisma dynamic again by rekindling it and setting it in motion. David's irresolute attempt to regain his charismatic self and leadership, however, was frustrated by his own aspiration to be re-established in his palace. The turmoil of Absalom's uprising did not sweep David away. Indeed it served as a shake-up for David to face the reality of his reign and as the backdrop for his charismatic re-emergence.[86] On the other hand David's re-emergence was not an unqualified success. David could probably not re-emerge as the charismatic leader of old, because he had passed the point of no return, i.e. he had irrevocably become accustomed to acting as an oriental despot. He did not re-establish himself as a charismatic leader, independent from anyone else. After his restoration to kingship David is the *old* king sitting in his palace and not venturing military operations on his own. David's attitude to kingship has not changed. To him regaining the throne (19:23; ET 19:22) means resumption of the oriental king concept. He is just as much in need of Joab's unlimited loyalty and determination as he was before the crisis. Now I shall study David's relationship with his strong man.

---

[85] To me 21:19 appears the narrator's "revenge". That is to say, being disillusioned by David's kingship, in an ironic twist he disclaims David's greatest bravery by ascribing it to one of his troops (similarly Goldingay 2000:304). (This is like the fate of Beethoven's Symphony No. 3, originally dedicated to Napoleon but its title-page torn apart in fury when Beethoven learned of Napoleon's coronation.) Adding insult to injury and so augmenting the reader's bafflement, the verbatim correspondence of 21:17bc with 1 Sam 17:50bc seems to suggest that Goliath's vanquisher might have been Abishai (cf. Fokkelman 1990:296). 2 Sam 21:17 is eye-catching from another angle too. It seems to be the counterpart to 1 Sam 3:3, as only these two verses employ כבה and נֵר together in the DH. Right at the beginning of the book, 1 Sam 3:3, "The lamp of God had not yet gone out", casts a ray of hope in the night and prepares the emergence of Samuel, the last judge. Here at the end of the book Israel, by retiring the once military king, takes measures "so that the lamp of Israel will not be extinguished." In this way the book is enclosed between the activities of Samuel, the greatest and last charismatic judge, and David, the paragon of kings. Whether David is the last charismatic king remains to be seen.

[86] Though from a very different perspective, Brueggemann in his "Kingship and Chaos" (1971) studies 2 Sam 15-20 and comes to a similar conclusion by stating that the narrative is about "the disrupting and reestablishing of life and *shalom*. It is the coming of weariness and then the return of strength, the coming of chaos and the return of order" (331; his italics).

Checks of Power

IN THE SHADOW OF THE GENERAL[87]

The most important and complex character in 2 Samuel, besides David, is undoubtedly Joab. It is he who, next to the king, not only appears most frequently, but whose role as the most senior and influential official assigns to him a major narrative role. Indeed on occasions he keeps the king in the background. Thus it is worth studying his role as a "supporting actor", because it may contribute to a better understanding of the relationship between "strong men" and charismatic leaders. As my focus is on David, I will not deal with the question how charismatic Joab was.

Apart from the reference in 26:6, Joab does not appear during David's emergence in 1 Samuel. This is no accident, as I shall show. Joab makes his debut right at the beginning of 2 Samuel, i.e. after David has emerged and is about to assume kingship.[88] His role in the cast will be a dominant one. The phraseology and events introducing him are telling. I shall now analyse his actions, words and the circumstances of his appearances.

Before Joab's introduction in 2 Samuel 2:13 the narrator devotes two sections to the rival kingdoms of Judah and Israel. 2:1-4 reports on David's inquiry of Yahweh and his subsequent election by Judah. In the first half of the section the protagonist is David. He engages in a conversation with Yahweh (v. 1), and it is David who "went up" to Hebron (v. 2) and "took the men who were with him" (v. 3). Subsequently "the men of Judah came to Hebron and there they anointed David king over the house of Judah" (v. 4). Their action is a response to David's previous actions.

As opposed to Judah's king, Israel's does not count for much. In 2:8-11 the protagonist is his general. Abner is the one who "takes him", "brings him over to Mahanaim" (v. 8) and "makes him king" (v. 9). In contrast to his southern rival, Ish-Bosheth is never the subject of a sentence[89] but always the object of Abner's handlings. His weakness is evident in that "he must rule from outside, i.e., beyond the borders in Transjordan" (Flanagan 1988:233).

---

[87] For a similar albeit shorter evaluation of Joab see Ishida 1982:181-85.
[88] Levanon has argued (referred to by Rosenberg 1986:167) that Joab's absence at the beginning of the Absalom revolt (between 15:1 and 18:2) can be explained by the hypothesis that Joab first sided with Absalom and only deserted him when Amasa was "appointed over the army in place of Joab" (17:25). Whether or not this is what historically happened, in narratological terms Joab's absence highlights David's charismatic re-emergence even more — up to the point where the king again abandons military leadership to his general (18:2ff).
[89] Except for 2:10c, "and he reigned two years". We have seen and shall see that he was a puppet. His dependence on his general is nicely highlighted on his next appearance and first action (3:7), when Ish-Bosheth reproaches Abner but is silenced by Abner's anger (3:11). Ish-Bosheth's only action is Michal's extradition in 3:15 (Fokkelman 1990:78).

Chs. 2-3 set the stage for military leadership in the rest of the book. Neither Ish-Bosheth nor, more importantly, David appear in the remainder of ch. 2, which shows the battle as initiated by the two generals, without the knowledge of their respective kings (contra Bietenhard 1998:116f). The account is clearly structured. 2:12-16 narrates Abner and Joab's encounter; vv. 17-23 focus on Abner and Asahel, whereas vv. 24-28 on the two generals again. As the counterpart to the account's beginning, in vv. 29-31 Abner and Joab depart. The major theme is fraternity and fratricide (Polzin 1993:26-35). Who is to blame for the ensuing civil war?

At their encounter, which seems to be pre-arranged, it is Abner who makes the suggestion to have the lads fight; Joab only accepts the proposal (v. 14). Thus Abner appears belligerent and Joab a dupe. Appearances, however, are deceptive. The second paragraph starts with a reference to Zeruiah's three sons, one of them Asahel (2:17). When the battle expands Asahel is eager to kill Abner, who tries twice to dissuade Asahel from chasing him — in vain. Finally Asahel's relentlessness takes its toll. He is killed by Abner, whose two futile dissuasions shed new light on the above question by portraying him rather positively, while Zeruiah's son dies because of his unyielding determination.

The next paragraph is again introduced by a reference to Zeruiah's two sons. When Abner realises the price of the initial "game", he addresses Joab (v. 26): "Don't you realise that this will end in bitterness?" There is more to this question as it can be translated quite differently by taking תִּהְיֶה as second singular masculine: "Don't you realise that you will end in bitterness?" Indeed David, though using another word, characterises the sons of Zeruiah as bitter, קָשִׁים, in 3:39, the word used for the battle in 2:17. Bietenhard considers the term "sons of Zeruiah" a reference to overt or covert opposition to David by them (1998:123-26). The sons of Zeruiah definitely are an epitome of relentlessness as well as of unreliability because of their violent opportunism.[90] The conflict will escalate accordingly. Abner does not realise Joab's relentless animosity towards him (3:27). Unaware of the literal truth of his utterance, Abner announces his own fate. In 2:28 Joab, putting an end to enmity for the time being, calls off the pursuit. It is he who controls events.[91]

The outcome of the battle, reported in 2:30f, epitomises the subsequent war and its outcome. When reading 3:1, the statement of Ish-Bosheth's power gradually diminishing while David's is increasing, the reader ponders how

---

[90] A more detailed study on their personalities would contribute to our understanding of psychological factors, such as paranoia or possible persecution complex (see 3:24f and the "symbolic" use of רדף in 2:24), developed during their early years on the run, which led to their belligerence as well as political expediency.

[91] Just as he did in two other civil wars, 18:16 and 20:22 (see Polzin 1993:183f). Ironically, at "hearing the sound of the trumpet" just after Solomon's anointing (1 Kgs 1:41) Joab is perplexed. The victorious general of civil wars now realises he will be the loser, as it is not he blowing the trumpet.

David's increasing power will materialise with his strong man in charge of the military.

Ch. 3 is about the showdown of the strong men. Before telling it, the narrator pauses for a while to report on David's family. Startlingly these reports are always set in a context of war. I have discussed what the implications of 5:11-16 in its context are. Whereas in 2:2 David was but a tribal chief with a moderate household, in 3:2-5 he has six wives. While Joab is busy on the battlefield David is apparently occupied at home either in founding a family (3:1-5) or in negotiations (3:22). The general is in charge of military operations, while David runs the kingdom.[92]

3:6-21 tells how Israel's general prevails over his king by deciding to go over to David. It is an exposition of v. 6 on Abner's power. 3:22-39 in turn is an exposition of v. 39 on the power of David's general (see Klaus 1999:144-52). 3:6-39 is thus sandwiched between two notes on the generals' power, pointing out that by violent deception Joab proves stronger than his rival. Abner's violent end condemns Joab for belligerence and vengeance. My subsequent reading will confirm that this is Joab's "character zone".

3:39 is interesting also from another point of view. Here the king realises his limited power and the big threat posed by the strong man to his rule.[93] David has taken pains to establish his rule legally and through ethical means. For this reason he had twice refrained from killing Saul, despite his men's urgings (1 Sam 24 and 26). Similarly, by his awareness of the need not to base the kingdom on blood (not by grasping but by being given, in Gunn's terms; 1975), he took great care to clear his name. Hence he had Saul's murderer killed in ch. 1, as he will have Ish-Bosheth's assassins in ch. 4. Though he does demonstrate his innocence of Abner's murder (3:36f), Joab gets away with impunity. The king only feels empowered to make the general participate in the burial (3:31).[94] All in all ethical government is not a viable option with violent and opportunistic strong men in the background. The attempts of charismatic David are frustrated by powerful men behind him. And strong men do not affect only policies and politics but eventually politicians too (cf. Gunn 1975; Perdue 1984).

The change of fortunes and who is at the helm is ominously hinted at in 3:24-26. "Joab's scathing remarks" in vv. 24f

---

[92] Fokkelman (1990:62) has noticed that the rising of the sun in 2:32 "stands for the increasing power of David's kingdom and for the career of Joab".

[93] David's weakness is exposed by literary means too. Similarly to Ish-Bosheth in 3:11 David does not respond to his general's rebuke in 3:24f (and later in 19:5-8, ET 19:4-7, on which see Gunn 1978:40). Notice also that the tension in both cases is caused by Abner's action, i.e. his "going in to" Rizpah (3:7) and David (3:24) respectively.

[94] Could David have ordered Joab to do so after ch. 11? On the sons of Zeruiah as David's adversaries see Gunn 1978:39f.

indicate the weakness of the king's position and also [...] hint at what is to be in the future, and at the array of relationships between David and Joab throughout: the impertinence and insolence of the military commander towards his king, the murders of the military commanders and the prince—Abner, Absalom and Amasa. (Klaus 1999:151)

V. 26 adds: "But David did not know it." This is the first occasion that David does not know something and is tricked by Joab. "In the long run what it is all about is whether or not, how and how far, David is losing grip on developments and is even a prey to continuing, fresh deception" (Fokkelman 1990:101).

Fokkelman's analysis of 2:1-11 (1990:38f) has shown how David makes an effort not to incite civil war and to preserve unity. He did not succeed (3:1), however, because of Joab's belligerent attitude and manoeuvres. Abner and Joab's roles in 2:12-32 hint at and foreshadow the importance of the generals and military — at the same time diminishing that of the rulers. Who is now actually in control? It is the generals' time.[95]

I have claimed that in 2 Samuel David's leadership style changes. With capturing Jerusalem, making it the capital and settling down there David becomes "settled", static as opposed to his dynamic self. He "goes out" more and more rarely to military operations, instead has his general direct them. By ch. 11 David has become an oriental king and Joab his proxy general (see Sternberg 1985:204; Bietenhard 1998:151f). The price of this change is considerable. I have demonstrated what it cost David after having abandoned military leadership for the model of oriental kingship. The other side of the coin, i.e. how Joab became too powerful for the king, was glimpsed above. 3:39 certainly does not record a sudden change in the king-general relationship but a phase in its development.

Sternberg (1985:213-17) has observed how Joab corrects David's hasty order as to how to have Uriah killed. Thanks to Joab's loyalty and shrewdness the affair and Uriah's murder are not revealed. In this way, however, David becomes increasingly indebted to Joab. Later in the narrative it will be Joab again who, by noticing his master's trouble, initiates Absalom's rehabilitation. And it is he who, by realising the political exigency, kills the rebel against the explicit order of the king. Joab acts "in the way in which he perceives to be correct, even if that does not comply with the wishes of the king" (Klaus 1999:175). Although his son's death was painful, David finally benefited from the elimination of Absalom.

Learning that the king mourns his son, the victory turns sour. Joab feels it is time to act. 19:6-9 (ET 19:5-8; cf. Sternberg 1985:252) signals the general's

---

[95] McCarter noticed that, while the two kings are passive, their generals are presented as powerful (1984:122). Fokkelman entitled his discussion of 2:1-3:5 "Who shall have dominion over Israel?" and that of 3:6-39 "The generals keep their kings occupied" (1990).

power. His rebuke can be read as a threat of "open revolt if David does not acknowledge the victory over Absalom and his followers" (Schley 1993:99; cf. Perdue 1984:73). Joab persuades David about the inappropriateness of his grief. He hits the nail on the head by reproaching the king for ignoring his army's victory and having distorted preferences (19:6f; ET 19:5f). "This is a typical example of a description of David's disqualification to be king, in which Joab's influence over the regime increases in inverse proportion to the decline of David's control over the kingship" (Ishida 1982:181). "Joab personifies the relentless state necessity, and, as in the murder of Absalom, here again he serves David's cause better than David himself" (Gressmann 1991:46). Although he is the most loyal man in the kingdom, Fokkelman (1981:338) correctly observes that Joab achieves the *shalom* of the state by destroying his rivals' *shalom*. While David's impotence in 2 Samuel is more or less counterbalanced by his piety, Joab's determination in political and personal matters alike is combined with ruthlessness.

At David's grief the general prompts David into action by using three verbs (19:8; ET 19:7). קוּם, i.e. stop mourning, find strength, face the reality. צֵא, i.e. at least pretend to be a military king by showing yourself, which seems an ironic use of the verb. The king, absent from the battle, is requested to "go out" after it. וְדַבֵּר to the men, i.e. appreciate their effort and victory as they expect you to do. The king at last musters the troops, which demonstrates the state of affairs: the king is in his general's pocket.[96] Bietenhard's conclusion is justified:

> When the narrator sends Joab to warn the king who then complies to the warning there seems to be a certain deception regarding the execution of authority not to be missed: regarding the passivity, the lack or false decision making ability of the ruler, his withdrawal into the private sphere, his abstinence from political and military risks. Responsibility is taken over by Joab: the general becomes the real driving force of David's rule. (1998:311f; AT)

The consequent narrative shows the inextricable entanglement of king and general. At the critical hour of Sheba's revolt, and probably having had enough of Joab's partisan actions,[97] David is determined to start afresh but makes crucial mistakes. He himself does not "go out" and he commissions the wrong man. In the end he is to see the out-of-favour general re-established (20:22f).

To begin with David intends to have his strong man replaced by Amasa

---

[96] As Gunn, albeit in another context, notes (1975:27): "With his appearance at the gate to review the troops we see that it is Joab's perspective, the norms of political necessity, that has won the day."

[97] By accounting for Joab's replacement mainly by Absalom's killing, which in my view was only the last straw, interpreters focus on the personal level and so fail to realise the political implication of David's decision.

(19:14; ET 19:13; 20:4).[98] When Amasa fails to execute the royal order, David turns to Joab's brother, not Joab himself, to recover the situation (20:6). From this point on David's attempt at a new beginning is doomed to failure, as Abishai, probably out of loyalty to Joab, relinquishes leadership to his brother. Joab is too shrewd and powerful to be so easily disposed of. His takeover is signalled by literary means. At David's command "Joab's men and the Kerethites and Pelethites and all the mighty warriors" go out "after him", וַיֵּצְאוּ אַחֲרָיו אַנְשֵׁי יוֹאָב (20:7). Historically they probably followed Abishai, but the text implies Joab's leadership from the beginning. Abishai is not mentioned in the chapter anymore, except for 20:10, and there only second to his brother. Joab's leadership is not questioned by troops or civilians. Standing beside Amasa's body one soldier says (v. 11): "Whoever favours Joab, and whoever is for David, let him follow Joab!" The irony of the words is unmistakable, as, according to Joab's man, whether one "is for David" will be manifest in his following Joab. Subsequently "all the men went on with Joab" (v. 13). Similarly the wise woman in the besieged town consults Joab (vv. 16-21). The story ends with the remark (v. 22), "And Joab went back to the king in Jerusalem." David's attempt to get rid of Joab obviously failed, the general is back in power. Indeed Joab emerges with renewed strength (cf. Schley 1993:99), which is confirmed in the list of royal officials that he heads (v. 23). His placing in the list seems to indicate his influential position, similarly to 8:16.

The end of the story (1 Kgs 1-2) is a paradox. By supporting Adonijah, Joab, for the first time, is on the wrong side. The irony is that David is able to prevail over Joab by having Solomon repay him for his wrongdoings only after his death; David himself will not benefit from the general's elimination.[99] With David dying Joab still commands sufficient authority not to be eliminated straight away, which is indicative of who really has been in charge. David is confined to his bed, at the mercy of his servants, inept and passive, while Joab acts vigorously. Their final hour thus finds David inactive, inert and devoid of his old charismatic ego, whereas Joab is very much his plotting and agile self. This last scene may be taken as a metaphor of their relationship and the development of David's personality.

Joab's character is equivocal. Rosenberg has argued that by murdering Abner, Joab "both contravened Davidic policy and committed a murder that

---

[98] 18:2 may also be a hint at David's attempt to restrict Joab's power (Rosenberg 1986:165).

[99] Fokkelman (1981:388) correctly attributes David's "unfathomable bitterness and rancour" to "the direct David-Joab relationship", but then, unfortunately, restricts it to "Joab's insufferably cruel treatment of his monarch during the latter's first mourning for Absalom and the equally insufferable deed immediately prior to and inseparable from the slaying of Absalom." As we shall see in the next chapter there might have been a political aspect to David's charge to Solomon.

was politically inconvenient to the king". This is repeated in the murder of Amasa. David obviously intended to "merge the feuding regions by incorporating the military leader of the opposed side into his court" which was frustrated by Joab. "In opposing the *union*, Joab in effect was opposing David" (1986:168; his emphasis).

In all these circumstances Joab exhibits cunning political discernment, which is often more accurate than the king's, as well as "parochial clan interest" in his opposition to union. Joab is portrayed as an opportunistic man, using violence to reach his ends[100]. Thus the general decides when and how Absalom should be pardoned or dispatched of. Repairing things broken by David's mismanagement, he is a real pragmatist, loyal to his king. At the same time this configuration reveals a major deficiency at the court. I have claimed that David emerged as a shrewd and, on occasions, deceitful strategist, resorting to any possible legal means to establish himself. That is what a charismatic leader must do. With his mission accomplished and in power (from 2 Sam 2 onwards), however, the king cannot use those qualities especially fit for gaining power. Realising how useful a loyal servant like Joab can be for him, he retires to his palace and has Joab fight his battles. Joab gradually takes over and becomes so powerful that he overshadows the king, who under Joab is no longer in need of his charismatic qualities. In shrewdness,[101] strategic thinking and deception the general is more than a match for his king by ch. 19 — without the necessary ethical disposition and political perspective.

"One of the king's fundamental obligations in the ancient Orient was the defense of his land and people. By relinquishing this function to Joab, David assured his nephew of a nearly unassailable position in the realm" (Schley 1993:102). Later on, by having military operations and dirty jobs done by his general, the king inadvertently transferred power to Joab and entrusted him with confidential matters, such as the plot to kill Uriah. Entrusting confidential matters and transferring power to Joab at the same time deprives the king of influence. The general takes over military leadership and becomes more and more powerful, so that by ch. 19 he overshadows the king. Finally the king finds himself in the general's grip, who overrules David's decision by killing Amasa, thus revealing his "anger against David who removed the faithful servant and replaced him with a rebel" (Hagan 1979:319f). After having reached the point of no return (ch. 11) David is unable to make a new start by eliminating the influential and crafty general — David is too weak to resume military leadership. It is indicative of their relationship that David never objects against Joab's criticisms (Bietenhard 1998:132).

---

[100] Rosenberg (1986:168) claims that Joab seems never to have used violence for its own sake.
[101] The ploy of recruiting the wise woman from Tekoa displays Joab's shrewdness, which David implicitly acknowledges in 14:19. Joab's tactics in delivering the message after the deaths of Uriah (11:19-21) and Absalom (18:19-21) also support this view.

The vicissitudes of David's relationship with Joab "are a sensitive indicator of David's overall power, or lack of it" (Rosenberg 1986:168). While emerging as a charismatic deliverer, David resolved all the difficulties by himself, without overreliance on human help — as a charismatic is supposed to. Joab, however, gradually took over military leadership from David right after his first introduction in 2 Samuel. This observation highlights that David, a successful military leader, as he was in 1 Samuel, did not really need a general of Joab's ilk. The charismatic deliverer did well without the help of strong men. Joab's first appearance in 2 Samuel 2:13ff, however, sets the stage for the remainder of 2 Samuel and David's military operations — David is absent while Joab is the protagonist who kills his antagonists. Without Joab David, now an oriental king, would definitely not have resolved crises in his kingdom; he needed his reckless and violent but loyal general to succeed (cf. Gunn 1978:40; Schley 1993:102).[102]

At the same time, I have claimed, Joab impedes David's efforts of unifying Israel. By lacking the ethical stance and political outlook and being violently opportunistic, Joab appears the opposite, on occasions adverse, character to David. Indeed Provan (1995:111f) suggests that the real reason of Joab's murder was his opposition to Israelite unity. David the king wanted to unite Israel; Joab his partisan general, representing the old guard (Walsh 1996:8), frustrated David's attempts (cf. Simon 1967:210). David's lament, "What do you and I have in common, you sons of Zeruiah?" (2 Sam 16:10; 19:22), remains rhetorical, never to attain resolution. For "these sons of Zeruiah are too strong for" the king (3:39).

Fokkelman drew attention to the conflict between David's fatherhood and being a king. "It is precisely because David cannot clearly keep these two modes of being apart that the erring and stagnating father extinguishes the king, so that a correction is possible from without", i.e. by Joab (1981:281). Subsequently the king is eclipsed and rendered impotent by his strong man. The king's dependence on Joab creates a rival centre of power. David's charismatic leadership diminishes in proportion to Joab's increasing influence. Joab got too big for his boots. A charismatic in someone else's shadow is doomed to misfortune and diminishing influence.

At the beginning of my discussion of Joab I suggested that the general was a "supporting actor" to David. Indeed his character highlights that of David, whose charismatic skills are emphasised first by Joab's absence in 1 Samuel, and then by the general's increasing presence. Joab's role is to facilitate the king's abandonment of charisma and charismatic leadership. In this respect Joab should be nominated for an Academy Award as the best supporting actor.

---

[102] Another interesting aspect is how much Joab, content with military leadership, needed a king like David in order to succeed.

IN THE SHADOW OF THE KING — WIVES

Although the aspect of David's wives as checks on his power may seem a bit unusual, recognising their role may shed light on David's power and personality, as "there is a correspondence between the public and private stages in David's life in terms of his responses to his wives" (Berlin 1982:79).

Despite their number David's wives play a marginal role in the narrative. In fact only three of them are cast in roles of some significance. His first wife is Michal, with the most elaborated personality. As generally recognised David's feelings towards Michal are ambiguous, to say the least. Likely Michal served as a stepping stone in David's career. With his political objectives achieved, she is easily disposed of. Thus Berlin (1982:79) characterises David's relationship with her as a "cold, calculated gaining of power".

Abigail is characterised not only as beautiful but intelligent as well (1 Sam 25:3). She acts and speaks according to this attribute. She is an excellent match for shrewd David, so the match is made. She is to strengthen the self-assurance of the increasingly powerful and popular leader (Berlin 1982:79).

At the beginning of his kingship in Hebron David has only two wives, Ahinoam and Abigail (2 Sam 2:2). During his Hebron years, however, David acquires at least four more wives (3:2-5) and even "more concubines and wives in Jerusalem" (5:13). David's polygamy signals his bent towards oriental kingship, and as such clashes with Yahwistic rule. The established David, as opposed to the emerging one, seems to be interested in physical appearance, possibly in huge quantities, and no longer in interior qualities. Therefore he takes "very beautiful" Bathsheba (11:2), who in 2 Samuel is used for different purposes by different people (Whybray 1968:40), "a complete non-person" and "simply part of the plot" (Berlin 1982:73; contra Nicol 1997). However, by 1 Kings 1-2 Bathsheba becomes a fully-fledged character from an agent (Berlin 1982:75f; 1983:27-30; contra Sternberg 1985:526, n. 10).[103] Apparently, years in the royal court transformed the simple-minded woman into an ambitious plotter.

Rosenberg (1986:152f) has observed that two women changed the fortunes of David at critical points of his career. Abigail's providential intervention prevented his fame from being harmed. Bathsheba was an unintentional *femme fatale* causing change for the worse. What concerns me is that David's relationship with her reveals his "desire to increase his holdings, expand his empire" (Berlin 1982:79). Moreover Nicol (1998) has demonstrated that David's acquiring of Bathsheba is in striking contrast to that of Abigail, connoting the change in the king's character and methods, so that "one can hardly avoid the conclusion that power and indolence can corrupt even one who began so promisingly as David" (140).

---

[103] To Berlin's perceptive analysis of Adonijah's request (75f) I would add that the use of על ("on behalf" or, alternatively, "against") in 1 Kgs 2:18f makes the scene even more ambiguous and Berlin's interpretation of Bathsheba as a schemer credible.

David's ageing, culminating in dementia, is best captured in 1 Kings 1. Ackerman (1990) has shown how the old king's not knowing of Abishag denotes his incompetence on several levels. In 1:18 "David does not know: he does not know Abishag as he had once known Bathsheba; nor does he know of Adonijah's ambitious preparations for coronation, because the waning king does not know good and evil" (Ackerman 1990:53). Preston has also pointed out the ironies that abound in David's relationship with Abishag.

> First, unlike Saul, who dies heroically on the battlefield, David, the celebrated soldier, lies unheroically dying in a bed, old and infirm, but in oriental despot fashion, comforted by a girl from the harem. But the irony increases, for he is not comforted in a sexual way, for David "knew her not". He is instead nursed by a beautiful girl whom he is not physically able "to know". The final irony, however, is that the punishment fits the crime. The "hot" David who seduces Bathsheba, and thereby sets in motion his downfall, suffers from cold chills, not able to repeat his sexual prowess any more effectively than his former military prowess. (1982:43)

In short David's impotence makes his "loss of control of the kingship" visible (Berlin 1982:79).

Alter (1981:61) has suggested that the total absence of a betrothal scene in the David narrative "may be a deliberate ploy of characterization and thematic argument." Since three of David's premarital episodes with women involve bloodshed, with the suppression of the pastoral motif (61), I would submit that marriage and wives for David are not essential and of no "sentimental value", but rather means to reach his objectives. The lack of a betrothal scene may anticipate David's career and relationship to women, just as Saul's parting with the girls and hurrying after Samuel in 1 Samuel 9 foreshadows Saul's fate (see Alter 1981:61f). Furthermore despite having several wives and concubines David's troubled relationship with them is well-known. In 1 Samuel 21:6 (ET 21:5) David claims that "women have been kept from us as always when I go on an expedition" (NRSV). It seems that David's life is a "constant expedition", *ipso facto* he is "womanless", as Clines puts it (1995:225). Indeed David does well without women (226f).

I have claimed that in 2 Samuel David opts for the oriental monarch image and abandons military leadership and with it his strategic shrewdness, which are subsequently appropriated by Joab. As a narrative clue for this development Michal is used to gain power, then clever Abigail is replaced by Bathsheba in 2 Samuel 11. This latter exchange might also be taken as the effect of David's psychological transformation under Joab's domination. If one is dominated by someone else, for example in his career, he will likely seek to compensate in his marriage by trying to assert himself as the master. Abigail's replacement by Bathsheba is certainly a sign of David's change in character, attitude and preferences — *noscitur e socio* (Sternberg 1985:357f; cf. Levenson 1982:237). Finally in 1 Kings 1-2 an oriental monarch is dying. Here David is reduced to utter impotence in every respect.

HOLY MEN — PROPHETS AND PRIESTS

Now I shall examine David's relationship to holy men, priests and, first and foremost, prophets, influential officials as they were. The narrative mentions three prophets — Samuel, Gad and Nathan. The first prophet in David's life is Samuel. His significance as the kingmaker anointing David is beyond doubt. But I have also claimed that his influence on David must have been limited, as he almost disappears after 1 Samuel 16. Thus David's anointing suggests that

> YHWH is impatient at Samuel's grief [for Saul] because he is still, for the old incomprehensible reasons, bent on having a real king. He is determined that Samuel will not a second time get a king he can control. This goes a long way toward explaining the kingmaking in 16:1-13, where Samuel is deprived of any real control over or even understanding of what is going on. He is needed as a functionary: continuity still requires that the last judge be the kingmaker. But this will be a new kind of king, one who is beyond Samuel's reach. (Jobling 1998:87)

The end of 1 Samuel 19, where David, as opposed to Saul, is not said to have been involved in the prophesying, reaffirms the impression that David managed to remain untouched by Samuel's manipulation and prophetic power. Miscall's observation that Samuel never speaks to David (1983:99) strengthens the argument. All in all in 1 Samuel David is presented as an independent hence increasingly successful and influential character — a charismatic leader.

Gad is first introduced in 1 Samuel 22:5, advising David in a dire situation. We do not know the historical significance of Gad's advice. What is important, however, is that by making David operate in Judah, Gad's counsel paves the way for David's influence and election. It also makes clear that at critical points in his life David could count on his aides' — on occasions critical — support. This also holds for 2 Samuel 24, where David faces God's punishment because of his oriental monarch undertaking. Gad, as opposed to Nathan, is critical about oriental kingship, and stops the king. Gad is for a Yahwistic monarchy.

Nathan's role is more ambiguous than Gad's. I have claimed that he is too uncritical, indeed supportive towards the king's centralisation project in 2 Samuel 7:3. Prompted by God, however, he corrects his mistake. In 1 Kings 1 Nathan plays the role of an influential court official, who, with Bathsheba's help, gets his way by deceiving the ageing king (Gunn 1975:30ff). On the other hand his courage in confronting the oriental monarch in 2 Samuel 12 is commendable.

My discussion of Abiathar and Zadok, the two priests, will be brief. After the massacre of the Shilohite priests Abiathar escapes (1 Sam 22:20) with the ephod, which he brings to David. This will profit David, who, by being able to inquire of God via the ephod, eludes Saul (1 Sam 23:9-13). Later Abiathar and Zadok become priests in the court (2 Sam 8:17; 20:25), obviously an influential position. During the revolt they successfully conspire against Absalom, confirming David's political insight in commissioning them.

SUMMARY

During his emergence David distinguishes himself in establishing the image of an independent charismatic leader. In 2 Samuel this picture changes in that David, by swapping military leadership for oriental kingship, is increasingly controlled by Joab and has very limited power. Abigail's disappearance and Bathsheba's influence may point in the same direction, as companions reveal each other's character. David was eclipsed by his general. Indeed in a sense Joab replaced Samuel by diminishing David as a military leader, while Saul remained a military king even under the prophet's mentorship, since Samuel did not lay claim to military leadership.

David's court prophets were also influential aides, who to a great extent retained their integrity. So even in the turmoil of the Absalom revolt, David could count on advisers, supporters and friends. No need to fear the king seems to have limited the prophets or prevented them from their prophetic activities when confronting him. Apparently David's was not an arrogant independence. Unlike Samuel to Saul, neither Nathan in 2 Samuel 12 (cf. v. 9 and 1 Sam 15:19) nor Gad behaved as the king's mentor. They only intervened when David's oriental king image threatened Yahwistic kingship, but they did not want to control the king. David was able throughout to maintain his independence from prophets whereas Saul was not.[104] Was it a sort of separation of state and religion, secular and religious authorities?

Even though the negative effect of David's reliance on Joab has been demonstrated, the other side of the coin has been noticed by Schley:

> It was probably one of the virtues of David's reign that he was surrounded by strong, independent lieutenants such as Joab, Abishai, and Nathan—men who could not be cowed, were possessed of their own integrity, and were willing to rely on their own judgment. (1993:103f)

Administration

Here I shall compare the lists of David's officials, in 2 Samuel 20:23-26 and 2 Samuel 8:16-18, in the light of what I have said. I hope to gain more insight into David's reign in this way. Both lists are headed by the senior officer of the monarchy. I claimed above that 20:23 implies Joab's restored position as the commander-in-chief of all the military. Yet David might have succeeded to limit his influence by strengthening Benaiah's position. This is suggested by

---

[104] I refer here to Polzin's insightful discussion of "Saul, David, and Prophecy" (1989:183-86), with which I am, however, not in total agreement, as he is generally somewhat biased towards prophecy and prophets.

Benaiah's occupying the second place, next to Joab in 20:23, (in 8:18 he was the fifth out of six).

Adoram's mention in 20:24, the only addition to the list in ch. 8, as the third officer of the monarchy may hint at a change in priorities in David's domestic policies. Whereas there is no reference in ch. 20 to David's executing justice, in contrast to 8:15, a royal officer in charge of forced labour, whether of Israelites or Canaanites, obviously damages the reputation of a "righteous king". Israel's king is engrossed in building projects, and his empire "is just like the Egypt from which Israel once escaped" (Goldingay 2000:299).

The roles of Jehoshaphat, Sheva, Zadok and Abiathar seem to be unchanged (I am not dealing with textual problems). Not so the "priests", if that is the correct reading; in 8:18 they are David's sons, whereas in 20:26 an unknown Ira is David's priest. 8:18 is a crux. Armerding (1975) examines it, along with other references to royal priests, in the context of the ideology of royal priesthood and considers this office positively. Fokkelman represents a different view by regarding the verse as "the first hint of David's approaching *hubris*. In which case the priesthood of his sons is a sequel to the corruption of the sons of two former people of integrity in Samuel, Eli and Samuel" (1990:262f; his italics). I am inclined to assess the office of David's sons similarly, but I should admit there is no explicit clue to this. Whether priests or palace stewards (so Wenham 1975) it is dangerously close to a family business, thus I see in it an extension of David's centralisation project. His sons being in the first list but missing from the second may suggest that David removed them from office. Or were they Amnon and Absalom? Whoever they were David did not replace them with royals — maybe a hint at his changed attitude.

The lists of David's officials may be regarded as confirmation of a double-sided David. While amending in one regard, he could neither overcome his imperial attitude in another nor could he successfully counterbalance Joab's power. This also sheds light on David's attitude, conscious or not, to royal power. Rosenberg (1986:127) remarks on 2 Samuel 11:1: "The rational and bureaucratic mode of statecraft that is David's specific innovation has better uses for the king than the charismatic and warlord functions that elevate a man to kingship in the first place."[105] In other words powerful oriental king David is not only the very opposite of young charismatic David but, as often happens with leaders who have emerged to power from a low status, he has become an obstacle to charismatic initiatives.

A Yahwist Military King or an Oriental Despot? — The Dilemma of the Charismatic

I have claimed that in 2 Samuel David's commitment to military leadership is challenged by the concept of oriental kingship. He wavers between the two and

---

[105] In Rosenberg's view this is positive, in mine rather negative.

frequently succumbs to the latter. Since David's dilemma in my view is an overarching theme in 2 Samuel, elaborating on it could prove insightful. I shall refrain from repeating what has been said so far. Instead I shall study the aspect of military versus oriental kingship by analysing 2 Samuel 21-24, a section which has been treated even by scholars of the synchronic approach rather unworthily (see Sternberg 1985:40, 42; Fokkelman 1990:13f). Through my analysis I hope to prove that the so-called "appendix" is an organic part of the David story and to gain a new understanding of David's rule and charismatic leadership.

Flanagan has observed (1983:361) that 5:13-8:18 is "a single literary unit woven together by content and structure". In his 1988 article Brueggemann elaborated on Flanagan's observation and contrasted the six units of 5:13-8:18 with the six in chs. 21-24. Klement (2000) has shown the thematic and structural coherence of chs. 21-24 with the preceding narrative. The following structuring is informed by Flanagan, Brueggemann and Childs (1979:273) and sheds light on the thematic arrangement of the units and their purpose.

The beginning of David's rule, 5:13-8:18:

A David's sons, 5:13-16
   B David's wars with the Philistines, 5:17-25
      C Transfer of the ark (centralisation-legitimation), 6:1-23
      C' Dynastic oracle (centralisation-legitimation), 7:1-29
   B' David's wars (general account), 8:1-14
A' David's officers, 8:15-18

The end of David's rule, chs. 21-24:

A Yahweh's wrath against Israel — due to Saul's violation of a covenant, 21:1-14
   B David's heroes in the Philistine wars, 21:15-22
      C David's psalm (legitimation), 22:1-51
      C' David's oracle (legitimation), 23:1-7
   B' David's heroes (general account), 23:8-39
A' Yahweh's wrath against Israel — due to David's violation of the covenant, 24:1-25

To sufficiently appreciate the first unit of 2 Samuel 21-24 and understand its main theme and contribution to the section and the book, I shall read it closely. 21:1-14 narrates an event of David's latter reign, definitely after ch. 9 (see 21:7).[106] First it is clear that Yahweh is angry because of Saul's destructive, שמד (v. 5), zeal against the Gibeonites, with whom Israel had made a treaty

---

[106] Contra Noll (1997:126), whose arguments, due to ignorance of basic textual evidence, are often circumstantial.

pledged by an oath, שׁבע (v. 2; cf. Josh 9:15). Therefore Yahweh's anger should be propitiated, and the Gibeonites come up with the suggestion to have seven descendants of Saul killed, to which David agrees (vv. 5f). We remember, however, that in 1 Samuel 24:22f (ET 24:21f) David also made a vow, שׁבע, not to wipe out, שׁמד, in contrast to oriental kings' practice, Saul's family when he becomes king. The king hands seven Saulides over to the Gibeonites, with Jonathan's son Mephibosheth spared, in line with his own oath (1 Sam 20:15-17). The Gibeonites then execute them, which, Gunn (1980:93-95) suggests, 1 Samuel 24:5 (ET 24:4) has envisaged by having David cut off Saul's seed in a symbolic way. Now can Saul's breach of an oath be undone and Yahweh be reconciled by breach of another oath on David's part?

Fokkelman (1990:285) pointed out that in v. 9 the plot comes to a conclusion. Yet the story is not concluded but carries on. "Paradoxically the end of the story is not the end but conceals a beginning" (284), as both v. 9, concluding the first plot, and v. 10, starting off the second plot, refer to "the beginning of the harvest", thus offering "a ray of hope" (285). The second plot starts with the unexpected appearance of two of the victims' mothers. Rizpah keeps vigil over the bodies "till the rain poured down from the heavens" (v. 10), which suggests that the rain arrives due to Rizpah's wake, putting an end to the famine (cf. Exum 1992:112f). What makes Rizpah act like this, asks Fokkelman. "She is not only motivated by the forces of yesterday and today (motherhood), but also by the decision to defy the present (the animals!) with an eye to the goal of tomorrow", which is decent burial, the prerequisite of rest for the soul (1990:286).

When news reaches David about Rizpah, he acts — out of compassion he demonstrates loyalty to Saul's house (vv. 11-14). The story ends with the note on the expiation. But the question arises: is Yahweh reconciled because of the sacrifice of the Saulides or rather because of the respectful burial of Saul, Jonathan and the seven sons? Apparently the sacrifice of the Saulides was what Yahweh expected. It appeased his anger. The resolution does not, however, come in v. 9, i.e. when the execution is done, but is anticipated in v. 10 and explicitly stated in 14d, which implies that Yahweh's reconciliation was brought about by the homage done to the Saulides, including Saul and Jonathan (see Fokkelman 1990:289f).[107]

The portrayal of David is double-sided. He relies on God and compassionately cares for his people — by breaking the oath to the victims' father (see also Exum 1992:112) as well as, apparently, Deuteronomy 21:22f. The story also presents two facets of God's character. In these narrated events both his inexplicable wrath and merciful reconciliation play a part. These facets of God and the king will figure as implicit themes in ch. 24.

---

[107] Saul finally rests in peace, which is "an illustration of the logical evolution toward comedy in the Bible" (Exum and Whedbee 1985:37, n. 12). Has Yahweh finally been reconciled to the first king granting his soul repose?

Now I turn to David's heroes. Regarding the list in 21:15-22 I claimed above that it is a disclaimer of David's military leadership. Indeed according to Goldingay the list

> threaten[s] to make David's story deconstruct. If David has one unequivocal achievement, it is in removing the Philistine threat. He gave the people military security. Except that here he is fighting Philistines again. And they are in exactly the same position that they were in when David first appeared as a fighter. They are represented by huge warriors kitted out with monumental shields and spears. Back at the beginning David faced them with energy and enthusiasm. But now David gets tired (21:15). (2000:304)

23:8-24:25, by juxtaposing two accounts of leadership, specifically talks about the aspect of military leadership versus oriental kingship. 23:8-39 is divided into two parts; vv. 8-23 report on the bravery of some of the mighty men, probably during the battles with the Philistines at David's emergence or early rule, while vv. 24-39 list their names. The list is headed by Asahel (v. 24), of whose death we read in ch. 2, and concludes with Uriah (v. 39), the only other mighty man reported killed in 2 Samuel. Thus the list would chronologically fit better before ch. 2, when Asahel was still alive, and certainly before ch. 11, with Uriah still living.

Most of the thirty-seven, except for Abishai (*passim*), Benaiah (20:23), Asahel (ch. 2), Uriah (ch. 11), are nowhere else referred to in 2 Samuel. Given the importance of David's military operations, the extraordinary deeds of the mighty men and their significance, implied by the phrase "the LORD brought about a great victory" (23:10, 12), this is inexplicable. This "failure" of the narrator is compounded by further obscurities such as who the Three were. 23:8-11 makes clear that the Three consisted of Josheb-Basshebeth, Eleazar and Shammah. But contrary to the assertion of v. 8, that the "chief of the Three" was Josheb-Basshebeth, v. 18 assigns this function to Abishai. Fokkelman considers the three in vv. 13-17, whose "identity is kept from us of all things" (1990:300), different from the Three of vv. 8-12. Who were the Three? A special unit or just warriors of exceptional bravery (cf. Schley 1990)? Why then does Benaiah not belong to them, despite his valour (23:20f) and being the chief of the bodyguard later (20:23)? Apart from textual problems the exact number of the Thirty, given as thirty-seven in 23:39, is rather problematic (see translations). Why are Jashen's sons not named and how many were they (23:32)? Finally why is the account placed here?

As I have argued, in 2 Samuel David wavers between military and oriental kingships. Military exploits are limited to a minimum (2 Sam 10; 21:15-22; with ch. 8 being a general overview), as opposed to 1 Samuel (17; 18; 23-27; 30), while oriental kingship gains the upper hand. The scattered placement of the accounts of David's military operations in 2 Samuel is also noteworthy. My suggestion is that the obscurity of 23:8-39 is a literary technique reflecting on

David's failure to perform sufficient and consistently distributed military action, in order to enhance and ensure his military leader image as well as the import of his mighty men. To put it differently the narrator's major focus is on how David established his oriental kingship, which did not allow for digressions on military exploits and heroes. With the monarchy established Yahweh's deliverance through military bravery is not needed anymore (see 23:10, 12, compared with 8:6, 14 by Fokkelman 1990:301), indeed a standing army conscripted via a census makes it redundant. The narrator, however, is uncomfortable with the result and feels compelled to devote a paragraph to David's heroes, who helped him and the kingdom emerge. He is at a loss because he has had no time and space for this, as he has been busy in reporting on David's wavering between military and oriental kingship and his gradual replacement by Joab. At last the narrator commemorates the mighty men, at the same time making clear the ambiguity and irony of their service to the kingdom. The Thirty became a legend, nostalgically remembered after they were no longer needed by the bureaucratic establishment of the monarchy. As signs of this the identity of the Thirty and, more to the point, the Three, became obscure, like the names of Jashen's sons, as if they had fallen into oblivion. The frame may suggest that the thirty odd mighty men are as dead as the two men at the head and foot of the list — the inclusio of the mighty men by the two killed, Asahel and Uriah, marks the end of an army based on bravery.[108]

Before turning to ch. 24 I notice that 23:13-17 foreshadowed a despotic David, unconcerned with his subjects' lives. This is the theme of 24:1-9.[109] The chapter starts with וַיֹּסֶף אַף־יְהוָה לַחֲרוֹת בְּיִשְׂרָאֵל. My question is: why is God angry again? What is the reference point to וַיֹּסֶף? Besides its obvious reference to 21:1-14 (see Polzin 1993:209-12) it may well refer back to 6:1, as in both cases Yahweh's punishment is provoked by David's attempts to enhance his oriental king !image. In ch. 6 David tried to achieve glory by centralising religion. Here he "acts like a tyrannical monarch capable of taxing production and conscripting soldiers and forced labor" (Flanagan 1988:266). This is also in startling contrast to his reliance on Yahweh's deliverance in 5:17ff. It meets with the disapproval of Yahweh. Joab also dislikes the idea. "The king's word, however, overruled Joab" (24:4). It is ironic that David's will proves stronger than Joab's and so causes a national disaster, as this is the only case when David prevails over Joab.

---

[108] The effect of 23:8-39 is similar to Ju 15:20 read together with 16:31. Had Samson continued his activity before 15:20, he would have been the greatest judge, not as equivocal as he becomes after 15:20. Had David continued his military leadership in the fashion of 1 Samuel, he would not have become an oriental despot in the shadow of his general.

[109] Fokkelman in his discussion of ch. 24 focuses on God's punishment and compassion (1990:308-31), which in my interpretation are activated by David's attitude of an oriental monarch and his piety respectively.

Between Charismatic Military Leadership and Oriental Kingship 161

To better appreciate the chapter and see with what וַיֹּסֶף is linked, the preceding chapter should not be forgotten. The theme of the previous section was David's warriors and their individual exploits, probably — I have claimed — dating back to the period of David's emergence. Since military actions and heroism were rendered unnecessary and unprofitable by and for David's oriental kingship, 23:8-39 has an ironically nostalgic or disenchanting effect: once David has established himself, no individual heroism is possible or desired. Given the linear sequence of the narrative, ch. 24 might be interpreted from this angle, i.e. the punishment came about because of God's anger and disillusionment at David's failure as a military king. That oriental kingship and military leadership are closely related is seen in 24:2 where the king is intent on setting up a standing army, replacing his mighty men's exploits. By relying on conscripts the "mighty-warriors" style of warfare is rendered redundant.

Waking up to what he has done, David humbly repents (v. 10).[110] When confronted by Gad he opts for a plague and not for a revolt (24:13f). "Rather than protect his people from disaster, David protects himself" (Linden 2000:193). This confirms that David is here an old monarch, unwilling to risk another rebellion, when on the run he may re-emerge and re-establish himself as a charismatic leader. His option, may it sound ever so pious, is that of a selfish oriental despot, who does not care for his people but wants to spare himself (Fokkelman 1990:326; Steussy 1999:64). Indeed Schenker (1982) argues that by not resisting God's incitement David misses the opportunity to reconcile Israel with Yahweh. In his conclusion Schenker regards the story as a "mirror for princes" (*Fürstenspiegel*):

> What makes a king a king is not his power but his compassion for his people. David became king when he renounced his royal dignity in order to save his people from disintegration. In this he was much more a king than when he, in the census, had his power determined with no regard to his people's increasing trouble at this. (28; AT)

---

[110] In his comment on 24:10 Brueggemann remarks (1990a:104, n. 13): "In this text, David has the remarkable and inexplicable capacity to be aware on his own of his violation of torah. This is unlike 2 Samuel 12, where his self-deception is much greater. In ch. 12, the persuasive, weighty confrontation of Nathan is required to make the point of David's guilt. This contrast between chapters 12 and 24 suggests that the David offered in the appendices is much more open to the old covenantal traditions that these chapters advocate." Is this openness "to the old covenantal traditions", that fell into oblivion in the reigns of his successors, why David, and not one of his successors, became the ideal king for Israel? It needs to be noted too that the idea of David as the best king might be based on popular perception. I shall make clear what I mean by an analogy. At the very beginning of the film industry there were only a few icons, like Charlie Chaplin, James Dean, Audrey Hepburn or Brigitte Bardot. With the commercialisation of the film industry now there are innumerable film stars, indeed every year brings new ones, but no icons. Is this similar with kings?

Finally the slaughter causes the king to repent (v. 17). Brueggemann (1990a:106) has noticed the intensified repentance of the confession. "In verse 10, David prayed for himself. Now, however, in verse 17, David gets beyond himself and prays for his people, for the ones against whom in verse 1, Yahweh had the initial anger." God acts out of anger in the first half of the chapter, but appears compassionate in the second, which resonates with 21:1-14.

The two psalms form the structural climax of the section, paralleling the inclusio; ch. 22 is juxtaposed with 23:1-7, David's early concept of ruling to that of his older days. The first psalm depicts a military deliverer, loyal to and relying on Yahweh. "David was able to work out his salvation because God was at work in him. God trained his hands for war (22:35). David won because he fought. But he won because God made him a fighter" (Goldingay 2000:306). Unfortunately, this attitude on David's part, as the inscription implies, did not last long.

The imagery of ch. 22, David's reliance on God's intervention arriving with terror and might in due time, is supported by its strategic placement. It is the parallel to Hannah's Song (1 Sam 2:1-10), echoing some of the phrases there (Childs 1979:272; Gordon 1984:26). Both songs point to a just king, who rose after Hannah's Song but diminished before David's. Outside the inclusio Israel is in dire and chaotic situations, first desiring a king (1 Sam 1; see Polzin 1989:18-54) then living with one — for better and for worse (2 Sam 23-24).

As opposed to 2 Samuel 22,[111] "the last words of David" (23:1-7) portray an old monarch concerned with power. While the focus of ch. 22 was on Yahweh and his deliverance (see Watts 1992:104), 23:1-7 stresses the king's role. Keil (1971:485) recognised that 23:1f "rests, both as to form and substance, upon the last sayings of Balaam concerning the future history of Israel". Not only the introduction but the whole poem might best be interpreted against the backdrop of Numbers 24:3-19. Balaam's oracle concerns Israel's future glory. God's people will live in peace and prosper (Num 5-7). In their strength they will conquer hostile nations (Num 8-9). Numbers 24:17-19 prophesies of a king who will utterly defeat Moab and Edom.

David's oracle in 2 Samuel 23:1-7 draws upon that of Balaam. However, David's main concern, unlike that of the Balaam oracle, is the justification of rule. He speaks of his person (v. 1-3), his house[112] and salvation (v. 5). The "evil men" (v. 6) are probably his personal enemies. David never mentions his people over which he rules; national aspects of government and military

---

[111] On the similarities between the two hymns see Noll 1997:155f; on the startling contrasts see Polzin 1993:204f. I do not share Polzin's negative view of ch. 22 but think the two hymns are juxtaposed to highlight David's opposing views at the beginning and end of his reign.

[112] Richardson (1971:259) restores 23:5a as "Truly, my house is established, כון, by God". If this is the correct reading, it corroborates my conclusion of a self-centered king (see my comments on כון above).

deliverance are totally ignored, unlike in ch. 22. Whether the psalm "is a self-satisfied reflection of the aging monarch" (Kruse 1985:148) or "wishful thinking" (Eslinger 1994:91, n. 2), the difference is trivial. Old David succeeds to spiritualise Balaam's oracle for his grandeur.

The last encounter with David in 2 Samuel reinforces the previous observations. At the (narrative) end of his rule David's picture is as double-sided as it has been throughout the book. The oriental monarch (24:1-9), abandoning military leadership and Yahweh's military intervention through a plan to establish a standing army (24:2), is juxtaposed with a pious Yahwist king (vv. 10-25; cf. Preston 1982:40f). The last chapter of 2 Samuel succinctly sums up the cost of the monarchy. At the end of his reign David realises the expense of oriental monarchy and the toll levied on the people for his grandiose projects. "This means that dramatically (not chronologically) the 'good' David is the early David, the one who lived prior to the seduction of the royal ideology" (Brueggemann 1988:394).[113] The contrast between young and old David is further substantiated by the discrepancy between his oriental kingship and how he taught King Saul the art of ruling in 1 Samuel 24 and 26 (see Rosenberg 1986:136f).

In 1-2 Samuel David is presented as a complex character, one who goes through some development. The emerging David is a strategist, occasionally

> a self-serving opportunist who nevertheless is able to charm story-bound characters and reader alike. [...] Ultimately, however, David's self-service becomes the reigning paradigm, and the narrative's dynamic follows the agenda set by his greed. The deeper David ensnares himself, the more of his ugly side surfaces, until the shrewd statesman has become an irrational murderer. (Noll 1997:61)

The thematic similitude and structural correspondence of the units of 2 Samuel 5:13-8:18 and chs. 21-24 are evident. I have demonstrated David's mixed attitude towards kingship. His dilemma between oriental kingship and military leadership is underlined in both units, with the old David much more susceptible to oriental despotism, which is further accentuated in 1 Kings 1-2. The four closing chapters of 2 Samuel thus constitute an "ending, or a series of endings", which can even be regarded as "a series of fragments, and their fragmentariness reflects the fragmentation of the man who is their focus" (Goldingay 2000:300). Rosenberg's observation (1986:173) on the Uriah affair holds true for the whole of 2 Samuel: "David the soldier, in retreat from soldiering at least since his elegy for Jonathan, has fully withdrawn behind the

---

[113] I disagree with nearly every observation of Brueggemann, because I find them more fanciful and tendentious than, as he claims (385), derived from the text, but, surprisingly, share his conclusion. This criticism also holds true of his 1990a:86-115.

mask of David the king."[114] Murray's remark on 2 Samuel 5-7 (1998:231) holds true of the whole of David's rule: "When at war in 5.17-25 David seems most at home with Yahweh, but his return home in 2 Samuel 6 and 7 is to a kind of war with Yahweh."

By having the principal discussion of David's clashing attitudes towards kingship embraced by the two units in 2 Samuel, the narrator's view has also become clearer: If a charismatic military deliverer does not lead his troops in battle but acts as an oriental king, God's dissatisfaction and wrath will inevitably follow.

Charisma and Character — The Deuteronomistic Criterion

David was elected by Yahweh and his spirit was bestowed upon him; this is beyond doubt. Other points are more equivocal. In 1 Samuel David's reliance on Yahweh's deliverance is tangible. Even though a shrewd strategist himself, David refuses to take violent action to secure the throne. Yahweh in his turn assists his undertakings, and everyone recognises this. In 2 Samuel David's Yahwistic stance might be seen in his hamstringing the chariot horses (8:4). On the other hand his bent towards oriental kingship is visible in his census.

The area where David comes worst off is obviously that of marriage. Even if he did not eventually resort to violence to get his way against Nabal, the outcome of the story is indicative of the way and the means with which David obtains women. His use of violent means in remarrying Michal and taking Bathsheba is indisputable. Taking Bathsheba and eliminating her husband were caused by the king's lust. David's reunion with Michal was politically motivated. David's feelings towards her (see Jobling 1998:159), and all his wives, are just as opaque as his political motivation.

More important is the question of polygamy. As I have noted it is not until David is elected king of Israel that he acquires a harem. While on the run David could not afford many wives, and I have argued that being powerless and charismatic correlate. The increasing number of wives and concubines, many of them of Canaanite origin, signals David's abandonment of charismatic Yahwistic kingship and his surrender to the oriental king image. Naturally many wives bear many sons, which in turn brings conflict to the royal house. Is the prohibition of many wives partly aimed at preventing warring heirs? Nurturing the oriental king image is an expensive business. Although we do not read any explicit condemnation of David's affluence, implicit denunciations might be found: David's children led a privileged royal lifestyle, never rebuked by their father.

---

[114] I refer here to Schwartz's claim (1991:45f) that sexual violence in David's house is not the public consequence of the king's private sin, but rather "politics and sexuality are so deeply and complexly integrated as to be one, and it is anachronistic to even understand them as two different spheres of life" (46).

Clearly Deuteronomy 17 is not a moralist warning, but rather concerned with royal power. Reliance on military power, in addition to costing much, renders Yahweh's intervention redundant. Similarly a harem and an affluent lifestyle are declarations of royal power, hence in conflict with what in fact makes a kingdom strong.

I stated above that emergency situations like the Absalom rebellion are opportunities when charismatics can prove themselves by being powerless. While on the run David subjects himself to God's mercy and acts morally, once settled (in his house) and in power, followed by immobility, he finds himself in predicaments.

> This immobility, however integral to the king's role as gatherer of intelligence and orchestrator of troops, closes him in, pressing him into an ever more cloistered and dependent state, ever more conducive to the king of luxuriating and personal sloth that the biblical narrator typically, as for Canaanite kings, epitomizes by the most private and compromised of daily actions. (Rosenberg 1986:139)

David's rule illustrates the confrontation between ethical and violent rule, a military king dependent on Yahweh's deliverance, and an oriental despot abusing royal power. David's kingship is a big step from Saul's rather tribal kingship towards an absolute monarchy.

Signs and Wonders

Similarly to Saul's, David's emergence is accompanied by signs and wonders. At his debut he delivers Israel by defeating Goliath miraculously and shrewdly. This in turn grants him increasing power and popularity. He enjoys God's assistance and intervening help, so that not even the king's envy can harm him. In fact Saul's attempts to kill David only witness to Yahweh's miraculous protection of David, making Saul frightened of his young rival. When on the run David's fortune is not changed, rather augmented. He is supported by benevolent people in the court (Jonathan, Michal), in the countryside (Abigail) and fugitives like him (see 1 Sam 22:2, 20). One of them (Abiathar) greatly improves his chances of survival and success (1 Sam 23:9; 30:7f) by providing him with the ephod. Yahweh's good will is visible in David's escape (cf. Klaus 1999:122-28). Even at the beginning of his Jerusalem reign David experiences Yahweh's wonderful military intervention (2 Sam 5:17ff). Wonderful rescues and success are hallmarks of David's early life. During all this Yahweh's intervention and deliverance are first and foremost related to military operations.

David's cleanness in various bloodlettings as well as "his outstanding *deeds* [...] prevented him and his kingdom from being undermined" (Klaus 1999:131; his italics). After being established as Israel's king, however, his deeds become kingship-centred (chs. 6-7), ambiguous (ch. 9) and despotic (ch. 11), unconcerned with justice (ch. 13), so undermining his rule and the monarchy (ch. 15). This change is indicative of what constituted David's authority and claim to power as well as of Yahweh's involvement in the kingdom.

Once established David's fortunes and his perception thereof change. He sees God's help in material wealth and not in military victory. With David established signs and wonders cease. In fact they are substituted by a sort of wealth theology[115] (from 2 Sam 5:12 on). Subsequently (after 2 Sam 5) God's wrath comes (cf. Exum 1992:137-42), so that in 2 Samuel 24 it is Yahweh who incites the king against himself and his people, which was unimaginable earlier in the narrative (Goldingay 2000:310). David's "story gains meaning as the conclusion of a process in which the relationship of the deity to David has gradually worsened" (Nielsen 1997:139). Since the state of affairs is linked to the tent, Rosenberg (1997:139) correctly observes that "2 Samuel thus ends where 1 Samuel began: with a stable and functioning shrine, albeit a troubled and haunted one."

Why did God confront David after the Bathsheba affair in the way he did? Goldingay's answer is that David was the man after God's heart (2000:247). This is certainly true as far as David the charismatic leader is concerned. The other side of the coin is that of the "charismatic movement". That is to say what matters is God's commitment to incipient charismatic movements, such as David's kingship was at the beginning. David was a charismatic leader, commissioned by Yahweh and leading a charismatic movement. Hence Yahweh's commitment had to be visible.

I have claimed that once God's interventions dwindle the leader is doomed to failure. David experienced Yahweh's intervention neither in a spectacular, explicit nor in an implicit way after the deliverance in 2 Samuel 5. Subsequently the king's leadership authority wasted away, so that by Absalom's coup only his most loyal men were prepared to share in his troubles. David seems to have recognised the cause and, in his resilience, was ready to make amends. He sent the ark back, thereby making clear his conviction that God cannot be forced to take David's side. By humbling and throwing himself upon Yahweh's mercy the king opened the way for God's voluntary intervention, which followed in an extraordinary manner. When regaining control after the civil war, the tribes' rivalry to re-establish the king testifies to their recognition of David's charismatic authority. Thus for a short period in the Absalom revolt David's attitude exemplified the postulate that the more charismatic leaders experience God's intervention the stronger their claim and authority are (cf. Weber 1968:242).

---

[115] I am referring to the emphasis on signs and wonders, characterising a number of Christian movements, Pentecostal and otherwise, which is swapped for a "prosperity" theology once they are established.

"Summer" — Israel's Hardships under David

The 1st movement's stillness and languor due to the heat, interrupted by birdsongs and breezes of wind, create apprehension. This apprehension takes shape in the man who has conventionally been regarded as a young shepherd apologising before his master, or, most recently by Everett (84), a peasant first anxious about, then lamenting, the loss of crops caused by hail. In this view "what might have been merely a transient, inconsequential feature of the weather proves to be a lasting and ultimately damaging one" (83). The peasant is like young David fearing for his life because of King Saul's fits of temper. My reading of the narrative has also pointed out the "lasting and ultimately damaging" nature of the antagonism between Saul's and David's houses. In the former interpretation the young shepherd might be young David defending himself from paranoid King Saul, who does not want to listen, does not forgive — he impatiently thunders. Whichever view is correct the "set of disarmingly 'slow' gestures, metrically dislocated, [...] must represent the lethargy of the anxious man at least as much as the oppressive heat of an airless day" (83). Consistent G minor implies the dominance of the fear-realisation theme (83). Thus similarly to *Spring* but in a more emphatic way there is an element of inauspiciousness. In fact Everett interprets Vivaldi by referring to John Milton's *L'allegro* and *Il penseroso*.

> According to the old superstition implicit in Milton's words, one is doomed to failure in love unless one hears the nightingale before the cuckoo — the point of departure for *Summer*, which fatally has the cuckoo first. Thereafter, Milton's harmless winds and honeyed bee become malevolent things. The outcome in *Summer* — the destructive storm that fills the sky — is a bitter parody of Milton's sweet music that brings 'all Heaven before mine eyes' (line 166). (79)

The parallel to David's marital life is too obvious. His "undisclosed" commitment and troublesome relationship to women had decisive implications not only for himself and his family but for the future of the entire nation.

The 2nd movement, similarly to that of *Spring*, depicts a sleeping man — this time one of troubled sleep because of the distant thunder. The virtual serenity and calmness is contrasted by the thunder of an approaching storm. This is like David's dormant charisma occasionally aroused in his early rule in 2 Samuel (including the Bathsheba affair), setting the stage for future troubles.

The storm finally arrives in the 3rd movement with a cloudburst. The man awakes from his sleep only to find the destruction of his hands' work by nature. The storm sent by forces ill-disposed to man is a destructive power, not unlike the storm and turmoil of Absalom's rebellion against old David. Similarly to the peasant of *Summer*, David, with rekindled charisma, woke up to see the destruction of his kingdom. Therefore "Summer's ruin" (82) not only fits Vivaldi's opus but partly David's reign.

The Leadership of the Charismatic

The Transition in Leadership

The narrator "is more interested in the persons causing the political transition than in the transition itself", Preston (1992:27) claims. This is certainly true. So I shall analyse David's charismatic leadership against the backdrop of Saul's by drawing upon their portrayals so far.

After his rejection Saul cannot effectively face the Philistine menace. He leads the army but is not able to deliver the nation. David comes to the stage in this situation. His emergence is triggered by the king's incompetence as a military leader. David soon proves to be a competent deliverer. The need for a change in leadership is clearly felt by the nation. Obviously Saul is not willing to abdicate. In his specific case this might be regarded as a virtue — he is finally acting as a king. However, his leadership is not indisputably beneficial to the nation. His unwillingness to step down, a characteristic of charismatic leaders, makes the transition as difficult as it is exciting.

George (1999) has made an excellent case to read 1 Samuel 17 from the angle of constructing identity. Saul, along with his armour, attitude and behaviour, represents the old identity, which is unable to meet Goliath's challenge to Israel. In contrast young David resolves the social and theological crisis by his belief in Yahweh and unconventional warfare, so offering a new identity to the nation in crisis. George's conclusion, though intended to bear on the post-exilic community, is relevant to the rise of the new from the midst of the old:

> Israel had faced overwhelming odds before (i.e., Goliath), and, although its traditional self-understanding (i.e., Saul) had failed to provide a solution to the crisis, a solution had been found, in an unexpected place (i.e., David). This solution required a new self-understanding and a new way of doing things (symbolized by the youth of David who confessed his faith and belief in YHWH), but it achieved the desired result. (411)

I have mentioned the surrogate father pattern in the Saul-David relationship, which is similar to the Samuel-Saul mentorship in that David's success induces the envy of his surrogate father. The once charismatic cannot stand the emerging one and wants David's life. But by chasing David away from the court, Saul unwillingly contributes to David's success. This is a fundamental difference to the Samuel-Saul relationship. Although "David's rise is accompanied by Saul's long-term presence", just as Saul's was accompanied by Samuel's (Preston 1982:38), David does not remain under Saul's (or Samuel's) control, as emphasised at his appearance in 1 Samuel 16. I have also stressed that David's independence is a basic factor in his success as a charismatic leader. He demonstrates autonomy in every respect. He does "not consult any man" (cf. Gal 1:17) when the nation's future, and accordingly his career, are at stake — in contrast to Saul. While Saul started out and remained a protégé of the prophet throughout his life, David becomes successful as a fugitive through strategic shrewdness and deception. Indeed Paul Borgman argues that after the three "trials" of 1 Samuel 24-26 in 26:7ff David self-confidently descends into Saul's camp — "David is too much in control" (1980:301). From this point "until he is anointed king of Judah (2 Sam. 2) David is easily in the ascendancy while Saul is pathetically on the decline" (301, n. 20). The basic difference between the leadership of David from that of Saul is that David gets his way, establishes himself as well as his autonomy, which both entails and presupposes Yahweh's support.

Saul surrendered to his surrogate father, whereas David does not do so but resorts to deception in order to prevail over his master. Saul was dominated by his mentor and could not dominate his protégé. So while the tense relationship between Samuel and Saul resulted in rejection and Saul's failure in charismatic leadership, that between Saul and David contributes even more to David's appropriating his charisma. In one respect the two relationships match: in both cases Saul is the underdog. From another angle Saul failed because of the jealousy and dominance of the prophet. Interestingly, in spite of or maybe because of Saul's jealousy David succeeds. David's resolve leads to success, while Saul's submission to his fall.

In 1 Samuel 18:10-19:10 Saul does not leave his palace. By doing so he inadvertently prepares David's military success, who in turn several times is said to "go out" to fight the Philistines. I have claimed that in this way David fulfils Saul's commission in 9:16. Saul first leaves his palace in 1 Samuel 19:22 to pursue David. He resumes his role as a military king and remains committed to his commission. By contrast David does not. Staying in the "palace" prepares a crisis for David as well. The difference is, however, that whereas after David's escape Saul resumes his military leadership and dies heroically in war, David does not and dies in bed (see Preston 1982). Still, David re-emerges and re-establishes himself when a rival emerges, albeit for a short period of time. Saul was doomed to failure in this respect. Saul, ironically, though deprived of Yahweh's spirit, remained a military king. David, though having the spirit all his life, ceases to act as a military king in 2 Samuel.

Military leadership is appropriated by David's general. Joab does not mentor David, still the effect is similar to Samuel's mentoring Saul: Joab overshadows and gradually replaces the king. Saul was not under the control of his general but of the prophet. He therefore became a religious bungler but remained a military king. David is under the control of his general. Therefore he becomes a puppet.[116]

Saul's jealousy of David takes on a new import. The old, when realising its decline and the emergence and success of the new, feels threatened, whether

---

[116] Joab is a reckless, ruthless opportunist. David cannot be caught at recklessness even though he was a strategist. Moreover, Joab is loyal to his master as David was to Saul. Is Joab the antitype of David?

due to paranoia or correct perception and behaves like Saul obstructing the emerging new with every possible means. The old is intent on eliminating the new. Moreover the old, despite promises, will never free the new to act as it wishes (see 1 Sam 17:25). The new must free itself from the suppression and tyranny of the old. The old cannot prevent God's new charismatic leader from emerging, but it can obstruct and delay it, as the Saul-David transition evinces. And even through its obstructing attempts the old assists the new as these attempts often go awry. Doubtless it is eventually God's mighty spirit at work behind the charismatic.

Fokkelman (1986:256) notes that 1 Samuel 19:4f (ET 19:3f) portrays David and his deed in unambiguously positive terms in that his deliverance, beneficial as it was for both nation and king, is contrasted with Saul's wish to kill. Jobling has correctly pointed out the contrast:

> Saul is shown negatively in almost every incident, but even more he is shown as frustrated—his plans to harm David are always turning out to David's advantage, his descent to the depths is the very cause of David's rule. David is shown positively, and as successful in what he intends. This is a first level in the contrast between the rejected and the elected; in character, bad *versus* good, in intentions, frustration *versus* success. […] A second level is the effect each character has on the relationship between them. Saul, as rejected, is disloyal to David, and tends to drive him away. David, as elected, is loyal to Saul, and tends to seek his presence. This sets up a great tension—the relationship finds no stability whether they are together or apart. (1986a:16f; his emphasis)

Although Jobling does not pursue his observation, its structuralist appropriation can be helpful again. That is, although the emerging new leader (or order) is said to be beneficial rather than harmful and because of their intrinsic antagonism, the old is not able or willing to understand and recognise the new and seeks to drive it away. The triumph and success of the new vex the old. The old is unreliable and capricious while the new is loyal. All the attempts of the old, however, backfire and only contribute to the success of the new, which is to replace the old.

Preston's pattern of the rise of the low and the fall of the mighty has an interesting implication. Viewing their succession with jealousy and as a power struggle both Samuel and Saul, though to different extents, succumb to persecution complex. I contended above that by this attitude Samuel makes Saul fail, while Saul aids David's emergence. David, however, seems to resist paranoia, even when threatened by his son.[117]

One of the most interesting and most difficult questions concerns Yahweh's involvement. As I have suggested 1 Samuel 16:13f is Yahweh's actions in a

---

[117] Or does he? In 1 Kgs 1 Bathsheba and Nathan seem to get their way by appealing to the king's conceit. Even if this is so, regarding paranoia David is far better off than his predecessors.

nutshell. By causing trouble and enmity between the former and the emerging charismatic leaders Yahweh's spirit makes sure that the Samuel-Saul mentorship with all its troubles will not be repeated. In other words Yahweh's spirit raises and establishes David as the new charismatic leader by maintaining alienation and animosity between the former and the new leader.

David's Attempts to Resolve Crises

I have claimed that David is only successful in trouble. Once at rest, i.e. charismatic "ideal" (cf. Weber 1968:1112f) achieved, trouble overcomes him. Obviously his charisma, like charisma in general, is related to crises. David demonstrates his charismatic leadership by resolving crises in 1 Samuel (see chs. 17-18, 24, 26, 30). Crises enable him to act as a charismatic. In fact he takes advantage of crisis situations and emerges from them with renewed power and authority.[118] This is a basic difference to Saul who, facing odds, could not remain in control. Now I shall survey a few crises and how David faced them.

The first is the Goliath crisis, vividly pictured in 1 Samuel 17:11, 24. In contrast to his countrymen David finds his way to defeat the giant. Secondly David delivers Keilah from the Philistines at Yahweh's behest, and despite his men's misgivings, he eludes his other enemy Saul once again (1 Sam 23). In 1 Samuel 30 David and his men are under a cloud on discovering that the Amalekites have plundered Ziklag. David's distress grows when his men want to stone him. In this decisive moment David finds "strength in the LORD his God" (30:6), indeed he takes advantage of the crisis by leading his troops to recover their families and goods. In both cases David's success is obtained through Yahweh of whom he inquires via the ephod.

In 2 Samuel the picture is more equivocal. Just after his enthronement David averts the Philistine threat in ch. 5. He does it, again, by inquiring of Yahweh who leads his military operation. Ch. 8 also ascribes to David's great military achievements. On the other hand, I have claimed that by becoming an oriental king David gradually and unknowingly relinquishes military leadership to Joab from ch. 2 onwards and does so openly in chs. 10-12. As I argued above, Joab's dubious role, i.e. his loyalty to the king but opposition to David's attempts at unification, was just as helpful in impeding David's success. "How universal can his reign be? How parochial must it remain? These are the questions posed by the presence of Joab in the story" (Rosenberg 1986:168). The ambiguous answer to these questions may be taken as an indication of Joab's character and involvement in establishing the Davidic monarchy.

The big crisis of the Absalom coup offers an extraordinary opportunity to David — he can re-emerge as a charismatic leader. Indeed David "goes out" (2 Sam 15:16f), resorting again to his leadership skills of rhetoric and military tactics. I have claimed that only by so doing can he rekindle his charisma and

---

[118] Is this the secret of his men's unwavering loyalty to him?

succeed. With the threat of his son's revolt averted, however, his oriental kingself prevails. He returns to his palace, resumes the rule of an oriental king who does not take seriously the new peril of secession. By reassuming his kingship, he again extinguishes his charisma. David has come full circle. He is the Churchill of ancient Israel — successful in wartime, while at odds with peace.

David emerges as a charismatic military leader in the crisis of Philistine oppression. Both on the run and in his early rule he considers military leadership his main task. This is also recognised and appreciated first by Judah and then by the northern tribes. His leadership is only a means to reach the objective: establishing an independent Israel. This he does with Yahweh's assistance. By 2 Samuel 8 Israel becomes an independent monarchy, a significant military power indeed.

The major threat to the young kingdom is secession and tribal rivalry. To avert these and hold the monarchy together takes much wisdom and political-diplomatic insight. David reveals such insight, even though seen from a theological angle it is rather dubious, in the centralisation project he undertakes in his early rule. By bringing the ark to the capital he establishes a central shrine. This is young David in his vigour. With the years passing by he will change for the worse.

I have indicated that Absalom's insinuation in 2 Samuel 15:3 was not totally baseless, and as the rebellion verified it Israel had grown discontent with David's reign. David apparently was not in touch with intertribal tensions and lost control of national developments. The state of affairs is alluded to by the Mahanaim motif. In 2 Samuel 2 (vv. 8, 12, 29) Mahanaim stands for the divided nation (Fokkelman 1990:61f), manifest in the civil war. David's rule entails another civil war, and David flees to Mahanaim (17:24, 27). Mahanaim has become the epitome of a warring nation. This is an evil war, in which "son is against father, cousin against cousin" as Conroy puts it referring to David, Absalom and the two generals (1978:48). Then, at the threat of another revolt, David's concern is his return to the palace. Little wonder that David's indifference re-ignites northern separatism. The civil war is averted by a woman's wisdom and, once again, Joab's resolution. At the end of his reign, David returns to where he started. His centralisation project does not bring about unity. Indeed this fiasco is exacerbated by an abandonment of basic attributes of Israelite religion, which in turn is aimed at bolstering the king's image (see Flanagan 1988:231f). Related to his project, David also misses the opportunity he so carefully prepared for (2 Sam 3:13f), to base the monarchy on a more inclusive foundation by producing an heir from Michal (2 Sam 6:23), thus establishing a firm union between North and South (Goldingay 2000:218; cf. Flanagan 1983a:55). David's success to unite Israel is as equivocal as his rule.

For all this I have blamed the king's seclusion and withdrawal into the palace. David's underlying motive, frustrating his attempts to keep the nation united and resolve the crisis, is to establish and nurture an oriental monarch image by abandoning military leadership. He fails as much in the latter part of his rule (from 2 Sam 9 on) as he is successful in the early years. David's attempt to play off Ziba against Mephibosheth might be taken as a metaphor of his divisive politics. Saul united the tribes in a much looser federal monarchy, and was able to mobilise them until the end of his rule. David delivers Israel from the Philistines, unites the nation and succeeds to centralise power, but cannot avoid civil war. He leaves a united nation behind — with tensions under the surface.

To What Extent Was David Charismatic?

To answer the question a distinction between the young and the old David should be made. Obviously David's charisma is related to military deliverance and leadership. David emerges as a shrewd strategist, often resorting to deception and ruse in order to get his way. He often deceives by sly rhetoric, another characteristic of a charismatic. I have pointed out that deception, as the weapon of the weak against the powerful, is essential in his emergence. David is deceptive when powerless — both under Saul and in the Absalom revolt, when he recovers his charisma. Deception seems to be a means of emerging charismatics to establish themselves in the face of the powerful.[119] Once in power, however, David does not resort to deception, but is often deceived himself. It follows that a powerful leader, not deceiving but being deceived, cannot be charismatic by definition. A king's misuse of power is an occupational hazard. Therefore becoming powerful poses a major threat to charismatic leadership. The main objective of a charismatic is to reach the charismatic ideal, in David's case emerging and becoming established as a military leader. Once in power his main objective becomes maintaining power.[120] Power is a major impediment for charismatics such as David to remain a charismatic leader. A "charismatic powerful" or "powerful charismatic" is a contradiction in terms in their case.

Two aspects making David's charisma manifest are his independence and, closely related, his determination. I have claimed that the narrative emphasises David's independence from both of his mentors, Samuel and Saul, during his emergence. Similarly in 1 Samuel David reveals resoluteness in making decisions. In 2 Samuel, however, David gradually loses independence and becomes overshadowed and controlled by his general. As a sign of and parallel to this either his role becomes marginal or he himself irresolute in a number of areas such as warfare, justice and family life. His charisma becomes inactive, so he cannot be considered charismatic in most of 2 Samuel. He becomes so impotent that his attempt to replace Joab fails ridiculously. David follows in Saul's footsteps — as Saul's charisma was killed by his irresoluteness and

---

[119] This is not a universal statement but rather one concerning a charismatic like David.
[120] This will be different with Solomon, the very opposite to his father's type.

reliance on Samuel, so is David's charisma extinguished by his wavering between his commission and oriental kingship. A wavering charismatic, therefore, is a contradiction in terms and bound to fail.

All these aspects are related to the objective of David's charisma — military deliverance. "Yahweh was with him", as it often reads, refers to his military success. A fugitive, David experiences Yahweh's deliverance and intervention. After 2 Samuel 8, however, Yahweh's direct interventions seem to decrease, even cease. Only when on the run during the Absalom revolt do references to them recur. Putting it differently David's preoccupation with maintaining royal power renders charisma dormant and static, and static charisma, again, is an oxymoron. The Absalom revolt shakes David up and makes his charisma dynamic by rekindling it. This proves that David's charisma, like charisma in general, functions only in emergency situations, i.e. when in need of Yahweh's help and intervention.

Charisma becoming dormant signals the impending end of the charismatic. The first step towards a dormant charisma is the fading commitment to the charismatic ideal on the part of the charismatic. David's vanishing commitment to the charismatic ideal, i.e. military leadership, is visible in his preoccupation with his palace and his abandoning the ideal of fighting Yahweh's battles (cf. 1 Sam 25:28). This is the more salient when compared with Saul, who, though abandoned by Yahweh, kept acting as a military king. A sign of diminishing commitment is the charismatic's failure to live up to the Deuteronomistic criterion. Again, Saul, though a religious bungler himself, is better off in this respect as his religious zeal never vanished. David's fading commitment, in contrast, is discernible in his gradual shift from righteousness and military leadership to oriental despotism in 2 Samuel, so that his priority ceases to be just government after 2 Samuel 8. Though for different reasons what I have claimed of Saul can be said of almost similar validity about David: his rise and fall as a charismatic leader puts him in the judges' company.

David's neglect and abandonment of charismatic leadership at the beginning of 2 Samuel first leads to a shift in commitment. Whereas in 1 Samuel David fights Yahweh's battles (25:28), in 2 Samuel he is more interested in his government, i.e. how to maintain power. Thus he begins his dubious centralisation project. Subsequently the institution of oriental kingship becomes all-important, and finally David's charisma is extinguished. If charismatic deliverers retreat into their palace and have their general run the monarchy, such an outcome will be unavoidable. David's reign demonstrates that charismatic and oriental kingships are incompatible. But is it the unavoidable fate of a charismatic leader to become a figurehead, like Saul under Samuel and David under Joab, and have his/her charisma extinguished? Charisma is bestowed by God's spirit, but emerging as a charismatic is as easy compared with remaining one as obtaining power in comparison with keeping it.

With David the era of charismatic military kings has come to an end. Who is next?

CHAPTER 4

From Redefined Charisma to Royal Pretension

After the vicissitudes of David's reign the monarchy enters its most peaceful era under Solomon. There are virtually no external or internal enemies threatening the idyllic harmony – Israel lives in peace and affluence. It is harvest time. Autumn's joy, the abundance and wealth of the harvest have superseded summer's toil. How does Solomon bring this about? Is he in need of charisma or does he manage without it? And whose abundance and riches are these: those of the people or the king's?

> In the case of hereditary charisma, recognition is no longer paid to the charismatic qualities of the individual, but to the legitimacy of the position he has acquired by hereditary succession. This may lead in the direction either of traditionalization or of legalization. The concept of divine right is fundamentally altered and now comes to mean authority by virtue of a personal right which is not dependent on the recognition of those subject to authority. Personal charisma may be totally absent.

It remains to be seen whether Weber's assertion (1968:248) holds true of Solomon.

Attaining Power – The Rise of the New Leader, 1 Kings 1-2

Setting the Stage – The Crisis of Leadership

I have shown how the first two kings of Israel came to power in crises when Israel was threatened by foreign nations. With no-one competent to face the threat both Saul and David emerged by the bestowal of Yahweh's spirit and with recourse to the appropriate means to resolve the crisis.

It is clear that this time the socio-political situation is very different from when Saul or David made their debuts. At Solomon's emergence there is no national emergency; if there is a crisis it is one in the royal court. King David is too old to control everything in his realm but not too senile not to play a decisive role in matters such as succession. With ageing David confined to his bedroom his environment is embroiled in a power struggle. The old monarch cannot properly run the kingdom and the stability of the monarchy is threatened by warring parties, because no successor has yet been appointed. In fact there is no-one really in charge of the monarchy – this is a crisis of leadership too, albeit very different from the previous ones. Now I shall study the first two chapters of 1 Kings in order to see how Solomon, his emergence, the transition in leadership and the consolidation of his rule are depicted.

My discussion of Solomon will be shorter than the previous chapters, partly because of the narrative's brevity. Also since the pattern of rise and fall has been established in the previous parts of my study, based on 1-2 Samuel, it will be easier to detect the causes of Solomon's change.

The Rise of the New Leader

The first section of the book paints a bedroom. It is David's bedroom but very different from that of David in his prime. Here an old monarch at the mercy of those around him is portrayed. His impotence is marked by his only "action", וְהַמֶּלֶךְ דָּוִד זָקֵן בָּא בַּיָּמִים, "When King David was old and well advanced in years" (1:1)[1], and his not knowing Abishag, וְהַמֶּלֶךְ לֹא יְדָעָהּ, "but the king had no intimate relations with her" (1:4). Otherwise David neither acts nor speaks in the introductory scene. On his deathbed the king "is hardly a source from which initiative or political power emanates" (Fokkelman 1981:345). A ruler suffering from dementia[2] easily becomes a pawn for others to reach their end. David will be no exception.

Next the atmosphere of a power struggle is created by the oscillation between references to Adonijah's followers (vv. 7, 9) and the Nathan party (vv. 8, 10). In v. 5 the limelight already shifted to the heir apparent Adonijah, who "put himself forward" or "exalted himself" (AT). This is his first characteristic, an ominous one considering the verb's import in Proverbs 30:32; Ezechiel 17:14; 29:15; Daniel 11:14 and Numbers 16:3 in particular. Adonijah acts in an arrogant way. In addition to repeating his brother Absalom's ambitious actions by getting a royal entourage of chariots, horses and 50 men, he deems his rule a *fait accompli*. This is evinced in his actions: he confers with powerful court officials (v. 7), and then appears to offer a sacrifice (v. 9). But his fundamental mistake is not to consult his father in the matter of succession. David is probably viewed by Adonijah as a figurehead king unable to make decisions. Adonijah "is fatally ignorant" (Provan 1997:21), and for this reason his plan will prove a deadly miscalculation, as David takes fully considered actions in vv. 28ff.

The ringleader of the other party is Nathan. He organises the plot to frustrate Adonijah's plan. As opposed to Adonijah, Nathan gets down to work with much caution. His first action is to get Solomon's mother Bathsheba to have a hearing with the king. He advises her what to say. Bathsheba bases her argument on David's alleged vow to her of Solomon's kingship (1:17). Whether or not David made such a vow is irrelevant as far as the outcome,

---

[1] If בָּא, literally "went", is a *qatal verbum finitum* and not a participle as Fokkelman suggests (1981:346). Unattributed Bible references in this chapter are to 1 Kings.

[2] Whether the Hebrew has an equivalent to "senile dementia" or not David is clearly characterised in ch. 1 as suffering from it. Ironically, not knowing has become a characteristic of the king; see vv. 11, 18, 27.

getting David's approval of Solomon, is concerned. Bathsheba claims that recent developments in the court threaten David's vow (vv. 18f). She also stresses that these are happening without the king's knowledge, but decisions are up to him (v. 20) – two powerful appeals. Finally she anticipates a purge should Adonijah prevail (v. 21).

Just when Bathsheba is done with her speech, Nathan arrives to drive home, by reiteration, what is going on and what their request is – that the king make the decision. To be sure having been manipulated David can make only the desired decision. Nathan employs powerful rhetoric, as a multitude of speech related words in reference to him and Bathsheba indicates – אמר, "to say", in vv. 11 (twice), 13, 24, 27; דבר, "to talk", in vv. 14 (twice) and 22.[3] Whereas Adonijah's plot is a series of high-flying actions, the counter-plot is based on rhetoric and personal contact with the king.[4] Obviously Nathan's action is a well-devised subterfuge meant to appeal to David's pride and perception of still being in control, totally ignored by Adonijah. Nathan also craftily plays on David's preoccupation with the loyalty expected from his subjects (Perdue 1984:79).

The rhetoric of Bathsheba and Nathan works well. David has been taken in by the scheme and from this point everything goes smoothly. David, for the first time in the narrative, really makes a vow (1:29). Indeed, belying his senility, David takes firm action by outlining the script of how to anoint Solomon king (1:32-37), officially approving of Solomon and disapproving of Adonijah. Senile David ostensibly is in control of his monarchy, not realising that by acknowledging him as king, Nathan's party takes advantage of his senility. This is the key to success and succession alike.[5]

One of the reasons David chooses Solomon might be David's recognition of the precariousness of being overshadowed and influenced by his general. Since Joab supports Adonijah, David wants to make sure his story is not going to be repeated (see Rosenberg 1986:167f). This might be an additional factor contributing to his order to kill Joab (see "to me" in 2:5), who is "the first victim of David's changed view of rule" (Perdue 1984:74); David wants a king independent of any court official.

---

[3] Notice also that they appeal to David's words in vv. 13, 16f, 20, 24.
[4] Note the references to coming to and doing obeisance before the king on the plotters' part in vv. 12, 14-16, 18, 22f.
[5] Provan (1995:27) comments on 1:39f, "The contrast with Adonijah's private dinner party for the few elite is evident. This is the proper way to become a king, the text tells us: out in the open, with mules, oil, and music, with popular involvement. Adonijah's attempted coup, by stealth and patronage, is an aberration." He is correct in pointing out the different ways taken by the two parties. I have claimed, however, that Nathan's was also a coup, even though a more calculating and circumspect one, and the text is more reticent and less transparent in its evaluation. A sign of this equivalence may be the use of "people" in vv. 39f, apparently taken by Provan as a reference to the nation or a major part thereof as is its normal use, which to me seems to refer to Solomon's adherents (see v. 45). If this is so the "popular involvement" was much more limited.

What interests me in all this is the way Solomon is involved in his anointing. Since he emerges in a coup orchestrated by court officials, it should not be a surprise that he is only referred to by different characters but does not himself appear before 1:38, nor does he act – except for his reported enthronement in 1:46 – or speak before the last two verses of the chapter (cf. Walsh 1995:473f). "Solomon is spoken about, but never speaks; he is alluded to, but not seen", in a word he is not a character (B.O. Long 1981:87) but made into a pawn by the coup. Will he remain like this?

Seeing the cast in ch. 2, the tables are turned. Whereas in ch. 1 Solomon appeared as a pawn amongst the machinations of Nathan and company, from ch. 2 Nathan, who masterminded Solomon's succession, and his "accomplices" will not appear again. Only Bathsheba takes the stage (2:13ff), but merely to confirm his son's power.

The chapter begins with David's charge to his son. 2:1-4 portray David as a pious Yahwist admonishing the new king to adhere to Yahweh. Vv. 5-9 are the voice of an opportunistic David advising Solomon how to eliminate potential threats to his throne by using his wisdom, i.e. engaging "in political deception" (Perdue 1984:79). The double personality of David of 2 Samuel makes his last appearance.[6] We do not learn of Solomon's reaction to what he has heard. He is a passive listener. The two admonitions are in obvious contradiction hence challenge the new king. Which of them will prevail? How will the new monarch execute David's will? Will he do it servilely or rather in an independent and self-reliant way? Will he be an obedient and pious king or a duplicate of his father?

With his father dead Solomon sets out to demonstrate his power in accord with David's will (2:2). The opportunity is given when Adonijah approaches Bathsheba with a fateful request. She mediates his request to the king. The scene is telling of Solomon's authority and personality.[7] When Bathsheba arrives before the king, it is not she making the obeisance (Walsh 1995:476) but he "stood up to meet her, bowed down to her and sat down on his throne." Then Solomon "had a throne brought for the king's mother, and she sat down at his right hand" (2:19). Bathsheba appears as a much respected mother figure with Solomon relying on her. She will certainly be able to get what Adonijah wants, will she not? Bathsheba tells Solomon she wants to ask for something and the king encourages her, "I will not refuse you" (2:20). On hearing Adonijah's request, however, the king's reaction exposes his independence, authority and determination to eliminate his rival (2:22-24). So does the execution of the main rival: it does not brook delay or compromise. Adonijah must be eliminated. His request might be innocuous; what matters, however, is

---

[6] This holds true in spite of Koopmans' argument (1991:447) that David's charges to Solomon are shown as "respect for the office of the anointed rather than a desire for revenge (2 Sam. i 13-16, iv 9-12)." On the political import of David's charges see also Provan 1995a.

[7] My focus here is Solomon, thus I am not dealing with Bathsheba's intention and personality.

how the king interprets it[8] – and he does so in a negative way. This marks the start of the showdown. Adonijah is only the first victim to the king's eagerness to establish his authority. Next is Joab who is killed in violation of the sanctity of the holy place. Then Shimei is avenged on technicalities (Provan 1997:113, n. 9). Solomon's authority is unquestionably established. In the way Solomon eliminates these men he demonstrates complete independence and ingenuity.[9] So he exiles Abiathar (2:26) though David did not give orders regarding him. Anyone not loyal to him must be disposed of.

Solomon's autonomy is hinted at already in his anointing as well as in his message to his rival. His anointing is introduced with the same words as his father's. Just as for David in 1 Samuel 16:13, a "horn of oil" is used to anoint him (1:39). Furthermore, similarly to David's, the verb לקח, "to take", is used to describe this.[10] There is also no follow-up on the part of those anointing him, Solomon refuses any control.

Secondly his first reported action in 1:52 is an ambiguous utterance, followed by verbs referring to royal power: שׁלח, "to send",[11] הוריד, "to bring down"[12] and השׁתחה, "to bow down", on Adonijah's part (1:53). The chapter concludes with Solomon's order to Adonijah, who is not named in vv. 52f nor is his reaction reported (Conroy 1985:63). This indicates who is in control. Solomon's very first words characterise him as a ruler of political expediency. Until the last scene of ch. 1 Solomon appeared as a pawn in the hands of the Nathan faction. 1:52f is the first hint at his independence and autonomous character. After ch. 1 Nathan and Zadok[13] play no significant role in Solomon's kingdom; we do not read of any action of theirs.

What can one say of Yahweh? How is the God of Israel involved in the appointment of the third king of his people? There are a number of references to him totalling thirty in chs. 1-2.[14] Many a major character (mis)uses Yahweh's name. Indeed the reader's impression is that they try hard to outdo each other in this respect. So, for example, Bathsheba mentions David's vow by Yahweh (1:17), who in his turn is keen on referring to the Almighty (1:29f, 48; 2:3f, 8). No wonder then that henchman Benaiah feels compelled to follow the court etiquette (1:36f; so do officials (1:47) and Adonijah (2:15). But the person making most use of the Almighty's name is the newly appointed king. It is a spectacular debut to refer to Yahweh/God nine times within nine verses

---

[8] This is suggested by the text's reticence about Adonijah's motives and focus on the king's response.

[9] Contra Fokkelman (1981:408) who unnecessarily psychologises by asserting that Solomon's "display of power [...] is [...] a sign of inner insecurity and weakness."

[10] Cf. also the resemblance of 1:33 to 1 Sam 16:11.

[11] See my remarks on the verb in 2 Sam 11.

[12] Note that in 1:33 Solomon is the object of the same verb as well as of another in *hiphil* in 1:38. הוריד, "to bring down", is also a key verb in David's instructions to his son about Joab and Shimei in 2:6, 9.

[13] In 4:4 Zadok is part of the state administration.

[14] As "Yahweh" he is referred to 23 times and as "God" 7 times.

(2:23f, 26, 32f, 42-45)! Of all the characters only Nathan refrains from using God's name.

Most startlingly, however, apart from 2:27 which has Solomon as its subject,[15] there is not one single reference by the narrator to God's involvement. Disregarding the ambiguous references to him by plotters and court officials Yahweh does not appear on stage in the first two chapters of the book. He neither acts nor speaks nor is he depicted as a background character.

In addition to what was observed above one of the underlying themes at the beginning of the book is the question of control. By his declaration Adonijah claims control of the monarchy (1:5; see also vv. 11, 18, 24f). This is counteracted by Nathan and Bathsheba's subtle and deceptive rhetoric, aiming at the king's perception of being in control of the kingdom (cf. Hagan 1979:320f). Being in control is a vexing question throughout. To this end ch. 1, exclusively in reference to David, 19 times (!) employs אָדוֹן, "lord", most often as אֲדֹנִי הַמֶּלֶךְ, "my lord the king". Nowhere else in the FT does the phrase occur so often in such proximity. At the same time, we remember, the self-styled king's name is a covert challenge to David's control and lordship (see Fokkelman 1981:352; Garsiel 1991:381).[16] That אָדוֹן is never used in reference to Yahweh is telling. By the plotting and self-declaration of the one called "my lord is Yahweh", by those who keep referring to David as "lord" and by both parties' negligence of *the* Lord, Yahweh's lordship is challenged. Thus the very name of Adonijah along with the manifold addresses to David's lordship become a paradox. The chapter presents claims about who is in control in Israel. Adonijah thinks he is, David ditto. And though those acknowledging David as lord will eventually prevail and gain control of happenings in the court, Yahweh is not involved in the events. Indeed Yahweh's lordship is indirectly disclaimed; the God of Israel is left out in the cold. The threat to his rule Yahweh was concerned about at the start of the monarchy has here come true – "they have rejected me as their king" (1 Sam 8:7), and lord as well. Thus Fokkelman's claim – aside from being based on rather accidental evidence – that "Solomon's kingship is a gift from God" is wide off the mark (1981:376). Israel's third king is appointed in a court intrigue and without the consent of its Sovereign who has been driven out of Israel's monarchy (cf. Exum 1992:140). This is not to say, however, that Solomon usurps the throne. Rather this depicts who and how is involved in making Solomon king.

The story ends with an ostensible statement about Solomon gaining control of the monarchy: וְהַמַּמְלָכָה נָכוֹנָה בְּיַד־שְׁלֹמֹה, "The kingdom was now firmly established in Solomon's hands" (2:46). It is ostensible because Solomon has established control over his kingdom, but, again, Yahweh's action and involvement in this are not disclosed, therefore one wonders whether it is true. Indeed the qualification of Solomon's established rule, "in/by his hand/power",

---

[15] When לְמַלֵּא, "fulfilling", is taken as a transitive verb.

[16] By the juxtaposition of "Adonijah" and "my lord the king" this motive is played upon in 1:18 and 24.

From Redefined Charisma to Royal Pretension 181

points to his share therein: Solomon managed to establish himself by the ruthless elimination of potential rivals (see Fokkelman 1981:408f; Rosenberg 1986:187; Eslinger 1989:125f; Walsh 1995:483) – without the help of Yahweh. His boast in 2:24 and 45, using כון, "to establish", again is probably as ostensible as it is self-confident. Moreover in 2:45 there is a development in his statement in relation to the similar assertion of 2:12, וַתִּכֹּן מַלְכֻתוֹ מְאֹד, "and his rule was firmly established", as the latter lacks the compromising qualification. 2:12 marks the irreversibility of the transition of government after the monarch's death.[17] After the elimination of threats to it Solomon's throne is firmly established and with it the power struggle is over (2:46). Similarly to 1 Samuel 14:48 (see my comments above) כון, "to establish", in these verses is a sort of *passivum divinum* to provide theological evaluation of character and development. I have also suggested that the verb has a static connotation. All in all Solomon's reign starts rather ambiguously.[18] What will follow?

Maintaining Power – King Solomon[19]

I have claimed that at Solomon's emergence no charisma was needed or involved. Now I turn to Solomon as an established monarch to see how he was first granted and how he used charisma. Chs. 3-11 are arranged in a clear way. The paragraphs in chs. 3-5 (Solomon's wife; God appears to the king; Solomon's charisma tested and confirmed; the officials of the monarchy; Solomon's court; Solomon and Hiram; forced labour) have their rough counterparts in chs. 9-11 (God appears to the king; Solomon and Pharaoh, Solomon and Hiram; forced labour; charisma tested and confirmed; Solomon's court; Solomon's wives; the adversaries of the monarchy).[20] These two units

---

[17] Thus my evaluation of the significance of כון, "to establish", is rather the opposite to that of Provan (1995:37).
[18] Weisman's article (1976) implies differences between the anointings of Saul and David on the one hand and Solomon on the other (secret vs. public anointing; location of the anointing; anointing by a prophet as opposed to one by a priest; bestowal of God's spirit; following demonstration of charisma and the lack of it). Though he does not deal with the question, one is wondering whether the abandonment of the anointing motif indicates Yahweh's involvement.
[19] Schäfer-Lichtenberger (1995:277-323) has organised her discussion of 3:16-8:66 under the title "The Test of the Charisma". Similarly Parker (1988) has suggested that chs. 6-8 demonstrate Solomon's recommendable attitude towards God, though she does not discuss the chapters at length. I disagree with them in that chs. 6-8 in my view do not belong to the demonstration of the charisma in the way they suggest (on Parker's study see Frisch 1991:5). Also chs. 6-8 are too long and thematically different to make up only a sub-section and not a section in its own right (similarly Brettler 1991:88; contra Williams 1999). For a reading accounting for both the positive and negative see Walsh 1995, 1996.
[20] Similarly Jobling 1991:61 (and 1997:475), whose essay, despite helpful observations and insights, I have found rather tendentious (see also Schäfer-Lichtenberger's critique

are related to Solomon's activity proper and make up the frame, with chs. 6-8, "the axis" in the middle, consisting of descriptions of the temple and the palace as well as Solomon's prayer. I shall study Solomon's rule by following the development of the narrative rather than in a thematic discussion. By analysing the axis after the discussion of chs. 3-5 and 9-11, however, I want to stress the similarities and differences of the two sections, as well as suggest that the axis provides the rationale for Solomon's change between the two units. On occasions I shall refer to implications of the text that are not so much literary yet still obvious enough to be worth paying attention to.

Solomon's Rule, 1 Kings 3-5

PROSPECTS, 1 KINGS 3:1-3

Clearly Solomon's marriage to Pharaoh's daughter (3:1) was motivated by political expediency to maintain good relations with one of the superpowers at that time. This must have entailed political stability and predictability.[21] Interestingly Solomon's marrying and bringing Pharaoh's daughter to Jerusalem are immediately followed by a comment on the building of "his palace and the temple of the LORD, and the wall around Jerusalem." The daughter of Pharaoh cannot live in a mediocre abode just as the god of a nation of increasing international recognition should not live in a tent. I have shown how God frustrated David's imperial ambitions in 2 Samuel 6-7. Obviously, however, worshipping Yahweh in a central shrine has its advantages as 3:2, 3c make clear. In spite of the rather critical cultic situation along with the potential of going astray and idolatry through marrying a non-Israelite, v. 3 is keen to state Solomon's loyalty to God (see Walsh 1995:478). His love towards Yahweh is beyond doubt; still, it is flanked by two statements of disapproval (vv. 2f), each introduced by רַק, "except".

In this brief section the key issues of Solomon's rule are listed: foreign women, treaties with neighbouring states, building projects, imperial ambition

---

1995:335, n. 613). Radday (1974) in a more general essay, Parker in a fine study (1988) as well as Newing (1994) have noticed the concentric structure of the Solomon narrative, and the latter has come to similar conclusions as I have. For an alternative and subtle discussion see Frisch 1991 and Brettler 1991, who argues that 9:26-11:10 is about Solomon's violation of Dt 17:14-17. I shall show that the anti-Solomonic section starts with 9:10, and chs. 6-8 are not clearly in favour of Solomon. Knoppers (1993) regards chs. 3-10 as unambiguously positive towards Solomon, but disregards some textual evidence I have shown to be negative and does not account for the abrupt change in ch. 11.

[21] I do not see in Solomon's marrying of Pharaoh's daughter an infringement of the Deuteronomic code as Provan (1995: *passim*) and Schäfer-Lichtenberger (1995:262f) suggest. Dt 17:1-6 in my view prohibits marriage to Canaanites only. To be sure the potential of apostasy was there. Eslinger's interpretation of 1 Kgs 3 in particular (1989:129-40) and the following chapters (140-81) is driven by an utterly negative tendentious approach. He also fails to show what causes the change from ch. 3 to ch. 4.

and the question of cult in the Israelite religion. In a nutshell here all the themes of chs. 3-11 are anticipated. These chapters will elaborate on the king's greatness and fall. Furthermore the arrangement of 3:1-3 and its implied assessment foreshadow the arrangement of and, more importantly, the assessment of various facets of Solomon's rule. To achieve greatness, first, what King Solomon really had to acquire was charisma he did not have at his emergence.

CHARISMA REDEFINED, 1 KINGS 3:4-15

To grasp the import of Solomon's request of God in 3:9 a short overview of the changed socio-political situation, as depicted in the narrative, is necessary. Whereas both Saul and David emerged in a situation of acute emergency, Solomon, I have claimed, came to power in a coup with no external threat to Israel visible. The only threat was that of civil war posed by rival factions. In the cases of Saul and David a charisma of strong military leadership was required to shake off foreign oppression and unite Israel. Once Israel has been established as a united nation under their military leaderships, a different leadership is wanted. Urgent in the new situation is the establishment of social and political institutions so that the welfare and security of the nation might be maintained. As I shall demonstrate this also takes charisma, though of a different sort – charisma to establish and maintain the state apparatus and the vital functions of the life of a state, such as diplomatic relationships with neighbouring states, centralisation, the control of society and taxation (cf. Clements 1992:104-09). In a word the new situation requires a new charisma – one of maintaining *shalom*, with all its related aspects. To see the significance and implications of God's visit to Solomon and the king's request the changed situation should be borne in mind.

It is important to note that in bestowing the charisma the initiative has so far been with God. On this occasion it is God again who visits the king and invites him to ask for something. In this respect the granting of charisma to Solomon is not very different from that in 1 Samuel 10 and 16. However, by his being offered to choose anything he fancies Solomon is given a unique opportunity. Though it is still God bestowing charisma, it will be Solomon who makes the decision regarding its nature. The king is almost treated as Yahweh's partner. Solomon's involvement in the decision making reveals his character, rule and developments in his kingdom.

David referred to Solomon's wisdom, i.e. political discernment, in 2:6, 9, which the new king subsequently demonstrated. Still 3:4-15 tells the story of the bestowal of the charisma of wisdom upon the king. Did the king possess charisma in chs. 1-2 or is he only given it in ch. 3? Schäfer-Lichtenberger (1995:268) observes that even though Solomon has demonstrated political astuteness his policies have so far (2:13-46) characterised him neither as a shining example nor as one who is able to distinguish between right and wrong, not to mention his failure to show religious integrity expected from someone who builds Yahweh's temple. This means that after God's bestowal of charisma Solomon changes.

Now I turn to Solomon's petition. His response to God's question consists of three parts. The first is about God's covenant with David (3:6). It is a powerful reminder of and appeal to God's loyalty and as such it is meant to drive home that the covenant should be upheld. Secondly Solomon outlines his situation as the new king on his father's throne (3:7f). Though Israel's king, he is "a little child", not knowing how to lead the nation (v. 7; see Kalugila 1980:110-12). Therefore Solomon recognising his position being less significant before Yahweh than that of his people wishes the qualities of a vizier and not the usual privileges of the kings (Schäfer-Lichtenberger 1995:268). What he needs is qualities to lead Israel – no longer in battles as his predecessors used to but in peace.[22] Last he voices the request proper, which is one for "a discerning heart to govern, שפט, your people and to distinguish between right and wrong" (3:9).[23] In fact Solomon is asking for two things: leadership skills and the right ethical attitude necessary for them. As a correcting intervention Yahweh grants the request to put the king on the right path (Schäfer-Lichtenberger 1995:360). The unfolding narrative will show how essential leadership skills and the right ethical attitude are for Israel's monarchy and monarch alike and whether Solomon can maintain them. Indeed these aspects will provide a basis to assess Solomon's rule.

What concerns me now is the nature of Solomon's request. By asking for leadership skills he clearly realises his limits and the need in his particular situation. Although as remarked above Solomon did not emerge in a crisis similar to those of Saul's or David's, his request does imply a crisis. He sees himself inadequate for the leadership task he is supposed to carry out and therefore requests what he lacks. This is a crisis of leadership and as such similar to those causing Saul and David to emerge.

What is different from previous charismata is the charisma's nature. Both in the case of Saul and that of David, charisma was linked to military leadership: God granted charisma so that the charismatic leader could deliver Israel. With Israel delivered from foreign oppressors and fratricide as well as being united under a central authority, the need, hence mandate for charismatic military leadership has expired. There is still need for charisma – but a different kind. While Saul and David's were wartime charismata, Solomon needs it in peace. This is the basic difference. He is in need of a charisma to properly exercise power (see Moberly 1999:16). By realising the changed socio-political situation and his need as Israel's leader Solomon "redefines" charisma. He needs a particular skill for his particular situation. This is what charisma is all about: recognising the situation and asking God to grant the skills to meet the need. For these reasons God is pleased to hear and grant Solomon's request.

What Solomon's leadership skills are related to is suggested by a network of interrelating phrases and allusions. In 3:9 Solomon requests of God "a discerning heart to govern your people and to distinguish between right and

---

[22] This is so whether or not Lingen's suggestion (1992) to render "going out and coming in" as a military term is correct.

[23] On Eslinger's rather far-fetched interpretation (1989:135f) see Walsh 1995:478, n. 14.

wrong", backed up with the obvious but interesting claim that Israel is a "great people" that no-one could count (3:8) and therefore in need of competent leadership. The reference to Israel's greatness recurs in a very different context in 4:20, "The people of Judah and Israel were as numerous as the sand on the seashore; they ate, they drank and they were happy." 5:9 (ET 4:29) repeats some of the phrases in 4:20 quite verbatim: "God gave Solomon wisdom and very great insight, and a breadth of understanding as measureless as the sand on the seashore."[24] In 3:9 Solomon asks for "a discerning heart" and immediately clarifies why he is asking for this. His concern is the welfare of Israel (cf. Kenik 1983:139f), a big nation. 4:20 restates the vastness of Israel. This statement follows the passage on the establishment of the districts, a step towards centralised power and a sign of Solomon's wisdom, and refers to Israel's content. 5:5 (ET 4:25) states that "Judah and Israel, from Dan to Beersheba, lived in safety, each man under his own vine and fig tree." The third reference to Solomon's wisdom in 5:9 (ET 4:29) once again emphasises the vast number of the chosen people, clearly reminiscent of the Abrahamic promise in Genesis 22:17 and implying its fulfilment (cf. Parker 1992:79). Similarly 5:14 (ET 4:34) is reminiscent of Genesis 18:18.[25] More importantly these references intimate that Solomon's need of wisdom is proportional to the size of the nation. This all suggests that what he is given should not be considered limited to "encyclopedic knowledge" (so DeVries 1985:74) nor merely judicial wisdom (so Mettinger 1976:241-44), but leadership skills in right proportion to the challenge and the objective the king is supposed to achieve. The enormous challenge of the vast number of people is met by the quality of Solomon's wisdom, i.e. leadership skills, given by God.

God is pleased at hearing Solomon's request. Schäfer-Lichtenberger has noticed that the phrase וַיִּיטַב הַדָּבָר בְּעֵינֵי יְהוָה, "The Lord was pleased", occurs only three times in the FT (Gen 38:10; 2 Sam 11:27; 1 Kgs 3:10). Here it stresses the validity of Yahweh's utterance on Solomon formulated in 2 Samuel 12:24 and cancels any effect of the preceding story out. Regarding this evaluation with respect to Solomon's lethal power politics so far Yahweh is offering a new beginning to the king (1995:273).

Various phrases are employed in reference to Solomon's charisma in God's commendation. Solomon asks for a "discerning heart", in 3:9. Von Rad in his study on *Wisdom in Israel* has remarked that what the king "wished for himself was not the authoritative reason which reigns supreme over dead natural matter, the reason of modern consciousness, but an 'understanding' reason, a feeling for the truth which emanates from the world and addresses man" (1972:296f; see also Moberly 1999:4f). God commends Solomon's wise request for having asked for "discernment", and not for self-seeking purposes (3:11). God is eager to grant "a wise and discerning heart" (3:12). At the demonstration of Solomon's charisma the people recognise that the king has been granted

---

[24] Knoppers (1993:84) has also noticed the link between 3:8 and 5:9.
[25] This reference is equivocal, because in Genesis the nations are said to be blessed by Abraham, while here they come "to listen to Solomon's wisdom".

"wisdom from God" (3:28). The various references to "wisdom" seem to be synonyms with no basic difference. What they have in common is their relationship with administering justice. Solomon realises the need and also his incapacity to administer justice, so he asks for the capacity to do so, "to govern your people" (3:9). On granting the request Yahweh acknowledges the objective of the charisma by referring, again, to "administering justice" (3:11). And in the narrator's sentence concluding 3:4-28, by the sixfold employment of the root שפט justice is stressed again. Solomon the petitioner, God the grantor and Israel the object of the request all acknowledge either the need or the bestowal of charisma. 1 Samuel 8:5, 20, where the elders wanted a king judging, שפט, them, also spring to mind. In Solomon Israel has got such a king. Yahweh's address right at the start (3:10-14) underlines this aspect of a new and exceptional beginning, Solomon's standing at a crossroads and his being fully aware of it very clearly. Solomon did not react as his royal colleagues in similar situations are wont (3:11). He has shown himself worthy his own request (Schäfer-Lichtenberger 1995:273). Will Solomon remain a king concerned about his people all his life?

At this point the question of why righteous rule in relation to the charisma given to Solomon is important seems in order. What is the aim of righteous rule? I have suggested that David was not very keen on and successful in resolving tribal tensions. Indeed he ignored them, thus fuelling discontent, intertribal conflicts and separatist striving. Therefore justice properly administered is necessary for Israel to become united under the leadership of a righteous king. This seems to be hinted at in 3:28 where seeing Solomon's verdict "all Israel" acknowledge the king's skill in administering justice by honouring him.

Clearly and not surprisingly Solomon has been given a charisma for the benefit of Israel. In contrast to the popular view, therefore, Solomon's skill has so far not been regarded by the narrative to have primarily consisted of universal proverbial wisdom. His is a down-to-earth wisdom, a leadership capacity related to establishing and maintaining power and royal authority. Who will benefit from this: the people or only the king?

Previously I underlined how vital the designation and approval of a leader is. Since Solomon emerged in a coup and as an heir to David, his designation and acclamation are more problematic than those of either Saul or David. Solomon enjoyed the support of influential court officials such as Nathan the prophet, Zadok the priest and Benaiah, the captain of David's bodyguard. As opposed to the Adonijah party, Solomon's mentors realised that without David's approval they would fail. Therefore they tried to make the king designate Solomon. Once this has been achieved (1:29-35) other court officials only approved it (1:47).

That my discussion of Solomon's charisma is not right after or linked with his emergence (cf. Saul and David), let alone "election", but in connection with his reign is indicative of an anomaly. As opposed to his two predecessors Solomon was designated by the reigning king and, subsequently, his courtiers. They were the foremost source of Solomon's legitimacy. To apply V.P. Long's model (1994), due to the anomalies mentioned above Solomon did not demonstrate his charisma immediately subsequent to and in connection with his designation. No wonder he did not as he is not said to have it at that point. I have also claimed that Yahweh, though frequently referred to, did not actively take part in Solomon's election, and the reader can only second-guess his view on whether Solomon's designation was legitimate.

With Solomon being a hereditary king, charisma was not expected or required by those designating him. Therefore the demonstration of his charisma happened, from this perspective, quite incidentally, but was welcomed by Israel. As usual it was bestowed at Yahweh's initiative. In 3:16-27 Solomon demonstrated his charisma and it was confirmed by "all Israel" (3:28), just as in Saul and David's case. In contrast to them, however, designation and confirmation were separated, hence one finds a conflict of interest between those designating and those confirming him. For this reason Solomon's succession establishes a precedent for hereditary succession where charisma is not required. If it is still granted, from the viewpoint of the designators it is a mere incident.

CHARISMA TESTED, 1 KINGS 3:16-28

The remainder of ch. 3 reports the first occasion Solomon publicly displays his charisma. The legal case of the two prostitutes is extremely difficult to settle by a proper ruling. This is probably hinted at by the narrator who does not divulge which of the two parties is the real mother and which is lying (similarly Provan 1995:51f). Solomon's "ability to distinguish between appearance and reality" (Moberly 1999:6) and skill to lead Israel by administering justice is revealed to all by his wise ruling, so that when "all Israel heard the verdict the king had given, they held the king in awe[26], because they saw that he had wisdom from God to administer justice" (3:28).

I have discussed how Saul and David were designated, how they demonstrated their charisma and how their charismatic leadership was subsequently confirmed. The sequence and the significance of when and at what stage designation and confirmation happened were the same in both cases. Both were privately designated by the religious leader and were empowered by Yahweh's spirit. Then both demonstrated leadership skills in military deliverance, whereupon confirmation on Israel's part followed.

With Solomon the pattern changes. Due to the tense political situation Solomon needed overt designation by both the acting king and the religious and secular authorities. As I have claimed Yahweh's guidance is not mentioned. Nor do we read of Yahweh's spirit coming upon Solomon after the designation. Actually the designation itself coalesces with Solomon's coming to power, two stages in the king's emergence clearly distinguishable previously. These facts and the coup in which Solomon emerges are indicative of changes in the emergence of (charismatic) leaders. Still Israel's God is loyal to David's house

---

[26] The meaning of the term here is, of course, "to respect" and not "to fear" (contra Eslinger 1989:149; Walsh 1995:489).

and the principle of making the mighty fall and raising the low. Lowly Solomon, not high-flying Adonijah, becomes king and he is given charisma in due course, which he publicly demonstrates and which Israel confirms. As a result "King Solomon ruled over all Israel" (4:1).[27]

CHARISMA DEMONSTRATED, 1 KINGS 4-5

I have pointed out that Solomon was given charisma for the benefit of Israel. I have also claimed that the new situation required a new leadership style. Now I shall further scrutinise for what Solomon's charisma was given and, not less importantly, how he used it. First I shall study chs. 4-5. Ch. 4 starts with a reference to Solomon's rule over Israel and is about his domestic policy. The next section is headed by a sentence on his rule over vassal states (5:1; ET 4:21) and discusses his foreign policy and its effect on Israel.

Instead of waging wars Solomon has to establish vital institutions to make the kingdom function. This is what he sets out to do right after the bestowal and confirmation of his charisma by appointing state officials (4:2-6) and district governors (4:7-19). The twelve districts are to replace the twelve tribes so dissolving the tribal system.[28] What makes Solomon do this? The tribes have functioned in an emergency as a federation by providing judges to deliver them. Thus despite its looseness, the federation has been a powerful means in Yahweh's hand to provide for Israel. It has also granted the individual Israelite a certain sense and framework of identity. Obviously in a monarchy there is no need for tribal deliverers. A standing army takes their role, so diminishing Yahweh's delivering activity. The "displacement of clans and tribes made state control more effective" (Brueggemann 1978:31).

On the other hand the tribal system has made Israel, as a nation of independent tribes, an easy prey to invading foreign powers as well as to animosity and rivalry between the tribes. A unified Israel under centralised power is inevitable if the nation is to survive (cf. Mettinger 1971:119f). With the replacement of Israel's tribal system by districts Solomon achieves two things at the same time – loss of tribal identity and a powerful modern centralised state.

4:20 makes clear that the beneficiaries of Solomon's administration are Israel and Judah: "they ate, they drank and they were happy." This state of affairs in Israel is further stressed in the following section on Solomon's foreign policy (5:1-14; ET 4:21-34), at first sight a miscellaneous paragraph on unrelated aspects of Solomon's reign.

Solomon rules over a number of vassal states that brings tribute (5:1; ET 4:21). Though his royal provision (5:2f; ET 4:22f) is mentioned in this context this is not so much the contribution of vassal states as the result of the peace between Solomon and his vassals. Put differently Israel's suzerainty materialises in socio-political security in which the economy can prosper. 5:4

---

[27] Notice the corresponding phrase "all Israel" in 3:28 and 4:1.
[28] With no explicit or implicit evaluation of this one has to resort to some sociological or historical framework.

(ET 4:24) relates the cause of Solomon's provision to his rule "over all the kingdoms west of the River", while v. 5 (ET 4:25) sees the result of Solomon's rule in Israel's welfare. Control over other countries is not possible without significant and sophisticated military power implied by v. 6 (ET 4:26). The provision of the horses is mentioned after the royal provision is referred to again (5:7f; ET 4:27f). The profit of Solomon's rule is restated in 5:9 (ET 4:29; see my comments above). Solomon's wisdom is said to exceed that of contemporary sages so that every king pays tribute to it (5:10-14; ET 4:30-34). This is a section on Solomon's wisdom.

    A Solomon's suzerainty over the nations, 5:1-4
      B The result of Solomon's rule: Israel's welfare and peace, 5:5
        C Solomon's horses, 5:6
          D Solomon's royal provision, 5:7
        C' The horses' provisions, 5:8
      B' Solomon's wisdom given by God – implicitly related to Israel, 5:9
    A' Solomon's reputation amongst the nations, 5:10-14

It is a rounded-off concentric structure whose focal point is clearly the reference to the royal provisions in v. 7 (ET 4:27). The reference to the royal provisions, כלכל, "supplied provisions", in v. 7 is detailed in vv. 2f (ET 4:22f) and followed by a reference to a sage called כַּלְכֹּל, Calcol (5:11; ET 4:31), as if to say that Solomon's charisma manifests itself in wisdom and royal provisions.[29] V. 7 is flanked by two remarks on the horses in vv. 6 and 8 (ET 4:26, 28), which, again, are flanked by the statements of Israel's welfare (vv. 5, 9; ET 4:25, 29), preceded and followed by the observations on Solomon's provision (5:2f; ET 4:22f) and wisdom (5:10-13; ET 4:20-23). The whole is framed by respective references to "all the kingdoms" bringing tribute (5:1; ET 4:21) and "all the kings" paying tribute to Solomon's wisdom (5:14; ET 4:34). Kings surround Solomon like courtiers.

As far as Israel is concerned Solomon's rule in this section is beneficial. They "lived in safety, each men under his own vine and fig-tree" (5:5; cf. 5:9; ET 4:25, 29). In the peace under Solomon Knoppers (1993:88; cf. Klaus 1999:133) sees the fulfilment of God's promise in 2 Samuel 7:10f. One should, however, account for the position of the two remarks; they are not at the centre of this section on Solomon's rule. Centrally placed are the royal provisions, so hinting at the king's inclinations. The toll of Israel's happiness, on the other hand, is high and mainly taken from surrounding nations. In other words Israel under Solomon's rule thrives at the expense of vassal states. The cast of the era of the judges, when Israel was exploited by foreign oppressors, is reversed here. This is intimated by the similar syntax of 4:20 and 5:1 (ET 4:21). In the second half of 4:20 three participles are employed in reference to Israel's *shalom*,

---

[29] Similarly Solomon's "breadth of understanding as measureless as the sand, כַּחוֹל, on the seashore" (5:9; ET 4:29) might be alluded to by another name, מָחוֹל, Mahol, in the list of the sages (5:11; ET 4:31).

while the second half of the next verse uses two participles to reflect on the nations' subject status.

The ostensible topic of 5:1-14 (ET 4:21-34) is Solomon's wise rule, while the arrangement discloses the underlying tendency of self-indulgence. So what at first glance seems to be a quite clear-cut picture of the benefits of Solomon's rule is challenged at the second glance at the section's arrangement climaxing in Solomon's provisions. Both the structure and the delicate intertwining of the parallel themes, the benefits and costs of Solomon's rule, suggest that any unequivocal criticism of Solomon's reign is inevitably hasty. Chs. 4-5 emphasise that Solomon's domestic rule as well as foreign policy are meant for the benefit of Israel. He uses his wisdom charisma to establish centralised royal power and *shalom* for his nation. The similarity of 5:4b and 11b (ET 4:24, 31) implies that it is his wisdom that causes both peace and his fame to spread at home and abroad.

The second half of ch. 5 focuses on a particular aspect of Solomon's foreign policy, his treaty with Hiram, king of Tyre. The treaty is meant to bring about the building of the temple. The necessary preparations are discussed here. A diplomatic relationship is first established between Israel and Tyre. On learning of Solomon's anointing Hiram sends to Israel's king who in his turn sends a message to Hiram (5:15f; ET 5:1). Solomon points out that his father could not build the temple, but with peace achieved he is resolute to build it and proposes a plan (5:16-20; ET 5:3-6). Hiram in his response expresses his joy about the plan and encourages Solomon to go ahead (5:21-23; ET 5:7-9).

At this point the narrator states that

> Hiram supplied, נתן, Solomon's every need for timber of cedar and cypress. Solomon in turn gave, נתן, Hiram twenty thousand cors of wheat as food for his household, and twenty cors of fine oil. Solomon gave, נתן, this to Hiram year by year. So the LORD gave, נתן, Solomon wisdom, as he promised him. There was peace between Hiram and Solomon; and the two of them made a treaty. (5:24-26; NRSV 5:10-12)

Thus both Hiram's supply of wood and Solomon's provisions are in a sense related to Yahweh's bestowal of wisdom on Solomon, which results in a co-operation between Israel and Tyre. Solomon's charisma achieves peace with a neighbour.[30] Solomon starts his building projects by conscripting labourers.[31]

Solomon's wisdom produces various, often opposing, achievements. The replacement of the tribal system by twelve districts aims at a strong, centralised

---

[30] We shall see in 9:10-14 that co-operation and peace between Israel and Tyre is not that unequivocal.

[31] Provan (1995:65) asserts that, in the light of 9:22, the forced labour consisted of non-Israelites. This interpretation makes Solomon just slightly better off, for Israel was not allowed to oppress aliens (Lev 19:33f). Schäfer-Lichtenberger claims (1995:332, n. 591), in disagreement with Soggin (1982), that to the successors of the Canaanites of Joshua's time Dt 20:11 was not applicable.

royal power, necessary to unite Israel. By establishing vital institutions Solomon reorganises society in Israel.[32] Furthermore, as I have suggested, the narrative makes one see that the major achievement of Solomon was peace, socio-political stability and economic growth. Solomon's use of wisdom is related to justice (see Moberly 1999:6-9). Solomon, on the other hand, uses his wisdom to make both Israel and vassals provide for his court. The preparations for the temple project highlight that Solomon uses his God-given charisma for his royal project and not just for the benefit of the nation that it has been given for. The benefit of peace between Israel and Tyre is explicitly mentioned. The "discerning heart" given to Solomon "to govern, עַמְּךָ, this great people of yours" (3:9) has been used to a great extent for Israel's benefit – and to some extent for royal pretension. How will he use his charisma in the latter part of his rule?

Solomon's Rule Revisited, 1 Kings 9-11

Now I turn to the second part of Solomon's rule. In a close reading I shall investigate the units familiar from chs. 3-5 and follow the development of Solomon's rule and leadership style. I shall also examine the question why Solomon's second test and "confirmation" of charisma do not directly follow God's second visit as they did on the first occasion.

SOLOMON REVISITED, 1 KINGS 9:1-9

In this section only God speaks, as opposed to Solomon's dream when the king was involved in the discussion and decision making. Does this imply that, since Solomon has used his charisma increasingly one-sidedly and for his own benefit, Yahweh has had enough and now communicates without expecting response? Also when God first appeared to Solomon in ch. 3, he was concerned about charisma, i.e. the king's leadership ability. This is what Yahweh addressed in his speech most emphatically (3:11-13), which renders 3:14 a contingency warning, i.e. relevant to Solomon only in case he misuses his charisma. New developments, however, make God concerned and force him to raise the issue of Solomon's leadership style more emphatically. What exactly makes God concerned and how does he address the new situation?

The first verse is telling in this respect as it places God's visit at the time when "Solomon had finished building the temple of the LORD and the royal palace, and had achieved all he had desired to do". It reveals the king's concerns and priorities. No wonder that God is concerned about Solomon's rule. Back in 3:9 Solomon's priority was Israel, "For who is able to govern this great people of yours?" What he lacked was skill in leadership, therefore he asked for "a discerning heart to govern your people and to distinguish between right and wrong." Apparently he has forgotten this during his rule.

In 9:3 God grants Solomon's request of ch. 8 as he did in ch. 3. This verse is crucial to understand God's response and intention. I shall claim that Yahweh's

---

[32] I do not elaborate on this as the text is reticent.

words to Solomon in 6:11-13 were disruptive and disillusioning. They prevented Solomon from misusing Israel's God, even though they did not stop him pursuing his royal ambitions. Yahweh's concern about this is revealed in his words couched in rather equivocal language: אֶת־הַבַּיִת הַזֶּה אֲשֶׁר בָּנִתָה לָשׂוּם־שְׁמִי שָׁם עַד־עוֹלָם הִקְדַּשְׁתִּי, "I have hallowed this house, which thou hast built, to put my name there for ever" (9:3; KJV). It is equivocal because it ostensibly means, as most translations render it, that by putting his name in the temple forever Yahweh has complied with Solomon's intention. In actual fact, though, in line with his principle divulged to the reader so far, Yahweh only refers to Solomon's intention and not what he did – the subject of 9:3f and 3e is the same.[33]

"My eyes and my heart will always be there"; God announces his commitment to the house. Or does he? Does he state his commitment or rather require awareness of the Lord of the temple for the people to maintain covenant loyalty, elaborated on in the following? Josipovici even hears "in this speech a gentle rebuke to Solomon for trying to raise himself above his father" (1988:101). Whereas Solomon wanted to make Yahweh dwell in the temple, he only gets Yahweh's eyes and heart to be present. Reaching the clear warning of v. 4, Yahweh's ambiguous utterances have come to an end. Here God introduces his unambiguous terms with a stress on the changed subject, Solomon, וְאַתָּה ("and you"), "I have granted your request; as for you now...", then the conditions listed (see Josipovici 1988:100f). As in 6:12 the stipulations are related to the appropriate use of charisma.

CHARISMA DEMONSTRATED – ROYAL PROJECTS, 1 KINGS 9:10-28

In the first discussion of how Solomon used his charisma I claimed that the king demonstrated his wisdom by using his charisma in a way that benefited Israel. In chs. 4-5 this wise use was manifest in state institutions established, which ensured political and social stability and economic prosperity for Israel. Likewise Israel's international relationships profited from Solomon's reign by mutually advantageous trade and treaties. Israel became a regional cultural and economic centre. How are political and social stability, economic prosperity and international relationships seen after the building projects? First I turn to the section on Solomon's charisma at work, 9:10-28. The section is made up of two sub-sections on the Solomon-Hiram economic relationship, which embrace the central discussion of Solomon's building projects.

9:10-14 discuss what happened after the completion of the temple and the

---

[33] It is likely that this is intended. That is to say, by resorting to equivocality, Yahweh bamboozles the high-flying king. The difference between 9:3 and 8:29, to which it refers back, may buttress this. Solomon asked for Yahweh's eyes to watch the temple of which – by taking 2 Sam 7:13, unless an interpolation, to mean this – he allegedly said: "My Name shall be there". In 9:3 Yahweh confirms his willingness to watch the temple but refrains from committing himself totally to the building by putting his name there. In other words by only "lending" his eyes and heart Yahweh tries to prevent Solomon from misusing his name (cf. Ex 20:7).

palace. In payment for Hiram's supply of timber and gold Solomon gives him 20 towns in Galilee. On seeing them, however, Hiram is not at all impressed, indicated by the naming of the area. If there has been limited co-operation between the two monarchs, it is here even more limited (see Provan 1995:64; Walsh 1996:96-99, 121f[34]). "The friendly, reciprocal relationship between the two kings" (Provan 1995:65) has changed for the worse (similarly Parker 1992:83f).[35] Thus Hiram sends, שלח, Solomon 120 talents of gold.[36] Whatever the explanation of this the beneficiary is obviously Solomon with Hiram probably acting as the junior partner of the treaty (Provan 1995:84f). As far as Israel is concerned, however, by losing territory to Tyre it is the victim of Solomon's politics.[37]

Gold is also becoming of major interest to Solomon. Whereas in chs. 4-5 it was not mentioned in the description of his wealth (Provan 1995:85), in "1 Kings 9:10-10:29 Solomon is a king who accumulates gold in extraordinarily large amounts—amounts that increase as we read (120 talents in 9:14; 420 in 9:28; 666 in 10:14 [...]) and that are collected from more and more exotic places (9:28; 10:22)" (85). In fact Porten (1967:111) observes the "progression in the frequency of the delivery": 9:28 reports the gold gained on a single voyage. The queen of Sheba brings spices, gold and precious stones (10:2, 10). From Ophir Solomon acquires gold, almug wood and precious stones (10:11). The Tarshish fleet triennially provides the king with gold, silver, ivory, apes and baboons (10:22). And finally the whole earth brings the king silver, gold, garments, myrrh, spices, horses and mules every year (10:25).[38]

The concluding part of the frame (vv. 26-28), again, addresses the economic aspect of the treaty between Israel and Tyre. Again, it is Hiram who sends,

---

[34] Walsh sees Solomon in the sections on the contract with Hiram in 5:22-26 (ET 5:8-12) and 9:10-14 negatively. In this section the "'wise' Solomon has not gotten a bargain" (99); the second passage depicts "Solomon as a shrewd and successful bargainer [...] able to turn a huge profit on relatively worthless land" (121f). I agree with Walsh, except that I view Solomon in the first section rather positively – as opposed to ch. 9, here he does not yet have imperialistic-exploitive tendencies.

[35] Here a word on Kuan's paper (1990) is necessary. He suggests that in their relationship Solomon was subordinate to Hiram. I think that this might be a feasible conjecture as far as ch. 5 is concerned (Cross though sees it differently; 1973:240). From ch. 9 on, however, the text is quite unambiguous about Solomon's increased power and superiority (see Knoppers 1993:87, n. 60), and I shall argue accordingly. Despite new insights in Kuan's article a great deal of it lacks textual evidence and remains a hypothesis.

[36] Nothing in the MT suggests, as do the NIV and NRSV, that 9:14 refers to a previous action and that the predicate is to be rendered by the pluperfect.

[37] Not to mention that the selling of Israelite land was a grave infringement of the Deuteronomic code. Schäfer-Lichtenberger (1995:332f) views Pharaoh's handing over Gezer to Solomon as an outstanding deed showing respect to Yahweh by a foreigner, an attitude the Deuteronomist occasionally exalts.

[38] Porten regards this "progression" as positive; I regard it as negative.

שלח, his servants to assist Solomon's in their maritime trade. And again it is Solomon who benefits from the trade.
The central part of the section (9:15-25) is arranged concentrically.

A Introduction to the section on forced labour conscripted, עלה, by Solomon; construction, בנה, of the temple, palace and the supporting terraces; Pharaoh's siege, introduced by עלה, "to go up", and gift to his daughter; vv. 15f[39]
    B Solomon's various projects built, בנה, (v. 17) by forced labour, עלה (v. 21); vv. 17-23
A' Pharaoh's daughter moves, עלה, into her palace, built, בנה, along with the supporting terraces and the temple by Solomon; Solomon's yearly offering, עלה, of sacrifice on the altar built, בנה, for Yahweh; vv. 24f

Conspicuously the verb עלה is employed five times – twice each in the frame, vv. 15-16 and 24-25, and once in the middle, v. 21 – with three different meanings. In vv. 15 and 21 it refers to the conscription of forced labour, in vv. 16 and 24 to the Pharaoh's coming up from Egypt and his daughter's to her palace respectively, while in v. 25 it denotes Solomon's sacrifices. בנה, "to build", is also used in reference to these three areas. Thus it is used in connection with the constructions by forced labour, Solomon's palace and the temple. These verbs are the keywords of the section. בנה, "to build", denotes Solomon's main focus and activity. עלה in *hiphil*, the verb of God's saving act from Egypt ("to bring out up"), is re-designed to fit royal projects. The subject of the verb is Solomon most of the time and never Yahweh, who is thus excluded from Israel's monarchy. In fact even Solomon's activities in v. 25 (העלה, "to offer offerings", and בנה, "to build"), by having the king as their subject, render the activity of the God of Israel, who redeemed, העלה, Israel from Egypt in the past and promised to build, בנה, a house for David in the future (2 Sam 7), redundant. Israel has become a self-sufficient and self-sustaining kingdom. In ch. 1 עלה, "to go up", was employed to mark Solomon's installation (vv. 35, 40, 45). I claimed that despite the manifold references to Yahweh Israel's God was remarkably absent from the events. Similarly to ch. 1, Yahweh is not mentioned in this section; the subject of the verb is always a royal person – Solomon (9:15, 21, 25, *hiphil*), Pharaoh (9:16,

---

[39] Discussing 9:16 Provan (1995:88, his emphasis) asks: "Why are we told of these Joshua-like exploits just at this point? Perhaps for this reason: that it helps us to see clearly just how easily *Solomon*, in all his glory and power, *could* have dealt with the Canaanites in the way deuteronomic law had commanded—if he had wished to. It points to the conclusion, in other words, that he continued to use them as labor *out of choice*, rather than out of necessity, because of his enthusiasm for building—and so willingly put himself at risk of their baneful influence." He is correct unless different rules apply to Solomon's period than to the conquest.

qal) or his daughter (9:24, *qal*). In ch. 1 the verb was used in relation to Solomon's emergence; in ch. 9 it is used in relation to his leadership style.[40] This usage will prevail in the rest of the Solomon narrative (see 10:5, 16f, 29). It is as if the verb has been appropriated for royal use by eliminating Yahweh and his action.

Parker (1988:24) has observed that whereas the forced labour in ch. 5 was conscripted for the temple project, here it is related to a number of building projects. As the number of projects increases so does that of the labourers (see also Chaney 1986:69).

The reference to Pharaoh's daughter is interesting for a couple of reasons. Firstly she is mentioned in the inner part of the frame, vv. 16 and 24. In v. 16 she is said to have been given Gezer "as a wedding gift" by his father. Likewise v. 24 sees her move into the palace specially built for her by her husband. Thus both verses concern her dowries.

Secondly she moves "from the City of David to the palace Solomon had built for her" (v. 24). In my discussion of 2 Samuel 5 I observed that the "City of David" referred to the centralisation motif. In line with the custom of ANE kings David re-named Jerusalem, made it his capital and subsequently intended to build a temple for his guardian deity. In comparison with Solomon, however, David was a tribal chief liberating Israel from foreign oppressors. From the very beginning Solomon has consciously acted as a monarch of international importance. As such he married the daughter of the most powerful neighbour. Of course a rural town is not worthy of the dignity of the emperor's daughter; hence major construction work is carried out to modernise it: palaces, temples and other buildings are built to welcome Pharaoh's daughter. The City of David is turned into the City of Solomon – a city of international fame, befitting her.

It is a difficult question how v. 25, which is rather positive as regards Solomon (see Dt 16:16), fits this arrangement.[41] I would suggest that there are at least two themes in the verse related to the section. The first is the building project theme I have elaborated on. Notice too that v. 24 concludes with the references to Solomon's wife's palace and the construction of the supporting terraces, whereas v. 25 ends with the note on the completion of the temple. The completion is referred to by the verb שׁלם. This concerns my second observation, because the root, either in verbal or nominal form, occurs three times: שְׁלֹמֹה, Solomon, שְׁלָמִים, "peace offerings", שָׁלֵם, "finished". Their connotation of "completeness" and the remark on the completion of the temple may imply what Solomon achieves by the building projects and his religious politics[42] – a complete and powerful centralised kingdom. Israel's שָׁלוֹם, *shalom*, is superseded by the temple being finished, שָׁלֵם.

By now the underlying theme of the section has become evident. The

---

[40] This is anticipated by 3:4, 15 and 5:27.
[41] See also Brettler 1991:90 who compares 9:24f with 3:1f and suggests that the former set of verses was "placed where they currently stand for structural reasons".
[42] Is he acting as a Pontifex Maximus here?

section's frame (vv. 10-14 and 26-28) informs of the business of two monarchs. Hiram is first discontent but then, presumably, profits from the trade. More importantly the focus is on Solomon who in both instances comes out as the beneficiary. This is the point of the section. In chs. 4-5 kings, though they were present, were rather generally referred to. Here royalty (Pharaoh, his daughter, Hiram and later the queen of Sheba) signal their increased weight. There Israel was said to benefit from Solomon's rule; here the nation does not play a role in the business of monarchs. The implication is that Solomon uses charisma for his own benefit. The central sub-section only reinforces this point. Again royals at work are presented; the forced labour, the construction work, the dowries to Pharaoh's daughter purport to imperial building projects. And although Israel benefits by not being conscripted to forced labour (9:22f), their benefit is undoubtedly as minimal as the weight of the reference.

All in all Solomon is depicted as a wise and shrewd oriental monarch who uses his wisdom charisma to take advantage of and exploit other nations. In this Israel seems to benefit little while the royal court grows extremely wealthy.

CHARISMA RE-TESTED, 1 KINGS 10:1-13

In ch. 3 Solomon was granted charisma for the benefit of Israel and the king used it accordingly by administering justice. I now turn to the paragraph I consider Solomon's second test, because of parallels with 3:16-28. In both sections, in front of women (Parker 1988:23), Solomon's skill is tested then affirmed. Minor similarities to be mentioned in due course also strengthen this observation. The question here is how the king uses charisma.

The story is about the encounter of two ANE monarchs. In line with royal protocol and pretension the queen of Sheba arrives with a huge amount of gifts to meet Israel's renowned king. She tests him and, on seeing its signs, is persuaded of Solomon's wisdom. Now what are those signs? The text is quite unequivocal when it states (10:4f): "When the queen of Sheba saw all the wisdom of Solomon and the palace he had built, the food on his table, the seating of his officials, the attending servants in their robes, his cupbearers, and the burnt offerings he made at the temple of the LORD, she was overwhelmed." The queen is persuaded on seeing the royal court, its wealth and what the king has achieved – the materialisation of Solomon's wisdom. The focus of ch. 10 "is very much upon the benefit that wisdom brings to the royal court and particularly to Solomon himself rather than upon any benefit that might flow out to the people" (Provan 1995:87; see also Parker 1992:85). It is as if the queen came with a demonstration of royal affluence, but seeing Solomon's she becomes convinced of the higher quality of Solomon's wisdom, i.e. that Solomon's wisdom achieves royal wealth more effectively. "She cannot eclipse him" (Provan 1995:89).

The queen's affirmation of Solomon's wisdom charisma is introduced by a reference to her "seeing" it and concluded with one to her "hearing" thereof. This catches the eye for various reasons. Firstly Solomon's charisma was affirmed by all Israel at "hearing", שמע, his verdict, "because they saw, ראה, that he had wisdom from God to administer justice" (3:28). Similarly here the queen "saw, ראה, all the wisdom of Solomon" (10:4) this time, however, visible in the set-up of the royal court. Then she reaffirms her impression of Solomon's wisdom by a reference to "having heard", שמע, of it (v. 6) and now "seeing", ראה, the authenticity of the hearsay (v. 7). A final parallel is 5:14 (ET 4:34) where people "of all nations came to listen, שמע, to Solomon's wisdom, sent by all the kings of the world, who had heard, שמע, of his wisdom."

Whereas in 3:28 wisdom became visible in a wise ruling and the administration of justice, i.e. for the people's benefit, for which Solomon's charisma was given, in ch. 10 the queen of Sheba perceives the king's wisdom in affluence and royal pretension. Israel was looking for a manifestation of just rule and they got it in justice administered. The queen is interested in the style (exterior manifestations) of ruling and she sees it in extensive wealth. Not surprisingly, as the king was given charisma for their benefit, Israel was concerned with how they could profit. The queen is concerned with how a monarch can. No wonder then that, whereas Israel both "heard" and "saw" the king's wisdom manifest in justice, the queen only "saw" it in his wealth and its manifestations. After all, gold, food, palaces and goblets can hardly be enjoyed by the ear. The queen benefited in a rather different way when receiving the king's presents. After hearing Solomon's wise request for wisdom Yahweh promised him "what you have not asked for—both riches and honour" (3:13). After hearing Solomon's wise answers the queen of Sheba honours him with riches (10:10). This "fulfilment" of the promise is ironic.

No less important is the confirmation of charisma. I have claimed that Solomon's charisma was eventually recognised and confirmed by Israel the beneficiary. At Solomon's second test his charisma is recognised and confirmed – this time, however, by an outsider to the charisma's supposed scope. His use of the charisma to benefit the queen and his political aspirations appears to diverge from the purpose for which it was requested.

I pointed out the close relation of Solomon's charisma with administering justice in the early chapters. Startlingly the only reference to justice in this section occurs in the queen's benediction of Solomon (10:9): "Because of the LORD's eternal love for Israel, he has made you king, to maintain justice and righteousness." In the light of these observations this is rather ironic, because it is a correct formulation of what the reign of Israel's monarch should be about, and, as a matter of fact, of what it is not. At least, apart from this, administration of justice is not mentioned in this section.[43] It is also strange to hear it uttered by one monarch to another as his only concern is manifestation of royal wealth (contra Jobling 1991:67).

The concentric conclusion to the section (vv. 10-13) only strengthens the impression of wealth as a royal priority.

    A The queen of Sheba gives presents to Solomon, 10a
        B "Never again were so many spices brought in…" 10bc

---

[43] The only other reference to justice after 3:11 and 28 is 7:7.

C Solomon's other acquisitions, 11-12a
B' "So much almug-wood has never been imported or seen since that day." 12bc
A' Solomon gives presents to the queen of Sheba, 13

A-A' are about the exchange of wealth as part of the diplomatic protocol of ANE monarchs. B-B' detail the extraordinary merchandise and wealth accumulated by trade. The arrangement and wording render C quite ambiguous by making Solomon's cultic activity subject to accumulating wealth and royal splendour.

My discussion has also answered the question why Solomon's second test and confirmation do not follow right after God's second visit but rather after the section on the use of charisma in 9:1-28. The emphasis on royal figures on the one hand and Solomon's relationship with Hiram, their trade and the building projects on the other make Solomon a wealthy king with a magnificent court. This is exactly what impresses the queen of Sheba. Their meeting is just another encounter of royals whose only interest is the demonstration of affluence. At the same time, Solomon's way of using charisma does not benefit Israel. God's people are left out of the royal business, in the cold. Brettler's claim (1991:90) that the focus of the story "is not Solomon's wisdom, as many scholars contend, but his wealth" is thus correct with the qualification that the story presents Solomon's wisdom in relation to his wealth and not to his subjects, and therefore criticises the king.

By reporting on the encounter of two royals, and this with reference to huge quantities of presents and kingly affluence, the themes of wealth and oriental kingship, those of 10:14-29, have been introduced.

CHARISMA DEMONSTRATED – SOLOMON'S GRANDEUR, 1 KINGS 10:14-29

The topic of this section is Solomon's grandeur; "it is Solomon's wealth that dominates" here (Walsh 1996:131). It is minutely described and every motif contributes to the picture – Solomon was a very affluent king. This is intimated by his trade activity. The huge amount of gold he received yearly, the horse trade from which he benefited, the luxury articles, the gifts presented to him by those coming to hear his wisdom all contributed to his wealth.

In the first half of the section "gold" occurs 10 times in total (10:14, 16 twice, 17 twice, 18, 21 twice, 22, 25), so revealing the king's main concern. Gold is used for the shields (vv. 16f) as well as the throne (v. 18). Both military and royal-judicial power may be emphasised in this way. The golden goblets (v. 21) were luxurious, and their mention, along with vv. 15, 22, 28f, stresses Solomon's economic power. Another contributor to Solomon's splendour is the horse trade. In addition to benefiting by mediating between Egypt, Kue and the North, Solomon acquires a great number of horses and chariots for military purposes. Unlike the references to gold and horses, silver is mentioned in asides or lists thus not making up a sub-section. Its sixfold occurrence (10:21f, 25, 27, 29) still highlights royal wealth. Solomon has become self-indulgent (contra Knoppers 1996:337-42).

From this section concerning Solomon's grandeur only two aspects are missing. Firstly there is no reference whatsoever to Israel for whose benefit Solomon's wisdom charisma was meant (similarly Walsh 1996:131f). Secondly, apart from v. 24, God is not referred to. V. 24 itself draws attention to a charisma originally given to benefit God's people but rather used as a tourist attraction, an aspect foreshadowed in 5:14 (ET 4:34).[44] Charisma is presented here as used to accumulate wealth and establish a lofty image of oriental kingship for the king's sake. Charisma has become an autonomous entity, with no reference to its original purpose of benefiting God's people. Solomon is portrayed as a self-sufficient king, not dependent on Yahweh and his power. Obviously "the king has changed: his own glory and wealth have become more important than the good of Yahweh's people" (Walsh 1996:132).

THE KING'S WIVES, 1 KINGS 11:1-13

Thus far King Solomon has mainly used charisma to accumulate wealth. With ch. 11 this changes. Here, with or without the use of charisma, he acquires many wives. The section is introduced by an ominous sentence on Solomon's changed priorities: "King Solomon, however, loved many foreign women" (11:1). This is in striking contrast to the claim of 3:3, which stated the king's covenant loyalty towards Yahweh. The change is further specified in 11:4, "his heart was not fully devoted, שָׁלֵם, to the LORD his God".[45] In 5:4 and 26 (ET 4:24 and 5:12) the root denoted the political stability Solomon's rule brought about by covenant obedience and the wise use of charisma. The rest of the narrative on Solomon will elaborate on the social and political unrest and discontent Solomon's disobedience and misuse of charisma causes. The mishap is even more salient with Solomon's claim in 2:33 in mind, "But on David and his descendants, his house and his throne, may there be the LORD's peace, שָׁלוֹם, forever."

Certainly Solomon's marriages are partly to be seen as politically expedient to secure peace with neighbours. On the other hand acquiring wives, particularly in this quantity, is but another expression of royal pretension. But it is definitely more than just demonstrating royal affluence and the status quo. It entails compromise and disobedience to the Sovereign of the covenant. Vv. 7f make clear that by marrying foreign wives Solomon opens the door to covenant disobedience. After a number of ambiguous and less ambiguous discussions on Solomon's reign this section presents the abyss of Solomon's deterioration in unambiguous language. No wonder that of the four addresses Yahweh delivers to the king the last one (11:9-13) is the most categorical: "Yahweh is angry and condemns Solomon for his failure to fulfill the conditions imposed on him" (Walsh 1996:154).

---

[44] Boff's rather general statement (1985:161) seems to fit here nonetheless. He claims that when improperly used charisma "loses its nature and becomes a spiritualistic curiosity."

[45] Thus the king is the first to break his own charge in 8:61 (cf. the same vocabulary).

THE AFTERMATH OF SOLOMON'S (MIS)USE OF CHARISMA, 1 KINGS 11:14-43

The last section on Solomon's rule is striking for at least two reasons. I have asserted that Yahweh has increasingly been sidelined in Solomon's monarchy. Here he reappears. Indeed he does so in a rather spectacular way – by raising up both external (Hadad, Rezon) and internal (Jeroboam) adversaries to Solomon. At the beginning of his reign Solomon had to face three adversaries; at the end of it he faces another three (Schäfer-Lichtenberger 1995:348; cf. Parker 1988:22). The king has come full circle.

Secondly Israel benefits less and less from the king's use of charisma. Therefore references to God's people dwindle as Solomon's story develops. Though we have not heard of Israel lately as affected by Solomon's use of charisma, in this last section Israel is finally in the focus. "Israel" is mentioned 6 times (vv. 25, 31f, 37f, 42); but the one concerned about Israel is not its king but its Suzerain.

Enemies and rebels are but the side-effect of Solomon's rule and the consequence of his disobedience and Yahweh's wrath. This makes it clear that he falls short of his request to "distinguish between right and wrong" (3:9), an essential quality of a Yahwistic ruler. What he gets here is adversaries versus the peace of his early rule (4:20; 5:4f; ET 4:24f).

The Axis: Yahweh's Conflict with Oriental Kingship, 1 Kings 6-8

The above interpretation has demonstrated that the temple and palace projects are positioned at a watershed in Solomon's rule, so that to speak of a "pre-temple" (charismatic) and a "post-temple" (misusing charisma) Solomon appears appropriate. Obviously this change should be shown or at least hinted at in the temple section. What role do the building projects play in this development? How do they contribute to a changed Solomon? I shall also attend to questions such as why the description of the temple is interrupted by Yahweh's words to Solomon in ch. 6 and by the description of the palace in ch. 7. I shall not deal with the lengthy descriptive part extensively, but rather focus on motifs related to the conflict between God and king, particularly on Yahweh's speech in ch. 6 and his appearance in ch. 8.

Building a temple for the patron deity was a common practice amongst ANE kings. Still the temple project is viewed by Yahweh and the narrator alike as Solomon's partisan action. A number of textual motifs as well as theological aspects show this. The first problem is that there is no reference in 2 Samuel 7 to Yahweh's delight in or approval of David's plan. This suggests that 1 Kings 8:18 might be an invented declaration. If so 8:17-21 is the king's presumptuous claim; as Eslinger puts it (1989:158), "'what you see before you—this temple and myself—are the fulfilment of God's promise to David. The age of the Davidic covenant is upon us.'"

The disagreement on the temple between Solomon and God is obvious once we remember the king's commissioning in ch. 3. There his concern was how his rule can sustain Israel's welfare. As a sign of God's delight in Solomon's request he was granted a charisma to this end. Obviously administration of justice to Israel did not necessitate a temple – that was designed to support ideological-political privileges. In other words the temple project is seen as a departure from Solomon's primary commitment to Israel's benefit towards a self-serving kingship.

God's word to Solomon (6:11-13) disrupts the description of the temple so dividing it into a more general section dealing mostly with the exterior (6:2-10) and one pertaining to the details, particularly of the interior layout (6:14-35). Vv. 36-38 conclude the chapter. What interests me is why God's warning is reported at that particular point.

God's word begins with, 'As for this temple you are building' (6:12). This introduction fits well the context of the description of the temple as well as Solomon's preoccupation with it. Still what ensues is a sort of *anacoluthon*, as there is no follow-up or conclusion to the introduction (cf. Walsh 1996:105). After the stipulation (6:12), which is couched in much stronger language than that in 3:14 (Eslinger 1989:142), Yahweh commits himself – not to the temple nor the dynasty, but to Israel (6:13): "I will live among the Israelites and will not abandon my people Israel." Two crucial issues have thus been raised: where Yahweh dwells, and on what condition he remains committed to his people. Solomon's major concern is to establish and maintain the royal image. To this end he uses the temple and religion. He builds the temple to make Yahweh dwell in it and in this way ensure his protection of Israel. Yahweh the Suzerain of the covenant, however, eschews this expectation by making clear his requirement of the inferior party. It is God who sets the agenda – Solomon is to comply.

Solomon's intention may be referred to right at the beginning of the temple account. The last clause of 6:1 states, וַיִּבֶן הַבַּיִת לַיהוָה. This is best rendered, in my view, as "and he [Solomon] began to build the temple for Yahweh", as "Yahweh's temple" is never referred to by this construction but always without the *lamed*. The next clause (6:2), וְהַבַּיִת אֲשֶׁר בָּנָה הַמֶּלֶךְ שְׁלֹמֹה לַיהוָה, "The temple that King Solomon built for the LORD", supports the impression of a temple being built to accommodate Yahweh. That this construction never again recurs after Yahweh's speech may be a sign that Solomon recognised his mistake. Yahweh's main concern is to get the king to maintain covenant loyalty by using his charisma properly. God's word not only disrupts the description of the temple but, containing an *anacoluthon*, is itself disrupted. Most significantly it disrupts Solomon's expectation to make Yahweh dwell in the building built for him. Only in 8:12f will the king realise that Yahweh cannot be subjected to projects of royal pretension.

As for the arrangement of the chapter, I suggest that the placement of God's message disrupts not only the description but also Solomon's intention, which was its purpose. Yahweh's warning was successful in this respect. Or was it? Ch. 8 and 9:1-9 make clear that Solomon did not relinquish and Yahweh is concerned about that – the issue is not settled satisfactorily. Though Solomon continues to maintain his royal image, on every occasion Yahweh ensures that he and his temple be not used to this end. Yahweh's contravention must disillusion Solomon each time.

To better see the implications of 1 Kings 6-8 for my theme I shall consult Gabriel Josipovici. In his book he devotes an entire chapter to the building of the tabernacle, the obvious backdrop to the temple project, and compares it with the text of 1 Kings 6 (1988:90-107). Josipovici argues that the detailed account of the tabernacle stresses the making process[46]: "What we are presented with here is the dramatization of making, not the description of a finished object" (103). He remarks on the important fact

> that the object is a tent and not a stone building. It is made of poles and curtains and is only itself when in action, so to speak, as an animal cannot be adequately understood in terms of bones and skin, but needs to be studied in movement, as a living whole. So the tent is always going to be more than the kit that makes up its parts. Each time it is erected, therefore, the process of making is renewed. And it is a process we readily accede to because for us too there has been a process: the process of reading. In neither case – the erecting of the tent or reading – do we have the finished object before us. (104)

In addition to the attempt of locating God in a solid building, here lies the basic difference between tabernacle and temple. I have frequently referred to the "description" of the temple. The Exodus account is not a description of a finished object, rather it is a presentation of an unending process. It does not describe a state but emphasises "the process of making as itself a sign of God's relation to man and man's to God" (105).

This also reveals the reason for God's unwillingness to "move" into a building. Whereas the tent was a constant reminder of the dynamic aspect of the God-Israel relationship built on Yahweh's dynamic character, a religion centred on a solid building infringes upon this aspect. With the temple project, a means of centralisation in Solomon's hand, Israelite religion goes through a major transformation. Religion is becoming a royal medium to maintain power.

Moreover the Exodus account stresses Yahweh's involvement and that everything should be, and in fact was, carried out according to his plan and command. To a similar extent the temple narrative makes Solomon the instigator of the project (see Josipovici 1988:100). Exodus 35 also points out the willingness of the people in making the tent. Josipovici (100) is probably wrong in his suggestion that the forced labour conscripted by Solomon was Israelite and as such "reminiscent of the Israelites in Egypt" (see Provan 1995:65), God's people, however, were not really involved in the project, nor eager to build the temple. As opposed to the Exodus account, here there is "no talk of divine inspiration or equipping of those directly involved in the building of the temple. To that extent the account of Solomon's activities is 'secular' as compared with the 'sacral' emphasis of the priestly tabernacle account" (Gordon 1995:100).

---

[46] See the abundance of *verbi finiti* in the Exodus account as opposed to the increased weight of nominal sentences in 1 Kgs 6.

The description of the temple suggests a magnificent shrine with elaborate splendour.[47] The 7 years spent building it were apparently not a waste of time. When compared with the minimal description of the royal palace that was built over 13 years, however, one cannot help wondering what the palace looked like if it took almost twice as long as the temple to finish (Josipovici 1988:100).

With this observation I shall go on to discuss the description of the palace (7:1-12), which interrupts that of the temple. The time it took to build the palace and some other details (like the excessive use of cedar) suggest that Solomon is more interested in it than in the temple. This may also be implied by the disruption to the account of the temple project. Provan has noticed "an emphatic contrast" between the two houses (1995:69; see also his comment on 3:1; 44f), which is

> implied in the double use of the verb *klh*. The key here lies in noting that the extra element in 7:1, when compared with 6:38, is the curious *kol* before *bêtô*: "He completed the temple... he completed *the whole of* his house." The implication is that Solomon not only spent more time on the palace project, but also pushed it through to completion before fully finishing his work on the temple. This explains why the account of the palace-building has been inserted between 6:38 and 7:13. The positioning is itself intended to indicate how Solomon's energies were diverted from temple- to palace-building, to the detriment of the former... (100; his italics)

The arrangement might indicate Solomon's disrupted interest in religion, maybe due to God's sobering message in 6:12f concerning the king's intention and attitude to use Yahwism to his own end. Ch. 8 exposes the most remarkable case of the king's attitude.

To introduce the new Solomonic order the ark is to be transferred from the tent to its proper dwelling place, the temple. As David's attempts has shown, this transfer "is a dangerous and unpredictable business" (Walsh 1996:110). Its unpredictability will be proved in due time (8:10f), and only God's mercy will avert the tragedy.

8:12 has Solomon facing the temple watching the priests bring the ark into it. Just when they are finished and about to perform their service, thus ready to complete Solomon's project, the cloud, the sign of Yahweh's presence, appears and interrupts all procedures. Interpreters take God's appearance as "a sure sign that the new arrangements for worship have the divine blessing" (Provan 1995:76). "The Mosaic covenant and the Davidic covenant were thereby intimately bound together", as the erection of the temple is compared to the erection of the tent (Ex 40:17ff) followed by the cloud of God's presence descending upon it (Porten 1967:120). While Porten might be correct, these explanations, by taking the reference to "the cloud" and/or the event's import for granted, imply that Solomon was in fact counting on God's appearance in

---

[47] The lavish use of gold in the temple may foreshadow Solomon's preoccupation with it in chs. 9-10.

the cloud – the God of the covenant took stage on schedule. What is puzzling in the account, though, is "the cloud" filling the temple (8:10f). "Cloud" is employed with the definite article, the lack of previous references notwithstanding. The effect of this is that, with the temple finished, the ark transferred into it and the priests prepared to perform their service, Yahweh's glory, as if waiting for the moment of intervention, frustrates Solomon's final act of ritual performance.[48] Solomon's reaction to the events (8:12f) can be read as supporting this interpretation.

It is also worth noting that the cloud referred to by the narrator as הֶעָנָן (vv. 10f), from the king's point of view is הָעֲרָפֶל, "dark cloud" (v. 12). The change is intriguing because this phrase occurs only 15 times in the FT, and is always related to God's numinous and terrible appearance. Its first occurrence is the most significant in relation to Solomon's use. Exodus 20:21 reads: "The people remained at a distance, while Moses approached the thick darkness, הָעֲרָפֶל, where God, הָאֱלֹהִים, was." This awesome godhead cannot be approached simply by anyone. The following rationale given by God (20:22-25) portrays him as a rather puritan god. In contrast Solomon's temple was anything but puritan. Solomon's reference to Yahweh who dwells in הָעֲרָפֶל (8:12) makes the king appear to realise the discrepancy between his project and God.

Solomon's speech consists of four distinct parts, each with an introduction (vv. 12, 14, 22f, 55). What concerns me is the king's first speech in 8:12f, which precedes his proper address. Facing the temple Solomon says: "The LORD has said that he would dwell in a dark cloud; I have indeed built a magnificent temple for you, a place for you to dwell forever."[49] Again, conventional interpretation regards it as a part of the ceremony, i.e. Solomon's introductory speech. However, 8:14 marks an interruption and introduces the address proper.[50] Thus in 8:12f, having been taken by surprise by Yahweh's unexpected action, the king is in a state of shock and murmurs to himself: "In vain have I built this magnificent temple, because the one I made it for dwells in clouds."[51] But he dare not admit it publicly, only to himself. Then he turns around to bless the people.

The following speech supports this "turn-around" in Solomon's thinking.

---

[48] Hurowitz (1992:269f) has noticed that the theme of 1 Kgs 8, the deity being brought into his temple, "has its closest parallel in 2 Samuel 6" (317). If so it is remarkable that in both accounts Yahweh resists the respective king's manipulation.

[49] DeVries (1985:125) argues for the restoration of the LXX rendering of vv. 12-14a, for it "is the best guide in restoring this *mangled* hymn" (my emphasis). The LXX's mention of the sun may make the hymn more complete, but I do not think it is indispensable. As for the reference to the "Book of the Upright One" I find it very awkward in this speech. The clause, "And the king turned away his face", is admittedly misplaced, as it "offers a poor preparation for Dtr's 'then he blessed....'" Why then retain it?

[50] Knoppers (1995:239), albeit in strictly literary-critical terms, lists vv. 10-13 under "Assymetry and Imbalance in 1 Kings 8". His observation may support my argument.

[51] Eslinger (1989:158) has come to a similar interpretation of 8:12f.

"Solomon's attitude toward Yahweh manifests grateful praise, reverence, and trust, as well as a realistic understanding of the role of obedience and repentance for sin in the life of the people", Walsh correctly asserts. Then he adds, "In short, we see here a dimension of Solomon's character we have not had occasion to witness before" (1996:115). Had we really had no occasion, we could blame the narrator for failure in Solomon's characterisation. However, I have demonstrated the temptation of royal pretension which Solomon grew increasingly too weak to resist. For a fading moment, here he has come to realise Yahweh's elusiveness and the vanity of his endeavour.

The centrality of the building projects in the chiastic arrangement implies that this is the axis upon which the previous and following sections turn. It demonstrates a delicate and implicit power struggle between king and god. Solomon, through various means, tries to establish himself as an oriental monarch. He builds the temple to make Yahweh dwell there (cf. Tsevat 1980:92), but the palace project soon takes his interest, revealing his main concern: furnishing an image of oriental kingship. The temple project is shown as an attempt to use Yahweh. Though Yahweh consistently refuses, his refusal only diminishes the king's resolution without totally destroying it. The disproportion between the discussion of the building projects and references to justice make evident the main emphasis of Solomon's reign. Solomon has gone a long way from being a modest ruler aware of his own incompetence and Yahweh's suzerainty (ch. 3) to the professional oriental monarch of chs. 6-8.

Yahweh's words in ch. 6 and his appearance in ch. 8[52] show his desire to thwart, in a rather low-key and moderate manner, Solomon's move towards a self-indulgent and autonomous oriental kingship; thus keeping the Israelite monarchy and its monarch within the boundary of the covenant. In other words Israel's God is determined to maintain his status as the Suzerain of Israel, his vassal, and to correct the course the king has taken. He is intent on sticking to the covenant, regardless of the self-seeking projects and obstructions by his servant Solomon.

Solomon's Rule Evaluated

I have argued that Solomon's reign is presented in three major blocks: chs. 3-5, 6-8 and 9-11. Having dealt with these units individually I shall now attempt to integrate them into the total picture to make sense of the whole.

The starting picture of Solomon's rule (3:1-3) foreshadows its most important aspects, elaborated on in the subsequent narrative. God's visit presents a unique opportunity to the king, who wisely chooses what he is in want of – skill to lead Israel (3:4-15). This skill is first tested and approved (3:16-28). So far so good. The picture of the benefits of Solomon's use of charisma in chs. 4-5 is slightly ambiguous. Even though the king's wisdom is manifest in "juridical brilliance, administrative efficiency, and encyclopedic

---

[52] And his words in chs. 3 and 9. On Yahweh's words in the Solomon story see Schäfer-Lichtenberger 1995:352-55.

knowledge" (Knoppers 1993:85) and it contributes to the nation's well-being (86), Solomon's use of charisma in the interest of obtaining royal provisions and furthering the horse trade, I have claimed, implies an inclination on his part towards a self-indulgent and self-seeking rule to make himself instead of Israel the beneficiary of his charisma. Still the general impression from this part of the narrative is that, since Israel's *shalom* is stressed, Solomon's rule benefited Israel to a high degree. "Israel experienced unprecedented unity and repose" (Knoppers 1993:86). Solomon's later rule will not be so beneficial for Israel.

The narrative on the projects, which I have called the axis, presents the attempts of the king to develop an oriental kingship as well as God's efforts to keep those attempts at bay and the kingdom in covenant relationship. And though Yahweh restrains Solomon, the king does not give up. Indeed chs. 9-11 present the final development of his leadership style. In these chapters the temple "no longer stands at the center of Solomon's world, and the projects described are undertaken for the king's own glory" (Savran 1997:157). Building projects, international treaties, trade enterprises, foreign relations (including the visit of the queen of Sheba and her ambiguous confirmation of Solomon's charisma) and the splendour of the court, including the enormous quantities of gold and wives, make his rule self-seeking and self-indulgent. As opposed to his early rule Israel is not benefiting now, in fact it is not even mentioned. The nation, the supposed beneficiary of the king's charisma, is not in its purview. Solomon has appropriated, actually confiscated, charisma and it is solely he who benefits from it. Thus chs. 3-5 narrate Solomon's rule hallmarked by a leadership charisma given and used for the benefit of his people. In contrast chs. 9-11, about the second half of Solomon's reign, are characterised by a misused charisma, with chs. 6-8 providing the clue to this transformation.

Charisma and Character – The Deuteronomistic Criterion

As generally acknowledged, Solomon is the first king in Israel's history to breach all the three major requirements of Deuteronomy 17:16f. He acquires "great numbers of horses for himself", takes many wives who lead him astray and accumulates "large amounts of silver and gold". In addition his election is rather dubious, making God's involvement unclear and the reader wonder whether Deuteronomy 17:15 is fulfilled. His increasingly self-indulgent rule and disobedience to God in several respects (cf. Schäfer-Lichtenberger 1995:356-64) also imply a breach of Deuteronomy 17:20. From Saul to Solomon a decline in living up to the standard can be seen. Solomon does not measure up to any of the requirements.

Administration and the Checks on Solomon's Power

The first officer mentioned in the list of 4:1-6 is "Azariah son of Zadok—the priest" (v. 2). The title הַכֹּהֵן usually refers to the high priest (Provan 1995:53). If Azariah was the high priest with the former high priests Zadok and

Abiathar[53] "relegated" to mere priesthood that has important implications. It may suggest that however grateful Solomon was to them for having helped him to power, he tried to limit their influence both upon himself and the kingdom. Solomon was determined to establish and maintain his autonomy. The absence of the ringleader Nathan from the list supports this hypothesis.

The replacement of Joab by Benaiah had two advantages for Solomon. Firstly he got rid of a very powerful officer who had often thwarted David's plans. Benaiah was as loyal as Joab but far less independent. This is implied at Benaiah's first appearance in 1:37 when he vowed allegiance to David and Solomon alike: "As the LORD was with my lord the king, so may he be with Solomon to make his throne even greater than the throne of my lord King David!" This statement reveals Benaiah's blind loyalty to the king. In ch. 2 he proved his loyalty, so that Whybray rightly calls him "Solomon's hatchet-man" (1968:45). In the discussion of 2 Samuel 7 I claimed that the term "Yahweh with someone" is of a military nature in the DH. Uttered by a military man, 1 Kings 1:37 is no exception. Benaiah's disappointment must have been the greater when he realised that Solomon was not the military king David had been. Thus Benaiah's role and power was certainly limited. With the elimination of Joab Solomon had "a loyal servant in Benaiah, but never again would one be found to serve the Davidic throne who had the strength to defy an errant royal will when necessary, yet who would not covet the throne for himself" (Schley 1993:103). The appointments of Benaiah and the Zadok clan were also meant to strengthen Solomon. "With the military and the cult under his control, Solomon has buttressed his position and come into his own as a ruler" (Savran 1997:155).

This raises the question whether there was any other centre of power in Solomon's monarchy. Apparently there was no prophet. Nathan, despite being Solomon's mentor, disappeared when his protégé became king.[54]

Signs and Wonders

In my discussions of Saul and David I claimed that charismatic military deliverers as they were, they witnessed God's many interventions in unbelievable military actions, bravery, victories and escapes. Once abandoned by God (in Saul's case) or having achieved the charismatic ideal (in David's) Yahweh's interventions decrease and cease. Indeed they are replaced by signs of God's wrath.

As for Solomon there are no extraordinary signs like those confirming his predecessors reported during his reign. His wise judgment in ch. 3 comes close to being an extraordinary sign by God and is followed by the affirmation of the

---

[53] Provan (1995:54; see also Schäfer-Lichtenberger 1995:267, 282f) suggests that, as a sign of a different Solomon, Abiathar was later restored to his former office (see 4:4).

[54] Cross's claim (1973:238) that with Nathan's "disappearance or death the prophetic office effectively disappeared form the Judean court" is an argument out of silence, nonetheless one not to be dismissed. See also Fuchs 1987.

people. This, however, has no follow-up which also highlights that, with their goal achieved, the time of military charismatics is over. While signs and wonders abounded in the incipient stage of the charismatic movement, they are not really needed anymore. Indeed what God's people are in want of is stability – the very opposite to the extraordinary. Solomon seems to be well aware of this as he builds his kingdom on the foundation of predictability and tries to avoid the peril of unexpectedness by both establishing vital institutions and centralising state and religion. So his policies are two-edged. On the one hand with his wisdom Solomon procures stability, and Israel subsequently prospers. On the other hand when the signs cease this stability not only diminishes the dynamism of an intervening and sovereign God but also entails a new court theology. Its chief representatives are the temple, demonstrating a stable, immutable religion and deity (see Brueggemann 1978:28-43), as well as Solomon's sapiential wisdom, easily used to rationalise the lack of Yahweh's interventions and actions.[55]

"Autumn" – Solomon's Undisturbed Reign

The 1st movement portrays harvest-time pleasures: "dancing after crops are gathered, drinking, story-telling and contented sleep" (77). One peasant's drunken antics, final collapse and undisturbed sleep are also vividly depicted. Harvest, wealth and affluence, prosperity and happiness, enjoying the fruits of one's work are motifs also found in Solomon's rule, which, after the hardships of his predecessors' reigns, brought about a long awaited *shalom*. At last the monarchy seems to have been established for the benefit of its populace. Both the splendour and wealth of the royal court as well as the safety and prosperity of the populace are explicit in the narrative (4:20; 5:5; ET 4:20, 25), like the season's happiness in the calm and harmonious music. "Autumn's revels" (85) – Everett entitled his chapter.

This ambience is reinforced in the 2nd movement. The sleep of inebriates in the pleasant air further stresses the general impression of a calm season. There are, however, disquieting sounds. "With frequent dissonance, unpredictable phrasing and extreme tonal dislocation, the Adagio seems rather to represent the fits and starts of confused dreams" comments Everett (86).

---

[55] Notice that Brueggemann discusses Proverbs under the heading "The Hiddenness of Yahweh" (1997:333-58). In this context a reference to C.R. Fontaine's study of "Proverb Performance in the Hebrew Bible" might be useful. She argues (1994:408) "that use of sayings and proverbs in social contexts was always purposeful, and acted to provide a form of verbal behavior which might diffuse potentially aggressive situations. In each case, ambiguous events which might be interpreted in a variety of ways served as the stimulus for proverb performance" (cf. Meyers 1983:425). *Mutatis mutandis* this can be claimed of wisdom as the "official ideology" of the Solomonic state in general. Thus the "potentially aggressive", because of possible resistance of the more traditional social classes to it, and "ambiguous" event of, e.g., the temple project could be presented as a manifestation of God given wisdom.

The uneasy dream is followed by the hunting scene of the 3rd movement – the culmination of the season. All this, however, may not be as positive as it appears.

> Struggle with Nature, so central to *Summer*, is a theme absent from *Autumn*. Having achieved a temporary victory by harnessing Nature's power, man may now enjoy the spoils (crops, ale, wild animals to be killed) in untroubled leisure. Selfish indulgence is hinted at both in the sonnet – which eschews the idea, present in *Spring*, that Nature ought gratefully to be honoured – and in music that concentrates on carousal and sport. (85)

From a sociological viewpoint hunting was undoubtedly the privilege of the well-off in the days of Vivaldi as in Solomon's. This implies social tension, which will become obvious after the monarch's death.

The Leadership of the Charismatic
The Transition in Leadership

Israel had gone through the crucial period of the founding of the state. To this end Yahweh raised up charismatic military deliverers. With the state of Israel firmly established, God's people needed a different type of leadership for a different socio-political situation – this was David's task. His successor Solomon emerged not in a national but in a court crisis, a coup. This, however, was not only a court crisis. What was going on in the royal palace revealed a national crisis, albeit different in character and degree from those in 1-2 Samuel. Then national survival was at stake, and David duly demonstrated his charisma by averting outside military threats and uniting the tribes in his kingdom. With the threats averted Israel became a regional power. What Solomon was to achieve was the social, political and economic stability of Israel and Judah, they were to become a powerful united nation. Thus Solomon's task was to usher Israel from wartime into peace. Accordingly his charisma was defined as peacetime leadership.

Regarding Israelite society David was the leader who made the transition from a traditional-tribal federation into a unified monarchic Israel possible. "In traditionalist periods, charisma is *the* great revolutionary force", in Weber's terms (1968:245; italics his). With a consolidated Israelite monarchy the traditional(ist) period of the tribal federation, along with its traditional values, became history. At the same time the charisma of the revolutionary kind, challenging the values of the traditionalist period, had to give way to one designed to maintain *shalom*.

The sooner one chooses his/her successor the better – this is a common-sense premise. David's failure to appoint his successor caused the crisis. Schäfer-Lichtenberger (1995:360) sees a crucial difference between the Moses-Joshua and David-Solomon relationships in the fact that whereas Moses prepared Joshua for the succession, David did not care. Only at the prompting and scheming of his officers and at the last possible minute did he choose

Solomon, thus averting the spectre of civil war. Neither David nor Solomon sought the kingdom, still, both received it and were the beneficiaries of the failures and conspiracy of others (Knoppers 1993:68).

What concerns me most is the aspect of charisma. The first two kings emerged due to the initiative of God who bestowed upon them his spirit. There was nothing of this sort about Solomon. To risk an understatement, God remained in the background in chs. 1-2 – he neither acted, nor spoke, nor was his spirit bestowed upon the successor. Better late than never: in ch. 3 Solomon was granted leadership charisma. From a different aspect, the demonstration and confirmation of Solomon's charisma were not preceded by the designation of God but only of a clique – an anomaly in Israel's charismatic leadership. This is not to disclaim Solomon's charisma but solely to highlight the changes in the emergence of this charismatic leader. That Solomon did not have charisma at his emergence, however, is indicative of an inherent problem of hereditary leadership.

It goes without saying that just as David was forced to master charismatic leadership without human assistance, on his own, so was his son. As opposed to his predecessors, however, Solomon did not have a surrogate father or mentor, indeed he was totally on his own in mastering and practising charismatic leadership. The surrogate father pattern so characteristic of 1-2 Samuel came to an abrupt end with Solomon. In his leadership style he demonstrated autonomy – for better and for worse. He maintained independence even from those who helped him to power. By establishing an absolutist kingship, occasionally challenging even Yahweh's suzerainty and without real checks of power, he defined Israelite monarchy in new terms, heretofore alien to it.

Bar-Efrat (1980:169) has observed that the transfers of leadership in 1 Samuel are increasingly discordant and fraught with conflict. If this holds true in 1 Samuel how much more so in Kings, starting with the transition from David to Solomon accompanied by violent deaths and nearly civil war. While David was meticulous in avoiding bloodshed when he ascended the throne, in Solomon's emergence violence was the norm.

Both Saul and David were hounded by the legacy of their respective predecessors (see Rosenberg 1997:139). Solomon, however, seems to have radically departed from this pattern, but at the expense of radical changes in Israelite society and finally the split in the monarchy.

The difference between Adonijah and Solomon is also noteworthy. I have observed that Solomon and his party did not deny David's authority, whereas Adonijah's arrogance was a challenge to it leading to his own fall. Thus Adonijah's failure and the key to Solomon's success alike were how they viewed the old system and defined their relation to it. In structuralist terms in a transition period like the one Solomon emerged in, with less external and more domestic threat, he/she who claims continuity will succeed.

Solomon's Attempts to Resolve the Crisis

I have stated that Solomon emerged in a very different socio-political situation from his predecessors. For them Israel's oppression by other ethnic groups constituted the crisis. With independence achieved, however, a new crisis was looming on the horizon. I have claimed that the crisis of the secession of the North was not adequately resolved under David, who, after having achieved the charismatic ideal of delivering Israel, relaxed and thus extinguished his charisma. The rivalry between Judah and Israel led to civil wars. Discontent due to the king's failure to administer justice fuelled this rivalry. Thus the crisis Solomon had to face was of a different kind, nonetheless one related to leadership and an effective charisma. The new king realised this and expressed his concern about the enormous responsibility and his incompetence to lead Israel (3:7-9). Yahweh in his turn was glad to grant him the necessary leadership charisma.

In the new situation Israel needed new institutions to make the monarchy work as well as firm international relationships. Solomon in his wisdom set them up (chs. 4-5). Social and political institutions were established, bringing welfare, security and peace for the nation. The building projects on the other hand were manifestations of royal affluence and pretension. The wisdom requested in 3:9 and demonstrated in 3:28 in a wise ruling was used to nurture the royal image. The people who originally benefited from the king's wisdom were pushed to the periphery of Solomon's interest, who became increasingly preoccupied with wealth.

One of the greatest challenges was to ensure national unity. David had already suggested this to Solomon on his deathbed (2:1-9). Provan (1995a) has pointed out that Joab and Shimei were major obstacles to national unity and therefore had to be eliminated, whereas Barzillai in his assistance to David embodied the ideal of a peaceful Israel, hence he was to be remembered.

Solomon started to solve the problem of secession by establishing twelve districts and so replacing the tribes as geographical and social units as well as by centralising religion. At the same time his foreign policy, by treaties, a powerful and modern military and taxation, gained political and economic stability for Israel, so that God's people "lived in safety, each man under his own vine and fig tree" (5:5; ET 4:25). His reign seems to have averted tribal rivalry, and the king succeeded in uniting Israel in a centralised monarchy. The discontent and rivalry, however, were only suppressed and not eradicated. They resurfaced in rebellions both from the outside and the inside (ch. 11), and after his death resulted in open revolt against Judahite lordship.

I have demonstrated that what led to this was the way in which Solomon used his charisma. Originally he was given wisdom to make him prepared for the challenges of leadership – for the benefit of Israel. I have noticed and traced a tension in the king's attitude and actions. At the beginning (chs. 3-5) he used his charisma properly; *shalom* so achieved benefited Israel. There was, however, an undercurrent, weak as it was at the beginning. Similarly to David's rule it was the temptation of oriental kingship (cf. Provan 1995: *passim*). I have discerned signs of Solomon's weakness to resist it: setting up a powerful army[56], the lavish lifestyle of the court and the starting of building projects. With the focus on the building projects (chs. 6-8) the undercurrent grew stronger. I showed there Solomon's attempt to use Yahweh for the purpose of royal pretension. However, Yahweh refused to become a tool in Solomon's hand.

The final chapters of Solomon's rule show the undercurrent becoming a torrent which the king was unable to withstand. His preoccupation with trade, accumulating wealth for himself, building projects and the demonstration of royal power by acquiring many wives swept him away. His wisdom charisma became self-serving, benefiting the court only and not Israel who is unnoticed (cf. Lasine 1997:383f). Israel and its king grew increasingly estranged. Solomon did not measure up to his commission to administer justice and establish *shalom* for Israel, because he was more concerned with his own *shalom* than that of his people.

To What Extent Was Solomon Charismatic?

Similarly to David here one needs to distinguish between the early (chs. 3-5) and late (chs. 9-11) Solomon. I have argued that in ch. 1 he was not a fully-fledged character, but by the end of ch. 2 he demonstrated determination and independence from everyone, including Yahweh. Independence from men and dependence on God are the hallmarks of a charismatic, so the outset of Solomon's reign is double-sided. Thanks to Yahweh's night-time "intervention" Solomon was given both leadership skills and the right attitude to leading Israel. It is not heroic military bravery, indispensable for Saul and David, that Solomon had to acquire. In the changed socio-political situation a redefinition of charisma was needed. In other words the leadership skills had to match the new situation. Though Solomon did not come to power in an obvious political crisis, he still had crises to resolve.

The references to Solomon's wisdom will give an overview of the narrative's view of his charismatic leadership and its progress. Solomon's wisdom is first mentioned by his father (2:6, 9). In the light of Solomon's actions in chs. 1-2 his wisdom was but political expediency. This, however, changed after God's visit, when the king asked for both proper leadership skills and the right attitude to governing (3:9-12), which he then demonstrated in his wise ruling. Though "wisdom" does not occur in ch. 4, clearly 5:5 (ET 4:25) is a summary statement of Israel's profit of its king's domestic and, to a lesser extent, foreign policies. This is further substantiated in 5:9f (ET 4:29f). That Solomon used his charisma to further international relationships was acknowledged by Hiram in 5:21 and the narrator in 5:26 (ET 5:7, 12).

In chs. 3-5 it is through his leadership charisma that Solomon established a peaceful socio-political situation and a thriving economy. The terminology applied in 3:9; 4:20; 5:9 (ET 4:29) also suggests that Solomon's wisdom was in

---

[56] Notice that Saul's and David's military powers were always mentioned with reference to Yahweh.

the first place related to and given for the benefit of all Israel. I have pointed out that after Israel gained independence what it really needed was this *shalom* secured by its monarch. Thus the king's charisma benefited his people. At the same time I have noticed the inclination on Solomon's part towards royal pretension manifest in building projects, the royal court and trade. But the real turning point in my view is to be seen in the axis (chs. 6-8), where the king displayed increasing independence from Yahweh, indeed opposition to God's ideal of Israelite kingship, so that God was compelled to warn the king. It is indicative of Solomon's use of his charisma that wisdom is not referred to in these chapters.

The eight explicit references to Solomon's wisdom in his early rule (3:9, 11f, 28; 5:9f, 21, 26) are counterbalanced by another six in his late rule (10:4, 6-8, 23f). I have demonstrated that the claims of Solomon's wisdom in the queen of Sheba story are rather ironic, as wisdom here is intimately linked to wealth: Solomon used his wisdom for personal benefit by accumulating wealth. This aspect is quite explicit in 10:23 and 24ff, by the juxtaposition of "wisdom" and "wealth", so that demonstration of wisdom before the international community became essential to him[57] – at the expense of Israel who was ignored. I have shown that already in ch. 9 Solomon did not use his charisma for the benefit of Israel but for exclusive royal pretension and at the cost of Israel and non-Israelite people alike. Solomon was a shrewd oriental monarch who took advantage of and exploited others. For Solomon kingship became a royal business, an end in itself.

Liver claims that in "the story of the Queen of Sheba the wisdom is specifically mentioned as being of a scholarly nature, and relating to sharpness of mind" (1967:83). I have argued that Solomon's wisdom seen by the queen was not related to Israel's well-being, justice or leading his people. Thus wisdom given to lead Israel was transformed by Solomon into a skill to subdue the people and to be established as an oriental monarch, as sapiential wisdom is often aimed at upholding the status quo.

Solomon's above mentioned independence, I have claimed, was a characteristic of a charismatic which, however, once uncontrolled, proved a breaking point between Yahweh and his deputy. Solomon's intensifying preoccupation with the oriental king image eliminated the wise use of his God given charisma. The reason for the lengthy discussion of Solomon's grandeur proves that he succumbed to every king's temptation. Solomon came full circle by becoming increasingly independent of God again.

I have claimed that Solomon's wisdom was by and large related to maintaining power while his predecessors' military charisma chiefly related to coming to power. In her socio-political study Carol Meyers states (1983:420): "The physical imposition of Israelite unity and dominion in the Levant

---

[57] From a sociological point of view, the mere fact that Solomon's wisdom acquires international reputation and attention is telling, as ordinary people, whether Israelite or of other nations, were not in the position to go and see for themselves. This was a royal privilege and quite different to what Israel was supposed to gain.

achieved under David through charismatic leadership and warfare [...] was sustained by Solomon for another forty years through diplomacy and ideology." In this way, however, his charisma was more prone to become static, institutionalised and finally extinguished than Saul's or David's who had a dynamic charisma by definition (cf. Brueggemann 1978:32).

Saul was a king with moderate pretensions. David's inclination to oriental despotism disabled David the military leader. Solomon was a monarch far away from the people and their needs. From the anarchic situation of the tribal federation Israel became a nation under the indulgent despotism of a centralised monarchy. The cost of the monarchy, that Samuel had warned the people of, became reality in three generations. In 1 Samuel 8 Samuel was worried about the dangers of monarchy. Solomon's late rule had all the characteristics of an exploitative and self-indulgent kingship that Samuel was worried about (cf. Frisch 2000:14f). Israel became like other nations (see Brueggemann 1982:20f, 42); Solomon became the king the elders requested – although very different from how they imagined. Yahweh's concern, "it is not you they have rejected, but they have rejected me as their king" (1 Sam 8:7), was finally justified. The inherent tendency of kingship towards self-indulgence, ignoring the nation and upholding autonomy dethroned Yahweh. Little wonder then that, to restore his sovereignty and indisputable authority over Israel, Yahweh had to resort to drastic means such as war and exile.[58]

By way of conclusion I will make a metaphoric remark. After Yahweh's night-time visit and the king's request for leadership charisma "Solomon awoke—and he realised it had been a dream" (3:15). Does this rather odd statement imply that he was given an opportunity to establish a Yahwistic monarchy, which, however, because of his inclination to oriental kingship, was never fully realised by Solomon and remained a dream? As far as Israel is concerned God's chosen people woke up too from the long sleep of monarchic rule – to exile. Only then did they realise that Solomon's dream was not translated into reality and started to look forward.[59]

---

[58] Is this because of kingship, the inherent potential to misuse charisma or the cessation of charisma?

[59] Of course this only holds if "dream" had the same semantic import to ancient Hebrews as it does to us.

CHAPTER 5

Conclusions

And What Came Then — "Winter"

"F minor, elsewhere having the unpleasant connotations of horror, vengeance and extreme grief, is entirely apt as a chilling backdrop for *Winter*" (Everett 1996:70). The key sets the tone. This is one of the most unpropitious and severe Allegros Vivaldi ever wrote. In the 1st movement calamities are knocking at the door: in the music a tempest — in Israel's monarchy social and political tensions and upheavals, unfaithfulness to Yahweh, sieges and wars prepared by Solomon's rule.

The 2nd movement introduces an indoor scene. The cheerful music makes the warmth of the fireplace tangible; it warms our souls — as does the new beginning by Jeroboam and the moments of victory and courage of a few individual kings and prophets in the divided kingdom. But only temporarily.

The gusts of wind in the 3rd movement reveal the illusoriness of our hope. The stumbling monarchies of Israel and Judah are aptly symbolised by the picture of skating people now falling over, now standing up. "In *Winter*, Nature is at her most terrifying in the bleakest of environments. This is evident in the tuneless opening ritornello, with cruel dissonance and icy articulation, and the fury of the wind that follows. It is certainly a vision of horror to Vivaldi's way of thinking", Everett concludes (87). So is it to ours. What is achieved by Nature in *Winter* is accomplished by History, whether one understands it as a narratological (DH) or a historical term (the historical developments), in the latter part of Kings.

Three seasons of charismatic leadership in Israel have passed. We looked forward to an auspicious new beginning in the spring, experienced the heat of the summer and enjoyed the tranquillity of autumn. Finally what will happen is glimpsed in anticipation. Now I shall devote myself to drawing conclusions concerning the seasons' nature (charismatic leadership), climate change (transition in leadership) and the involvement of the supernatural in nature (signs and wonders). I shall also consider further prospects as well as the relevance of this study.

Charismatic Leadership

Having finished my study of three seasons of charismatic leadership in Israel I am now in the position to summarise and draw conclusions from my observations and analyses as well as address more universal questions of charismatic leadership. I hope I have made clear that the "three seasons" do not necessarily imply a sequence, although they may. They are rather meant to refer to three different leaderships — each growing out of the previous leadership and succeeded by the next.

I have claimed that charisma was always given for the benefit of God's people. In order to resolve a crisis God raised a man and bestowed upon him his spirit, i.e. equipped him with the skills needed in the particular situation. Thus Saul was raised to deliver Israel from its enemies, the Philistines in particular. He was a military king. So was David in the first place. In addition to liberating Israel from Philistine overlordship he was to emerge and establish himself under Saul's kingship.

Resolution and commitment to the charismatic ideal were crucial for the charismatic leaders' success. At the beginning of their activity both Saul and David demonstrated these qualities. "As Saul left his oxen to deliver Israel, so [...] David left his sheep to deliver Israel", Campbell comments (1986:39). A commitment to Israel's welfare was also the driving force behind Solomon's petition in 1 Kings 3. The abandonment of this resolution and commitment entailed the charismatic's failure.

I have shown how charismatic David used once-charismatic Saul's failures for his own benefit. With Israel established as a sovereign nation, however, David abandoned his commission of military leadership and turned to establish himself as an oriental monarch. In contrast to his predecessors Solomon emerged in a court crisis with no outside threat on the horizon. Though Yahweh was not involved in his emergence, he assisted Solomon's rule by granting him the necessary charismatic gift of wise leadership.

As far as the use of charisma is concerned, only Saul was consistent, as long as he was allowed, in using it for the benefit of Israel. His successors, with their mission accomplished, ceased using charisma as intended by God and became less committed to their commission. In different ways, however, all three "put out the Spirit's fire" (cf. 1 Thess 5:19) — Saul by submission to Samuel; David by wavering between charismatic military leadership and oriental kingship and abandoning the former; Solomon by relinquishing the charismatic leadership of leading Israel for projects of oriental kingship. I have found that charisma was often not used to the end it was given. A charisma not used to the end it has been given, for the benefit of God's people, is misused.

With this I have touched upon another significant issue. Both in popular understanding and in the presupposition of theologians (see e.g. Soggin 1959, 1963; Boff 1985) the antipode to charisma is institution. This view is not to be dismissed, as institution, in this framework, often stands for stasis, rigidity and unchangeability, which is the very opposite to the dynamic, indeed often subversive and revolutionary force of charisma. I have, however, argued that, in the cases of David and Solomon, what threatens charismatic leadership is not institution in the first place. Indeed David and Solomon in particular were keen to establish institutions and give the Israelite monarchy stability. In doing so they demonstrated charismatic competence and benefited Israel. The shortcoming I criticised them for was the alternative ideology to their charismatic leadership and commissioning — oriental kingship. It was this which encroached upon the territory of their charismatic leadership and changed it profoundly.

In this context there is an interesting configuration. I have claimed that Saul's charisma was extinguished by his mentor. Saul was a reluctant king, and a reluctant charismatic is destined to failure. As opposed to him David was ambitious and successful. He used charisma, but with charismatic ideal achieved he abandoned it and was overshadowed by Joab. Solomon's leadership is a case of charisma used and misused. Where did the stories of David and Solomon go wrong?[1] — when they were no longer committed to their commission and so the concept of oriental kingship took over the agenda. This observation not only resonates with the pattern of the rise-of-the-low-fall-of-the-mighty, but makes it less accidental by revealing potential threats to charismatic leadership. In more general, almost trite, terms power is the greatest threat to charismatic leadership.

What has been said concerns the human element of and divine involvement in charisma. Will God permanently be involved with the charismatic because charisma has been granted? The basic thrust of this study is that reliance on God and his Spirit's intervention cannot be abandoned or substituted for. Saul's leadership is the clearest example of the sovereignty of God's Spirit, who departed from his chosen one. With his objective achieved, David stopped relying on God's deliverance. Solomon exchanged reliance on God's help for a stable and predictable rule based on temple ideology, oriental kingship and wealth. Indeed I have claimed that the abandonment of relying on God seems to have been the built-in factor of monarchy. All in all charisma does not know stasis but is a dynamic force to be used, appropriated and never to be laid to rest. Therefore the abandonment of a reliance on God's Spirit is a real threat to charismatic leaders in particular.

I have stated that defining (Saul and David) or redefining (Solomon) charisma is vital for both the charismatic leader and her/his followers. Failure to do so led to Saul's fall, while its awareness and appropriation to David's and Solomon's success. The differences between Solomon's and his predecessors' charismata follow from the fact that Saul and David were granted charisma at their emergence, so that they could establish their authority. Solomon, however, was in need of and was granted charisma to maintain power. Therefore charisma was redefined and adapted to the changed socio-political situation.

I have also made it clear, especially in the study of David and Solomon, that charisma only achieves what it is supposed to, if it retains its dynamic

---

[1] Saul's is different from this angle.

character. To put it differently once it is ignored, charisma becomes static and God's gift is extinguished. In a different context Miscall employs a metaphor:

> To read OT narrative is to follow the way of the Lord, but the way is a labyrinth, a network, without a beginning, a center, or an end. To follow means movement, not stasis; to follow is to traverse a path, not to arrive at a destination—the meaning, the explanation, the word of the Lord. (1986:184)

Mutatis mutandis this applies to leadership, which is to be dynamic instead of static. Once a charismatic leader or movement becomes static, it is in need of a dynamic start-over and the intervention of God's dynamic and uncontrollable Spirit. And as the Spirit is as unpredictable as English weather and because charismatic leaders are led by the very dynamic Spirit of God who does not know stasis, a charismatic should never sit back but be open to the Spirit's guidance.

Transition in Leadership — From a Structuralist Point of View

I have shown that the transition in leadership is a significant aspect of charismatic leadership. I have suggested that different leaderships and eras presuppose different transition models. In this study each transition was unique. The Samuel-Saul transition is encumbered by the mentor's hegemony and authoritative self-imposition on Saul. The Saul-David transition is characterised by animosity between the old and the new leaders. Finally David's failure to designate his successor almost leads to civil war. Now I shall elaborate on these aspects in a structuralist framework of binary oppositions[2]. I am not going to claim that these observations are absolute. Rather they are determined by setting and models of transition.

In the relationship between Samuel and Saul mentor-protégé relationships matter. I have suggested that an old, orthodox order never lets the new and charismatic leader establish her/himself or have her/his own way. As is often the case the old sticks to power by manipulation, deceit, selfish rhetoric and suppressing differing views. In this model the new is doomed to failure. As Jobling puts it (1998:100), "Saul cannot become a real king because he cannot shake free of the premonarchical order embodied in Samuel." Therefore it is understandable that David and in particular Solomon established themselves and their monarchy independently from any prophet.

Whereas tension is not overt but suppressed in the Samuel-Saul transition, it is not hidden in the Saul-David model. Animosity is covert in the Samuel-Saul transition, in the Saul-David it is overt. Here again the old is not willing to yield to the new order, therefore breaches inevitably follow. And since the new is not willing to relinquish its demands and objectives, it often turns against the old.

---

[2] See my methodology on how I use structuralism.

In this model conflict is inevitable.[3] The big question is how and in what way will the new assert its claim to power. With a more confrontational stance Saul might have escaped from Samuel's dominance and prevented his own fall. On the other hand David succeeded partly because he avoided confrontation with Saul's overt enmity.

I have suggested that a charismatic leader can only prevail if he/she is determined to achieve his/her goals by any decent means, and subordinates everything to them. The establishment is not interested in making way to the new, for that would be a suicidal action. Ultimately the transition is dependent on the charismatic's attitude and actions, the old is not at the disposal of the new. The new must emerge on its own and in opposition to the old.[4] To put it in the way Jesus did, old wineskins are not suitable for new wine (Mt 9:17); the two are totally incompatible because they jeopardise each other's existence. Therefore the new needs something entirely new which can contain it. This is the main reason for Saul's failure as well as David's and Solomon's success.

Secondly the old cannot get rid of the new and the new of the old. They must live together; they are condemned to coexistence. The more peaceful the coexistence the better it is for the community. But this seldom happens. On the other hand the more successful the new wants to be the more radical it tends to be, which means tension and opposition.

Preston's pattern (the rise of the low, the fall of the mighty) has an interesting implication. Viewing their succession with envy and as a power struggle both Samuel and Saul succumb to persecution complex, though to different extents.[5] Of course the paranoia is fuelled by the old's failure and the new's success, which in turn results in admiration of the new on the part of various people (cf. 1 Sam 18:1, 3, 16, 20, 28). Another important aspect is that of a charismatic leader under the mentorship of "paranoid" strong men such as Samuel or Joab. Neither once-charismatics nor strong men are likely to retire, and this makes the job of the new more difficult.

Thirdly the minimal preparation for transition rendered the start of Solomon's rule difficult. Absence of reference to God, popular support and

---

[3] As the Hungarian saying goes, there is no space for two bagpipers in one pub.

[4] David, by not killing his predecessor but patiently waiting, set a precedent for his house — none of the assassins of Judah's kings succeeded. By contrast successful coups d'état became the norm in the northern kingdom. Jeroboam rebels against Solomon (1 Kgs 11:26; though the reference of the phrase is obscure) after having been anointed king and not being able to wait until Solomon is dead. Jeroboam epitomises an emerging charismatic new order discontent with the rigid and oppressive institution of the old.

[5] The clearest sign of Saul's paranoia can be seen in the spear motif (1 Sam 18:10; 19:9, 33; 22:6; introduced in 14:2). The spear as his weapon is often considered something related to the constant characterisation of Saul (Stoebe 1973:201; startlingly Fokkelman 1986:219 deems it "suitable as a phallic symbol") but not recognised as a weapon of self-defence in his persecution complex. Interestingly in 1 Sam 26:22 David returns Saul the spear but not the water jar.

confirmation make transitions of this sort suspect. Being unprepared for leadership forced Solomon to take actions like eliminating rivals and opposition, which would have been avoidable if David had taken the effort to prepare Solomon for leadership. By appointing him in the last possible moment David hindered him gaining experience of statecraft. Also the lack of checks of power indicates an autocratic rule, confirmed by the narrative as a whole, and the events and implications of 1 Kings 11-12 in particular. This only underlines the truism that charismatic movements can easily and quickly (from David to Solomon) become the establishment, obstructing new charismatic movements. And then, God willing, the whole process, often in baffling ways, starts all over.[6]

Careful evaluation of the particular context will definitely help realise which model fits a situation as well as make a decision as to how to encounter the old, face challenges and implement changes.

Signs and Wonders

There may be truth in the literary critic [sic] conclusion that the role of Yahweh as a visible actor in human history tends to fade in the later writings of the Hebrew Bible. There may, however, also be a purely literary reason for his involvement or non-involvement in human affairs. When a story has to move quickly, Yahweh enters the scene in a "deus ex machina" fashion. But when a story becomes more reflective and philosophical, Yahweh moves into the background, "directing" affairs as if from a distance, without losing control.

Deist's claim (his abstract; 1993:7) is intriguing, especially if compared with Jobling's observation of Yahweh's decreasing interventions in the DH, upon which I have elaborated. I have remarked on how Yahweh intervened in the Saul, David and Solomon narratives. Even though the topic of Yahweh's interventions, or signs and wonders, is not strictly related to charismatic leadership, it seems to have crucial implications hence is fundamental for a better understanding of the evolving story of charismatic leadership. Therefore I shall develop this idea.

To do so I first refer to the claim I have made that the intervention of God's spirit by signs and wonders is distinctive of charismatic movements. This aspect might be refined by referring to the difference between Homer's *deus ex machina* and that of the DH. In the Iliad and the Odyssey Homer resorts to *deus ex machina* to make the invisible forces of and behind the plot visible. With it he explains changes of fortune, peaceful or violent. The actions and

---

[6] In his discussion of 1 Kings 11:14-43 Walsh (1996:138-42) has observed that the way God raises Hadad and Rezon (11:14, 23), two Gentiles, is reminiscent of the emergence of Moses and David. "The God of Israel is able and willing to manipulate events in far-flung countries in order to achieve his purposes in Israel" (142).

interventions of Homer's deities are, however, subject to and determined by the plans of humans. In other words the sovereignty of Greek gods is quite limited. More importantly divine interventions abound. For Homer there are no "dispensations", i.e. anyone at any time can experience *deus ex machina*. That is what renders it more unreal and makes us identifying with it or entering its world more difficult (see Auerbach 1953:18-23; Gamzu's, 1984, and Josipovici's discussions thereof, 1988:218-30, 300; see also Gunn and Fewell 1993:47).

The DH's resort to *deus ex machina* is different from Homer's in that mention of God's intervention and spirit is hardly ever made to explain happenings by recourse to behind-the-scene operations. Thus *deus ex machina* is used by the Hebrew writers to highlight God's sovereignty. More importantly, in this way it is linked to charisma and charismatic leadership. *In the DH charismatic movements are defined by* deus ex machina. That is to say *deus ex machina* occurring intermittently results in "dispensations" of God's presence by the interventions of his spirit and God's absence when the extraordinary ceases. That is what makes it more real and helps us, who also live between God's extraordinary interventions and absence identify with and enter into the world of the DH. It is in this context that Josipovici (1988:218ff) asks what the qualitative difference between the account of the Gospels and of the apocryphal gospels is. He concludes that the Gospels force us to enter their world and so to "experience what it means to be a human being in this world of ours" (230), while the apocryphal ones by a rather schematic plot and incessant flow of miracles deny us entry into their world, which is different from our experienced world.[7]

By saying this I am claiming that signs and wonders in the DH are indicative of charismatic leadership, through which God's spirit is present in an extraordinary way. In fact the theme of signs and wonders constitutes a unique biblical characteristic as far as charismatic leadership is concerned. God's presence (the manifestations of God's power, miracles and interventions) and absence constitute the ebb and flow of the life of God's people. A shortage of charismatic leadership points to God's absence and punishment (see Jeremiah). No less importantly we can gain entry into the biblical world through the door of God's presence and absence and this door links the biblical world to the world we live in.

The emergence of a charismatic leader is antithetical to disruption and

---

[7] Similarly Paul Borgman in his study comparing Homeric and biblical storytelling comments that whereas in Homer's world things "are the way they are, and no other", the Bible's world is "very difficult to name or fix: this has the texture of history, after all, realm of the unexpected and genuinely new" (1980:297). And as "there exists in this open world the possibility for the emergence of an unexpected moral point of view" (309f), so there is in ours the possibility of the unexpected arrival and intervention of God's Spirit.

tragedy, God's wrath and rejection. Rather, charismatic movements witness God's grace, mercy and support. Indeed when facing challenges and threats charismatic leaders can prove themselves. Therefore David as an emerging charismatic leader did not face calamities, while as a "retired" charismatic he did (2 Sam 21:1-14; 24:1-25). Once a charismatic leader is established and "sits in his palace", miracles and charismatic manifestations are replaced by troubles. The absence of charisma, signs and wonders implies that God's Spirit is not present, which in turn indicates that charismatic leaders are wanted. Similarly once settled charismatic leaders become complacent, charismatic deeds occur more rarely, for charisma likes unsettledness, temporariness and vicissitudes to prove itself. After God's Spirit withdraws, signs and wonders cease and give way to God's discontent and wrath. Then God withdraws completely — no signs, no wonders, but no wrath either. Human narrative becomes *a-theos*, i.e. one without God. To amplify Auerbach's concept, there will be no relation to the divine world. "Far from seeking, like Homer, merely to make us forget our own reality for a few hours, it [the Bible] seeks to overcome our reality: we are to fit our own life into its world, feel ourselves to be elements in its structure of universal history" (Auerbach 1953:15).

Auerbach concludes his comparison of Homeric and FT storytelling (22f), "The sublime influence of God [...] reaches so deeply into the everyday that the two realms of the sublime and the everyday are not only actually unseparated but basically inseparable." What Auerbach says of the FT, perhaps even more markedly distinguishes charismatic movements: at their rise the "sublime influence of God", by signs and wonders, deeply reaches into the everyday thereby making the sublime and the everyday inseparable. To be really overcome by God's sublime reality, without deserting this world, we need the presence and intervention of his mighty Spirit. God's empowering presence in a charismatic movement will transform the yearning of Psalm 74:9, "We are given no miraculous signs; no prophets are left, and none of us knows how long this will be", into the confidence of Hebrews 2:4, "God also testified to it [God's deliverance by Jesus] by signs, wonders and various miracles, and gifts of the Holy Spirit distributed according to his will."

For the success of a charismatic movement God's presence is indispensable (see Brueggemann 1978:37). To be a successful (charismatic) leader, whether a David or an Odysseus, one needs the deity's approval, indeed good will and active help, not only the skills and valour of a Saul or a Hector. Signs and wonders are also needed in emergency situations and for new systems at their emergence to replace the old. This is why Solomon could make do without them.

Weber claims that charisma is a volatile force (1968:1114, 1121). In this regard a remark of Robert Polzin takes on some new implications. Commenting on the "perhaps" of 1 Samuel 9:6 he concludes (1989:125): "Thus the Deuteronomist offers no absolute certainties concerning the path that leads away from exile toward a regaining of the land; otherwise the author would be denying to the LORD the very freedom of action that merely human characters are shown to possess." Here Polzin is tackling humanity's dilemma of certainty vs. "perhaps". As far as the exilic community is concerned Polzin is undoubtedly correct. Charismatic communities, however, long for certainty. With signs and wonders, extraordinary interventions by God's Spirit this is granted, despite the unstable nature of charisma (or, rather, that of the charismatic).

This may help explain a couple of apparently unrelated issues. In the first place God's resistance to kingship appears less whimsical. In judgeship God's intervention was a built-in factor, which, however, kingship rendered redundant by a standing army, centralised power and administration — by self-reliance. God's dynamic character and Israel's dynamic relationship to its Suzerain were profoundly shaken.

Here the opposition of the static and the dynamic seems to be of great significance. I have shown how by retiring David rendered his charisma static and so extinguished it. Similarly Solomon's royal pretension and misuse of charisma resulted in a static temple with a static state religion, where God's intervention was not welcome. As I have claimed the very thing a charismatic cannot afford is stasis; charisma must be constantly used and used to the end it has been given for.

The signs-and-wonders motif extends even beyond the FT. As far as the ST is concerned the early church experienced God's manifest presence and support, and occasionally God's wrath (Acts 5) like David in 2 Samuel 6 (see Goldingay 2000:213). Even though suffering and persecution are characteristics of the followers of Jesus,[8] in the ST there is a lack of FT aspects of the dark side of God such as unreliability on God's part or God's wrath against his people. This makes the ST appear rather triumphalist compared to the FT. This I suggest might partly be explained by the realisation that the ST witnessed the emergence and climax of a triumphant charismatic movement demonstrating God's positive presence and the manifestations of God's Spirit.

Josephus somewhere claims that the work of God's prophetic spirit has ceased. The Christian movement of the ST, however, obviously viewed itself as heir to that prophetic spirit. Indeed for 1st century Judaism the notion of the Holy Spirit was well-known. Still, only Christianity claimed to be a charismatic movement, which heavily resorted to the person, presence and work of the Spirit.[9]

Prospects

In the "Introduction" I claimed that the focus of the studies I had reviewed was

---

[8] This needs further elaboration in this framework.

[9] The Bar-Kochba revolution of the early 2nd century AD may be another candidate. I do not know, however, whether it made any reference to the Spirit.

either the narrative or charisma; charismatic leadership has been neglected. I have studied the narrative from the perspective of character and plot development in particular in order to see the story's view of charismatic leadership. I have attempted to present a consistent plot with "real-life" characters and their motives, ambitions and challenges, that contribute to the picture of charismatic leadership. My study, though not a conventional commentary, has produced, I hope, a coherent and comprehensive reading. If my argument was coherent and I presented my methodology compellingly, methodologies need to take the dynamism of characters, plot and their development more seriously into account, as these aspects are essential to understand narratives. Similarly the narrator's view should more consistently be distinguished from that of characters.

Now what is 1-2 Samuel all about? Goldingay suggests (2000:3) that 1-2 Samuel is a study on leadership. Having finished my analysis it is tempting to consider 1-2 Samuel a narrative on charismatic leadership in the first place, and I am more and more convinced that this is 1-2 Samuel's main theme. I hope I have argued this convincingly.[10]

My study raises some questions for further study. God's uneasiness about the monarchy was a recurring motif from 1 Samuel 8. Was God opposed to monarchy because it eventually eliminated charismatic leadership as became increasingly clear after the rule of David? It would also be worth researching whether and how much it is related to (or took the place of) another theme in the Bible: God's primordial conflict with chaos and its representatives. The application to the FT and ST of my suggestion of signs and wonders in the DH should be studied further. Power is a major aspect of charismatic leadership, I have claimed; more study on this is also needed. Whether the bigger unit is Deuteronomy-2 Kings or, as more recently proposed by scholars (e.g. Rosenberg 1986; Bar-Efrat 1989:139; Miscall 1993; Goldingay 2000:2), Genesis-2 Kings, these topics need to be addressed.

From Saul to Solomon there is a development from a state with hardly any institutions to a highly institutionalised monarchy. How "issues of 'charismatic empowerment' on the one hand and 'institutional authorization' on the other relate to one another" (Hutton 1994:24), charisma and institution, their correlation and interaction, the transition and underlying forces are worth being studied. For scholars of the diachronic approach my study may imply that in tradition-historical terms there was a "charismatic" tradition; again, a possible area of research. Also the problem of anti- and pro-Davidic sources may need

---

[10] That 1-2 Samuel was intended as a study of charismatic leadership may seem too exclusive a claim. Hence I also sympathise with Gunn's proposal (1978:61f) that the narrative is entertainment, although serious entertainment. I would qualify Gunn's proposal by adding the adjective "theological". Entertainment is still a broad enough category to include themes such as tragedy, charismatic leadership and various other issues one should study.

be revisited. Certainly, studying the different transitions in leadership of the FT (e.g. Eli-Samuel; Solomon-Jeroboam) and the ST (e.g. Jesus-apostles; Paul-Timothy) will be rewarding too.

More importantly God's intermittent interventions by his Spirit can rightly be considered an overarching theme in the Bible. The theme's presence in historical and prophetic books is obvious. In a sense even the Psalms witness to what it is like, most frequently in personal terms, when God's spirit is present or absent. More problematic, from the viewpoint of a biblical theology, is the virtual absence of explicit references to the spirit in the wisdom literature.[11] The problem may be addressed from a historical perspective though. That is to say the ebb in the work of God's presence might be explained as a possible reaction to theological, social and political developments like the exile, the misuse of Deuteronomistic theology and power issues — and lack of charismatic leadership. It can also be argued that those books not explicitly referring to God's mighty acts in history implicitly do so — the absence of the theme may imply the need for God's intervention. In a different context Goldingay argues (1994:134) that the Hebrew scriptures "seek to keep alive both founding events and charismatic impulse without leading either to bureaucratization or sectarianism." Thus the concept of charismatic leadership may prove a good starting point for a biblical theology or a study of the Bible in the fashion of Josipovici. Alternatively the concept can be developed elaborating on Terrien's theme.

In the subsequent DH after Solomon there is a decrease or even a disintegration of the theme of charismatic leadership. In the northern kingdom Jeroboam, the next charismatic leader after Solomon, is referred to as an Ephrathite in 1 Kings 11:26 — as David was in 1 Samuel 17:12, and as the Samuel-Saul story was introduced in 1 Samuel 1:1[12]. Is Jeroboam considered by the narrator the next charismatic leader like David and not like Solomon? Given the civil war-like situation of 1 Kings 12, similar to when David was made king in 2 Samuel, and what Jeroboam is expected to achieve, this is likely. After Jeroboam there is the emergence of charismatic Jehu (2 Kgs 9). The text, however, does not stress this point very much. Jehu is rather a man acting rashly — he becomes an Israelite king not very different from his predecessors and successors. Is the lack of emphasis on charismatic leadership indicative of its diminishing significance?

Regarding Judah the reigns of Joash, Hezekiah and, especially, Josiah are worth studying from the viewpoint of charismatic leadership. Kings of a doomed kingdom, their reigns are not accompanied by God's good will to the

---

[11] To be sure God's spirit is referred to, e.g., in Job 32:8, 18; 33:4, 34:14. The spirit, however, appears to be the "organising principle" of the cosmos.
[12] The phrase's only two other and rather insignificant occurrences are Ju 12:5 and Ruth 1:2.

degree David's or even Solomon's was.[13] In fact the way the end of their reigns is narrated is ambiguous to say the least. Also the narrator's focus on good as opposed to bad ruler rather than on charismatic leadership may make a study of charismatic leadership in Kings difficult.

Only in the ST is charismatic leadership emphasised to the extent it was in the earlier parts of the DH (particularly in the Lucan corpus;[14] see also motifs borrowed from 1-2 Samuel, e.g. in Lk 2:52). The role of the Holy Spirit is significant throughout Luke-Acts, not decreasing in relevance; then Paul develops a theology of the presence and work of the Holy Spirit. In the witness of the ST the early church's claim is that in them a new charismatic movement was emerging. Indeed charismatic empowerment and its ramifications (the concept of priesthood and prophethood of all members of God's people, i.e. everyone can be endowed by God's Spirit) is fully realised in the ST.

Other implications for ST studies, particularly the Lucan corpus, and biblical theology might be found in the idea of emerging charismatic leaders (John the Baptist, Jesus, the apostles, the early church) and their endowment by the Spirit. Indeed this might be intentional in Luke, since he undoubtedly used 1-2 Samuel to shape his own work. The theme is present in Revelation: only God's coming rule will establish just rule, as God is the only righteous leader and deliverer, not subject to mentorship, royal pretension, misuse of power and sin. To put it differently the DH's pessimism towards charismatic leaders and kings forces the Bible to project the dream of charismatic leadership into the future and into the apocalyptic figure of the Messiah.

The Relevance of This Study

At one point during my research I phoned my godmother. She insinuated her "disapproval" by the question: "Why did you not choose a topic more profitable to your church?" And with some anti-Semitic sentiment she added: "Why on earth are you studying those Jewish kings?" I hope to have demonstrated that "studying those Jewish kings" need not be idealistic or impractical as it has often been, but can be a down-to-earth endeavour with much relevance to life, people, church, politics, power and of course charismatic leadership. My hope and wish is that the church, both worldwide and the Reformed Church in Hungary, may benefit from this study. To this end I shall make the possible profits of this study more explicit.

Having studied at different seminaries and now studying charismatic leadership I have come to realise a basic shortcoming as far as the philosophy and curriculum of training are concerned. Though the institutions I have studied at were dedicated to training pastors, i.e. leaders of local churches, the intention

---

[13] See my discussion of *Signs and wonders*.
[14] See terms like "filled with the Holy Spirit"; 1:15, 35, 41, 67; 2:25-27; 3:16, 22; 4:1, 14, 18; Acts 1:5, 8; 2:4, 33, 38; 4:8, 31; 8:15-19; 9:17; 10:38-47; 13:9, 52.

to train future leaders was somehow missing. For obvious reasons we studied Hebrew, Greek, Latin, church history, systematic theology and for less obvious reasons architecture (in case we become involved in building a church), hymnology and playing the organ (to lead singing). Charisma and leadership, let alone charismatic leadership, were not on the curriculum. At the time of my studies I did not realise this. I only noticed it recently and it shocked me: How is it possible to train future leaders without preparing them for the leadership position they are expected to perform? What will be the quality of leadership of those graduating from seminaries?

The church cannot afford to ignore the training of charismatic leaders. I am aware that this is a strong and, at the same time, ambiguous statement. It is ambiguous firstly because humans cannot grant charisma. Secondly it is ambiguous because it can refer either to recognised or to prospective charismatic leaders. If understood in the latter sense, it may appear as a rather presumptuous goal.[15]

Whether one likes it or not, in the Bible, both the FT and the ST, God's usual way of intervention and dealing with his people is by appointing and equipping leaders in order to help his people. Deficiency in leadership training implies a deficient vision of how God acts. God has always been keen to raise leaders by his Spirit and equip them with skills particularly needed in the given crisis. Without leaders God rarely intervenes. To be sure we cannot grant charisma, but we are responsible for asking for it, just as we are to train leaders. In this we most often fall short. I am convinced that the inefficiency of Christian training programmes is a result of our lack of focus on and unawareness of the importance of charismatic leadership.

Though God's preferred way of deliverance is raising charismatic leaders, theologians have not been keen to study or elaborate on this. It is indicative of the general situation that references in Gottwald's monumental volume *The Tribes of Yahweh* (1979) to "charisma" or "charismatic" are insignificant[16]. Nearly quarter of a century ago Samuel Terrien observed (2000:64) that 20th century theology had "generally believed that the Hebrew cultus gradually emerged as an impersonal and sociological phenomenon in the course of many generations." What he adds I hope is not wishful thinking: "Today, a balanced view of the interaction between individual and society is gaining ground. Attention is again being paid to the intensely personal character of Hebrew faith."

For the above reasons it is not groundless to say that the greater the ignorance about leadership, the stronger the tendency to both authoritarianism, which is but another form of leadership, and chaos. Authoritarian and suppressive leadership is often the main external obstacle to charismatic leadership, particularly of the radical kind. The implications for church

---

[15] By the ambiguity I intended to create some "undecidability".
[16] To "charisma" or "charismatic" there are as few as seven references in the index.

leadership, specifically in more authoritarian climates like Eastern Europe, are immense. The major threat to charisma and charismatic leadership is a self-serving and self-indulgent leadership, which compromises its commissioning, office and responsibility. Therefore the most important question is not whether charisma has been bestowed but how it is being used after its bestowal. Charisma, though being God's free gift, is to be used and mastered wisely. In other words charisma needs to be viewed in its dynamism and never as a static concept.

I hope this study has also made it clear that with God's supernatural gift individuals are capable of overcoming enormous challenges. Hopeless situations and desperate crises are surmounted by the wise use of charisma. What Boff (1985:157) observes with the Roman Catholic Church in mind has universal validity and may be encouraging for those longing for the activity of the Spirit, which "never takes place as a part of the state, an established order, or the people as a whole. The reality of the Spirit is found in the arena of creativity, of the unconventional, in the interruption of something new, on the level of the individual."

Jobling's assertion of the turn in biblical studies may equally be applied to my investigation:

> A revolution is going on in biblical studies and the turn towards literature, or "reading," is a major part of it. But unless this revolution stays linked with political transformation, it can only be seen as the work of an intellectual class which accepts its leisured marginalization. The reader for whom I have tried in this essay to assess the value of Solomon's age is not, therefore, some "general reader" with no particular location, but one who is asking questions about what it means to read the Bible within the culture we all inhabit. (1997:491f)

The following "charismatic typology" may help us see charismatic leadership in context. My study suggests three basic types, which is not to say that only three exist, nor that they are pure types.[17] The Saul type charismatic leader is subordinated, suppressed and likely to end up with his charisma extinguished. He/she is the charismatic leader never able to use charisma in the unrestrained and mastered way charisma is supposed to be used. He/she is probably surrounded by authoritarian (traditional and institutionalised) structures and a rather unstable socio-political situation.

The David type is an accomplished, fulfilled leader, who, however, extinguishes his charisma by not using it. In this way her/his leadership is rendered meaningless. "Davids" emerge in acute emergencies when tactfulness, sharp insight, strategic thinking and the character of a diplomat are needed to avert national crises. On the other hand she/he is the leader who, sits back after big achievements, retires to her/his palace and relinquishes leadership to her/his right-hand man and will thus be controlled by him. Again this all presupposes a

---

[17] In addition to my three types, the Eli-Samuel transition presents another type.

rather volatile context.

The Solomon type emerges due to his/her predecessor's failure to designate his/her successor. This failure may cause rivalry, mayhem and faction. A "Solomon's" charisma is to provide order, welfare and unity. With no checks on her/his power, however, charisma may be compromised and misused. The transition in leadership assumes a stable government and a well-established ruling class distinct from the grass roots that is not involved in policy making.

The need for new leadership, quite explicit in the transition from Samuel to Saul and in that from Saul to David, creates a tension between the old and the new leadership. It follows that the same leadership cannot be sustained beyond one generation. This observation only verifies the different but related claim that a renewal cannot be sustained beyond one generation. If so then charismatic leaders had better watch out not to canonise the methods of their success. A greater degree of awareness of the limits of one's leadership must be demonstrated. We may also look at church history, past or contemporary, differently. Furthermore the David-Solomon transition implies that the more hierarchic and routinised the institution is, the more difficult it is for it to produce charismatic leaders. God willing, charisma can still be bestowed, but it is not inherent in the system. Again a demonstration of one's awareness of the limits, indeed the downside, of authoritarian and rigid structures is desirable.

Other questions: What are the implications of the "charismatic typology" for traditional churches and movements? And for emerging churches and movements? What are the implications for recognising, selecting and training prospective (charismatic) leaders? And for seminary curricula? Given the difference between charismatic leaders, how are we supposed to deal with transitions in leadership? By raising these questions I have reached the point where stating a few basic practice principles seems to be in order.

1. My study of the transition in leadership from Samuel to Saul and Saul to David has suggested that, since the authoritarian old does not tolerate the emerging new, covert or overt animosity often marks the transition in leadership. A recognition of whether the animosity is covert or overt and of the tension between the old and new may prepare one to face the animosity with the correct attitude and skills and make one successful.
2. My analyses of Saul, David and Solomon imply that awareness of the nature of the crisis as well as that of the needed leadership is a precondition to resolving the crisis. Without this awareness both the old and the emerging new make the transition only more difficult.
3. The circumstances of Solomon's ascending the throne evinces that the transition in leadership should be prepared and implemented with great care. Whether mission agencies, seminaries, church legislative and executive bodies, or congregations, it is in the interest of everyone involved that the transition take place smoothly and quickly, with minimal conflict and maximal consensus.
4. In my study of 1 Samuel 13-15 I claimed that as old Samuel made Saul fail,

so the old obstructs the initiatives of the new by unrealisable requirements. This is a relevant observation for church and service. Since young people are the most venturing and creative, youth should be given maximal freedom to worship God in their own way. Any expectation to measure up to the standards of the older generation is likely to cause frustration and alienation. Good youth leaders are by definition autonomous and creative people with a vision, open to new initiatives and lacking rigidity. This too must be taken into account when training and appointing youth leaders.[18]

5. My study of David suggests that independence and determination are two requirements for the emerging charismatic leader. Without these qualities the new will not succeed. These qualities make charismatic leaders dissenters. In *Refounding the Church: Dissent for Leadership* Gerald Arbuckle argues that a conscious encouragement to dissent is valuable for the emerging new leadership. Such encouragement will result in "loyal dissent" (2f). Since each leadership faces new challenges, it is reasonable, in fact imperative for the old leadership to nourish dissent in the emerging leadership. Arbuckle quotes John Paul II (3; citing Swidler 1987:312): "'Conformity means death for any community. A loyal opposition is a necessity in any community.'" The aim of this is autonomous and competent leadership that confidently embarks on new ventures (cf. 6f).

6. In my study of David and Solomon I have suggested that the real challenge to charismatic leadership is oriental kingship, or, in more general terms, power. If that is so institutions as well as leaders had better consider how to avoid compromises of charismatic leadership and how to keep the charismatic committed to the charismatic ideal. A charismatic leader should be given freedom to bring about her/his vision. The institution is to make sure that the leader's attempts are not impeded by lack of time and duties that other people can do. A support team checking the leader's agenda seems desirable, "strong men", however, can make him/her fail.

7. The Saul and David narratives also imply that careful and manifold examination of prospective leaders is inevitable *in order to recognise* their potential leadership skills. These skills might be suppressed and dormant, waiting to be recognised and mastered. Their examination and recognition are the first steps towards mastering them. Similarly practice is necessary for the leadership skills to be mastered. To be sure, there are differences between one charismatic leader and another, between one leadership charisma and another. Which leader fits what situation, which charisma is suitable for a certain setting needs careful evaluation. People lacking leadership skills are not necessarily disqualified from ministry. The recognition, however, of this lack may prevent future conflicts and

---

[18] Cf. Arbuckle's observation (1993:2): "Creative people are anathema to totalitarian systems. Eventually these totalitarian systems collapse, killed by their own refusal to accept needed innovation under the inspiration of dissenters at all levels of society."

disasters, whether personal, familial or communal.
8. Finally two important and universal principles have emerged from my study. Firstly I have tried to show from the narrative that charisma is always granted for the benefit of God's people and must be used accordingly. Indeed the basis for evaluating a charismatic's activity and success is how he/she uses the charisma. The charismatic's leadership should constantly be checked: How is charisma used? Who benefits from it? Is the charismatic's commitment to his/her commission fading? If so what measures should be taken so as to reinvigorate it?
9. Secondly my analysis of David's call and rise implies that an openness towards the initiative of the Spirit and the granting of charisma is required as well as an awareness of the Spirit's sovereignty. We cannot forestall the Spirit's action. When praying and waiting for God's intervention and renewal, expect the unexpected!

Unfortunately theologians have abandoned leadership studies to sociologists, businessmen and managers. The church has at best focused on leadership from the angles of character and individual ethics. It is time to "repent" and reclaim the neglected area of charismatic leadership to theology as well as the church.

For a Hungarian Reformed, as I am, to come to these conclusions is I think quite an achievement. For this I am grateful to God's Spirit.

Bibliography

Abramski, S. "The Beginning of the Israelite Monarchy and Its Impact upon Leadership in Israel", *Imm* 19 (Winter 1984-85), 7-21.
Ackerman, J.S. "Knowing Good and Evil: A Literary Analysis of the Court History in 2 Samuel 9-20 and 1 Kings 1-2", *JBL* 109 (1990), 41-60.
— "Who Can Stand Before Yahweh (1Sam 1-15)?" *Proof* 11 (1991), 1-24.
Ackroyd, P.R. "The Succession Narrative (so-called)", *Int* 35 (1981), 383-96.
Ahlström, G.W. "Solomon, the Chosen One", *HR* 8 (1968), 93-110.
Alt, A. "The Formation of the Israelite State in Palestine", *Essays on Old Testament History and Religion* (Sheffield: JSOT Press, 1989), 171-237.
— "The Monarchy in Israel and Judah", *Essays on Old Testament History and Religion* (Sheffield: JSOT Press, 1989), 239-59. 1989a
Alter, R. *The Art of Biblical Narrative* (New York: Basic Books, 1981).
— *The David Story: A Translation with Commentary of 1 and 2 Samuel* (New York: W.W. Norton & Company, 1999).
— *The World of Biblical Literature* (London: SPCK, 1992).
Amit, Y. *Hidden Polemics in Biblical Narrative* (BIS 25, Leiden: Brill, 2000).
Anderson, A.A. *2 Samuel* (WBC 11, Dallas: Word Books, 1989).
Arbuckle, G.A. *Refounding the Church: Dissent for Leadership* (London: Geoffrey Chapman, 1993).
Armerding, C.E. "Were David's Sons Really Priests?" *Current Issues in Biblical and Patristic Interpretation: Studies in Honor of Merrill C. Tenney* (ed. G.F. Hawthorne, Grand Rapids: Wm.B. Eerdmans, 1975), 75-86.
Auerbach, E. *Mimesis: The Representation of Reality in Western Literature* (Princeton: Princeton University Press, 1953).
Auld, A.G. and Ho, C.Y.S. "The Making of David and Goliath" *JSOT* 56 (1992), 19-39.
Bach, A. "The Pleasure of Her Text", *The Pleasure of Her Text: Feminist Readings of Biblical and Historical Texts* (Philadelphia: Trinity Press International, 1990), 25-44.
Bach, R. *Die Aufforderungen zur Flucht und zum Kampf im alttestamentlichen Prophetenspruch* (WMANT 9, Neukirchen: Neukirchener Verlag, 1962).
Bar-Efrat, S. *Narrative Art in the Bible* (JSOTSup 70, Sheffield: Academic Press, 1989).
— "Some Observations on the Analysis of Structure in Biblical Narrative", *VT* 30 (1980), 154-73.
Barr, J. *The Concept of Biblical Theology* (London: SCM, 1999).
— *The Garden of Eden and the Hope of Immortality: The Read-Tuckwell Lectures for 1990* (London: SCM Press, 1992).
Barthélemy, D.; Gooding, D.W.; Lust, J. and Tov, E. *The Story of David and Goliath: Textual and Literary Criticism; Papers of a Joint Research Venture* (OBO 73, Fribourg: Éditions Universitaires—Göttingen: Vandenhoeck & Ruprecht, 1986).
Berges, U. *Die Verwerfung Sauls: Eine thematische Untersuchung* (Würzburg: Echter, 1989).
Berlin, A. "Characterization in Biblical Narrative: David's Wives", *JSOT* 23 (1982), 69-85.

— *Poetics and Interpretation of Biblical Narrative* (BLS 9, Sheffield: The Almond Press, 1983).
Beuken, W.A.M. "I Samuel 28: The Prophet as 'Hammer of Witches'", *JSOT* 6 (1978), 3-17.
Beyerlin, W. "Das Königcharisma bei Saul", *ZAW* 73 (1961), 186-201.
Bietenhard, S.K. *Des Königs General: Die Heerführertraditionen in der vorstaatlichen und frühen staatlichen Zeit und die Joabgestalt in 2 Sam 2-20; 1 Kön 1-2* (OBO 163, Freiburg: Universitätsverlag—Göttingen: Vandenhoeck & Ruprecht, 1998).
Boff, L. *Church: Charism and Power. Liberation Theology and the Institutional Church* (London: SCM Press, 1985).
Borgman, P. "Story Shapes That Tell a World: Biblical, Homeric, and Modern Narrative", *Christian Scholar's Review* 9 (1980), 291-316.
Bowman, R.G. "The Fortune of King David/The Fate of Queen Michal: A literary Critical Analysis of 2 Samuel 1-8", *Telling Queen Michal's Story, An Experiment in Comparative Interpretation* (eds. D.J.A. Clines and T.C. Eskenazi, JSOTSup 119, Sheffield: Academic Press, 1991), 97-120.
Brauner, R.A. "'To Grasp the Hem', and 1 Sam 15:27", *JANESCU* 6 (1974), 35-38.
Brettler, M. "The Structure of 1 Kings 1-11", *JSOT* 49 (1991), 87-97.
Brongers, H.A. "Bemerkungen zum Gebrauch des adverbialen *we'attah* im AT (ein lexikologischer Beitrag)", *VT* 15 (1965), 289-99.
Brooks, S.S. "Saul and the Samson Narrative", *JSOT* 71 (1996), 19-25.
Brueggemann, W. *David's Truth in Israel's Imagination and Memory* (Philadelphia: Fortress Press, 1985).
— *First and Second Samuel* (Interpretation, Louisville: John Knox Press, 1990).
— "Israel's Moment of Freedom", *The Bible Today* 42 (April 1969), 2917-25.
— "Kingship and Chaos (A Study in Tenth Century Theology)", *CBQ* 33 (1971), 317
— "Narrative Coherence and Theological Intentionality in 1Samuel 18", *CBQ* 55 (1993), 225-43.
— "On Coping with Curse: A Study of 2 Sam 16:5-14", *CBQ* 36 (1974), 175-92.
— *Power, Providence, and Personality: Biblical Insight Into Life and Ministry* (Louisville: Westminster-John Knox Press, 1990). 1990a
— *Theology of the Old Testament: Testimony, Dispute, Advocacy* (Minneapolis: Fortress Press, 1997).
— *The Prophetic Imagination* (Philadelphia: Fortress Press, 1978).
— *1 Kings* (KPG, Atlanta: John Knox Press, 1982).
— "2 Samuel 21-24: An Appendix of Deconstruction?" *CBQ* 50 (1988), 383-97.
Buber, M. "Der Gesalbte", *Werke*, Vol. 2 (München: Kosel—Heidelberg: Lambert, 1964), 725-845.
— "Die Erzählung von Sauls Königswahl", *VT* 6 (1956), 113-73.
Campbell, A.F. *Of Prophets & Kings: A Late Ninth Century Document (1 Samuel 1–2 Kings 10)* (CBQMS 17, Washington DC: CBAA, 1986).
— "Yahweh and the Ark: A Case Study in Narrative," *JBL* 98 (1979), 31-43.
Cannon, W.W. "The Reign of Saul", *Theology* 25 (1932), 326-35.
Cargill, J. "David in History: A Secular Approach", *Judaism* 35 (1986), 211-22.
Carlson, R.A. *David, the Chosen King: A Traditio-Historical Approach to the Second Book of Samuel*, (Stockholm: Almqvist & Wiksell, 1964).
Caspari, W. "The Literary Type and Historical Value of 2 Samuel 15-20", *Narrative and Novella in Samuel* (ed. D.M. Gunn, JSOTSup 116, Sheffield: The Almond Press,

1991), 59-88.
Ceresko, A.R. "A Rhetorical Analysis of David's 'Boast' (1 Samuel 17:34-37): Some Reflections on Method", *CBQ* 47 (1985), 58-74.
Chaney, M.L. "Systemic Study of the Israelite Monarchy", *Semeia* 37 (1986), 53-76.
Childs, B.S. *Introduction to the Old Testament as Scripture* (London: SCM Press, 1979).
Clements, R.E. *God and Temple* (Oxford: Basil Blackwell, 1965).
— *Wisdom in Theology* (Carlisle: Paternoster—Grand Rapids: Wm.B. Eerdmans, 1992).
Clines, D.J.A. "David the Man: The Construction of Masculinity in the Hebrew Bible", *Interested Parties: The Ideology of Writers and Readers of the Hebrew Bible* (JSOTSup 205, Sheffield: Academic Press, 1995), 212-43.
— "The Story of Michal, Wife of David, in Its Sequential Unfolding", *Telling Queen Michal's Story, An Experiment in Comparative Interpretation* (eds. D.J.A. Clines and T.C. Eskenazi, JSOTSup 119, Sheffield: Academic Press, 1991), 129-40.
Cohen, K.I. "King Saul — A Bungler from the Beginning", *Bible Review* 10/5 (1994), 34-39, 56-57.
— "The Rebellions During the Reign of David. An Inquiry into Social Dynamics in Ancient Israel", *Studies in Jewish Bibliography, History, and Literature in Honor of I. Edward Kiev* (ed. C. Berlin, New York: KTAV Publishing House, 1971), 91-112.
Conroy, C. *Absalom, Absalom! Narrative and Language in 2 Sam. 13-20* (Analecta Biblica 81, Rome: Biblical Institute Press, 1978).
— "A Literary Analysis of 1 Kings i 41-53, with Methodological Reflections", *VTSup* 36 (1985), 54-66.
Craig, K.M. "Rhetorical Aspects of Questions Answered with Silence in 1 Samuel 14:37 and 28:6", *CBQ* 56 (1994), 221-39.
Cross, F.M. "The Ammonite Oppression of the Tribes of Gad and Reuben: Missing Verses from 1 Sam. 11 Found in 4Q Sam^a", *History, Historiography and Interpretation: Studies in Biblical and Cuneiform Literature* (eds. H. Tadmor and M. Weinfeld, Jerusalem: Magnes Press, 1983), 148-58.
— "The Ideologies of Kingship in the Era of the Empire: Conditional Covenant and Eternal Decree", *Canaanite Myth and Hebrew Epic: Essays in the History of Religion of Israel* (Cambridge: Harvard University Press, 1973), 219-73.
Crüsemann, F. *Der Widerstand gegen das Königtum* (WMANT 49, Neukirchen-Vluyn: Neukirchener Verlag, 1978).
Cryer, F.H. "David's Rise to Power and the Death of Abner: An Analysis of 1 Samuel xxvi 14-16 and its Redaction-Critical Implications", *VT* 35 (1985), 385-94.
Culpepper, R.A. "Narrative Criticism as a Tool for Proclamation: 1 Samuel 13", *RE* 84 (1987), 33-40.
Czövek, T. *Some Peculiarities in the Book of Judges* (Unpublished ThM thesis, Decatur, 1997).
Deist, F. "Coincidence as a Motif of Divine Intervention in 1 Samuel 9", *OTE* 6 (1993), 7-18.
DeVries, S.J. *1 Kings* (WBC 12, Waco, TX: Word Books, 1985).
Dietrich, W. "Die Erzählungen von David und Goliat in I Sam 17", *ZAW* 108 (1996), 172-91.
Donner, H. "Art und Herkunft des Amtes der Königinmutter im Alten Testament", *Festschrift Johannes Friedrich* (eds. R. von Kienle et al., Heidelberg: Carl Winter, 1959), 105-45.
Dragga, S. "In the Shadow of the Judges: The Failure of Saul", *JSOT* 38 (1987), 39-46.

Edelman, D. *King Saul in the Historiography of Judah* (JSOTSup 121, Sheffield: JSOT Press, 1991).

Edenburg, C. "How (not) to Murder a King: Variations on a Theme in 1 Sam 24; 26", *SJOT* 12 (1998), 64-85.

Eslinger, L. "A Change of Heart: 1 Samuel 16", *Ascribe to the Lord: Biblical & Other Studies in Memory of Peter C. Craigie* (eds. L. Eslinger and G. Taylor, JSOTSup 67, Sheffield: Academic Press, 1988), 341-61.

— *House of God or House of David: The Rhetoric of 2 Samuel 7* (JSOTSup 164, Sheffield: Academic Press, 1994).

— *Into the Hands of the Living God* (JSOTSup 84, Sheffield: The Almond Press, 1989).

— *Kingship of God in Crisis: A Close Reading of 1 Samuel 1-12* (BLS 10, Sheffield: The Almond Press, 1985).

— "Viewpoints and Points of View in 1 Samuel 8-12", *JSOT* 26 (1983), 61-76.

Everett, P. *Vivaldi:* The Four Seasons *and Other Concertos, op. 8* (Cambridge: Cambridge University Press, 1996).

Exum, J.C. *Tragedy and Biblical Narrative: Arrows of the Almighty* (Cambridge: Cambridge University Press, 1992).

Exum, J.C. and Whedbee, J.W. "Isaac, Samson, and Saul: Reflections on the Comic and Tragic Visions", *Tragedy and Comedy in the Bible* (ed. J.C. Exum, Semeia 32, Decatur: Scholars Press, 1985), 5-40.

Flanagan, J.W. "Chiefs in Israel", *JSOT* 20 (1981), 47-73.

— *David's Social Drama: A Hologram of Israel's Early Iron Age* (SWBAS 7, Sheffield: The Almond Press, 1988).

— "Social Transformation and Ritual in 2 Samuel 6", *The Word of the Lord Shall Go Forth: Essays in Honor of David Noel Freedman in Celebration of his sixtieth Birthday* (eds. C.L. Meyers and M. O'Connor, Winona Lake: Eisenbrauns, 1983), 361-72.

— "Succession and Genealogy in the Davidic Dynasty", *The Quest for the Kingdom of God: Studies in Honor of George E. Mendenhall* (eds. H.B. Huffmon, F.A. Spina and A.R.W. Green, Winona Lake: Eisenbrauns, 1983), 35-55. 1983a

Fokkelman, J.P. *Narrative Art and Poetry in the Books of Samuel*, Vol. 1. *King David* (Assen: Van Gorcum, 1981).

— *Narrative Art and Poetry in the Books of Samuel*, Vol. 2. *The Crossing Fates* (Assen: Van Gorcum, 1986).

— *Narrative Art and Poetry in the Books of Samuel*, Vol. 3. *Throne and City* (Assen: Van Gorcum, 1990).

— *Narrative Art and Poetry in the Books of Samuel*, Vol. 4. *Vow and Desire* (Assen: Van Gorcum, 1993).

Fontaine, C.R. "Proverb Performance in the Hebrew Bible", *Wise Words: Essays on the Proverbs* (ed. W. Mieder, New York & London: Garland Publishing, 1994), 393-413.

Foresti, F. *The Rejection of Saul in the Perspective of the Deuteronomistic School: A Study of 1 Sm 15 and Related Texts* (Studia Theologica-Teresianum 5, Roma: Edizioni del Teresianum, 1984).

Fowler, H.W and Fowler, F.G. (eds.) *The Concise Oxford Dictionary of Current English* (Oxford: Oxford University Press, 1990).

Fretheim, T.E. "Divine Foreknowledge, Divine Constancy, and the Rejection of Saul's Kingship", *CBQ* 47 (1985), 595-602.

Frisch, A. "'For I Feared the People, and I Yielded to Them' (I Sam 15,24) — Is Saul's

Guilt Attenuated or Intensified", *ZAW* 108 (1996), 98-104.
— "Structure and its Significance: The Narrative of Solomon's Reign (1 Kgs 1-12.24)", *JSOT* 51 (1991), 3-14.
— "The Exodus Motif in 1 Kings 1-14", *JSOT* 87 (2000), 3-21.
Fuchs, S. "Solomon—The King Without a Prophet", *BRev* 3/2 (1987), 46-47.
Gamzu, Y. "The Semitic and the Hellenic Types of Narrative", *Semitics* 9 (1984), 58-85.
Garsiel, M. "Puns Upon Names as a Literary Device in 1 Kings 1-2", *Bib* 72 (1991), 379-86.
— *The First Book of Samuel: A Literary Study of Comparative Structures, Analogies and Parallels* (Ramat-Gan: Revivim Publishing House, 1985).
— "The Story of David and Bathsheba: A Different Approach", *CBQ* 55 (1993), 244-62.
George, M.K. "Constructing Identity in 1 Samuel 17", *BibInt* 7 (1999), 389-412.
Gillingham, S.E. *One Bible, Many Voices: Different Approaches to Biblical Studies* (London: SPCK, 1998).
Goldingay, J. *Men Behaving Badly* (Carlisle: Paternoster, 2000).
— *Models for Interpretation of Scripture* (Grand Rapids: Wm.B. Eerdmans—Carlisle: Paternoster, 1995).
— *Models for Scripture* (Grand Rapids: Wm.B. Eerdmans—Carlisle: Paternoster, 1994).
Good, E.M. *Irony in the Old Testament* (London: SPCK, 1965).
Gordon, R.P. "A house divided: wisdom in Old Testament narrative traditions", *Wisdom in ancient Israel: Essays in honour of J. A. Emerton* (eds. J. Day, R.P. Gordon and H.G.M. Williamson, Cambridge: Cambridge University Press, 1995), 94-105.
— "Aleph Apologeticum", *JQR* 69 (1978), 112-16.
— "David's Rise and Saul's Demise: Narrative Analogy in 1 Samuel 24-26", *TB* 31 (1980), 37-64.
— *1 & 2 Samuel* (OTG, Sheffield: JSOT Press, 1984).
— *I & II Samuel: A Commentary* (Exeter: Paternoster, 1986).
Gottwald, N.K. *The Tribes of Yahweh: A Sociology of the Religion of Liberated Israel, 1250-1050 B.C.E.* (Maryknoll: Orbis, 1979).
Gressmann, H. "The Oldest History Writing in Israel", *Narrative Art and Novella in Samuel* (ed. D.M. Gunn, JSOTSup 116, Sheffield: The Almond Press, 1991), 9-58.
Grottanelli, C. "Charismatic Possession and Monarchic Rationalization: The Folly of Saul", *Kings & Prophets: Monarchic Power, Inspired Leadership & Sacred Text in Biblical Narrative* (Oxford: Oxford University Press, 1999), 87-109.
Gunn, D.M. "A Man Given Over to Trouble: The Story of King Saul", *Images of Man and God: Old Testament Short Stories in Literary Focus* (ed. B.O. Long, BLS 1, Sheffield: The Almond Press, 1981), 89-112.
— "From Jerusalem to the Jordan and Back: Symmetry in 2 Samuel XV-XX", *VT* 30 (1980), 109-13. 1980a
— "In Security: The David of Biblical Narrative", *Signs and Wonders: Biblical Texts in Literary Focus* (ed. J.C. Exum, Decatur: Scholars Press, 1989), 133-51.
— "Narrative Patterns and Oral Tradition in Judges and Samuel", *VT* 24 (1974), 286-317.
— "New Directions in the Study of Biblical Hebrew Narrative" *JSOT* 39 (1987), 65-75.
— "Reading Right: Reliable and Omniscient Narrator, Omniscient God, and Foolproof Composition in the Hebrew Bible", *The Bible in Three Dimensions: Essays in Celebration of Forty Years of Biblical Studies in the University of Sheffield* (eds.

D.J.A. Clines, S.E. Fowl and S.E Porter, JSOTSup 87, Sheffield: Sheffield Academic Press, 1990), 53-64.
— "The 'Battle Report': Oral or Scribal Convention?" *JBL* 93 (1974), 513-18. 1974a
"David and the Gift of the Kingdom (2 Sam 2-4, 9-20, 1 Kgs 1-2)", *Semeia* 3 (1975), 14-45.
— *The Fate of King Saul: An Interpretation of a Biblical Story* (JSOTSup 14, Sheffield: JSOT Press, 1980).
— *The Story of King David: Genre and Interpretation* (JSOTSup 6, Sheffield: JSOT Press, 1978).
Gunn, D.M. and Fewell, D.N. *Narrative in the Bible* (OBL, Oxford: Oxford University Press, 1993).
Hagan, H. "Deception as Motif and Theme in 2 Sm 9-20; 1 Kgs 1-2", *Bib* 60 (1979), 301-26.
Hauer, C.E. "The Shape of Saulide Strategy", *CBQ* 31 (1969), 153-67.
Hawk, L.D. "Saul as Sacrifice: The Tragedy of Israel's First Monarch", *BRev* 12/6 (1996), 20-25, 56.
Hertzberg, H.W. *I & II Samuel: A Commentary* (OTL, London: SCM Press, 1964).
Hong, Y.-G. *Dynamism and Dilemma: The Nature of Charismatic Pastoral Leadership in the Korean Mega-churches* (Unpublished PhD thesis, Oxford: OCMS, 2000).
Howard, D.M. "The Transfer of Power from Saul to David in 1Sam 16:13-14", *JETS* 32 (1989), 473-83.
Humphreys, W.L. "From Tragic Hero to Villain: A Study of the Figure of Saul and the Development of 1 Samuel", *JSOT* 22 (1982), 95-117.
— "The Rise and Fall of King Saul: A Study of an Ancient Narrative Stratum in 1 Samuel", *JSOT* 18 (1980), 74-90.
Hurowitz, V. *I Have Built You an Exalted House: Temple Building in the Bible in Light of Mesopotamian and Northwest Semitic Writings* (JSOTSup 115, Sheffield: JSOT Press, 1992).
Hutton, R.R. *Charisma and Authority in Israelite Society* (Minneapolis: Fortress Press, 1994).
Ishida, T. "Solomon's Succession to the Throne of David—A Political Analysis", *Studies in the Period of David and Solomon and Other Essays: Papers Read at the International Symposium for Biblical Studies, Tokyo, 5-7 December, 1979* (ed. T. Ishida, Tokyo: Yamakawa-Shuppansha, 1982), 175-87.
— "The Story of Abner's Murder: A Problem Posed by the Solomonic Apologist", *Eretz-Israel* 24 (1993), 109-13.
Jeremias, J. *Die Reue Gottes: Aspekte der alttestamentlichen Gottesvorstellung* (Biblische Studien 65, Neukirchen-Vluyn: Neukirchener Verlag, 1975).
Jobling, D. "Deuteronomic Political Theory in Judges and 1 Samuel 1-12", *The Sense of Biblical Narrative: Structural Analyses in the Hebrew Bible,* Vol. 2 (JSOTSup 39, Sheffield: JSOT Press, 1986), 44-87.
— "'Forced Labor': Solomon's Golden Age and the Question of Literary Representation", *Semeia* 54 (1991), 57-76.
— "Jonathan: A Structural Study in 1 Samuel", *The Sense of Biblical Narrative: Structural Analyses in the Hebrew Bible,* Vol. 1 (JSOTSup 7, Sheffield: JSOT Press, 1986), 12-30. 1986a
— "Saul's Fall and Jonathan's Rise: Tradition and Redaction in 1 Samuel 14:1-46", *JBL* 95 (1976), 367-76.

— "The Value of Solomon's Age for the Biblical Reader", *The Age of Solomon: Scholarship at the Turn of the Millennium* (ed. L.K. Handy, SHCANE 11, Leiden: Brill, 1997), 470-92.
— *1 Samuel* (Berit Olam: Studies in Hebrew Narrative & Poetry, Collegeville: The Liturgical Press, 1998).
Josipovici, G. *The Book of God: A Response to the Bible* (New Haven: Yale University Press, 1988).
Kalugila, L. *The Wise King: Studies in Royal Wisdom as Divine Revelation in the Old Testament and Its Environment* (CBOTS 15, Lund: CWK Gleerup, 1980).
Kapelrud, S. "King David and the Sons of Saul", *ZAW* 67 (1955), 198-205.
Keil, C.F. *The Books of Samuel* (Grand Rapids: Wm.B. Eerdmans, reprint, 1971).
Kenik, H.A. *Design for Kingship: The Deuteronomistic Narrative Technique in 1 Kings 3:4-15* (SBLDS 69, Chico: Scholars Press, 1983).
Keys, G. *The Wages of Sin: A Reappraisal of the "Succession Narrative"* (JSOTSup 221, Sheffield: Academic Press, 1996).
Klaus, N. *Pivot Patterns in the Former Prophets* (JSOTSup 247, Sheffield: Sheffield Academic Press, 1999).
Klein, R.W. *1 Samuel* (WBC 10, Waco: Word Books, 1983).
Klement, H.H. *II Samuel 21-24. Context, Structure and Meaning in the Samuel Conclusion* (EUS 23, Frankfurt: Peter Lang, 2000).
Knoppers, G.N. "Prayer and Propaganda: Solomon's Dedication of the Temple and the Deuteronomist's Program", *CBQ* 57 (1995), 229-54.
— "The Deuteronomist and the Deuteronomic Law of the King: A Reexamination of a Relationship", *ZAW* 108 (1996), 329-46.
— *Two Nations under God: The Deuteronomistic History of Solomon and the Dual Monarchies*, Vol. 1, *The Reign of Solomon and the Rise of Jeroboam* (HSMM 52, Atlanta: Scholars Press, 1993).
Koopmans, W.T. "The Testament of David in 1 Kings ii 1-10", *VT* 41 (1991), 429-49.
Kruse, H. "David's Covenant", *VT* 35 (1985), 139-64.
Kuan, J.K. "Third Kingdoms 5.1 and Israelite-Tyrian Relations During the Reign of Solomon", *JSOT* 46 (1990), 31-46.
Lasine, S. "Solomon and the Wizard of Oz", *The Age of Solomon: Scholarship at the Turn of the Millennium* (ed. L.K. Handy, SHCANE 11, Leiden: Brill, 1997), 375-91.
Lawton, R.B. "Saul, Jonathan and the 'Son of Jesse'", *JSOT* 58 (1993), 35-46.
Lemche, N.P. "David's Rise", *JSOT* 10 (1978), 2-25.
Levanon, A. *Yo'av: 'Iyyun besefer Shemu'el* (Jerusalem: Moses and Jacob Levanon Memorial Association, n.d.).
Levenson, J.D. *Creation and the Persistence of Evil: The Jewish Drama of Divine Omnipotence* (Princeton: Princeton University Press, 1994).
— "1Samuel 25 as Literature and as History", *Literary Interpretations of Biblical Narratives*, Vol. 2 (eds. K.R.R. Gros Louis and J.S. Ackerman, Nashville: Abingdon, 1982), 220-42.
Linafelt, T. "Taking Women in Samuel: Readers/Responses/Responsibility", *Reading Between Texts: Intertextuality and the Hebrew Bible* (ed. D.N. Fewell, Louisville: Westminster-John Knox Press, 1992), 99-113.
Linden, N. ter *The Story Goes... III. The Stories of Judges and Kings* (London: SCM Press, 2000).
Lingen, A. van der "$Bw^\jmath$-$y\c{s}^\jmath$ ('To Go Out and To Come In') as a Military Term", *VT* 42

(1992), 59-66.
Liver, J. "The Book of the Acts of Solomon", *Bib* 48 (1967), 75-101.
Long, B.O. "A Darkness Between Brothers: Solomon and Adonijah", *JSOT* 19 (1981), 79-94.
Long, V.P. "How Did Saul Become King? Literary Reading and Historical Reconstruction", *Faith, Tradition, and History: Old Testament Historiography in Its Near Eastern Context* (eds. A.R. Millard, J.K. Hoffmeier and D.W. Baker, Winona Lake: Eisenbrauns, 1994), 271-84.
— *The Reign and Rejection of King Saul: A Case for Literary and Theological Coherence* (SBLDS 118, Atlanta: Scholars Press, 1989).
Malamat, A. "Charismatic Leadership in the Book of Judges", *Magnalia Dei: The Mighty Acts of God. Essays on the Bible and Archaeology in Memory of G. Ernest Wright* (eds. F.M. Cross et al., Garden City: Doubleday, 1976), 152-68.
Malul, M. "Was David Involved in the Death of Saul on the Gilboa Mountain?" *RB* 103 (1996), 517-45.
Marguerat, D. and Bourquin, Y. *How to Read Bible Stories: An Introduction to Narrative Criticism* (London: SCM Press, 1999).
Marcus, D. "David the Deceiver and David the Dupe", *Proof* 6 (1986), 163-71.
Martin, J.A. "The Literary Quality of 1 and 2 Samuel", *Bibliotheca Sacra* 141 (1984), 131-45.
Mauchline, J. *1 and 2 Samuel* (NCB, London: Oliphants, 1971).
McCarter, P.K., Jr. "The Ritual Dedication of the City of David in 2 Samuel 6", *The Word of the Lord Shall Go Forth: Essays in Honor of David Noel Freedman in Celebration of his sixtieth Birthday* (eds. C.L. Meyers and M. O'Connor, Winona Lake: Eisenbrauns, 1983), 273-78.
— *I Samuel* (AB, 8, Garden City: Doubleday, 1980).
— *II Samuel* (AB, 9, Garden City: Doubleday, 1984).
McFall, L. *The Enigma of the Hebrew Verbal System: Solutions from Ewald to the Present Day* (HTIBS, 2, Sheffield: The Almond Press, 1982).
McGinnis, C.M. "Swimming with the Divine Tide: An Ignatian Reading of 1 Samuel", *Theological Exegesis: Essays in Honor of Brevard S. Childs* (eds. C. Seitz and K.Greene-McCreight, Grand Rapids: Wm.B. Eerdmans, 1999), 240-70.
Mettinger, T.N.D. *King and Messiah: The Civil and Sacral Legitimation of the Israelite King* (CBOTS 8, Lund: CWK Gleerup, 1976).
— *Solomonic State Officials: A Study of the Civil Government Officials of the Israelite Monarchy* (CBOTS 5, Lund: CWK Gleerup, 1971).
Meyers, C. "The Israelite Empire: In Defense of King Solomon", *Michigan Quarterly Review* 22 (1983), 412-28.
Miles, J. *God: A Biography* (London: Touchstone, 1995).
Miscall, P.D. "Moses and David: Myth and Monarchy", *The New Literary Criticism and the Hebrew Bible* (eds. J.C. Exum and D.J.A. Clines, JSOTSup 143, Sheffield: Academic Press, 1993), 184-200.
—*The Workings of Old Testament Narrative* (Semeia Studies, Philadelphia: Fortress Press—Chico: Scholars Press, 1983).
— *1 Samuel: A Literary Reading* (Bloomington: Indiana University Press, 1986).
Moberly, R.W.L. "Solomon and Job: Divine Wisdom in Human Life", *Where Shall Wisdom Be Found?* (ed. S.C. Barton, Edinburgh: T&T Clark, 1999), 3-17.
Muilenburg, J. "Isaiah 40-66", *The Interpreter's Bible,* Vol. 5 (ed. G.A. Buttrick, New

York: Abingdon Press, 1956), 422-773.
Murray, D.F. *Divine Prerogative and Royal Pretension: Pragmatics, Poetics and Polemics in a Narrative Sequence about David (2 Samuel 5.17-7.29)* (JSOTSup 264, Sheffield: Academic Press, 1998).
Newing, E.G. "Rhetorical art of the Deuteronomist: Lampooning Solomon in First Kings", *OTE* 7 (1994), 247-60.
Niccacci, A. *The Syntax of the Verb in Classical Hebrew Prose* (JSOTSup 86, Sheffield: Sheffield Academic Press, 1990).
Nicol, G.G. "David, Abigail and Bathsheba, Nabal and Uriah: Transformations within a Triangle", *SJOT* 12 (1998), 130-45.
— "The Alleged Rape of Bathsheba: Some Observations on Ambiguity in Biblical Narrative", *JSOT* 73 (1997), 43-54.
Nielsen, F.A.J. *The Tragedy in History: Herodotus and the Deuteronomistic History* (JSOTSup 251, Sheffield: Sheffield Academic Press, 1997).
Noll, K.L. *The Faces of David* (JSOTSup 242, Sheffield: Academic Press, 1997).
Noth, M. "Office and Vocation in the Old Testament", *The Laws in the Pentateuch and Other Studies* (London: SCM Press, 1984), 229-49.
— *The Deuteronomistic History* (JSOTSup 15, Sheffield: JSOT Press, 1991).
Overholt, T.W. "Thoughts on the Use of Charisma in Old Testament Studies", *In the Shelter of Elyon: Essays on Ancient Palestinian Life and Literature in Honour of G.W. Ahlström* (eds. N.B. Barrich and J.R. Spencer, JSOTSup 31, Sheffield: JSOT Press, 1984), 287-303.
Parker, K.I. "Repetition as a Structuring Device in 1 Kings 1-11", *JSOT* 42 (1988), 19-27.
— "Solomon as Philosopher King? The Nexus of Law and Wisdom in 1 Kings 1-11", *JSOT* 53 (1992), 75-91.
— "The Limits to Solomon's Reign: A Response to Amos Frisch", *JSOT* 51 (1991), 15-21.
Patte, D. and Patte, A. *Structural Exegesis: From Theory to Practice* (Philadelphia: Fortress Press, 1978).
Payne, D.F. "Estimates of the Character of David", *IBS* 6 (1984), 54-70.
Perdue, L.G. "'Is There Anyone Left of the House of Saul...?' Ambiguity and the Characterization of David in the Succession Narrative", *JSOT* 30 (1984), 67-84.
Petersen, D.L. "Portraits of David: Canonical and Otherwise", *Int* 40 (1986), 130-42.
Polzin, R. *Biblical Structuralism: Method and Subjectivity in the Study of Ancient Texts* (Philadelphia: Fortress Press—Missoula: Scholars Press, 1977).
— *David and the Deuteronomist: A Literary Study of the Deuteronomic History. Part Three: 2 Samuel* (Bloomington & Indianapolis: Indiana University Press, 1993).
— *Moses and the Deuteronomist: A Literary Study of the Deuteronomic History. Part One: Deuteronomy, Joshua, Judges* (Bloomington & Indianapolis: Indiana University Press, 1980).
— *Samuel and the Deuteronomist: A Literary Study of the Deuteronomic History. Part Two: 1 Samuel* (Bloomington & Indianapolis: Indiana University Press, 1989).
Popović, A. "Saul's Fault in 1Sam 13-15", *Antonianum* 68 (1993), 153-70.
Porten, B. "The Structure and Theme of the Solomon Narrative (I Kings 3-11)", *HUCA* 38 (1967), 93-128.
Porton, G.G. "Midrash", *The Anchor Bible Dictionary*, Vol. 4 (ed. D.N. Freedman, New York: Doubleday, 1992), 818-22.

Powell, M.A. *What is Narrative Criticism? A New Approach to the Bible* (London: SPCK, 1990).
Praag, H.M. van "The Downfall of King Saul: The Neurobiological Consequences of Losing Hope", *Judaism* 35 (1986), 414-28.
Preston, T.R. "The Heroism of Saul: Patterns of Meaning in the Narrative of the Early Kingship", *JSOT* 24 (1982), 27-46.
Prouser, O.H. "Suited to the Throne: The Symbolic Use of Clothing in the David and Saul Narratives", *JSOT* 71 (1996), 27-37.
Provan, I.W. "Why Barzillai of Gilead (1 Kings 2:7)? Narrative Art and the Hermeneutics of Suspicion in 1 Kings 1-2", *TB* 46 (1995), 103-16. 1995a
— *1 and 2 Kings* (NIBC, Peabody: Hendrickson, 1995).
— *1 & 2 Kings* (OTG, Sheffield: Academic Press, 1997).
Pyper, H.S. "The Enticement to Re-Read: Repetition as Parody in 2 Samuel", *BibInt* 1 (1993), 153-66.
Rad, G. von *Old Testament Theology: The Theology of Israel's Historical Traditions*, Vol. 1 (Edinburgh-London: Oliver and Boyd, 1962).
— *Wisdom in Israel* (London: SCM Press, 1972).
Radday, Y.T. "Chiasm in Kings", *Linguistica Biblica* 31 (1974), 52-67.
Richardson, H.N. "The Last Words of David: Some Notes on II Samuel 23:1-7", *JBL* 90 (1971), 257-66.
Ridout, G. *Prose Compositional Techniques in the Succession Narrative (2 Sam. 7, 9-20; 1 Kings 1-2)* (Diss. Graduate Theological Union, Ann Arbor, 1971).
Roberts, J. "The Legal Basis for Saul's Slaughter of the Priests of Nob (1Sam 21-22)", *JNSL* 25 (1999), 21-29.
Robertson, E. *Samuel and Saul* (Manchester: The Manchester University Press and The John Rylands Library, 1944).
Robinson, B.P. *Israel's Mysterious God: An Analysis of some Old Testament Narratives* (Newcastle upon Tyne: Grevatt & Grevatt, 1986).
Rose, A.S. "The 'Principles' of Divine Election: Wisdom in 1 Samuel 16", *Rhetorical Criticism: Essays in Honor of James Muilenburg* (eds. J.J. Jackson and M. Kessler, Pittsburgh: Pickwick, 1974), 43-67.
Rosenberg, J. *King and Kin: Political Allegory in the Hebrew Bible* (ISBL, Bloomington & Indianapolis: Indiana University Press, 1986).
— "1 and 2 Samuel", *The Literary Guide to the Bible* (eds. R. Alter and F. Kermode, London: Fontana Press, 1997), 122-45.
Rost, L. *The Succession to the Throne of David* (HTIBS 1, Sheffield: The Almond Press, 1982).
Rudman, D. "The Commissioning Stories of Saul and David as Theological Allegory", *VT* 50 (2000), 519-30.
Savran, G.W. *Telling and Retelling: Quotation in Biblical Narrative* (Bloomington: Indiana University Press, 1988).
— "1 and 2 Kings", *The Literary Guide to the Bible* (eds. R. Alter and F. Kermode, London: Fontana Press, 1997), 146-64.
Sawyer, J. "What Was a mošia‛?" *VT* 15 (1965), 475-86.
Schäfer-Lichtenberger, C. *Josua und Salomo: Eine Studie zu Autorität und Legitimität des Nachfolgers im Alten Testament* (VTSup 58, Leiden: Brill, 1995).
Schenker, A. *Der Mächtige im Schmelzofen des Mitleids: eine Interpretation von 2 Sam 24* (OBO 42, Freiburg: Universitätsverlag—Göttingen: Vandenhoeck & Ruprecht,

1982).

Schley, D.G. "Joab and David: Ties of Blood and Power", *History and Interpretation: Essays in Honour of John H. Hayes* (eds. M.P. Graham, W.P. Brown and J.K. Kuan, JSOTSup 173, Sheffield: JSOT Press, 1993), 90-105.

— "The šālîšîm: Officers or Special Three-Man Squads?" *VT* 40 (1990), 321-26.

Schulz, A. "Narrative Art in the Books of Samuel", *Narrative and Novella in Samuel: Studies by Hugo Gressmann and other Scholars 1906-1923* (ed. D.M. Gunn, JSOTSup 116, Sheffield: The Almond Press, 1991), 119-70.

Schwartz, R.M. "Adultery in the House of David: The Metanarrative of Biblical Scholarship and the Narratives of the Bible", *Semeia* 54 (1991), 35-55.

Seebass, H. *David, Saul und das Wesen des biblischen Glaubens* (Neukirchen-Vluyn: Neukirchener Verlag, 1980).

Shils, E. "Charisma, Order, and Status", *American Sociological Review* 30/1 (1965), 199-213.

Simon, U. "A Balanced Story: The Stern Prophet and the Kind Witch", *Proof* 8 (1988), 159-71.

— "The Poor Man's Ewe-Lamb: An Example of a Juridicial Parable", *Bib* 48 (1967), 207-42.

Smith, J. "The Discourse Structure of the Rape of Tamar (2 Samuel 13:1-22)", *VE* 20 (1990), 21-42.

Soggin, J.A. "Charisma und Institution im Königtum Sauls", *ZAW* 75 (1963), 54-65.

— "Compulsory Labor under David and Solomon", *Studies in the Period of David and Solomon and other Essays: Papers Read at the International Symposium for Biblical Studies, Tokyo, 5-7 December, 1979* (ed. T. Ishida, Tokyo: Yamakawa-Shuppansha, 1982), 259-67.

— *Das Königtum in Israel. Ursprünge, Spannungen, Entwicklung* (BZAW, 104, Berlin: Alfred Töpelmann, 1967).

— "Zur Entwicklung des alttestamentlichen Königtums", *TZ* 15 (1959), 401-18.

Spengler, O. *The Decline of the West* (London: Allen & Unwin, 1926-28).

Sternberg, M. *The Poetics of Biblical Narrative: Ideological Literature and the Drama of Reading* (ILBS, Bloomington: Indiana University Press, 1985).

Steussy, M.J. *David: Biblical Portraits of Power* (Columbia: University of South Carolina Press, 1999).

Stoebe, H.J. *Das erste Buch Samuelis* (KAT 8/1, Gütersloh: Mohn, 1973).

— "Die Thronnachfolge Salomos. Überlegungen und Fragen", *Vielseitigkeit des Alten Testaments: Festschrift für Georg Sauer zum 70. Geburtstag* (eds. J.A. Loader and H.V. Kieweler, Frankfurt am Main: Peter Lang, 1999), 63-78.

Stone, G.R. "Grasping the Fringe", *Buried History* 31(1995), 4-20, 36-47.

Stone, K. *Sex, Honor, and Power in the Deuteronomistic History* (JSOTSup 234, Sheffield: Sheffield Academic Press, 1996).

Swidler, L. "Democracy, Dissent, and Dialogue", *The Church in Anguish* (eds. H. Küng and L. Swidler, San Francisco: Harper & Row, 1987).

Terrien, S. *The Elusive Presence: Toward a New Biblical Theology* (Eugene: Wipf and Stock Publishers, 2000).

Thompson, J.A. "The Significance of the Verb *Love* in the David-Jonathan Narratives in 1 Samuel", *VT* 24 (1974), 334-38.

Thornton, T.C.G. "Charismatic Kingship in Israel and Judah", *JTS* 14 (1963), 1-11.

Trible, P. *God and the Rhetoric of Sexuality* (OBT, Philadelphia: Fortress Press, 1978).

— *Texts of Terror: Literary-Feminist Readings of Biblical Narratives* (OBT 13, Philadelphia: Fortress Press, 1984).
Tsevat, M. "The Biblical Account of the Foundation of the Monarchy in Israel", *The Meaning of the Book of Job and Other Biblical Studies* (New York: KTAV, 1980), 77-99.
Uffenheimer, B. *Early Prophecy in Israel* (Jerusalem: The Magnes Press, 1999).
VanderKam, J.C. "Davidic Complicity in the Deaths of Abner and Eshbaal: A Historical and Redactional Study", *JBL* 99 (1980), 521-39.
Walsh, J.T. "The Characterization of Solomon in 1 Kings 1-5", *CBQ* 57 (1995), 471-93.
— *1 Kings* (Berit Olam: Studies in Hebrew Narrative & Poetry, Collegeville: The Liturgical Press, 1996).
Waltke, B.K. and O'Connor, M. *An Introduction to Biblical Hebrew Syntax* (Winona Lake: Eisenbrauns, 1990).
Watts, J.W. *Psalm and Story: Inset Hymns in Hebrew Narrative* (JSOTSup 139, Sheffield: Academic Press, 1992).
Weber, M. *Economy and Society: An Outline of Interpretive Sociology* (eds. G. Roth and C. Wittich, New York: Bedminster, 1968).
Weisman, Z. "Anointing as a Motif in the Making of the Charismatic King", *Bib* 57 (1976), 378-98.
— "Charismatic Leaders in the Era of the Judges", *ZAW* 89 (1977), 399-411.
— *Political Satire in the Bible* (SBLSS 32, Atlanta, GA: Scholars Press, 1998).
— "The Personal Spirit as Imparting Authority", *ZAW* 93 (1981), 225-34.
Weiss, M. "Einiges über die Bauformen des Erzählens in der Bibel", *VT* 13 (1963), 456-75.
— "Wege der neuen Dichtungswissenschaft in ihrer Anwendung auf die Psalmenforschung", *Bib* 42 (1961), 255-302.
— "Weiteres über die Bauformen des Erzählens in der Bibel", *Bib* 46 (1965), 181-206.
Wenham, G.J. *Story as Torah: Reading the Old Testament Ethically* (OTS, Edinburgh: T&T Clark, 2000).
— "Were David's Sons Priests?" *ZAW* 87 (1975), 79-82.
Wesselius, J.W. "Joab's Death and the Central Theme of the Succession Narrative (2 Samuel IX-1 Kings II)", *VT* 40 (1990), 336-51.
Whedbee, J.W. "On Divine and Human Bonds: The Tragedy of the House of David", *Canon, Theology and Old Testament Interpretation: Essays in Honor of Brevard S. Childs* (eds. G.M. Tucker, D.L. Petersen and R.R. Wilson, Philadelphia: Fortress, 1988), 147-65.
Whybray, R.N. *The Succession Narrative: A Study of II Sam. 9-20 and I Kings 1 and 2* (SBT, SS 9, London: SCM Press, 1968).
Williams, D.S. "Once Again: The Structure of the Narrative of Solomon's Reign", *JSOT* 86 (1999), 49-66.
Williams, J.G. "Sacrifice and the Beginning of Kingship", *Semeia* 67 (1994), 73-92.
Wong, G.C.I. "Who Loved Whom? A Note on 1 Samuel xvi 21", *VT* 47 (1997), 554-56.
Zakovitch, Y. "The First Stages of Jerusalem's Sanctification under David: A Literary and Ideological Analysis", *Jerusalem: Its Sanctity and Centrality to Judaism, Christianity, and Islam* (ed. L.I. Levine, New York: Continuum, 1999).

Author Index

Abramski, S. 50, 97.
Ackerman, J.S. 4, 42-43, 45, 53, 55, 58-59, 61-62, 69, 79, 128, 135, 139, 141, 153.
Ackroyd, P.R. 127.
Ahlström, G.W. 20, 23-24, 28-29.
Alt, A. 20-23, 28-29, 124.
Alter, R. 11, 35, 70, 80-81, 85.
Amit, Y. 39, 70, 84, 86.
Anderson, A.A. 132.
Arbuckle, G.A. 230.
Armerding, C.E. xix, 2, 94, 108, 110, 127, 156.
Auerbach, E. 34, 37, 221-22.
Auld, A.G. 107.
Bach, A. 131.
Bach, R. 49, 65.
Bar-Efrat, S. 34, 37, 39, 131, 137, 210, 224.
Barr, J. 40, 91.
Berges, U. 79, 108-09.
Berlin, A. 37, 93, 152-53.
Beuken, W.A.M. 47.
Beyerlin, W. 20, 22, 29, 53.
Bietenhard, S.K. 145, 147-48, 150.
Boff, L. 199, 216, 228.
Borgman, P. 108, 111, 169, 221.
Bourquin, Y. 91.
Bowman, R.G. 112.
Brauner, R.A. 84.
Brettler, M. 36, 181-82, 195, 198.
Brongers, H.A. 62.
Brooks, S.S. 58.
Brueggemann, W. 40, 66, 68-69, 78, 91, 109-12, 137, 143, 157, 161-63, 188, 208, 214, 222.
Buber, M. 2, 42, 45, 57.
Campbell, A.F. 108, 122, 216.
Cannon, W.W. 97.
Cargill, J. 113.
Carlson, R.A. 39, 121.
Caspari, W. 32.

Ceresko, A.R. 113.
Chaney, M.L. 195.
Childs, B.S. 157, 162.
Clements, R.E. 123, 183.
Clines, D.J.A. 112, 153.
Cohen, K.I. 89, 136.
Conroy, C. 32, 40, 126, 135, 141, 172, 179.
Craig, K.M. 59, 92.
Cross, F.M. 51, 117-18, 193, 207.
Crüsemann, F. 136, 141.
Culpepper, R.A. 50.
Czövek, T. xiii, xiv, xv, 123.
Deist, F. 46, 55, 220.
DeVries, S.J. 30, 185, 204.
Dietrich, W. 104, 106-07.
Donner, H. 20-21, 29.
Dragga, S. 62, 76.
Edelman, D. 5, 15-18, 20, 42-43, 54, 56, 59, 67, 74, 82, 103, 107.
Edenburg, C. 111.
Eslinger, L. 3-7, 15-16, 19, 33, 36, 40, 43, 46, 48-49, 52, 59, 62-63, 89, 102, 122, 124, 126, 163, 181-82, 184, 187, 200-01, 204.
Everett, P. 93-94, 167, 208, 215.
Exum, J.C. 4, 58, 87, 89, 95, 97-98, 107, 158, 166, 180.
Fewell, D.N. 34-38, 221.
Flanagan, J.W. 114, 120, 123, 140, 144, 157, 160, 172.
Fokkelman, J.P. 4-5, 8, 10-14, 16, 20, 25, 33, 35, 43, 45, 48, 51-52, 56, 58, 60-61, 63-65, 67-69, 72-80, 82, 84-85, 89, 105, 107, 109, 113-15, 121-22, 127-28, 130, 132-35, 139, 141-44, 146-49, 151, 156-61, 170, 172, 176, 179-81, 219.
Fontaine, C.R. 208.
Foresti, F. 80.
Fowler, F.G. 3.
Fowler, H.W. 3.
Fretheim, T.E. 84.

Frisch, A. 83, 181-82, 214.
Fuchs, S. 207.
Gamzu, Y. 221.
Garsiel, M. 43-44, 50, 130, 180.
George, M.K. 105, 168.
Gillingham, S.E. 31.
Goldingay, J. 3, 35, 101-02, 120, 124, 126, 136, 143, 156, 159, 162-63, 166, 172, 223-25.
Good, E.M. 52, 72.
Gooding, D.W. 18, 101-02, 106, 109-10, 117.
Gordon, R.P. xix, 33, 43, 54, 56, 89, 111, 162, 202.
Gottwald, N.K. 227.
Gressmann, H. 32, 148.
Grottanelli, C. 95.
Gunn, D.M. 3-5, 11-12, 19, 33-38, 55, 62, 65, 70, 72-73, 75, 79-82, 84, 86-87, 114, 116-17, 132, 136, 140-41, 146, 148, 151, 154, 158, 221, 224.
Hagan, H. 112, 150, 180.
Hauer, C.E. 98.
Hawk, L.D. 89.
Hertzberg, H.W. 81, 109.
Ho, C.Y.S. 107.
Hong, Y.-G. 30.
Howard, D.M. 103.
Humphreys, W.L. 87.
Hurowitz, V. 204.
Hutton, R.R. 20, 24-26, 29, 31, 224.
Ishida, T. 113, 132, 144, 148.
Jeremias, J. 79.
Jobling, D. 2, 7-9, 14, 19-20, 35, 41, 47, 54, 58-59, 65, 69-70, 72, 76, 80-81, 85, 87-92, 94-95, 97, 109, 112, 154, 164, 170, 181, 197, 218, 220, 228.
Josipovici, G. 116, 192, 202-03, 221, 225.
Kalugila, L. 184.
Kapelrud, S. 112.
Keil, C.F. 3, 113, 162.
Kenik, H.A. 32, 185.
Keys, G. 12.
Klaus, N. 42, 146-47, 165, 189.
Klein, R.W. 3, 113.
Klement, H.H. 9, 157.
Knoppers, G.N. 182, 185, 189, 193, 198, 204, 206, 210.

Koopmans, W.T. 178.
Kruse, H. 163.
Kuan, J.K. 193.
Lasine, S. 212.
Lawton, R.B. 75, 109.
Lemche, N.P. 113.
Levanon, A. 144.
Levenson, J.D. 91, 153.
Linafelt, T. 48, 91.
Linden, N. ter 52, 58, 75, 122, 161.
Lingen, A. van der 184.
Liver, J. 213.
Long, B.O. 178.
Long, V.P. 15-16, 18, 20, 25, 33-34, 46-51, 54-56, 58-59, 61, 65-70, 76, 78-81, 83-86, 88-89, 117, 186.
Malamat, A. 26-30, 99.
Malul, M. 113, 115.
Marguerat, D. 91.
Marcus, D. 111-12, 131, 138.
Martin, J.A. 44.
Mauchline, J. 68, 89.
McCarter, P.K., Jr. 38, 41, 68, 102, 118, 121-22, 132, 147.
McFall, L. 36.
McGinnis, C.M. 38-39, 87.
Mettinger, T.N.D. 30, 141, 185, 188.
Meyers, C. 208, 213.
Miles, J. xvii, 42, 90-91.
Miscall, P.D. 3, 6-7, 19, 33-34, 56, 82, 89, 97, 103-04, 106, 112-15, 154, 218, 224.
Moberly, R.W.L. 184-85, 187, 191.
Muilenburg, J. 47.
Murray, D.F. 119, 121-26, 164.
Newing, E.G. 11, 182.
Niccacci, A. 36.
Nicol, G.G. 152.
Nielsen, F.A.J. 80, 89, 166.
Noll, K.L. 157, 162-63.
Noth, M. 2, 30, 66.
O'Connor, M. 138.
Overholt, T.W. 24, 28.
Parker, K.I. 39, 181-82, 185, 193, 195-96, 200.
Patte, A. 34.
Patte, D. 34.
Payne, D.F. 114.

Perdue, L.G. 34, 127, 129, 141, 146, 148, 177-78.
Petersen, D.L. 93, 132.
Polzin, R. xvii, 5, 7, 9-13, 15-16, 20, 25, 32-36, 39, 43-44, 46, 48, 53-59, 61, 63-64, 69-70, 74, 76, 83, 87-90, 108, 114-16, 119, 122, 124-26, 128-29, 139-40, 145, 155, 160, 162, 222-23.
Popović, A. 69.
Porten, B. 39, 193, 203.
Porton, G.G. 34.
Powell, M.A. 38, 86.
Praag, H.M. van 88, 91.
Preston, T.R. 17, 34, 41, 44, 70, 97, 118, 153, 163, 168-70, 219.
Prouser, O.H. 111.
Provan, I.W. 6, 15, 18-20, 151, 176-79, 181-82, 187, 190, 193-94, 196, 202-03, 206-07, 211.
Pyper, H.S. 132
Rad, G. von 2, 69, 81, 185.
Radday, Y.T. 182.
Richardson, H.N. 162.
Ridout, G. 11.
Roberts, J. 112.
Robertson, E. 91.
Robinson, B.P. 69, 73.
Rose, A.S. 104.
Rosenberg, J. 11, 106-09, 119, 123, 130, 132-33, 144, 149-52, 156, 163, 165-66, 171, 177, 181, 210, 224.
Rost, L. 4, 12, 19, 39.
Rudman, D. 49, 108.
Savran, G.W. 61, 63, 79, 83, 89, 138, 206-07.
Sawyer, J. 51.
Schäfer-Lichtenberg, C. 15, 19-20, 30-31, 181-86, 190, 193, 200, 205-07, 209.
Schenker, A. 161.
Schley, D.G. 148-51, 155, 159, 207.
Schulz, A. 32.
Schwartz, R.M. 124, 164.
Seebass, H. 83, 91.
Shils, E. 25.
Simon, U. 88, 97, 131, 151.
Smith, J. 132.
Soggin, J.A. 53, 90, 190, 216.
Spengler, O. 93.

Sternberg, M. 18, 38, 66, 79, 81, 114, 123, 128, 130, 132, 139, 147, 152-53, 157.
Steussy, M.J. 43, 45, 63, 120, 124, 161.
Stoebe, H.J. 4, 12, 69, 219.
Stone, G.R. 84.
Stone, K. 131.
Swidler, L. 230.
Terrien, S. 225, 227.
Thompson, J.A. 110.
Thornton, T.C.G. 20, 22-23, 28-29, 42.
Trible, P. xvii, 133.
Tsevat, M. 44, 205.
Uffenheimer, B. 43.
VanderKam, J.C. 113, 115.
Walsh, J.T. 14, 151, 178, 181-82, 184, 187, 193, 198-99, 201, 203, 205, 220.
Waltke, B.K. 138.
Watts, J.W. 162.
Weber, M. xiii, xv, 20, 23, 26-29, 41, 53, 71, 94, 101, 112, 115, 117, 166, 171, 175, 209, 222.
Weisman, Z. 2, 26-28, 59, 111, 181.
Weiss, M. 76, 96-97, 120.
Wenham, G.J. 104, 156.
Wesselius, J.W. 115.
Whedbee, J.W. 87, 95, 132, 141, 158.
Whybray, R.N. 152, 207.
Williams, J.G. 89, 181.
Wong, G.C.I. 110.
Zakovitch, Y. 122.

Subject Index

Abiathar 95, 137, 154, 156, 165, 179, 207.
Abigail 117, 152-53, 155, 165.
Ability xvii, 42, 97, 148, 187, 191.
Abimelech 9.
Abishag 153, 176.
Abishai 18, 139, 141, 143, 149, 155, 159.
Abner 22, 107, 115-16, 132, 144-47, 149.
Abrahamic 185.
Absalom 118, 121, 129-39, 142-44, 147-50, 155-56, 165-67, 171-74, 176.
Abusive 44, 48.
Accusation 15, 61, 63, 69, 81, 140.
Accusatory 60, 62, 68-69.
Achish 103, 111.
Acknowledge xix, 12, 30, 37, 55, 57, 109, 148, 150, 186, 206, 212.
Acts 226.
Adam 12.
Adonijah 24, 149, 152-53, 176-80, 186, 188, 210.
Adoram 156.
Agag 78, 80-82, 86.
Agenda xvii, 6, 163, 201, 217, 231.
Agent 125, 130, 137, 152.
Ahijah 22, 73-74..
Ahinoam 152.
Ahithophel 137.
Ai 80, 86.
Alienation 171, 230.
Altruistic 106, 114.
Amalek 55, 77-78, 80.
Amalekite 82, 86, 109, 171.
Amasa 141-42, 144, 147-50.
Ambiguity 7, 12, 34, 58, 73, 79, 114, 120, 123, 160, 227.
Ambiguous 34, 50, 57, 64, 69-71, 73, 77, 84, 86, 88, 90-91, 106, 112-15, 126, 129, 134-35, 141, 152, 154, 166, 171, 179-80, 192, 198-99, 205-06, 208, 226-27.
Ambition 106, 114, 122, 182, 192.
Ambitious 6, 10, 106, 114-15, 152-53, 177, 217.
Ammon 51, 54, 90, 108, 129.
Ammonite 51, 53, 61, 64, 67, 71, 93, 128-30, 139.
Amnon 131-35, 156.
Animosity 145, 171, 188, 218, 229.
Antagonism 8, 17, 167, 170.
Antagonist 89, 151.
Antecedent 72, 77-78, 118.
Apostle 225-26.
Appearance 1, 7-8, 19, 45-46, 48, 54, 58, 60, 94, 102, 105, 107, 135, 137-38, 144, 148, 151-52, 158, 168, 178, 187, 200, 203-05, 207.
Appendix 12, 157, 161.
Appointment 24, 28, 50-51, 141, 179, 207.
Aramean 6.
Arrogance 83-84, 91, 137, 210.
Arrogant 82-83, 155, 176.
Asahel 145, 159-60.
Audience xv, 17-18, 26, 63.
Author 5, 7, 14, 17-18, 25-26, 34, 39, 45, 88, 90, 127, 222.
Authoritarian 9, 48, 54, 56, 88, 227-29.
Authority xiii, xv, 14, 16, 19, 21-22, 24-28, 39, 41, 43, 64, 66, 68-71, 76-77, 84, 88, 90, 92, 98, 101, 103, 130, 148-49, 166, 171, 175, 178-79, 184, 186, 210, 214, 217.
Autonomous 101, 179, 199, 205, 230.
Autonomy 46, 53, 66, 70, 99, 102-03, 124, 168-69, 179, 207, 210.
Azariah 206.
Balaam 162-63.
Bardot 161.
Bar-Kochba 223.
Barzillai 141, 211.
Bathsheba 13, 129, 131, 134, 152-55, 164, 166-67, 170, 176-80.
Battlefield 97, 106, 109, 129-31, 136, 142, 146, 153.
Beersheba 185.

Subject Index

Beethoven 143.
Benaiah 155-56, 159, 179, 186, 207.
Beneficiary 188, 193, 196-97, 206, 210.
Benefit 1, 15, 59, 71, 104, 111-13, 115, 132, 147, 149, 186, 188, 190-92, 194, 196-201, 205-06, 208, 211-13, 216-17, 226, 231.
Benevolence 90.
Benevolent 78, 123, 138, 165.
Benjamin 45, 57.
Benjaminite 57, 141.
Bestow 2, 21, 27-29, 53, 104, 117, 122, 125, 164, 174, 183, 187, 210, 216, 228-29.
Bestowal 22, 175, 181, 183, 186, 189-90, 228.
Beth Aven 68.
Bethel 68.
Bethlehem 102, 105.
Blame 6, 59, 62, 69, 91, 111-12, 130, 133, 139, 145, 172, 205.
Blunder 67, 69, 86, 91.
Blunderer 76, 98.
Boundary 9, 114, 205.
Bungler 86, 92, 169, 174.
Canaanite 22, 60, 156, 164-65, 182, 190, 194.
Capricious 122, 170.
Centralisation 121-23, 125-26, 134, 154, 156-57, 172, 174, 183, 195, 202.
Centralise 44, 110, 125, 127, 137, 160, 173, 185, 188, 190, 195, 208, 211, 214, 223.
Challenge 42, 45, 50, 52, 54, 62, 69, 98, 101, 105-06, 108, 119, 136, 141, 156, 168, 178, 180, 185, 190, 210-11, 220, 222, 224, 228, 230.
Chaplin 161.
Character development 12, 15-16, 36-37, 129.
Character xiv, xvii, 3-8, 12-13, 16, 19, 22, 30, 33-41, 44-46, 48-49, 53-56, 65, 74-75, 79-81, 86-87, 89, 92-93, 96, 107-08, 110, 114-15, 118, 120, 126, 130, 135, 144, 149, 151-55, 158, 163-64, 170-71, 178-81, 183, 202, 205-06, 209, 212, 218, 223-24, 227-28, 231.
Character zone 10, 20, 46, 107, 146.

Characterisation 3, 8, 10, 12-13, 20, 25, 34, 37-39, 77, 82, 108, 114, 118, 153, 205, 220.
Charge 41, 46, 54, 59, 77-78, 83, 87, 137, 140, 146, 149, 156, 175, 178, 199.
Charisma xiii, xvii, 1-3, 19-31, 34, 42, 52-54, 61, 66-67, 71, 76, 85, 88, 91-92, 99, 101, 111, 117-18, 129, 136, 138-39, 143, 151, 164, 167, 169, 171-75, 181, 183-92, 196-201, 205-06, 209-14, 216-18, 221-24, 227-31.
Charismatic leader xiii, xv, xix, 2, 20, 27-28, 40-41, 49-50, 52-54, 56, 65-66, 71, 75, 88, 90-92, 94, 96, 98-99, 101-03, 105-06, 108, 111, 114-17, 131, 135-36, 139, 143-44, 150, 154-55, 161, 166, 168, 170-71, 173-74, 184, 210, 216-19, 221-22, 225-30.
Charismatic leadership xiii-xv, xvii, xix, 1-3, 19, 21-22, 24, 26-28, 30-31, 34-35, 39-40, 52, 55, 67, 71, 85-86, 92-93, 95, 98, 101, 104, 118, 151, 157, 168-69, 171, 173-74, 187, 210, 212, 214-18, 220-21, 224-28, 230-31.
Chiasm 33, 103.
Chiastic 6, 56, 205.
Christian 3, 37, 166, 223, 227.
Christianity 20, 223.
Chronicles 124.
Church xv, xvii, xix, 1, 29, 32, 35, 223, 226-31.
Churchill xiii, 172.
Civil war 45, 51, 98, 135, 139, 141, 145, 147, 166, 172-73, 183, 210-11, 218, 225.
Climax 15, 48, 57, 62-63, 78, 92, 162, 190, 223.
Coherence 9-10, 15-16, 19-20, 32-33, 38-39, 77, 80, 157.
Coherent xx, 9, 13, 16, 18-19, 33, 36-38, 40, 77, 83, 224.
Commission 21, 49-50, 55, 58-59, 66-67, 71, 77, 86, 94, 98, 169, 174, 212, 216-17, 231.
Commitment 25, 32, 60, 69, 109-10, 115, 125, 131, 137, 156, 166-67, 174, 192, 201, 217, 231.
Community xx, 1, 168, 213, 219, 223,

230.
Competence 9, 52, 61, 69, 108, 217.
Competent xvii, 74, 168, 175, 185, 230.
Concentric 12, 182, 189, 197.
Concubine 92, 120, 130, 142, 152-53, 164.
Condemn 10, 36, 63, 69-70, 79, 81, 83, 90, 122-23, 146, 164, 199, 219.
Condemnation 15, 37, 39, 60, 68-69, 72, 76-77, 81-82, 89, 131, 164.
Confidence 49, 52, 68, 91, 222.
Confident 51, 108, 150, 169, 181, 230.
Confirmation xvii, 20, 25, 30, 53, 85, 115-17, 151, 187-88, 191, 197-98, 206, 210, 220.
Conflict xvii, 9, 50, 72, 80, 88, 94, 124, 132, 141, 145, 151, 164-65, 186-87, 200, 210, 219, 224, 229-30.
Confrontation 76, 106, 142, 161, 165, 219.
Confusion 13, 17, 21, 31, 58-59, 115.
Consecration 79.
Consistency 12, 77, 80.
Consistent 7, 10, 13, 20, 36, 75, 77, 81, 116, 167, 216, 224.
Conspiracy 48, 129, 135-36, 138-39, 210.
Continuity 8, 93, 98, 126, 154, 210.
Control 16, 47, 49, 56, 59, 61-67, 69-70, 88-89, 99, 105, 121, 126, 136-38, 140, 147-48, 153-55, 166, 168-69, 171-72, 175, 177, 179-80, 183, 188-89, 207, 220.
Conventional 1, 3, 6-7, 10, 19, 36, 42, 77, 107, 113, 204, 224.
Corleone 78.
Corrupt 41, 51, 66, 152.
Corruption 41, 95, 156.
Covenant xiv, 9, 41, 60, 65, 112, 114, 127, 132, 157, 161, 184, 192, 199-201, 203-206.
Crisis 2, 21, 26, 30, 41-42, 49, 51-54, 63-64, 67, 71, 75, 96, 98-99, 101, 107-08, 112, 118, 129, 131, 133, 136-39, 142-43, 151, 168-69, 171-72, 175, 184, 209-12, 216, 227, 229.
Culprit 79, 89.
Cycle 9, 93, 140.
Dagon 122.
Dan 185.
Dean 161.

Death 8, 25, 57-58, 66, 76, 85, 88, 91, 95, 97-99, 109, 112, 115, 117, 119, 124, 128, 134-35, 142, 147, 149-50, 159, 182, 209-11, 207, 230.
Deceit 139, 218.
Deceitful 133, 138, 150.
Deceive 112, 116, 131-32, 138, 173.
Deception 14, 53, 107, 112, 120, 131-32, 138, 146-48, 150, 161, 169, 173, 178.
Deceptive 14, 102, 120, 132, 135-36, 145, 173, 180.
Decision making 87, 148, 183, 191.
Decline 26, 74, 93, 95, 111, 148, 169, 206.
Deductive 8, 35.
Deference 37, 63, 69, 86, 88.
Deferential 54, 68.
Delay 55, 67-68, 70-71, 75, 86, 95, 170, 178.
Deliverance 44, 49, 51, 53, 85, 102, 118, 123, 160, 162-66, 170, 173-74, 187, 217, 222, 227.
Deliverer 26, 44-45, 50-53, 58, 65, 71, 92, 105, 107-09, 116-18, 126, 138, 151, 162, 164, 168, 174, 188, 207, 209, 226.
Demise 85, 105.
Democratic 43-44.
Demonstrate 2, 6-7, 13, 15-16, 20, 22, 25-26, 33, 35-36, 39-40, 43, 46, 51, 53-54, 63-64, 66, 73-77, 86, 91-92, 97, 110, 112, 117-18, 137, 141, 146-48, 152, 155, 158, 163, 168, 171, 174, 178-79, 183, 187-88, 192, 198, 200, 205, 207, 209-13, 216-17, 226, 229.
Demonstration 6, 16, 20, 53, 63, 107, 120, 181, 185, 187, 196, 198, 210, 212-13, 229.
Denouncement 69-70, 73.
Denunciation 60, 68, 74, 164.
Dependence 46, 59, 61, 65, 83-84, 88, 91-92, 98, 111, 144, 151, 212.
Dependent 26, 28, 46-47, 64-66, 84, 88, 95, 112, 128, 165, 175, 199, 219.
Deprivation 85.
Descriptive 2, 4, 11, 32, 40, 200.
Designate 2, 21, 34, 54, 117, 186-87, 218, 229.
Designation 20-23, 27, 29-30, 115, 186-87, 210.

Subject Index 251

Despot 45, 92, 131, 136, 141, 143, 153, 156, 160-61, 165, 174.
Despotism 163, 174, 214.
Destiny 46, 48, 61, 73, 102, 104, 114-15.
Determination 71, 74-75, 116, 143, 145, 148, 173, 178, 212, 230.
Determined 14, 49, 52, 67, 72, 75, 84, 87, 99, 106, 115, 121, 148, 154, 161, 205, 207, 218-19, 221.
Deuteronomic 182, 193-94.
Deuteronomist History (DH) 9, 20, 26, 58, 60, 66, 80, 104, 119, 122-24, 133-34, 143, 207, 215, 220-21, 224-26.
Deuteronomist xvii, 92, 193, 222.
Deuteronomistic 24, 26, 92, 164, 174, 206, 225.
Diachronic 12-18, 32, 53, 224.
Dilemma 27, 119, 134, 156-57, 163, 223.
Disapproval 30, 42, 75, 81, 83, 160, 182, 226.
Discrepancy 46, 108, 131, 163, 204.
Disloyal 170.
Disobedience 10, 60, 62, 69, 78, 82-83, 199-200, 206.
Disobedient 83.
Distrust 78-79.
Division 1, 9, 11, 49-50, 52, 59, 65, 70, 139.
Doctrinal 12.
Doeg 134.
Domestic policy 156, 188.
Dubious 78, 120, 129, 132, 171-72, 174, 206.
Dues ex machina 220-21.
Dupe 57, 89, 145.
Dynamic 3, 8, 25, 36-38, 52, 118-19, 126, 136, 143, 147, 163, 174, 202, 214, 216-18, 223.
Eclectic 7, 35.
Edom 162.
Effect 14, 38, 43, 48-50, 58-60, 62, 64, 73, 78-79, 85, 96-97, 113, 120, 133-37, 140, 143, 150, 153, 155, 160-61, 169-70, 185, 188, 200, 203.
Effective 30, 55, 73, 98-99, 103-04, 112, 114, 139, 188, 211.
Efficiency 86, 205, 227.
Egypt 49, 60, 78, 124, 140, 156, 194, 198, 202.
Ehud 45, 53, 116.
Eleazar 159.
Election xvii, 22, 24, 28, 43, 49-51, 55, 57, 77, 96, 102, 117-19, 129, 139, 144, 154, 186-87, 206.
Eli 41, 54, 68, 90, 156, 225, 228.
Eliab 104, 106, 114.
Elusive 7, 71, 107, 114, 124, 126.
Elusiveness 205.
Emerging 26, 38, 58, 90, 94-97, 99, 101, 106, 115-16, 136, 151-52, 163, 168, 170-71, 173-74, 219, 222, 226, 229-30.
Envy 111, 165, 168, 219.
Ephraim 45.
Ephrathite 105, 225.
Epithet 74, 104.
Everlasting 9, 41.
Exodus 6, 109, 202.
Expectation 45, 50, 55, 58, 62, 80, 88, 97-98, 109, 201, 230.
Explicit 10-11, 13, 19, 22, 28-29, 32-35, 37-38, 51, 61, 81, 109, 119, 122, 128, 134, 142, 147, 156, 158, 164, 166, 188, 191, 208, 213, 225-26, 229.
Failure 13, 20, 37, 49, 62-63, 66-67, 70-71, 73-74, 76, 79-82, 85-86, 90-92, 102, 105, 107, 116-117, 132-33, 135, 139-40, 149, 159-61, 166-67, 169, 174, 183, 199, 205, 209-11, 216-19, 229.
Fate 4, 53, 76, 83, 87, 91, 94, 96-99, 101, 126, 134-35, 143, 145, 153, 174.
First Testament (FT) 3, 7, 15, 19, 37-38, 40, 44, 90, 96, 123, 133, 180, 185, 204, 222-25, 227.
Flaw 4, 13, 25, 56, 74, 87.
Forced labour 156, 160, 181, 190, 194-96, 202.
Foreign policy 30, 188, 190, 211-12.
Fratricide 145, 184.
Frustrated 32, 76, 115, 132, 143, 146, 150-51, 170, 182.
Frustration 125, 170, 230.
Gad 154-55, 161.
Gap 5, 7, 9, 13-14, 18, 33, 36.
Gebah 67.
Genesis 6, 11, 18, 185, 224.
Geshur 135.

Gezer 193, 195.
Gibeah 51-52, 58-59.
Gibeon, 19.
Gibeonite 157-58.
Gideon 9, 22, 25, 49-50, 53-54, 60, 105, 108, 116, 123.
Gilead 51, 128, 139.
Gileadite 52.
Gilgal 50, 54, 64, 67-68, 70, 72, 75, 79-82, 84-87, 140.
Gittite 137.
Goliath 101, 104-09, 112-13, 115, 119, 135, 143, 165, 168, 171.
Gorbachev 96.
Government 9, 41, 44, 49, 55, 90, 95, 98, 129, 146, 162, 174, 181, 219.
Governor 50, 58, 67, 71, 188.
Grammar 12.
Grammatical 10, 97.
Grósz 96.
Guilt 4, 6, 17, 79, 161.
Guilty 6, 69, 79, 81, 87.
Hadad 200, 220.
Handicap 74.
Handicapped 38, 72-73, 83, 105.
Hannah 42, 162.
Harem 92, 120, 123, 142, 153, 164-65.
Harsh 56, 60, 68-69, 84, 117.
Hebron 119-20, 130, 139, 144, 152.
Hector 222.
Hepburn 161.
Hereditary 21-22, 41, 44, 175, 187, 210.
Herem 78, 80, 86.
Hero 3, 45, 51-52, 86, 89, 114, 157, 159-60.
Heroic 58, 68, 71, 97, 153, 169, 212.
Heroism 41, 53, 161.
Hezekiah 225.
Hiram 119, 181, 190, 192-93, 196, 198, 212.
Historical xiv, 3-4, 9, 13, 17-18, 27-28, 32-33, 121, 144, 149, 154, 188, 215, 224-25.
Historical criticism 4, 32-33.
Historical-critical 12, 91.
Historiography 8, 18.
History xiii, xiv, 8, 19, 59, 62, 64, 91, 133, 162, 206, 209, 215, 220-22, 225, 227, 229.
Hittite 6.
Holy Spirit 222-23, 226.
Homer 37, 220-22.
Homeric 221-22.
Hostile 141, 162.
Hostility 4, 141.
House 21, 41, 54, 68, 76, 90, 104, 107-12, 118, 122-27, 131-32, 135, 139, 141-42, 144, 158, 162, 164-65, 167, 177, 187, 192, 194, 199, 203, 219.
Humble 54, 83, 137.
Humility 83.
Hushai 133, 137-38, 141.
Hypocrisy 84-85.
Hypocrite 82.
Ideal 9, 23, 94, 115, 130, 161, 171, 173-74, 207, 211, 216-17, 230.
Ideological 9, 14, 18-19, 23, 32, 140, 201.
Ideology 10, 23-24, 39-40, 156, 163, 208, 214, 217.
Idolatrous 122.
Idolatry 55, 83, 123, 182.
Iliad 220.
Illegitimate 117.
Implicit 10, 13, 19, 24, 28-29, 32-37, 62, 89, 105, 119, 122, 134, 150, 158, 164, 166-67, 188-89, 205, 225.
Impotence 105, 107-08, 148, 153-54, 176.
Impotent 52, 151, 173.
Inclusio 77, 96-97, 103, 160, 162.
Incompetence 108-09, 118, 121, 153, 168, 205, 211.
Incompetent 56.
Inconsistency 7, 12-13, 38, 80, 110.
Inconsistent 8-9, 12, 30, 38, 82, 84, 122.
Independence 49, 59, 65-66, 70-71, 91, 98, 103-08, 110, 115, 155, 168, 173, 178-79, 210-13, 230.
Independent 16, 25, 31, 47, 50, 52, 69, 71, 82, 88, 98, 102-03, 143, 154-55, 172, 177-78, 188, 207, 213, 218.
Indifference 141-42, 172.
Indifferent 90, 133.
Indignant 61, 89.
Indispensability 63.
Inductive 8, 35.
Inefficiency 227.

Subject Index

Inefficient 106.
Infidelity 60.
Influence 3, 7, 22, 29-30, 35, 37, 55, 63, 75, 87, 90, 103-04, 148, 150-51, 154-55, 177, 194, 207, 222.
Initiative xvii, 21, 44, 46-50, 56, 68, 73, 92, 98-99, 119, 123-24, 140, 156, 176, 183, 187, 210, 230-31.
Innocence 62, 69, 87, 111, 114-15, 125, 128, 146.
Innocent 6, 76, 89, 91, 114, 139.
Insecure 46, 91.
Insecurity 44, 73, 98, 179.
Instability 44.
Institution xiii, xx, 21, 23-24, 28-29, 44, 93, 98, 126, 174, 183, 188, 191-92, 208, 211, 216-17, 219, 224, 226, 229-30.
Institutional 26, 28, 54, 133, 224.
Institutionalise 22, 44, 214, 224, 228.
Insubordinate 83.
Integrity 41, 63, 79, 82-83, 155-56, 183.
Intent 12, 31, 62, 65-67, 70, 75, 84, 89, 102, 104, 115, 127, 161, 170, 205.
Intention 2, 5, 7, 33, 48, 64, 71, 76-78, 80-81, 86-87, 111, 114, 117, 127-29, 138, 141, 170, 178, 191-92, 201, 203, 226.
Intentional 13, 56, 66, 70.
Interior monologue 120.
Intermittent 221, 225.
Intertribal 172, 186.
Intervention 42, 44, 53, 64, 75, 83, 88, 92-93, 118, 121, 152, 162-63, 165-66, 174, 184, 204, 207-08, 212, 217-18, 220-23, 225, 227, 231.
Ira 156.
Ironic 14, 26, 37, 41, 43-44, 47, 65, 105, 113, 122-24, 131, 133, 136, 148, 160-61, 169, 176, 197, 213.
Irony 61, 75, 105, 122, 124, 126, 131, 135, 149, 153, 160.
Irresolute 49, 102, 143, 173.
Ish-Bosheth 115, 139, 144-46.
Israelite 20-21, 25, 27, 42, 50, 53, 64, 66-68, 75, 80, 85, 93, 97, 105-06, 112, 119, 122, 124, 130, 134, 136, 139, 151, 156, 172, 182-83, 188, 190, 193, 201-02, 205, 209-10, 213, 217, 225.

Ittai 137-38, 141.
Jabesh Gilead 51-52, 64, 107-108, 116.
Jashen 159-60.
Jealousy 51, 65-66, 90, 94, 109, 169-70.
Jebusite 120.
Jehoshaphat 133, 156.
Jehu 225.
Jeremiah 221.
Jericho 80, 130.
Jeroboam 108, 200, 215, 219, 225.
Jerusalem 118-121, 129-30, 132, 135, 139-42, 147, 149, 152, 165, 182, 195.
Jesse 46, 102, 105, 109-10.
Jesus xv, xx, 112, 115, 219, 222-23, 225-26.
Joab 95, 116, 129-32, 134-35, 142-51, 153, 155-56, 160, 169, 171-74, 177, 179, 207, 211, 217, 219.
Joash 225.
John Paul II 230.
John the Baptist 226.
Jonadab 132.
Jonathan 9, 13, 17, 41, 63, 73-76, 105, 109, 112, 116-17, 127, 129, 158, 163, 165.
Jordan 51, 140, 144.
Joseph 133.
Josephus 223.
Josheb-Basshebeth 159.
Joshua 31, 45, 80, 145, 190, 194, 209.
Josiah 225.
Judaism 223.
Judge xiv, 8, 25-26, 41-42, 51, 53-55, 58, 61, 65-67, 92, 94-95, 116, 127, 133, 143, 154, 160, 174, 188-89.
Judges (book) 2, 9, 22, 26, 45, 51, 58, 60-61, 121, 123.
Judgeship 8-9, 20-21, 41-42, 44, 54, 62, 65-66, 94, 101, 223.
Judgment 5, 39, 54, 60, 61, 68, 70, 77, 79, 84-85, 90, 97, 102, 135, 155, 207.
Justice 26, 43, 56, 87, 132-33, 156, 166, 173, 186-87, 191, 196-97, 201, 205, 211-13.
Keilah 171.
Kenite 78.
Kerethites and Pelethites 149.
Kings (book) 3, 6, 12-13, 18-19, 22, 24,

40, 42, 66, 134, 176, 210, 215, 224, 226.
Kingship 8-9, 20-24, 28, 41, 43-45, 52-54, 61, 65, 67, 69, 73, 79, 89, 94, 97, 101, 103, 112, 115, 117, 121-22, 124-27, 131, 133-34, 136-44, 147-48, 152-57, 159-61, 163-66, 172, 174, 176, 180, 198-201, 205-06, 210-11, 213-14, 216-17, 223, 230.
Kish 46, 57-58.
Kue 198.
Language 2, 5-6, 9-10, 14, 192, 199, 201.
Legal-rational 20.
Legitimate 9, 187.
Levant 213.
Lévi-Strauss 7-8.
Levite 134.
Liberal 36, 113.
Literary critical 25, 32.
Literary criticism 10, 12, 17, 32-33, 40.
Literary device 10, 13, 15, 33, 35, 120.
Literary technique 79, 81, 96, 159.
Literature xix, 3, 5, 8, 11, 17-18, 37, 91, 93, 225, 228.
Loyal 127, 133, 136, 138-39, 141, 148, 150-51, 162, 166, 169-70, 179, 187, 207, 230.
Loyalty 17, 63, 109-10, 112, 127, 137, 141, 143, 147, 149, 158, 171, 177, 182, 184, 192, 199, 201, 207.
Luke 226.
LXX 21, 43, 82, 91, 107, 130, 204.
Mafioso 78.
Mahanaim 139, 144, 172.
Malevolence 90, 141.
Malevolent 167.
Mandate 52, 86, 101, 184.
Manipulate 5, 16, 61, 63, 65, 108, 110, 177, 220.
Manipulation 16, 39, 48, 59, 61, 65, 73, 76, 98, 154, 204, 218.
Manipulative 48, 62, 65, 73.
Manoeuvre 68, 117, 138, 147.
Masoretic Text (MT) 10, 46-47, 51, 53, 63-64, 66, 80, 96, 107, 115, 130, 137, 193.
Mazière 96.
Mediator 7, 28, 50, 62-63, 66.

Mentor xix, 46, 48-49, 65-66, 69, 71-76, 88, 91, 98-99, 103, 111, 155, 169, 173, 186, 207, 210, 217-18.
Mentorship 94, 99, 155, 168, 171, 219, 226.
Mephibosheth 127-30, 132, 138, 141, 158, 173.
Merab 127.
Metaphor 9-10, 110, 114, 135, 149, 173, 218.
Metaphoric 10, 66, 214.
Method 2-3, 8, 12, 14, 16-18, 32, 34-35, 40, 152, 229.
Methodological xvii, 4, 10, 14-15, 25, 27, 34-35.
Methodology xix, 2, 4, 7-8, 12-13, 17-19, 29, 31, 33, 35, 218, 224.
Meticulous 83, 86, 210.
Metonym 119, 129, 142.
Michal 112, 117, 127, 144, 152-53, 164-65, 172.
Michmas 68.
Midianite 23.
Mighty 17, 106, 149, 159-61, 170, 188, 217, 219, 222, 225.
Military king 45, 92, 96, 98, 109, 118-22, 126-27, 130, 132, 139, 143, 148, 155-56, 161, 165, 169, 174, 207, 216.
Military leader xiii, 49-50, 54-55, 58-59, 71, 98, 104-05, 108, 118, 121, 150-51, 155, 160, 168, 172, 172-74, 214.
Military leadership 16, 30, 54, 97, 99, 101, 109, 117, 119, 129, 131, 144-45, 147, 150-51, 153, 155-156, 159-61, 163, 169, 171-74, 183-84, 216.
Milton 167.
Misperception 69, 123-26, 130.
Misunderstanding 5, 47, 73, 115.
Misuse 114, 173, 191-92, 199-200, 206, 214, 216-17, 223, 225-26, 229.
Mizpah 59, 61.
Moab 162.
Moses 3, 31, 43, 49-50, 56, 80, 89, 104, 140, 204, 209, 220.
Motif 5, 8-10, 14-15, 17-18, 20, 33, 35, 48, 58, 103-06, 110, 118-19, 121, 123, 127, 132-35, 138, 142, 153, 172, 181, 195, 198, 200, 208, 219, 223-24, 226.

Subject Index

Motivation 12, 23, 36, 42, 55, 65-66, 88, 110, 114-15, 123, 127, 164.
Motive xvii, 6-7, 19-20, 33, 35, 37, 40, 55, 65, 71, 75, 78-79, 82, 89-91, 106-07, 111, 113-15, 128, 172, 179-80, 224.
Nabal 108, 117, 164.
Nacon 125.
Nahash 51, 64.
Napoleon 143.
Nathan 13-14, 39, 95, 124, 131-33, 135, 154-55, 161, 170, 176-80, 186, 207.
Negative 3-4, 6, 19, 30, 43, 54, 56, 73, 77-79, 81-82, 84, 86, 89, 96-97, 103, 115, 121, 128, 134, 140, 155-56, 162, 179, 181-82, 193.
New Testament 3.
Nob 105, 112.
Obed-Edom 122.
Obedience 17, 50, 60, 65, 88, 199, 205.
Obedient 68, 178.
Obscure 34, 49-50, 73, 102, 114, 160, 219.
Obstruct 66, 70, 91, 170, 220, 230.
Obstruction 94, 111, 205.
Obstructive 74.
Odysseus 222.
Odyssey 220.
Old Testament (OT) xv, 7, 12.
Omniscient narrator 80, 82.
Ophir 193.
Ophrah 123.
Opponent 6, 75, 98.
Opportunist 114-15, 163, 169.
Opportunistic 146, 150-51, 178.
Opposition 8-9, 19-20, 34-35, 78, 134, 145, 150-51, 171, 213, 218-20, 223, 230.
Oppression 22, 44, 51, 133, 172, 183, 211.
Oppressive 44, 167, 219.
Oriental despot 45, 92, 131, 136, 141, 143, 153, 156, 160-61, 165.
Oriental king 118-19, 121-22, 130-31, 137, 142-43, 147, 151, 155-56, 158, 160, 164, 171-72, 213.
Oriental kingship 101, 117, 121-22, 125, 127, 136, 142, 147, 152, 154-57, 159-61, 163-64, 174, 198-200, 205-06, 211, 214, 216-17, 230.
Oriental monarch 118, 120-21, 127, 129, 131, 137, 139, 141, 153-54, 160, 163, 172, 196, 205, 213, 216.
Oriental monarchy 163.
Palace 6, 23, 118-21, 123, 125, 129-31, 133-34, 136-37, 142-43, 150, 156, 169, 172, 174, 182, 191, 193-97, 200, 203, 205, 209, 222, 228.
Paradox 9, 27, 149, 180.
Paranoid 9, 97, 167, 219.
Pattern 11, 17, 20, 41, 62, 80, 101, 130, 138, 168, 170, 176, 187, 210, 217, 219.
Paul 225-26.
Pawn 176, 178-79.
Peace 22, 158, 162, 172, 175, 184, 188-91, 195, 199-200, 209, 211.
Pentateuch 45, 80.
Pentecostal 166.
Persecution 75, 105, 145, 170, 219, 223.
Pharaoh 6, 181-82, 193-96.
Philistine 9, 72-74, 77, 86, 98, 101, 105, 107, 109, 111, 113, 117-18, 121-22, 136, 142, 157, 159, 168-69, 171-73, 216.
Plot 3, 5, 8, 11, 13, 19-20, 25, 33-39, 44, 53, 93, 111, 149-50, 152, 158, 176-77, 180, 220-21, 224.
Plot development 4, 12-13, 15-16, 19, 34, 37, 224.
Political xv, 2, 4, 10, 18, 20, 23, 27-28, 30, 44, 52, 71, 96, 103-04, 110, 112-13, 115-17, 121-22, 126, 136-37, 145, 147-52, 155, 164, 168, 172, 175-76, 178-79, 182-84, 187-88, 191-92, 197, 199, 201, 209-13, 215, 217, 225, 228.
Politics 32-33, 44, 109, 116, 122, 129, 146, 164, 173, 185, 193, 195, 226.
Portrayal 9, 13, 36, 38, 40, 47, 55, 74, 77-78, 81, 83-84, 86, 88, 90, 96-97, 105, 108, 110, 113-14, 118, 129, 132, 138, 158, 168.
Positive 3-4, 14-15, 39, 43-44, 67, 80, 82, 84, 86, 96-97, 103-04, 112, 134, 145, 156, 170, 181-82, 193, 209, 223.
Postmodern xv, 36, 113.
Predictability 182, 208.
Predictable 44, 129, 217.
Prophecy 10, 57, 155.
Protagonist 4, 25, 115, 144, 151.

Protégé 48, 65, 99, 103, 108, 119, 168-69, 207, 218.
Prowess 93, 109, 113, 153.
Psalms 24, 162, 225.
Psychological 12, 20, 34-36, 48, 81, 91, 142, 145, 153.
Psychologise 13, 16, 35, 82, 179.
Pun 5, 9, 20.
Punishment 60-61, 86, 91, 153-54, 160-61, 221.
Puppet 144, 169.
Qohelet 125.
Rachel 57.
Reaction 4, 28, 32-33, 101, 178-79, 204, 225.
Realpolitik 113.
Rebuke 11, 34, 51, 76, 85, 134, 146, 148, 164, 192.
Recalcitrant 83.
Recognise 12, 17, 24, 28, 30, 36, 46, 53-54, 72, 84, 86, 89, 94, 110-12, 115-17, 119, 121-22, 128, 134, 141, 152, 162, 164, 166, 170, 172, 184-85, 197, 201, 219, 227, 229-30.
Recognition xvii, 22, 30, 35, 57, 63, 108, 117, 137, 166, 175, 177, 182, 229.
Reformed 1-2, 29, 35, 226, 231.
Refusal 5, 11, 44, 55, 60, 83, 97, 117, 134, 205, 230.
Refuse 2, 5, 17, 43-44, 47, 77, 85, 87, 104, 134-36, 139-40, 164, 178-79, 205, 212.
Rejected 9, 41-42, 54, 66, 71-72, 76, 79, 87, 89, 93, 97, 170, 180, 214.
Rejection 3-4, 8, 15-16, 19, 30, 37, 49, 55, 66, 70-75, 79-80, 84-86, 88-92, 94-95, 97-98, 101-03, 106, 168-69, 222.
Relentless 69, 83, 145, 148.
Relentlessness 145.
Reliability 7, 10, 137.
Reluctance 51, 54, 67, 73, 86-87, 91, 98.
Reluctant 47, 52, 54, 98, 217.
Repentance 10, 60, 63, 68, 77, 84, 86-87, 89, 162, 205.
Repetition 7, 15, 33, 36, 79, 125, 127-28.
Resentment 65, 91.
Resolute 52, 71, 87, 98, 101, 117, 190.
Resoluteness 52, 173.
Resolution 8, 30, 106, 151, 158, 172, 205, 216.
Resolve 8, 42, 49, 96, 114, 119, 151, 168-69, 171-72, 175, 210-12, 216.
Resourceful 112.
Restrain 49, 66, 68, 83, 105, 116, 133, 206.
Revelation (book) 226.
Revolutionary 209, 216.
Rezon 200, 220.
Rhetoric xvii, 5-6, 40, 43-44, 61-62, 106, 112, 139, 171, 173, 177, 180, 218.
Rhetorical 5, 9, 15, 33, 40, 51, 69, 113, 140, 151.
Ritual 50, 65, 69, 73-76, 85-86, 89, 122, 140, 204.
Ritualistic 74, 76, 140.
Rival 54, 71, 90, 101, 111, 116-17, 139, 141-42, 144, 146, 148, 151, 165, 169, 178-79, 181, 183, 204, 220.
Rivalry 66, 140-41, 166, 172, 188, 211, 229.
Rizpah 92, 146, 158.
Royal image 118, 120, 126, 142, 201, 211.
Royal pretension 124-25, 175, 191, 197, 199, 201, 205, 212-13, 223, 226.
Ruse 53, 106, 108, 128-29, 131-32, 173.
Sacrifice 5, 58, 68-69, 81-82, 86, 89, 158, 176, 194.
Salvation 12, 26-27, 162.
Samuel xiv, 3-5, 7-10, 15-16, 19-20, 35, 37, 39-50, 52-56, 58, 60-73, 75-78, 80-99, 101-05, 108, 110-11, 115-17, 123, 131, 133, 143, 153-56, 168-71, 173-74, 214, 216, 218-19, 225, 228-29.
Samuel (book) 2-3, 6-13, 15-16, 18, 20, 31, 40-42, 54, 60, 89, 92, 101, 109-10, 116, 118, 120-21, 124-25, 129, 134, 136, 144, 147-48, 151-57, 159-60, 163-64, 166-67, 169, 171, 173, 176-78, 209-10, 224-26.
Saulide 158.
Scene 11, 15, 44-48, 55, 65, 70, 82, 84, 87, 91, 105, 107, 115, 136, 142, 149, 152-53, 176, 178-79, 209, 215, 220-21.
Scripture xv, 225.
Secession 141, 172, 211.
Second Testament (ST) 3, 38, 112, 223-27.

Subject Index

Security 43, 62, 75, 122, 159, 183, 188, 211.
Separatist 186.
Sequentiality 12.
Shaalim 45.
Shalisha 45.
Shalom 43, 48, 83, 89-90, 95, 206, 208-09, 211-13.
Shammah 159.
Sheba 24, 141-42, 148, 193, 196-98, 206, 213.
Sheva 156.
Shilohite 154.
Shimei 136, 138-41, 179, 211.
Shobi 139.
Shrewdness 147, 150, 153, 169.
Skill 1-2, 52-54, 113, 140, 151, 171, 184-87, 191, 196, 205, 212-13, 216, 222, 227, 229-30.
Skilled 54, 97.
Solomon xiv-xv, 2-4, 6, 19-20, 23-24, 28, 30-31, 36-40, 119, 121, 124, 145, 149, 173, 175-220, 222-26, 228-30.
Solomonic 182, 203, 208.
Speculation 9, 18, 20, 36, 115.
Speculative 11, 18, 30.
Spirit xv, xvii, xx, 1-3, 17, 22-26, 28, 44, 52-54, 57-58, 72, 75-76, 91-93, 98-99, 101, 103-04, 107, 117, 135, 138, 164, 169-71, 174-75, 181, 187, 210, 216-18, 220-23, 225-28, 231.
Stability 21, 23, 93, 98, 124, 126, 129, 170, 175, 182, 191-92, 199, 208-09, 217.
Static 3, 6, 13, 21, 24, 36-37, 119, 126, 136-37, 143, 147, 174, 181, 214, 218, 223, 228.
Status quo 98, 199, 213.
Stipulation 42-43, 60, 63, 133, 192, 201.
Stratagem 106, 137.
Strategist 54, 104, 109, 112, 115-16, 132, 137, 139, 150, 163-64, 169, 173.
Strategy 5, 68, 78-79, 98, 107, 116, 138.
Structural 5, 8, 10, 15, 157, 162-63, 195.
Structuralism 9, 35, 218.
Structuralist xvii, 7-9, 19-20, 35, 94, 170, 210, 215, 218.
Structure xiv-xv, 10-11, 33, 40, 48, 55-56, 59, 69, 96, 101, 106, 119, 127, 157, 182, 189-90, 222, 228-29.
Structured 2, 11, 61, 121, 145.
Style xix, 10, 15, 34, 40, 56, 82, 129, 147, 161, 188, 191, 195, 197, 206, 210.
Submission 50, 84, 87, 99, 169, 216.
Submissive 83, 88, 91, 99, 125.
Subordinate 4, 10, 48, 69, 75, 83, 91, 110, 193, 219, 228.
Subordination 91, 110.
Subservient 69, 83.
Subversive 56, 125, 216.
Success 3, 48-49, 52-53, 66, 71-72, 74-75, 89-90, 98, 102, 104, 107, 111-15, 117, 119-20, 126-27, 143, 165, 168-72, 174, 177, 210, 216-17, 219, 222, 229, 231.
Succession Narrative (SN) 4, 12, 18, 31.
Suppressive 47-48, 227.
Surrogate father 110, 168-69, 210.
Suspicion 3, 5, 6, 11, 17, 37, 55, 65, 76, 78-80, 91, 113, 128.
Suspicious 7, 12, 19, 36, 45, 55, 113, 138.
Suzerain 200-01, 205, 223.
Suzerainty 188-89, 205, 210.
Sword 106, 112-15, 142.
Symbolic 13, 34, 103, 111-12, 125, 137, 145, 158.
Sympathy xiv, 25, 86, 120.
Synchronic 3, 10, 12, 15-16, 18-20, 25, 31-33, 35, 37, 53, 157.
Syrian 129.
Tactician 102, 112.
Tamar 131-35.
Tarshish 193.
Tautology 59.
Tautological 88.
Taxation 183, 211.
Technique 12, 17, 79, 81, 96, 159.
Tekoa 132, 150.
Tension xvii, 24-25, 57, 59, 118, 121, 128, 141, 146, 170, 172-73, 186, 209, 211, 215, 218-19, 229.
Thematic 10, 13, 121-22, 153, 157, 163, 181-82.
Theocracy 4, 42-43, 62.
Theocratic 4, 27, 42, 48, 62, 66, 90.
Timothy 225.
Traditional 20, 25-26, 31, 168, 208-09,

228-29.
Tragedy 4, 43, 89-90, 94, 112, 133-34, 203, 222, 224.
Tragic xiv, 25, 86-87, 89.
Transfer 103-04, 109-10, 150, 157, 203-04, 210.
Transform 2, 5, 34, 52-54, 86, 92, 98, 102, 152, 213, 222.
Transformation 5, 20, 22, 30, 153, 202, 206.
Transition xvii, 1-2, 4, 20, 31, 75, 94-96, 101, 130, 168, 170, 176, 181, 209-10, 215, 218-20, 224-25, 228-29.
Transitional 8.
Transjordan 144.
Tyre 190, 191, 193.
Unification 171.
Unintentional 69, 122, 152.
Unity 3, 33, 64, 147, 151, 172, 206, 211, 213, 229.
Unpredictability 114-15, 203.
Uriah 130-31, 134, 247, 150, 159-60, 163.
Uzzah 123, 125.
Verdict 68-69, 186-87, 196.
Victim 4, 89-91, 123, 125, 131-32, 134, 158, 177, 179, 193.
Victory 53-54, 64, 71, 74-75, 78-80, 96-97, 102, 105-06, 109, 113-14, 118-19, 121, 127, 129, 140, 147-48, 159, 166, 207, 209, 215.
Victorious 39, 86, 96-97, 145.
Viewpoint xiv, 19, 53, 79, 138, 187, 209, 225.
Villain 6, 37, 90, 134.
Vindication 62-63.
Violation 108, 157, 161, 179, 182.
Violence 113, 150, 164, 210.
Violent 134-35, 140, 145-46, 151, 164-65, 210-20.
Vivaldi 93, 167, 209, 215.
Walesa 96.
Warrior 2, 74, 91, 97, 106, 149, 159, 161.
Wealth 3, 92, 108, 118, 127, 129, 133, 166, 175, 193, 196-99, 208, 211-13, 217.
Welfare 63, 124, 183, 189, 200, 211, 216, 229.
Wisdom 6, 39, 53, 172, 178, 183, 185-87, 189-92, 196-99, 205, 208, 211-13, 225.
Yahwist 108, 113, 131, 156, 163, 178.
Yahwistic 52, 54-55, 64, 200, 214.
Zadok 154, 156, 179, 186, 206-07.
Zeruiah 145-46, 151.
Ziba 128, 132, 138, 141, 173.
Ziklag 171.
Zion 121.
Zuph 45.

Scripture Index

Genesis
chs. 2-3, *91*
3:13, *69*
18:18, *185*
22:17, *185*
28:11ff, *57*
37:3, *133*
37:23, *133*
37:32, *133*
38:10, *185*

Exodus
2:23, *44*
3:7, *44*
3:7-9, *49*
3:9, *44*
4:1-9, *56*
4:10-16, *104*
10:29, *95*
12:31ff, *95*
ch. 17, *81*
17:15, *80*
17:16, *80*
20:7, *192*
20:21, *204*
20:22-25, *204*
22:16, *132*
ch. 35, *202*
40:17ff, *203*

Leviticus
19:33, *190*
19:34, *190*

Numbers
16:3, *176*
24:3-19, *162*
24:5-7, *162*
24:8-9, *162*
24:17-19, *162*
27:12-23, *1*

Deuteronomy
1:26, *134*
2:30, *134*
7:2, *87*
10:10, *134*
12:10, *123*
12:11, *123*
16:16, *195*
ch. 17, *165*
17:1-6, *182*
17:14-17, *182*
17:14-20, *42-43*
17:15, *24, 206*
17:15-17, *92*
17:16, *206*
17:17, *206*
17:20, *206*
18:3, *42*
20:11, *190*
21:22, *158*
21:23, *158*
23:6, *133*
25:7, *133*
25:17-19, *77*
25:19, *77*
28:68, *78*

Joshua
chs. 3-4, *140*
5:3ff, *140*
5:9, *140*
ch. 6, *80*
7:19, *69*
ch. 8, *81*
8:2, *80*
8:23, *80*
8:29, *80*
9:15, *158*
24:10, *133*

Judges
1:22, *124*
chs. 2-11, *9*
2:1-3, *59-60*
2:1-6, *51*
2:3, *60*
2:4, *51*
2:18, *124*
2:22, *60*
ch. 3, *45*
3:10, *52, 58*
3:15, *45*
3:15-30, *53*
3:30, *121*
4:17-22, *53*
4:23, *121*
ch. 6, *60*
6:8, *60*
6:8-10, *51, 59*
6:9, *60*
6:10, *60*
6:11-24, *105*
6:12, *108, 124*
6:13, *124*
6:34, *52, 58*
6:37, *123*
7:5, *123*
7:8, *63*
7:19-23, *53*
8:23, *54*
8:27, *123*
8:28, *121*
8:30, *123*
ch. 10, *60*
10:11-14, *59*
10:13, *60*
10:14, *60, 63*
11:1, *108*
11:17, *133*
11:29, *52, 58*
11:33, *121*
12:5, *225*
14:6, *52, 58*
14:19, *52, 58*
15:14, *52, 58*
15:20, *160*
16:31, *160*
chs. 17-19, *45*

ch. 19, *45*
19:10, *134*
19:25, *134*
chs. 20-21, *45, 64*
20:3, *64*
20:13, *134*
ch. 21, *52, 53*
21:25, *53*

Ruth
1:2, *225*

1 Samuel
ch. 1, *162*
chs. 1-12, *4*
1:1, *44-45, 105, 225*
1:20, *42*
chs. 2-7, *56*
2:1-10, *162*
2:13, *42*
2:27, *122*
2:27-36, *7, 68*
2:30, *68, 122*
ch. 3, *54-55*
3:3, *143*
3:8, *45*
3:18, *90*
ch. 4, *54, 90, 122*
chs. 4-6, *122*
4:1, *54, 90*
4:1ff, *54*
4:3, *137*
4:4, *124, 137*
ch. 5, *122*
ch. 6, *122*
ch. 7, *54, 95*
7:15, *94*
ch. 8, *16, 41-42, 44, 45, 47, 49, 54, 56, 61-64, 82, 89, 130, 133, 214, 225*
chs. 8-9, *35, 120*
chs. 8-12, *67*
8:1, *56*
8:5, *42, 55-56, 186*
8:6, *123, 143*
8:7, *42, 180, 214*
8:7-9, *55*
8:8, *60*
8:9, *42-43*

Scripture Index

8:10, *43, 45*
8:11, *43*
8:11-18, *43, 55, 62*
8:12, *44*
8:13, *43, 48*
8:14, *43*
8:15, *43*
8:16, *43, 45, 48*
8:17, *43, 131*
8:18, *44, 60*
8:19, *43-44*
8:20, *44, 109, 186*
8:21, *55*
8:22, *42, 55*
ch. 9, *5, 16-17, 44, 46, 53, 56, 88, 105, 153*
chs. 9-10, *49, 52, 108*
chs. 9-11, *46, 75*
chs. 9-15, *15*
9:1, *45, 105, 108*
9:1-4, *45*
9:1-10, *21*
9:1-10:8, *44*
9:1-10:16, *22*
9:1ff, *102*
9:2, *45, 98, 105, 108, 135*
9:4, *45*
9:5, *45, 46, 57*
9:5-10:8, *45-46*
9:6, *46, 222*
9:7, *46*
9:7-9, *9*
9:8, *46*
9:11, *47*
9:11-14, *47*
9:13, *69*
9:14, *47*
9:14-21, *47*
9:15, *5*
9:16, *5, 21, 44, 49, 51, 54, 101, 169*
9:17, *66*
9:18, *46, 47*
9:19, *47*
9:20, *45, 57*
9:21, *46-47, 83, 105*
9:22, *5, 45-48, 84, 90, 104*
9:22-24, *65*
9:22-26, *47, 49*

9:23, *5, 48*
9:24, *5*
9:26, *48*
9:27, *49, 56*
ch. 10, *45, 51, 54, 56, 66- 67, 183*
10:1, *21, 49, 56, 59*
10:1-8, *59*
10:1-13, *26*
10:1ff, *77*
10:2, *49, 57-58*
10:2-6, *56*
10:2-8, *56*
10:3, *57*
10:4, *57, 105*
10:5, *50, 57-59, 67, 70, 73, 86*
10:5-7, *57-58*
10:5-8, *50, 55, 59, 67*
10:5-16, *22*
10:6, *57, 84*
10:7, *57-59, 65, 67, 70-71, 73, 86, 91, 95*
10:8, *50, 57-59, 67-68, 70-73, 75*
10:9, *57*
10:10, *52*
10:11, *58*
10:12, *58*
10:14, *48*
10:16, *115*
10:17, *61*
10:17-19, *61*
10:17-27, *61, 86*
10:18, *43, 51, 59-61*
10:19, *51, 53, 59-61*
10:20, *60*
10:21, *60*
10:22, *60, 83*
10:23, *60, 98*
10:24, *22, 61*
10:25, *54, 133*
10:26, *54*
10:27, *51*
ch. 11, *16, 21-22, 37, 51, 53-54, 58, 63-64, 68, 71, 74-76, 81, 92-93, 98, 105, 107-108, 118, 122*
chs. 11-12, *63*
11:1-11, *53-54, 61*
11:2, *64*
11:3, *51, 53, 64*
11:4, *51*

11:5, *51, 86*
11:6, *52, 54, 91, 97*
11:7, *52, 64*
11:9, *53*
11:10, *51*
11:11, *105*
11:12, *53-54, 64*
11:13, *53, 61*
11:14, *54, 61, 64-65, 79*
11:15, *54, 64, 72, 79, 85*
ch. 12, *9, 16, 44, 61, 66, 73, 75-76, 89, 95*
12:1, *62, 64*
12:1-25, *64*
12:2, *62, 73, 84*
12:2-5, *62*
12:3, *62, 73, 84*
12:4, *62, 63*
12:5, *62*
12:6, *62, 65*
12:6-17, *62*
12:7, *62*
12:7-12, *62*
12:9-25, *64*
12:10, *44*
12:11, *62*
12:12, *42*
12:13, *45, 62-63*
12:13-15, *62*
12:14, *63*
12:15, *63*
12:16, *62*
12:16-18, *62*
12:17, *62*
12:18, *63, 65*
12:19, *63, 65, 88*
12:20, *65*
12:20-25, *63, 65*
12:23, *69*
ch. 13, *9, 38, 40, 47, 50, 64-67, 72, 74-77, 80-82, 86-88, 93, 95, 98*
chs. 13-14, *60, 86, 88, 116*
chs. 13-15, *10, 22, 37, 55, 66, 89-90, 118, 122, 229*
chs. 13ff, *46*
13:1, *66-67, 85, 95*
13:2, *67*
13:2-4, *67*
13:2-7, *72*

13:3, *67*
13:4, *67-68*
13:5, *67*
13:5-15, *71*
13:6, *68*
13:6-8, *67*
13:7, *67-68, 70*
13:7-15, *67*
13:8, *68, 97*
13:8-12, *95*
13:8-16, *72*
13:8ff, *74*
13:9, *68, 73*
13:10, *68-69*
13:10-15, *73*
13:11, *68-69*
13:11-15, *81*
13:12, *68-69, 73, 85, 97*
13:13, *68-69, 71-73, 82, 85*
13:14, *68, 71-73, 81-82, 85, 89, 116, 133*
13:15, *73, 81*
13:16, *133*
13:17-22, *72*
13:18, *133*
13:19, *133*
13:20, *133*
13:21, *133*
13:23, *133*
13:25, *133*
13:31, *133*
13:36, *133*
ch. 14, *10, 38, 72-76, 85-86, 88, 92, 98, 105*
chs. 14-15, *101*
14:1, *74*
14:2, *219*
14:3, *74*
14:17-19, *75*
14:18, *16, 74*
14:19, *16, 74*
14:24, *74*
14:24ff, *75*
14:29, *133*
14:32, *80*
14:33, *74*
14:34, *74*
14:36, *74-75*
14:37, *75*

14:38, *75*
14:39, *75*
14:41, *75*
14:43, *17, 69*
14:44, *75*
14:47, *96-98*
14:47-52, *96-97*
14:47ff, *40*
14:48, *86, 96, 181*
14:49-51, *96*
14:52, *96-98, 108*
ch. 15, *7, 10, 16, 38-40, 47, 50, 64, 71, 73, 75-77, 80, 83, 86, 89-90, 93, 98*
15:1, *50, 88, 133*
15:1-3, *77*
15:1-12, *77, 79*
15:2, *77-78*
15:3, *77, 82*
15:4, *78, 88*
15:6, *78*
15:7, *78*
15:8, *78, 80*
15:9, *78-79, 81, 133*
15:11, *78-79, 81-83, 85, 88-89, 125*
15:12, *79, 81, 86*
15:13, *80-81, 88*
15:13-35, *77*
15:14, *81*
15:15, *63, 79, 81-82, 87-88*
15:16, *83, 88*
15:17, *82-83, 85, 87, 105*
15:17-19, *82*
15:19, *83, 88, 155*
15:20, *81, 83, 87-88*
15:21, *63, 83, 87-88*
15:22, *83, 88*
15:23, *83, 88*
15:24, *78, 81, 83, 87-88*
15:25, *83-85, 87*
15:26, *84-85, 88*
15:27, *84*
15:28, *84*
15:29, *84, 87*
15:30, *63, 84-85, 88*
15:32, *80, 133*
15:33, *85*
15:35, *67, 77, 85, 89, 95*
ch. 16, *17, 97, 101, 105, 120, 154, 168, 183*
chs. 16-17, *17, 46, 99, 101, 108*
16:1, *89*
16:1-13, *101-02, 154*
16:2, *94*
16:4, *82-83*
16:7, *102*
16:11, *104-06, 179*
16:12, *102, 104, 107, 135*
16:13, *56, 103, 107, 169, 179*
16:14, *38, 75, 81, 92, 99, 103, 169*
16:14-23, *101, 103*
16:17, *104*
16:18, *102, 104, 108, 113, 124, 137-38*
16:19, *104-05*
16:20, *105*
16:21, *104, 110*
16:22, *104*
ch. 17, *18, 34, 101, 104-05, 107-08, 113, 159, 168*
chs. 17-18, *171*
17:1-11, *101*
17:10, *135*
17:11, *97, 171*
17:12, *105, 225*
17:12ff, *102*
17:14, *105*
17:15, *105-06*
17:17, *46, 106*
17:18, *46, 106*
17:19, *106*
17:20, *106*
17:21, *106*
17:22, *106*
17:24, *171*
17:25, *105, 169*
17:25-40, *113*
17:26, *106-08, 110*
17:28, *106*
17:32-37, *106*
17:33, *97*
17:34-37, *113*
17:35, *106*
17:37, *97, 124*
17:37-47, *113*
17:38, *105-06*
17:39, *105-06*
17:41, *107*

17:42, *107*
17:42ff, *102*
17:43, *106*
17:45, *106, 109*
17:45-47, *106, 108*
17:47, *106*
17:48, *106-07*
17:50, *109, 113, 143*
17:51, *109, 113*
17:54, *119*
17:55-58, *13, 17, 107, 110*
17:56, *115*
ch. 18, *17-18, 116, 159*
18:1, *112, 219*
18:1-4, *117*
18:2, *104, 108*
18:3, *117, 219*
18:4, *112, 117*
18:5, *117*
18:5-7, *108*
18:6, *117*
18:7, *117*
18:10, *219*
18:10-19:10, *169*
18:11, *18*
18:12, *124*
18:13, *109, 130*
18:13-16, *108*
18:14, *124*
18:16, *109, 219*
18:17, *109*
18:19, *127*
18:20, *112, 219*
18:22, *117*
18:28, *124, 219*
18:30, *109, 117*
ch. 19, *71, 154*
chs. 19-20, *112*
19:4, *94, 169*
19:5, *169*
19:8, *109, 136*
19:9, *219*
19:10, *18, 109*
19:22, *169*
19:24, *95*
19:33, *219*
ch. 20, *112*
20:13, *124*

20:14-17, *112, 117, 127*
20:15, *127*
20:15-17, *158*
20:16, *127*
20:17, *112*
20:23, *112*
20:29ff, *108*
20:35-21:1, *13*
20:42, *112*
chs. 21-22, *112*
21:3-6, *105*
21:6, *153*
21:11, *117*
21:12, *109*
ch. 22, *76, 97*
22:2, *117, 132, 165*
22:3, *105, 110*
22:4, *105, 110*
22:5, *154*
22:6, *219*
22:17, *134*
22:18, *94*
22:19, *94*
22:20, *154, 165*
22:20ff, *137*
ch. 23, *171*
chs. 23-27, *159*
23:1-5, *109*
23:2, *109*
23:5, *109*
23:9, *165*
23:9-12, *121*
23:9-13, *154*
ch. 24, *127, 146, 163, 171*
chs. 24-26, *111, 169*
24:5, *7, 111, 158*
24:20, *117*
24:21, *112*
24:22, *158*
24:23, *158*
ch. 25, *117*
25:3, *152*
25:7, *117*
25:8, *117*
25:10, *108*
25:28, *109, 117, 174*
25:28-30, *111*
25:30, *117*

25:31, *117*
25:39, *7*
25:44, *127*
ch. 26, *127, 146, 163, 171*
26:6, *144*
26:7ff, *169*
26:8, *18*
26:22, *219*
26:23, *134*
ch. 27, *116*
27:8, *109*
27:9, *109*
ch. 28, *47, 49, 88, 92, 95*
chs. 28-31, *109*
28:3, *75*
28:5, *97*
28:15, *59*
28:16-19, *47*
29:8, *111*
ch. 30, *159, 171*
30:6, *171*
30:7, *165*
30:8, *121, 165*
30:17-20, *109*
30:26, *109, 117*
30:26-31, *117*
ch. 31, *18, 97, 99*
31:4, *99, 133*

2 Samuel
ch. 1, *16, 97, 127, 146*
1:10, *130*
ch. 2, *145, 150, 159, 169, 171-72*
chs. 2-3, *145*
chs. 2-5, *98*
2:1, *117, 144*
2:1-4, *144*
2:1-11, *147*
2:1-3:5, *147*
2:2, *117, 119, 144, 146, 152*
2:3, *144*
2:4, *117, 144*
2:7, *117*
2:8, *139, 144, 172*
2:8-11, *144*
2:9, *144*
2:10, *144*
2:12, *139, 172*

2:12-16, *145*
2:12-32, *147*
2:13, *144*
2:13ff, *151*
2:14, *145*
2:17, *145*
2:17-23, *145*
2:21, *134*
2:24, *145*
2:24-28, *145*
2:28, *145*
2:29, *139, 172*
2:29-31, *145*
2:30, *145*
2:31, *145*
2:32, *146*
ch. 3, *146*
3:1, *145, 147*
3:1-5, *146*
3:2-5, *146, 152*
3:6, *146*
3:6-21, *146*
3:6-39, *146-47*
3:7, *144, 146*
3:11, *144, 146*
3:13, *112, 117, 172*
3:14, *112, 172*
3:15, *144*
3:22, *146*
3:22-39, *146*
3:24, *145, 146*
3:24-26, *146*
3:25, *145-46*
3:26, *147*
3:27, *145*
3:31, *146*
3:36, *146*
3:37, *146*
3:39, *146-47, 151*
ch. 4, *146*
4:9-12, *127*
ch. 5, *102, 121, 123, 125, 127, 165, 171, 195*
chs. 5-7, *119, 126, 134, 164*
chs. 5-10, *118, 142*
5:1-5, *117-18*
5:2, *108, 111, 117, 130*
5:3, *102*

5:6, *121*
5:6-8, *118*
5:7, *121*
5:9, *119, 121*
5:9-16, *119*
5:10, *36, 119-20, 126*
5:11, *119, 122, 123*
5:11-15, *121*
5:11-16, *146*
5:12, *36, 119-20, 123, 125, 165*
5:13, *120, 152*
5:13-16, *157*
5:13-8:18, *157, 163*
5:17, *121*
5:17-25, *118, 157, 164*
5:17ff, *121, 160, 165*
5:19, *121*
5:20, *122*
5:22, *121*
5:23, *121*
ch. 6, *121-23, 125, 129, 136, 160, 164, 204, 223*
chs. 6-7, *121, 126, 137, 165, 182*
6:1, *160*
6:1-23, *157*
6:2, *124*
6:6, *34, 125-26*
6:7, *122*
6:8, *125*
6:9, *122*
6:10, *121-22, 134*
6:12, *121, 134*
6:13, *122*
6:14, *122*
6:16, *121-22*
6:16-23, *122*
6:17, *123*
6:17-19, *122*
6:20, *122, 125*
6:22, *122*
6:23, *172*
ch. 7, *5, 9, 11, 41, 123, 125-26, 164, 194, 200, 207*
chs. 7-8, *137*
7:1, *119, 123, 129*
7:1-3, *123*
7:1-29, *157*
7:2, *123*

7:3, *124, 154*
7:4-10, *124*
7:5-11, *124*
7:6, *124*
7:7, *124*
7:10, *189*
7:11, *189*
7:12, *124-26*
7:12ff, *23, 125*
7:13, *125-26, 192*
7:14, *90*
7:14-16, *124*
7:29, *125*
ch. 8, *96-97, 122, 126-29, 159, 171-72, 174*
chs. 8-10, *129*
8:1-6, *126*
8:1-14, *126, 157*
8:4, *164*
8:6, *96-7, 120, 127, 160*
8:7, *129*
8:7-10, *126*
8:7-12, *126*
8:8, *129*
8:11, *127*
8:13, *127*
8:14, *96-97, 120, 127, 160*
8:15, *132, 156*
8:15-18, *127, 157*
8:16, *149*
8:16-18, *155*
8:17, *154*
8:18, *156*
ch. 9, *31, 127, 129, 157, 165, 173*
chs. 9-10, *127*
chs. 9-20, *12*
9:1, *128-29*
9:2, *128*
9:3, *128*
9:4, *128*
9:6, *128*
9:7, *128*
9:8, *128*
9:9, *128*
9:10, *128*
9:11, *128*
9:12, *128*
9:13, *130*

ch. 10, *128-29, 159*
chs. 10-12, *171*
10:2, *128-29*
10:5, *130*
10:7, *129*
10:10, *137*
10:11, *137*
10:14, *130*
10:17, *129-30, 139, 143*
ch. 11, *37-39, 118, 129-32, 146-47, 150, 153, 159, 165, 179*
chs. 11-12, *130*
chs. 11-17, *131*
11:1, *33, 129-31, 156*
11:1-15:12, *129*
11:2, *119, 131, 152*
11:9, *119*
11:11, *123*
11:12, *130*
11:14-27, *124*
11:19-21, *150*
11:27, *185*
ch. 12, *154-55, 161*
12:1-6, *132*
12:9, *155*
12:10-12, *131*
12:11, *129*
12:13, *131*
12:17, *133*
12:20, *119*
12:24, *185*
12:27, *130*
12:28, *130-31*
12:30, *130*
ch. 13, *131, 165*
13:1-15:12, *131*
13:6, *131*
13:7, *119, 131*
13:12, *131*
13:13, *132*
13:14, *132, 134*
13:15, *135*
13:17, *134*
13:20, *132, 135*
13:21, *131-32, 135*
13:22, *135*
13:25, *130, 134, 136*
13:26, *131*

13:27, *131, 134*
13:28, *134*
13:32, *132*
13:34, *135*
13:36, *131*
13:37, *135*
13:39, *135*
ch. 14, *132*
14:19, *150*
14:25, *135*
14:26, *135*
14:29, *134-35*
14:29-33, *134*
14:31, *135*
14:32, *135*
14:33, *132, 135*
ch. 15, *135, 137, 165*
chs. 15-20, *143*
15:1, *144*
15:1-12, *129*
15:3, *132, 136, 172*
15:4, *136*
15:7, *132*
15:8, *132*
15:9, *130, 136*
15:13-17:29, *131*
15:13-19:1, *136*
15:14, *136-37*
15:15, *137*
15:16, *130, 136, 142, 171*
15:17, *136-37, 171*
15:18, *138*
15:18-22, *138*
15:18-37, *138*
15:19-22, *137*
15:19-16:13, *141*
15:22, *138*
15:23, *138*
15:23-29, *138*
15:25, *136-37*
15:26, *136-37*
15:27, *137*
15:28, *137*
15:30, *138*
15:30-37, *138*
15:31, *137*
15:32-36, *137*
16:1, *138*

16:1-4, *128*
16:1-14, *138*
16:5, *138*
16:7, *136, 139*
16:10, *129, 139, 151*
16:11, *129*
16:14, *138*
17:8, *138*
17:14, *122*
17:24, *139, 172*
17:25, *144*
17:27-29, *139*
18:1, *137*
18:2, *137, 139, 144, 149*
18:2ff, *144*
18:3, *139, 143*
18:4, *139*
18:6, *139*
18:9, *12, 134-35*
18:10-15, *134*
18:16, *145*
18:19-21, *150*
ch. 19, *150*
19:2-20:26, *140*
19:5-8, *146*
19:6, *142, 148*
19:6-9, *147*
19:7, *148*
19:8, *148*
19:9, *140*
19:11, *140*
19:12, *140, 142*
19:13, *140*
19:14, *141, 149*
19:15, *140*
19:16, *140*
19:17-41, *141*
19:19, *140, 142*
19:22, *151*
19:23, *140-41, 143*
19:24, *141*
19:24-30, *128*
19:25, *138*
19:25-31, *141*
19:29, *128*
19:42, *142*
19:42-44, *141*
19:44, *142*

ch. 20, *156*
20:1, *141*
20:2, *142*
20:3, *119, 130, 142*
20:4, *142, 149*
20:6, *149*
20:7, *149*
20:10, *149*
20:11, *149*
20:13, *149*
20:16-21, *149*
20:22, *145, 148-49*
20:23, *148-49, 155-56, 159*
20:23-26, *132, 155*
20:24, *156*
20:25, *154*
20:26, *156*
ch. 21, *76, 115, 122*
chs. 21-24, *12-13, 142, 157, 163*
21:1, *75*
21:1-14, *157, 160, 162, 222*
21:2, *75, 158*
21:5, *157-58*
21:6, *158*
21:7, *157*
21:9, *158*
21:10, *158*
21:11-14, *158*
21:14, *158*
21:15, *159*
21:15-17, *142*
21:15-22, *142, 157, 159*
21:17, *143*
21:19, *143*
21:22, *143*
ch. 22, *13, 162-63*
22:1-51, *157*
22:35, *162*
chs. 23-24, *162*
23:1, *162*
23:1-3, *162*
23:1-7, *157, 162*
23:2, *162*
23:5, *162*
23:6, *162*
23:8, *159*
23:8-11, *159*
23:8-12, *159*

Scripture Index

23:8-23, *159*
23:8-39, *157, 159-61*
23:8-24:25, *159*
23:10, *159, 160*
23:12, *159, 160*
23:13-17, *159-60*
23:16, *134*
23:17, *134*
23:18, *159*
23:20, *159*
23:21, *159*
23:24, *159*
23:24-39, *159*
23:32, *159*
23:39, *159*
ch. 24, *122, 154, 158, 160-61, 165*
24:1, *162*
24:1-9, *160, 163*
24:1-25, *157, 222*
24:2, *161, 163*
24:4, *160*
24:10, *161-62*
24:10-25, *163*
24:13, *161*
24:14, *161*
24:17, *162*
24:18ff, *142*

1 Kings
ch. 1, *13-14, 138, 153-54, 169, 176, 178-80, 195, 212*
chs. 1-2, *12-13, 18-19, 39, 149, 152-53, 163, 175, 179, 183, 210, 212*
1:1, *176*
1:1-3:15, *19*
1:4, *176*
1:5, *176, 180*
1:7, *176*
1:8, *176*
1:9, *176*
1:10, *176*
1:11, *176-77, 180*
1:12, *177*
1:13, *177*
1:13-16, *178*
1:14, *177*
1:14-16, *177*
1:16, *177*

1:17, *176, 177, 179*
1:17-24, *13*
1:18, *153, 176-77, 180*
1:19, *177*
1:20, *177*
1:21, *177*
1:22, *177*
1:23, *177*
1:24, *177, 180*
1:25, *180*
1:27, *176-77*
1:28ff, *176*
1:29, *177, 179*
1:29-35, *186*
1:30, *13, 179*
1:32-37, *177*
1:33, *179*
1:35, *194*
1:36, *179*
1:37, *124, 179, 207*
1:38, *178-79*
1:39, *177, 179*
1:40, *177, 194*
1:41, *145*
1:45, *177, 194*
1:46, *178*
1:47, *179, 186*
1:48, *23, 179*
1:52, *179*
1:53, *179*
ch. 2, *31, 178, 207, 212*
2:1-4, *178*
2:1-9, *211*
2:2, *178*
2:3, *179*
2:4, *179*
2:5, *177*
2:5-9, *178*
2:6, *179, 183, 212*
2:8, *179*
2:9, *114, 179, 183, 212*
2:12, *181*
2:13-46, *183*
2:13ff, *178*
2:15, *179*
2:18, *152*
2:19, *152, 178*
2:20, *178*

2:22-24, *178*
2:23, *180*
2:24, *180-81*
2:26, *179-80*
2:27, *180*
2:28, *134*
2:32, *180*
2:33, *180, 199*
2:34, *134*
2:42-45, *180*
2:45, *181*
2:46, *180-81*
ch. 3, *6, 182-83, 187, 191, 196, 200, 205, 207, 210, 216*
chs. 3-5, *181-82, 191, 205-06, 211-12*
chs. 3-10, *182*
chs. 3-11, *181, 183*
3:1, *182, 195, 203*
3:1-3, *182-83, 205*
3:2, *182, 195*
3:3, *182, 199*
3:4, *195*
3:4-15, *183, 205*
3:4-28, *186*
3:6, *184*
3:7, *184*
3:7-9, *211*
3:7-12, *39*
3:8, *6, 184-85*
3:9, *6, 183-86, 191, 200, 211-13*
3:9-12, *212*
3:10, *185*
3:10-14, *186*
3:11, *185-86, 197, 213*
3:11-13, *191*
3:12, *185, 213*
3:13, *197*
3:14, *191, 201*
3:15, *195, 214*
3:16-27, *187*
3:16-28, *187, 196, 205*
3:16-8:66, *19, 181*
3:28, *186-88, 196-97, 211, 213*
ch. 4, *182, 188, 212*
chs. 4-5, *188, 190, 192-93, 196, 205, 211*
4:1, *188*
4:1-6, *206*
4:2, *206*

4:2-6, *188*
4:4, *179, 207*
4:7-19, *188*
4:9-12, *178*
4:20, *185, 188-89, 200, 208, 212*
ch. 5, *190, 193, 195*
5:1, *188-89*
5:1-4, *189*
5:1-10, *119*
5:1-14, *188, 190*
5:2, *188-89*
5:3, *188-89*
5:4, *188, 190, 199-200*
5:5, *185, 189, 200, 208, 211-12*
5:6, *189*
5:7, *189*
5:8, *189*
5:9, *185, 189, 212-13*
5:10, *212, 213*
5:10-13, *189*
5:10-14, *189*
5:11, *189-90*
5:14, *185, 189, 197, 199*
5:15, *190*
5:16, *190*
5:16-20, *190*
5:17, *31*
5:18, *31*
5:19, *31*
5:21, *31, 212-13*
5:21-23, *190*
5:22-26, *193*
5:24-26, *190*
5:26, *199, 212-13*
5:27, *195*
ch. 6, *200, 202, 205*
chs. 6-8, *39, 181-82, 200, 202, 205-06, 212-13*
6:1, *201*
6:2, *201*
6:2-10, *201*
6:11-13, *192, 201*
6:12, *192, 201, 203*
6:13, *201, 203*
6:14-35, *201*
6:36-38, *201*
6:38, *203*
ch. 7, *200*

Scripture Index

7:1, *203*
7:1-12, *203*
7:7, *197*
7:13, *203*
ch. 8, *122, 191, 200-01, 203-05*
8:9, *124*
8:10, *203-04*
8:10-13, *204*
8:11, *203-04*
8:12, *201, 203-04*
8:12-14, *204*
8:13, *201, 204*
8:14, *204*
8:17-21, *200*
8:18, *200*
8:22, *204*
8:23, *204*
8:29, *192*
8:55, *204*
8:61, *199*
ch. 9, *193, 195, 205, 213*
chs. 9-10, *203*
chs. 9-11, *181-82, 191, 205-06, 212*
9:1-9, *19, 191, 201*
9:1-28, *198*
9:1-10:29, *19*
9:3, *191-92*
9:4, *192*
9:10, *182*
9:10-14, *190, 192-93, 196*
9:10-28, *192*
9:10-10:29, *193*
9:14, *193*
9:15, *194*
9:15-25, *194*
9:16, *194-95*
9:17, *194*
9:17-23, *194*
9:21, *194*
9:22, *190, 196*
9:23, *196*
9:24, *194-95*
9:25, *194-95*
9:26-28, *196*
9:26-11:10, *182*
9:28, *193*
ch. 10, *196-97*
10:1-13, *196*
10:2, *193*
10:4, *196-97, 213*
10:5, *195-96*
10:6, *197*
10:6-8, *213*
10:7, *197*
10:9, *197*
10:10, *193, 197*
10:10-13, *197*
10:11, *193, 198*
10:12, *198*
10:13, *198*
10:14, *193, 198*
10:14-29, *198*
10:15, *198*
10:16, *195, 198*
10:17, *195, 198*
10:18, *198*
10:21, *198*
10:22, *193, 198*
10:23, *213*
10:24, *199, 213*
10:24ff, *213*
10:25, *193, 198*
10:26-28, *193*
10:27, *198*
10:28, *198*
10:29, *6, 195, 198*
ch. 11, *6, 37, 39, 182, 199, 211*
chs. 11-12, *220*
11:1, *199*
11:1-13, *199*
11:4, *6, 199*
11:7, *199*
11:8, *199*
11:9-13, *199*
11:14, *220*
11:14-43, *200, 220*
11:23, *220*
11:25, *200*
11:26, *219, 225*
11:28, *108*
11:31, *200*
11:32, *200*
11:37, *200*
11:38, *200*
11:42, *200*
ch. 12, *225*

22:50, *133*

2 Kings
8:19, *133*
ch. 9, *225*
9:1-3, *56*
13:23, *134*
17:14, *66*
18:7, *124*
24:4, *133*

Job
32:8, *225*
32:18, *225*
33:4, *225*
34:14, *225*
39:9, *133*

Psalms
1:6, *96*
ch. 12, *96*
74:9, *222*

Proverbs
30:32, *176*

Ezechiel
17:14, *176*
29:15, *176*

Daniel
11:14, *176*

Hosea
13:11, *89*

Jesus Sirach
47:4, *113*
47:5, *113*

Matthew
9:17, *219*
17:24-27, *115*

Mark
2:23-28, *115*
3:1-6, *115*

Luke
1:15, *226*
1:35, *226*
1:41, *226*
1:67, *226*
2:25-27, *226*
2:52, *226*
3:16, *226*
3:22, *226*
4:1, *226*
4:14, *226*
4:18, *226*

Acts
1:5, *226*
1:8, *226*
2:4, *226*
2:33, *226*
2:38, *226*
4:8, *226*
4:31, *226*
ch. 5, *223*
8:15-19, *226*
9:17, *226*
10:38-47, *226*
13:9, *226*
13:52, *226*

1 Corinthians
12:11, *29*

Galatians
1:17, *168*

1 Thessalonians
5:19, *216*

Hebrews
2:4, *222*

Regnum Studies in Mission
Academic Monographs on Missiological Themes
(All titles paperback, 229 x 152mm)

Allan Anderson and Edmond Tang (Eds.)
Asian and Pentecostal
The Charismatic Face of Christianity in Asia
(Published jointly with Asia Pacific Theological Seminary)
This book provides a thematic discussion and pioneering case studies on the history and development of Pentecostal and Charismatic churches in the countries of South Asia, South East Asia and East Asia.
2005 / 1-870345-43-6 / approx. 600pp

I. Mark Beaumont
Christology in Dialogue with Muslims
A Critical Analysis of Christian Presentations of Christ for Muslims from the Ninth and Twentieth Centuries
This book analyses Christian presentations of Christ for Muslims in the most creative periods of Christian-Muslim dialogue, the first half of the ninth century and the second half of the twentieth century. In these two periods, Christians made serious attempts to present their faith in Christ in terms that take into account Muslim perceptions of him, with a view to bridging the gap between Muslim and Christian convictions.
2005 / 1-870345-46-0 / xxvi + 228pp

Kwame Bediako
Theology and Identity
The Impact of Culture upon Christian Thought in the Second Century and in Modern Africa
The author examines the question of Christian identity in the context of the Graeco–Roman culture of the early Roman Empire. He then addresses the modern African predicament of quests for identity and integration.
1992 / 1-870345-10-X / xviii + 508pp

July 2005

Gene Early
Leadership Expectations
How Executive Expectations are Created and Used in a Non-Profit Setting
The author creates an Expectation Enactment Analysis to study the role of the Chancellor of the University of the Nations-Kona, Hawaii, and is grounded in the field of managerial work, jobs, and behaviour, drawing on symbolic interactionism, role theory, role identity theory, and enactment theory. The result is a conceptual framework for further developing an understanding of managerial roles.
2005 / 1-870345-30-4 / xxiv + 276pp

Keith E. Eitel
Paradigm Wars
The Southern Baptist International Mission Board Faces the Third Millennium
The International Mission Board of the Southern Baptist Convention is the largest denominational mission agency in North America. This volume chronicles the historic and contemporary forces that led to the IMB's recent extensive reorganization, providing the most comprehensive case study to date of a historic mission agency restructuring to continue its mission purpose into the twenty-first century more effectively.
1999 / 1-870345-12-6 / x + 140pp

Tharcisse Gatwa
The Churches and Ethnic Ideology in the Rwandan Crises 1900-1994
Since the early years of the twentieth century Christianity has become a new factor in Rwandan society. This book investigates the role Christian churches played in the formulation and development of the racial ideology that culminated in the 1994 genocide.
2005 / 1-870345-24-X / approx 300pp

Gideon Githiga
The Church as the Bulwark against Authoritarianism
Development of Church and State Relations in Kenya, with Particular Reference to the Years after Political Independence 1963-1992
'All who care for love, peace and unity in Kenyan society will want to read this careful history by Bishop Githiga of how Kenyan Christians, drawing on the Bible, have sought to share the love of God, bring his peace and build up the unity of the nation, often in the face of great difficulties and opposition.' Canon Dr Chris Sugden, Oxford Centre for Mission Studies.
2002 / 1-870345-38-X / xviii + 218pp

Samuel Jayakumar
Dalit Consciousness and Christian Conversion
Historical Resources for a Contemporary Debate
(Published jointly with ISPCK)
The main focus of this historical study is social change and transformation among the Dalit Christian communities in India. Historiography tests the evidence in the light of the conclusions of the modern Dalit liberation theologians.
1999 / 81-7214-497-0 / xxiv + 434pp

Samuel Jayakumar
Mission Reader
Historical Models for Wholistic Mission in the Indian Context
(Published jointly with ISPCK)
This book is written from an evangelical point of view revalidating and reaffirming the Christian commitment to wholistic mission. According to Jayakumar, the roots of the 'wholistic mission' combining 'evangelism and social concerns' are to be located in the history and tradition of Christian evangelism in the past; and the civilizing purpose of evangelism is compatible with modernity as an instrument in nation building.
2003 / 1-870345-42-8 / x + 250pp

Julie Ma
Mission Possible
Biblical Strategies for Reaching the Lost
Written as Julie Ma hiked the mountains to share God's news, this is a missiology book for the church which liberates missiology from the specialists for every believer. Nevertheless, it serves as a textbook that is simple and friendly, and yet solid in biblical interpretation. This book links the biblical teaching to the actual and contemporary missiological setting, thus serving two important purposes. Examples are clearly given which aid understanding, and the biblical development is brought in to our contemporary setting, thus making the Bible come alive.
2005 / 1-870345-37-1 / xvi + 142pp

Myung Sung-Hoon and Hong Young-Gi (eds.)
Charis and Charisma
David Yonggi Cho and the Growth of Yoido Full Gospel Church
This book discusses the factors responsible for the growth of the world's largest church. It expounds the role of the Holy Spirit, the leadership, prayer, preaching, cell groups and creativity in promoting church growth. It focuses on God's grace (charis) and inspiring leadership (charisma) as the two essential factors and the book's purpose is to present a model for church growth worldwide.
2003 / 1-870345-45-2 / xxii + 218pp

Bernhard Ott
Beyond Fragmentation: Integrating Mission and Theological Education
A Critical Assessment of some Recent Developments in Evangelical Theological Education
Beyond Fragmentation is an enquiry into the development of Mission Studies in evangelical theological education in Germany and German-speaking Switzerland between 1960 and 1995. This is carried out by a detailed examination of the paradigm shifts which have taken place in recent years in both the theology of mission and the understanding of theological education.
2001 / 1-870345-14-2 / xxviii + 382pp

Bob Robinson
Christians Meeting Hindus
An Analysis and Theological Critique of the Hindu-Christian Encounter in India
This book focuses on the Hindu-Christian encounter, especially the intentional meeting called dialogue, mainly during the last four decades of the twentieth century, and mainly in India itself.
2004 / 1-870345-39-8 / xviii + 392pp

Christopher Sugden
Seeking the Asian Face of Jesus
The Practice and Theology of Christian Social Witness in Indonesia and India 1974–1996
This study focuses on contemporary wholistic mission with the poor in India and Indonesia combined with the call to transformation of all life in Christ with micro-credit enterprise schemes. 'The literature on contextual theology now has a new standard to rise to' – Lamin Sanneh (Yale University, USA).
1997 / 1-870345-26-6 / xx + 496pp

Christopher Sugden
Gospel, Culture and Transformation
A Reprint, with a New Introduction, of Part Two of Seeking the Asian Face of Jesus
Gospel, Culture and Transformation explores the practice of mission especially in relation to transforming cultures and communities. Vinay Samuel has played a leading role in developing the understanding of mission as transformation, which he defines as follows: 'Transformation is to enable God's vision of society to be actualised in all relationships: social, economic and spiritual, so that God's will may be reflected in human society and his love experienced by all communities, especially the poor.'
2000 / 1-870345-32-0 / viii + 152pp

Hwa Yung
Mangoes or Bananas?
The Quest for an Authentic Asian Christian Theology
Asian Christian thought remains largely captive to Greek dualism and Enlightenment rationalism because of the overwhelming dominance of Western culture. Authentic contextual Christian theologies will emerge within Asian Christianity with a dual recovery of confidence in culture and the gospel.
1997 / 1-870345-25-8 / xii + 274pp

regnum

Regnum Books International
9 Holdom Avenue,
Bletchley,
Milton Keynes MK1 1QR,
United Kingdom
Web: www.authenticmedia.co.uk/paternoster

July 2005